AMERICANA LIBRARY

ROBERT E. BURKE, EDITOR

Revolt
on the Campus

BY JAMES WECHSLER

Introduction to the Original Edition
by Robert Morss Lovett

Introduction to the Americana Library Edition
by the Author

UNIVERSITY OF WASHINGTON PRESS
Seattle and London

Copyright © 1935 by James Wechsler
Originally published by Covici-Friede
University of Washington Press Americana
Library edition 1973
"Introduction to the 1973 Edition"
copyright © 1973
by the University of Washington Press
Printed in the United States of America

Library of Congress Cataloging in Publication Data

Wechsler, James Arthur, 1915–
    Revolt on the campus.

    (Americana library, AL-26)
    Reprint of the ed. published by Covici, Friede,
New York; with new introd.
    1. Universities and colleges—United States,
2. College students—United States—Political
activities. I. Title.
LA229.W4   1973   378.1'98'10973   73-8748
ISBN   0-295-95296-2

INTRODUCTION
TO THE 1973 EDITION

For the author, a reading of this book more than thirty-five years after its appearance was alternately a nostalgic, poignant, and even melancholy exercise; it is, after all, a cruel documentation of the passage of time in one man's life, and a reminder of what in many ways were golden days of high passion and virtuous certitude. It was written in the summer months immediately following my graduation from Columbia (an event which I attended bearing a picket sign rather than cap and gown in protest against the expulsion of an anti-war group at the university's medical school). I was not quite twenty when these words were hastily composed and rushed into print; to the extent that there are many matters of both style and substance that I wish could be retrieved, that chronology may be considered apologia. Yet I confess a certain vanity about the resurrection of a work that, so remote in time, has been deemed to have any modern relevance. For that I am presumably indebted to a new generation of student activists, with some of whom I have had warm personal relationships and to others of whom I have been a target of the epithet "old-fashioned liberalism." After a television confrontation with Jerry Rubin and Abbie Hoffman in 1970, in which they suggested my brand of ADA politics was somewhat more sinister than that of Spiro T. Agnew, some of my Columbia

v

classmates suggested that I had received long-merited punishment for the intolerances I had inflicted on the university community in the thirties.

In a volume called *The Age of Suspicion,* published in 1953 after I had been summoned before Senator Joseph McCarthy's investigating committee and belatedly confronted with the record of my undergraduate involvements, as well as ensuing political offenses, I tried to recapture and reappraise some aspects of the student movement, and mood, that produced *Revolt on the Campus.* Those who are curious about my subsequent political evolution will find that described in the same volume.

It was not until the latter part of the 1960's that there occurred any student upheavals on American campuses comparable to those recorded here. Some contrasts will be self-evident to the reader. Militant as was our image of our radicalism, it had an almost muted tone when viewed against the tactics employed by some factions of the Students for a Democratic Society and their fellow-travelers. I do not recall any occasion when it occurred to us to occupy buildings, imprison deans, and even, as in the dubious heyday of the Weathermen sect, to engage in the amateur production of bombs. "Disruption" generally took the form of student strikes of brief duration in which violence was almost invariably confined to small bands of right-wing students who thought the "good name" of their institutions could be most effectively preserved by assaults on radicals. I do not mean to suggest that our language was wholly unprovocative, or that we were exemplars of civilized discourse; indeed, we were highly capable of arguing that the rights of free speech we claimed for Communists, for example, should not be extended to Fascists, a selective interpretation of the Bill of Rights that was to find favor three decades later among disciples of Herbert Marcuse.

Ironically, I believe the difference in tactical operation between the student movement of that period and the high point of the "New Left" operations in the late 1960's was the consequence of our predominantly Marxist orientation. Again I am talking primarily of the leaders rather than of many who joined us in specific engagements, such as the national anti-war strikes of 1934-36. And where this book is most disingenuous is in its failure to identify those political commitments. I, for example, joined the Young Communist League in 1934 (and left in early 1937), and most of those in the forefront of the Columbia upheavals—as well as those at other places—were either YCL members or enrolled in the Young People's Socialist League and some of the smaller Marxist sects.

Few of us may have been skilled students of the gospel, but most of us had absorbed the ancient Leninist principle that "individual terrorism" was futile and even counterproductive. Where we were the victims of attack, we relentlessly exploited the fact; many of our largest mobilizations were the product of instinctive anger aroused among instinctive libertarians by the vigilante behavior of some of our adversaries. There were occasions when we tended to be almost recklessly provocative. But bombings or take-overs were not the order of the day or night.

To dwell further on the disparities between student insurgence in the thirties and the sixties may be an excessive exercise in reverie. Perhaps, however, one additional reflection is warranted. Those of us who entered college in the

vii

years of what is now remembered as the Great Depression were primarily products of that setting. We had seemingly good reason to believe that the American system had lost control over events; and many of those disposed to think much about the chaos were capitvated by the view that the Soviet "experiment" showed us how to resolve the grotesquerie of poverty in a country so richly endowed as ours. The Moscow mystique largely guided much of our ensuing activity; when the Kremlin decreed in 1935 that traditional revolutionary dogma must give way to the concept of a Popular Front against fascism, all the signals were changed. The pacifist overtones of the student movement were slowly transformed into the gospel of collective security; by 1936 —when I was serving as a post-graduate functionary for the American Student Union—defense of the Spanish republic had largely pre-empted the anti-war slogans, and muted the revolutionary music at home. Spain became almost in reverse the obsession that Vietnam was to become for many thirty years later; it was, ironically, our hope that the United States would provide, as it never did, the aid for the embattled Spanish regime that it was to supply for Saigon while students in growing numbers demonstrated for American withdrawal from the Indo-China wasteland.

I do not mean to suggest now that the cause of Madrid (stained as it later proved to be by disclosure of factional Stalinist ruthlessness) can be remotely likened to that of Thieu's despotism in Saigon, but only to emphasize what Reinhold Neibuhr detected as the underlying irony of history.

If too much of this has a defensive tone, let me reiterate that a re-reading of this book was not a joyous enterprise

viii

for the author. It is unpleasant to be reminded of how self-righteously wrong I was in my assessment of some wholly decent men who happened to differ with the conventional radical wisdom of that time.

But I would also contend that there has been one valid continuity between the upheavals of the two eras. In both instances young Americans were reacting against what seemed to be the blind-alley blandness and sterility of national and world leadership. This was as true of the campus movement for Norman Thomas in 1932 as it was for the Eugene McCarthy crusade of 1968 (and the McGovern upsurge of 1972).

In both times large numbers of students were unaffected and uninspired by the sights and sounds of protest. But that is generally true of the mass of mankind, at least until circumstances beyond individual control create large-scale involvement. On balance the spectacle of concerned students who refuse to accept the bleakness of things as they are still seems to me more appealing than the deadness that prevailed on campuses during what is recalled as "the silent generation" of the 1950's. In the same sense I derived no satisfaction from the widespread reports in the winter of 1972 (somewhat challenged by events in the spring) that "a new calm" had settled over our colleges and universities, with students turning inward and losing all confidence in their ability to influence public affairs—or even the conduct of the institutions they attend. Nor do I derive any satisfaction from widely published reports in this spring of 1973 that the campuses have reverted to the "quiet" cherished by some academics.

Without reverence for much that is recorded here, I

ix

submit that it exhibits an involvement in "the actions and passions of our time" without which, Justice Holmes reminded us, man can be judged not to have lived. I know it has long been fashionable to assume that the activist undergraduate is some kind of psychological freak; one might argue at least as convincingly that education is an unrewarding sedative if its model specimens are those who do not give a damn, or have acquired the spurious maturity of cynical disengagement. A tolerance for diversity of view —so conspicuously missing from this volume—is a poor excuse for passivity. In so far as we were moved then, as other young men and women are now, by an impulse "to comfort the afflicted and afflict the comfortable," I should like to believe that many of us were engaged in something more meaningful than ego-trips. Many of us were to move from those days of dogma toward a democratic humanism to which we still adhere. In doing so we have perhaps at least refuted the smug bromide that young radicals are hopelessly destined to become aged reactionaries.

JAMES A. WECHSLER

New York
March 1973

ACKNOWLEDGMENTS

It is impossible for me to list here those teachers and students who have aided me in the completion of this work by furnishing data, by detailing their own impressions and correlating them with others, by reporting facts and trends in areas with which they are most familiar. To record their names would require far more space than is feasible; moreover, their association with the main premises and conclusions of this book would, in many cases, result in academic discipline. For that reason I have also been compelled, in the discussion of specific colleges, to preserve the anonymity of those who have submitted material to me. I can make only this blanket acknowledgment to them for assistance which was both a prerequisite and a guide.

I am deeply indebted to George D. Pratt for the files of *The New Student,* to Mrs. Lucille Millner and the office staff of the Civil Liberties Union for ready co-operation and access to many relevant documents, to Ernest Johnson of the Committee on Militarism in Education for similar help, to Joseph P. Lash of the Student League for Industrial Democracy, Adam Lapin of the National Student League and John Lang of the National Student Federation for files, mailing-lists and suggestions and especially to Nancy Fraenkel for constant and invaluable aid throughout the preparation of this manuscript.

J. W.

INTRODUCTION
TO THE ORIGINAL EDITION

It was long a matter of surprise to foreign students that their contemporaries in American colleges and universities manifested so little interest in public affairs, and exerted practically no influence on the conduct of them. This indifference was easily explained by the intellectual immaturity of American undergraduates, comparable rather with pupils of the lycée or gymnasium than with those of the foreign university, by the absorption of graduate and professional students in studies promotive of their later careers, and especially by the expanding economy of the country which made conventional education in the form of discipline or acquirement almost a passport to success in life. Education in America came to have the authority of the mediaeval church. It was sought by the individual at whatever sacrifice as a way of salvation, and it was endowed by the rich as a means of acquiring merit and distinction, much as their forebears had founded monasteries and contributed to cathedrals. Professor Veblen pointed out the inevitable trend of this system toward unqualified support of the *status quo,* in *The Higher Learning in America,* and Professor Kirkpatrick followed with *The American College and its Rulers,* but for the most part the academic world dwelt like the Sidonians, "quiet and secure."

The free silver campaign of 1896 caused the first break in this serenity since the civil war, and a few professors lost their jobs for doubting the divine inspiration of the gold standard, notably President E. Benjamin Andrews, who had to leave Brown for Nebraska. The World War brought its casualties; Professor Simon Patten was dismissed by the trustees of the University of Pennsylvania, and President Butler expelled Professor Cattell from Columbia for writing to Congressmen protesting against the selective service law. Some young instructors, among them Carl Haessler, went from the campus to prison as conscientious objectors. The post-war hysteria was used to advantage in such purges as that at the University of Minnesota under the judicial direction of Mr. Pierce Butler. The American Association of University Professors, under the initiative of its founders, displayed some activity in defending its members in their constitutional rights of free speech. These were faculty matters, however, and for the most part the student body remained acquiescent and patriotic, carried by the wave of nationalism which swept all classes. The movement of the present, of which Mr. Wechsler gives striking examples, is mainly a rank and file development. He deals with some outstanding cases of professional expulsion, such as that of Professor Miller at Ohio State, and Professor Turner at Pittsburgh, but in the main he is concerned with a stirring of thought and feeling among the students, not only in the classroom but on the campus. And this agitation has been only in small part the result of faculty inspiration, but has arisen from the contact of students with phenomena and influences outside of college. Of these, there have been three, the War, Soviet Russia, and the depression.

It is only to be expected that the youth of today should look back on the World War as the supreme instance of the folly and cruelty of the past. We know now that the part which the United States played in that war was that of dupe, a rôle which is insulting to any intelligence. It is no wonder that students of the generation which will have to fight the next war refuse in advance to be sacrificed to the stupidity of government and the greed of business. It is no wonder that they protest against the presence on the campus of a military organization which perpetuates the memory of that past in propaganda backed by appeals to military glory and feminine favor. The annual repudiation of war by the student body throughout the world is a reminder of the solemn covenant signed by sixty-three nations to discard war as an instrument of national policy. It is amazing that college authorities should select this ground of all others on which to discourage the free expression of student opinion.

The example of the Soviet Union, which Jane Addams called the greatest laboratory experiment in social science of all time, is similarly a challenge to intelligence. Who would wish students of today to ignore it? We should despise them if they did. Academic authorities today might well take the advice which their predecessor Gamaliel gave to his country-men in Jerusalem: "If this counsel or this work be of men, it will come to nought; But if it be of God ye cannot over-throw it, lest haply ye be found even to fight against God."

The depression is undoubtedly a more immediate and general cause of unrest among students who are forced to look forward to entering a world which at the moment has no place for them. An instinct of self-preservation impels them to question an economic order which results in such a catas-trophe as war, and to which various theories of planned economy, of collectivism, of production for use rather than profit offer more or less plausible alternatives. Again, we should find students who remain complacent and inert in the face of such exigencies and occasions as justifying the cynical charge that they are essentially uneducable.

Mr. Wechsler has written a challenging book. I do not entirely agree with it. I feel that he is less than fair to President Frank, President Wilkins, President Hutchins, too little considerate of the difficulties of those in positions of responsibility who would agree with him on the main issue. Yet in the light of his own experience and that of others in being subjected to violence countenanced or encouraged by college authorities for the sin of holding opinions at variance with those accounted orthodox, it is difficult to blame him for some asperity. It is a disconcerting book for those of us who have had the responsibility of college teachers during these late crucial years. Mr. Wechsler reminds us how we joined in the insane cry of hate in wartime and flung the young lives entrusted to our care into the carnage as cannon fodder, how we took advantage of the lethargy of disillusionment and prosperity of subsequent years to forget all our promises to the dead, how impatient we were at having our repose broken by somewhat rude demands for advice and support in directions which we recognized as those which give ultimate meaning to education in the application of reason and intelligence to human affairs. Perhaps if we had given that advice and support more constantly and more willingly in the past the demands would sound today less rudely in our ears.

One effect of Mr. Wechsler's book is to remind us how far we of the faculty have removed ourselves from the discipline of the institution in procedures affecting the activities of students in respect to questions which are vital to their future. Surely it might be expected that the professors should

xvi

take as much interest in groups of students formed for social and political discussion and action as in fraternities and athletic teams. Especially is intervention by the faculty called for when administrative authorities resort to violent means to rid themselves of the nuisance of student criticism. Sometimes this violence is personal, as when a college president undertakes to disperse a demonstration with an umbrella. Sometimes it is vicarious, as when police are called in, or, most reprehensible of all, when attacks of students upon their fellows are invited or tolerated. Mr. Wechsler gives many instances in which R.O.T.C. men led in such attacks. One asks what becomes of the arguments in favor of the R.O.T.C. as promoting obedience, discipline, and conduct expected of officers and gentlemen.

The great danger in this country at present is the increasing practice of violence in disputes of every kind. The colleges should be free from it. Undoubtedly a responsibility rests upon those of us who welcome the campus revolt as a hopeful sign for the future, to discourage practices which have no objective except provocation to disorder and reprisals. Such caution as this, however, seems to be only a feeble commonplace in the light of the overwhelming evidence submitted by Mr. Wechsler of suppression, discrimination, and violence, official and officially inspired and countenanced, against which the revolt on the campus is making its way.

ROBERT MORSS LOVETT

xvii

CONTENTS

xix

CONTENTS

CONTENTS

CONTENTS

CONTENTS

CONTENTS

REVOLT ON THE CAMPUS

PART I
PANORAMA

1. Signs of Revolt

THE university has traditionally been viewed as the most stable, unwavering phase of American life. It was designed, we were told, to provide dispassionate study and appraisal of outside turmoil while refraining from partisan interest in the outcome. That notion has been sharply dispelled; academic aloofness and calm are an ancient legend.

Even as I write,* four students prominent in the espousal of anti-war doctrines at the University of Michigan are "denied readmission" to the institution. Although they were unmistakably proficient in their studies, President Ruthven explains that they are "not the type of students wanted on a university campus."

Returning from a congress of the Carnegie Endowment for International Peace at Paris, Nicholas Murray Butler discourses on the crisis in international affairs. When a reporter questions him about the dismissal of nine leaders of the peace committee at the Columbia University Medical School, Dr. Butler denies the irony, denouncing the "sensational turn" which the press has given the episode. In the same city the Chairman of the Board of Examiners condemns "unrest" and "defiance of rulings" in the city colleges; he warns that those adjudged guilty will be barred from posts in the teaching system.

In the face of a remorseless inquisition by local die-hards, one of that diminishing handful of progressive, forthright administrators—the president of Omaha's Municipal University—commits suicide. *The New York Times* recounts his passing in an unobtrusive paragraph.

* In July, 1935.

3

At Rutgers University an investigating committee sustains the dismissal of an outspoken anti-nazi professor in the German department. Despite abundant evidence that his ouster was engineered for political reasons by the head of his department, an avowed disciple of the Nazi regime, the committee blandly defends its verdict.

Simultaneously Congressman Dickstein renews his demand for a nationwide probe into "subversive activities in the colleges," aimed to "weed out un-American elements." His is not a solitary voice. Seconding the proposal is a chain of newspapers which reaches into the homes of nearly twenty million American people.

And, in the annual summary of its endeavors, the American Civil Liberties Union reports that "attacks on academic freedom are greater in number and more dangerous than ever before in our history."

These are the interludes of a Summer in the midst of the stormiest period in American academic life.

Shortly after the onset of economic decline, Walter Lippmann admonished the American student "not to let himself be absorbed by distractions about which as a scholar he can do almost nothing. For this is not the last crisis in human affairs. The world will go on somehow." But his auditors did not keep the faith. Above the incessant clamor which has subsequently surrounded the campus, there has been sober judgment on at least one premise: that the undergraduate of 1935, for better or worse, is a distinctly different specimen from his predecessor of a decade before. Only recently Professor Irwin Edman cited the "extraordinary change in viewpoint and climate" to be discerned among students.* The annual report of the Carnegie Foundation notes the passing of the "blase, sophisticated student of the twenties." Writing in *The New York World-Telegram*, Mrs. Dorothy Dunbar Bromley observes that at last "large groups

* From an article in *The New York Times*, April 14, 1935.

4

of students are beginning to think and talk seriously about such momentous subjects as war and peace." Another commentator echoes her view, perceiving that "enrollment in the social studies is way up and a growing concern with social questions is apparent." * An educational convention in the midwest is told that the contemporary college would be "unrecognizable to the graduate of 1925."

Almost every contemporary journal has occupied itself with some phase of the metamorphosis. But beyond recognizing its existence, there has been relatively little understanding of the roots of the change or the beliefs and aspirations of those most intimately involved in it. Certainly there have been unique currents generated on the campus; in essence they mirror what is taking place in spheres far beyond the educational horizon. That much is usually acknowledged. The extent to which it has been broadcast is, in fact, an almost disproportionate tribute to the phenomenon. Accompanying these testimonials, however, there has been a deluge of deliberate distortion, of bewilderment, of avowed or inferential hostility. Functionaries within the universities have been as guilty as righteous-minded citizens without. The undergraduate dissenter has been mercilessly damned or cynically patronized. Almost invariably his efforts have received the judgment of discipline, whether it be outright or concealed. But even while his mind has become suspect and his motives deemed sinister, the fact of recognition endures. The outcries of those whom he has offended only serve to emphasize larger crises about him.

The setting has ample historic precedent. Following the popular uprisings of 1849, Nicholas I was seized with an hysteria not uncommon in the present day. He contemplated a general shut-down of the colleges; pride forbidding so sweeping an edict, he ordered the schools reorganized along military lines with six hours a week of military drill. At the

* Evelyn Seeley, writing in *The Literary Digest*, May 25, 1935.

5

University of Kiev, the students of the Medical Faculty were warned by the governor general:

"You gentlemen may dance, play cards, flirt with other men's wives, frequent women and beat women, but stay away from politics or I will throw you out of the University."

On another occasion he told an assembly of professors and students:

"You professors may call on each other but only for the purpose of playing cards; while, as for you students, remember that I shall regard leniently your dissipations, but a soldier's cap awaits anyone of you suspected of free thinking." *

In the stress of the present, these utterances are revived. Thus Hugh Fullerton declares in an article syndicated from coast to coast:

"The trend of thought—and action—among the younger generation is a thing which the United States ought to study more seriously than ever before. For the first time in its history the country faces the danger of student leadership. Every one of the older countries of Europe and many of the South American Republics have felt the power of student opinion and leadership which has frequently, and one might say invariably, led to revolution."

Heralding his perception, one periodical adds:

"The college rebels are today aware of the fact and in their feline manner are creeping upon the sons and

* Quoted from *The Social Frontier*.

6

daughters of these inalert parents. Everywhere one reads of bloody revolutions in other countries and, as the smoke clouds lift, one invariably finds a misled but carefully regimented university student group taking the leading part in the fiasco." *

Even more succinct is the ultimatum of *The Raleigh Times:*

"Let the students think their heads off if they are so inclined. . . . But somehow or other they must be constrained to stop short of 'direct action.' "

The most pronounced voice in the chorus has been the Hearst press and its subsidiaries, decrying "attempts to bootleg Old World doctrines into our colleges," the "nefarious meddling of professorial nincompoops" and "the declining American colonies" in the undergraduate population. Its anguish is equalled only by that of Mr. Ralph Easley and his National Civic Federation who envisage "red co-eds" luring away their innocent colleagues into strange fields of thought. Around them have sprung up a coterie of aides, haunted by the same spectre which afflicted Nicholas I eighty-five years ago.

They are the vanguard whose inanity is paralleled only by their influence, exerted through a hundred channels of American life. More complacently hostile notes can be detected even where the antics of the Hearstlings are derided. The columnist in "Topics of the Times," consistently annoyed by student agitation, wrote at the termination of the school year:

"Another week or two and the dove of peace will be brooding over some of the nation's most conspicuous sore spots. Arms will be laid down. . . . Provocative

* From *The National Republic,* an organ of "Americanism."

7

demonstrations will be a thing of the past. . . . The undergraduates, sappers and miners of the country's foundations, will let up on prexy and concentrate on the young women in the English swimming suits."

One educator deplores the "ill-mannered outbursts of undergraduates"; another sees "the destruction of the calm and detachment in which the university once flourished"; still a third is distraught because "our pupils are jumping to conclusions without consulting the wisdom of ages."

However much the volume and tone of the response may differ, its essence is the same. On one hand it assumes the form of loud convulsions and incitements to repression; elsewhere, of condescension to "impractical idealists," mingled with cynical contempt for those who ought to know better.

These fragments may indicate how widespread—and noisy —is the confusion. An unceasing din has been created by those who, through choice or the dictates of salary, have set out to "explain" the "rebellious student." If they have satisfied the fears of their employers, or augmented them, depending upon their findings, few have contributed anything to genuine enlightenment.

Amidst the uproar, certain definite and relevant fields of inquiry may be discerned which, upon exploration, may serve to clarify the stream of events. The first bears upon the fact of the revolt itself—to discover its roots, to verify the impulse behind the startling revision in the outlook and preoccupations of those thousands, for example, who joined a nationwide strike against war. To what extent—in scope, perspective and purpose—is their uprising distinct from the murmurings of the iconoclasts of the 1920's? If we ascertain the origins and aspirations of the revolt, its permanence or decline can then be estimated in terms of the apparent possibility of solving those dissatisfactions which underly the ferment.

8

This is one side of a broad panorama; the other is inseparable from it. For the fact of reaction is, in many realms, even more palpable than the "enemy" against whom it has been invoked. Its sponsors are many and widely distributed; although certain of their more rhetorical spokesmen have already been cited, the network extends far beyond them. Their existence, of course, is generally sensed; the impetus behind them, however, is not so well-known. Why, for instance, are educators striving so desperately to stifle a passionate concern for social issues among their students? That such an attempt is on foot cannot be doubted; again, however, there is appalling ignorance of its real meaning or that which it presages for the future. Repression, I think it will be shown, is not a unique or unprecedented arrival to the campus; but there are special, novel aspects to the latest outbreak of restrictive devices whose importance is only dimly realized; of these, the large-scale appearance of expulsions and dismissals is perhaps the most pronounced.

At the outset one reservation should be set forth. Although there are large and highly significant numbers involved in these events, there are thousands more in American colleges only remotely connected with them. In many places the latter group constitutes a majority; it betrays only passing interest in the affairs which absorb more alert contemporaries. To visualize the nature of this complacence, I quote from the student newspaper at the University of Nebraska which, in May, 1935, announced:

> "Pent-up Spring pep will find an outlet in the all-university torch parade to be held Friday night, May 17, in honor of Big Six cinder artists with secondary homage going to Henry F. 'Indian' Schulte for fifteen years of service as Nebraska's track mentor. Backed by a majority of the top-notch organizations on the campus . . . the rally committee promises a lively program."

From the University of Minnesota comes similar testimony to the existence of sound, clean American thinking:

"Female hearts beat normally again today as 14 male students at the University of Minnesota sang the jailhouse blues in an iron-barred cell, the aftermath of the annual pajama parade in which about three hundred men participated. Some were big, all were bold and, Dean Nicholson said, a few perhaps were bad as they snakedanced through the campus in multicolored pajamas to the first sorority house." *

I cite these incidents because they are far more typical than might be imagined. An extravagant picture of the meaning and scope of the rebellion—the term which, in the absence of a more scientific description of so diverse a situation, will be frequently used—will deceive no one, accomplish nothing and invalidate the entire significance of what is taking place. Hence, for the solace of the tender-hearted and an accurate appraisal of the scene, these items have been recorded.†

One final explanation is required. The entire approach of this study will be lost without reference to the contrast and experiences on the campus provided by the decade preceding the present unrest. Although I cannot hope to present a comprehensive document of those years in the colleges, at least certain rough outlines can be drawn. They are important as points of departure; there are, moreover, certain basic principles about the structure of our universities, their growth and inherent nature which flow from that period and provide the bridge between it and the present. Some of these details have been recounted before; many, including the rise of "The New Student" are not so widely known. In the light of the

* From an Associated Press dispatch, May 21, 1935.
† A chapter will be devoted to a discussion of colleges where such "incidents" are still the major phase of undergraduate activity.

events we are now witnessing, they serve as an illuminating counter-point. Thus, at a time when the omens of a new war are so acute, the behavior of our citadels of learning in the last conflict should be deeply engraved upon the minds of their current inhabitants; similarly, when the advocates of peace are hounded from the campus as they are today, that earlier outburst of righteousness has an immediate relevance. It is equally essential to an insight into the affairs of the post-war generation and the precursors of the depression revolt. This continuity of development, the constant interplay between the campus and its environs provide the structure without which the revolt would be shorn of stature and permanent meaning.

II. Learning Goes to War

IN one of Woodrow Wilson's portfolios there was placed, early in 1917, a secret cablegram from Ambassador Page, warning that "the pressure of this approaching crisis . . . has gone beyond the ability of the Morgan financial agency for the British and French governments. . . . It is not improbable that the only way of maintaining our pre-eminent trade position and averting a panic is by declaring war on Germany."

Official Washington had long before sensed the exigency; now it hurried through the last formalities preparatory to a declaration of war. Although the contents of that and similar cablegrams were not disclosed until nearly twenty years later, their effects were instantaneous. The press releases of the State Department made clear how urgent was the plight of all that was good, noble and democratic in mankind.

In the same month a crowd of several hundred people gathered in a Baltimore meeting-hall. They had come, at the behest of a local peace league, for one fleeting and forlorn

11

gesture against the inevitable. For days their purpose had been whispered about the city, causing fierce resentment in a citizenry which already envisaged itself at war. Among the most vehement in the indignation chorus was a large group of students in neighboring colleges, banded together in one of the hundred patriotic societies of the day. They issued manifestos to the sponsors of the meeting; they advised cancellation in unequivocal terms and threatened "direct action" if their wishes were unheeded.

But on a torrid April night the hall was crowded when David Starr Jordan, elderly president emeritus of Stanford University, stepped to the platform. He was a unique figure in that hour. Almost all his colleagues in administrative posts were clamoring for our entrance into the war. He was surrounded in the academic world by blustering, aggressive righteousness. In the midst of the turmoil, he was one of that pitifully isolated few bold enough to speak out.

As he began his address, there was a restive murmuring in the audience. It was evident that the student-patriots had responded to the summons; many of them were jammed into the meeting-room; others stood outside in hostile, angry groups. Those inside did not wait long to announce their mission. Each of Dr. Jordan's utterances was punctuated by bitter epithets from the undergraduate throng. They denounced him as an agent of the kaiser, a foreign emissary and a godless traitor. When he sought to remonstrate with them, they bellowed more furiously or shrieked selections from "The Star Spangled Banner."

Dr. Jordan did not finish his address. The din had grown too overpowering—and too ominous. Irritated by any voice of reason in its midst, the mob several times warned him to halt; when he refused, its leaders advanced toward him with loud bravado. They announced that they would be compelled to use force since "reason" had made no headway.

Several of the speaker's friends, aware how imminent was an outbreak, rushed to the platform and prevailed upon him to leave. The aged, bewildered man was sped out of the hall before his capture could be effected.

All that night the streets of Baltimore were filled with hysterical, high-pitched sounds, the cries of students searching for their victim. Until dawn they patrolled the streets and alleys, hoping that he would reappear or his hideout be discovered. In the morning the vain pursuit ended.

Although they had failed to seize their prey, the students were nevertheless saluted by the populace for a noble effort. It was agreed that the boys were academic heroes, a credit to their colleges, scholars and good fellows who would make their way in the world—if they survived the war.

Nine years later tranquillity had returned. Carter Osburn had been one of the leaders of the embryonic lynch-mob that Sunday night in Baltimore and in 1926 he wrote his confessional. In "An Open Letter to David Starr Jordan" he declared:

"Much has happened in the last ten years. I spent part of them overseas and saw something of the actuality of war. . . . Maturity and experience have brought me the poignant realization that on that Sunday evening of long ago, you were motivated by the principles of civilization while I was motivated by the passion of barbarism."

Vincent Sheehan was a student at the University of Chicago during the war. It ended before he went overseas, postponing his enlightenment for several years. Long afterward he recalled his own impression of the period:

"We were all patriots then. We knew nothing about the horror and degradation which our elders who had been through the war were to put before us so unremittingly for the next fifteen years." *

* From *Personal History*, Sheehan's autobiography.

13

They were the thousands who heard the summons when the higher learning blew its own horn and went to war.

The crude humor of the war psychosis had its academic counterparts. There was the professor of Geology at the University of Michigan who abandoned all his researches to compose a series of prose poems about 'the enemy of mankind'; Professor Josiah Royce of Harvard, the quiet, meditative prototype of the philosophic spirit who overnight became the mentor of a "Citizens' League for America and the Allies"; the picturesque pronouncements of Dr. Vernon Kellogg of Stanford, predicting that forever after mankind will "shrink aside" when a German passes "or stoop for stones to drive him from its path"; the warning delivered to professors by one periodical: "conform or get out"; the patriotic orgy of the American Association of University Professors which "warmed the heart of Attorney General A. Mitchell Palmer." * These were everyday items which have been frequently recited to the discomfort of the participants. But the deliverance of the universities to the War Department encompassed more than the familiar outcries of the academic mind set free. It invaded the curriculum, the laboratory, every university facility allegedly devoted to the quest for truth.† "Even staid old colleges," wrote Kolbe in 1919, "which had formerly put up rigid bars between themselves and the modern ideas of the community . . . awoke to the call of patriotism and introduced unheard-of innovations in the matters of courses and credits." Another com-

---

* For a more detailed study of the performance of the professors, see "The Higher Learning Goes to War," in *The American Mercury* of May, 1927.

† This transference of every academic agency to the War Department should appear peculiarly noteworthy in later sections when we encounter the attacks of educators on the current movement against war—because, they lament, it "disrupts academic routine" or "introduces irrelevant considerations into the life of a university."

14

mentator noted that "the first effect of America's entrance into the war was to paralyze ordinary academic work while spurring into furious activity the technical courses of a military or semi-military character."

This "shift of emphasis" in the curriculum was large-scale with scarcely an institution exempt from the procedure. The University of Wisconsin assured the Bureau of Education that "practically all scientific research has been directed into war channels." At the Case School of Applied Science "all courses are taught with more or less of a war view." Yale was even more lavish in its endeavors, providing a new three-year course on subjects relating exclusively to "the military career, as an alternative to the regular college course." With the Reed College catalogue appeared a twelve-page supplement outlining its "war studies." Out at the University of Washington an entirely new division of the college was added to furnish instruction in naval, military and aeronautical science under the direction of government officers. One professor in the East urged the abandonment of "all activities not contributing to the winning of the war."

How extensive were the "revisions" in the curriculum was glowingly described by Paul Boyd, dean of Kentucky University: "We have learned to our benefit that our educational system is still virile enough to make of itself a tool for a special purpose."

With fitting flourishes he depicted the evidences of "virility" in each field. In philosophy were "made plain the roots of present day Teutonic madness." English professors presented their material with an eye to service "as a tool for the transfer of exact information." "War chemicals" became the major pre-occupation of the Chemistry Department. "History," he explained quite succinctly, "was made more definite." In the Art Department "the principles of camouflage" were the source of primary concern. And "agriculture, home economics, engineering and law all found plenty to do that

15

contributed toward the one great problem of organizing a nation for war." *

Augmenting these "adjustments" in the curriculum was the direct transfer of the educational plant into the hands of the War Department. President Thomson of Ohio State swiftly responded to the call: "The faculty and trustees pledge you their loyal support in your leadership. The resources of the University in scientific and research laboratories and in men will be at your command."

The Princeton *Alumni Weekly* boasted that "every day Princeton becomes less an academic college and more a school of war." Most distinguished was the generosity of the American University in Washington; placing all its buildings and equipment at the disposal of the national executives, the school "virtually ceased its own work in consequence." At Worcester Polytechnic Institute, commercial shops were employed for the actual manufacture of army and navy machinery; the testing laboratory was surrendered for experimentation with war materials. Government chemists took over the laboratory at Lafayette. Due to the "rapid expansion of government work," Georgetown University submitted half of its law buildings for war purposes. Yale was again extravagant in its fervor, pouring out $250,000 for military instruction and equipment. Out of this disbursement was erected "the best equipped artillery armory outside of Fort Sill, Nebraska." "As time goes on," remarked Kolbe, "it seems inevitable that the great reserves of college plant and equipment in this country will be called upon to an ever-increasing degree for such service." †

Those who sought to combat the uproar were quickly sacrificed on the altar of "truth." The casualty list was monumental. Because he had attended a meeting of the People's

* Quoted from *School and Society*, 1919.
† Kolbe's book, *The Colleges in War Time and After*, was published in 1919 as an ardent eulogy of "patriotic education." Much of the data in this chapter is based upon his enthusiastic researches.

16

Council in 1917, Allan Eaton, an instructor at the University
of Oregon, was summarily dismissed. Three professors were
driven from the University of Nebraska: they lacked "aggressive Americanism," were suspected of "internationalism"
and they "disbelieved German atrocities." That vague but
apparently contagious disease, "pro-German leanings," precipitated the removal of seven professors at Michigan. After
eighteen years of service, Professor William E. Walz was
banished from the University of Maine because "he had
been so unfortunate, to put it mildly, as to create the impression that in this war his sympathies as well as his convictions
are with Germany." Another ground for academic execution
was discovered at Rice Institute where Dr. Lyford Edwards,
a sociologist "possessed certain views in respect to Russia so
contrary to the fundamental principles of our government as
utterly to destroy his further usefulness." Illinois warned
that stern punishment would be meted to those guilty of
"deriding Liberty bond salesmen" but apparently this threat
sufficed; there were no dismissals. On Morningside Heights
Nicholas Murray Butler conducted his celebrated purge,
resulting in the departure of Professors Charles Beard,
H. W. L. Dana and James Cattell and the permanent fright
of those who remained behind. His example was hailed
throughout the land as the epitome of conduct to which college presidents should aspire; they did. Nor did it require
any considerable sabotage on the part of the dissenters to
bring down the wrath of their overseers. A word, a hint, a
suggestion at a dinner-table, a momentary display of boredom
or scepticism was sufficient incitement to the servants of the
war to preserve freedom.

The Osburns went to the front, supremely certain of the
glamor, the nobility and rewards of their adventure; others
followed them because it was the thing to do; and the Shee-
hans, left behind, were impatient and disgruntled at their
own misfortune. Those who, by political or religious con-

17

viction, opposed the war were hopelessly buried in the avalanche of ballyhoo. They had neither a compact organization nor any substantial number of followers; a few held firm, seeking to resist the tide, and were quickly set upon by their hysteria-ridden cohorts. The great body of undergraduates needed no such compulsion.

"With all the impetuosity of youth he threw himself into the emergency as he conceived it in terms of immediate action. However much . . . we may deprecate the loss of so much potentially trained material, we cannot for an instant begrudge the praise due that high-minded patriotism which drove thousands of American college students out to fight their country's war. . . ." *

A sharp slump in university enrollment figures testified to the exodus. In the liberal arts colleges the loss was estimated at about twenty per cent; in the graduate schools the decline was even more marked.† Every detachment for France had its quota of feverish, expectant young men who had readily dropped Aristotle for this more provocative task. One periodical hailed them as "recruits from the cloister," who were first looked upon by the soldiers as "dreamers and theorists" but soon, by their enthusiasm, wrought a "perceptible change in the attitude of those with whom they were associated." At zero hour the boys who had "prepped" at Groton could not be distinguished from the hardened longshoremen.

Meanwhile, for those not yet summoned to active duty, the Student Army Training Corps had been established; its official inauguration was celebrated in 400 colleges with 140,000 students dedicating themselves to "the service of their country."

* See Kolbe.
† See Slosson, *The Great Crusade and After.*

18

"It was an impressive occasion and one of deep moment for the higher educational system in the United States, for it represented the official culmination of collegiate effort for official recognition. . . . Education . . . now assumed its rightful place . . . as a vital and properly organized factor toward the winning of the war."

The curriculum of the corps was "naturally determined by the policy of the War Department." Its program was "along lines either directly or indirectly related to war service." The only required course was a study of "the issues of the war."

Deprived of the opportunity for actual combat, the members of the S.A.T.C. staged their own sham battle, played at being generals and looked wistfully toward the distant scene of struggle.

The Trustees and their underlings paid ready homage to the war; they turned their universities into armed camps; the vast majority of professors assented willingly to the transformation, lending their own voices to the tumult. Meanwhile, the students did what they were told to do and thought what they were supposed to think. Most of them had never emerged from their grammar-school diapers; having no comprehension of the real issues involved, they behaved with the obedience to which they had been trained. Some were fervent and others were luke-warm; but there was fairly general agreement that since the War Department, the President of the University, the Trustees and the Faculty possessed full knowledge of their students' activities, these activities must have been right and worthwhile. If any felt resentment against the war, it was because the football season had been interrupted and there was only a handful of scrub-teams to perform.

As the conflict progressed, those who had been the first to volunteer became "statistics of sacrifice"; those who remained behind were apprised, in brief bulletins, that their brothers and companions would not return. It was a jarring succession of disclosures. The American student, it was reported, "displayed unyielding courage and faith."

Several months after the Armistice a writer in *School and Society* estimated that "the rate of loss among college men was probably as great as was the case in any other body of Americans of equal number." One incomplete survey placed the number of dead at 6,500 with thousands more wounded. Yale discovered that, of 700 volunteers from the classes of '18 and '19, close to 100 had been slain. Similar revelations were emerging from scores of institutions whose sons had made the grade. And those who came back from the carnage seemed subdued, resentful, out of place in the flag-draped furor.

"Commencement time this year," remarked *The Literary Digest* in June, 1919, "is a season of memorials as well as reunions and we are impressed with the cost in promising young life that was exacted."

Pausing after two years of delirium, *The New York Tribune* murmured, "They may well stand for that vast body of college bred heroism . . . that played so large a part in leading our forces to battle." At Yale President Hadley orated: "Those who died have protected democracy against the attacks of those who conceived themselves above the law."

Addressing the graduating class at Princeton, President Hibben pointed to those "whose place today among their comrades is vacant. They have freely given their lives for the great cause."

No one, in the multitude of nationwide memorials, mentioned that scores of new millionaires had emerged from the crusade; no one remarked that a large group of University trustees had made proportionately large profits out of the holocaust. It was unanimously agreed that the bright, able

20

young men had not died in vain and that plaques should be erected in their memory.

III. The Boom in Culture

AT last the guns were stilled; but their reverberations on the campus were far more enduring than had been realized during the siege. The shock was most visible in the demeanor of those returning to renew their studies. Their heroic buoyancy, their flip, self-assured eagerness had vanished; deluged by testimonials, by back-slapping, by community acclaim, they maintained an indifferent, resentful silence. The feeling was quickly communicated, especially to those who, while playing at war in the S.A.T.C., had chafed at the confinement. In this aftermath the game seemed a frivolous, unwarranted impudence, a barometer of their own insensitivity. To the non-combatants the war years had been an unreal interlude in which they were robbed of the natural culmination of their fervor—actual war service. When they saw the faces of the fortunate, their chagrin disappeared.

This debacle of the spirit was not, of course, uniform; many retained their enthusiasm at least long enough to join in the post-war Red Scare; others, only mildly let down, went back to the routine course of their lives. To an extraordinary number, however, it had been a severe ordeal, the stress of which was most poignantly felt when the battle had subsided. Suddenly their certainties, their aggressive conviction were gone. They had fought, or wanted to fight, to make the world a secure, liveable place. Now they found it a less inviting spectacle than ever before. The shelter in which they had so blithely rested was no longer attainable, rudely invaded by a circumstance more profound than they had ever imagined. "Lost Generation" was the phrase. Utterly unprepared for so vast a crisis in human affairs, they had been propelled into its midst; once the intensity of their ardor diminished, they awoke with a dull, remorseful headache to discover that all was neither so simple nor so appealing as they had at first fancied.

But 1919, a year of demobilization, saw the dawn of the Red-hunt and this, for a time, transcended all else in popular distractions. In college towns as everywhere, the bloodhounds, wrapped in American flags, were scenting treason. Gripped by the carefully-nurtured fear mania of 1917, they did not desist even when the national honor and the democratic spirit had been officially preserved. The authors of *Middletown* quoted a lone dissenter as murmuring in surrender: "I just run away from it all to my books." According to Frederick Lewis Allen:

"As for the schools and colleges, here the danger was more far-reaching and insidious still. According to Mr. Whitney, Professors Felix Frankfurter and Zacharia Chaffee of Harvard and Frederick Wells Williams and Max Solomon Mandell of Yale were too wise . . . not to know that their words . . . are, to put it conservatively, decidedly encouraging to the communists." *

A writer in *The Forum*, appalled by the desertions of his colleagues from the patriotic bandwagon, urged college Trustees to stump the universities and, by the persuasiveness of their own personalities, "refute the radicals." His admonition went unheeded but the jitters became a countrywide affliction. Even as late as June, 1921, Howard Elliott, former President of the Northern Pacific Railways and of the New York, New Haven and Hartford line was declaring at a Harvard alumni luncheon:

". . . In schools, colleges, even in our beloved Harvard, there is some of this atmosphere (of unrest and dis-

* From Frederick Lewis Allen's *Only Yesterday*.

22

content) and it is disturbing some of the best friends of education and progress in the country. In giving mental nourishment, why lay before young and impressionable men and women un-American doctrines and ideas that take mental time and energy from the study and consideration of the great fundamental truths?"

But the search for heresy had lost a legion of followers. The post-war undergraduate could display no avidity for the sham battle. Even as it was being waged, his own distemper, his loss of faith and zeal, was crystallizing into his first, groping assault on all that he was presumably supposed to cherish.

Out of the dislocation in spirit emerged two undergraduate uprisings, of considerable magnitude and duration. Their credo was uttered by John F. Carter, writing in *The Atlantic Monthly*. "The older generation has pretty well ruined the world before passing it on to us. They gave us this thing, knocked to pieces, leaky-red-hot, threatening to blow up; and then they are surprised that we don't accept it with the same attitude of pretty, decorous enthusiasm with which they received it way back in the eighties."

And F. Scott Fitzgerald echoed him: "Here was a new generation . . . grown up to find all gods dead, all wars fought, all faiths in men shaken."

Although the origins of the two rebellions were identical, their manifestations were palpably divergent. One, the "revolt in manners and morals," was chaotic, disorganized guerilla warfare; the other, "The New Student," * experienced a bewildering succession of changes but adhered to an intellectualized framework. The first represented a blunt, decisive surrender to despair, expressing itself in a desperate quest for emotional relief; the other sought to sing of renewed hope, to discover, in the ruins, a promise of a better future. It

* This became the title of the group's periodical; it was also vaguely characteristic of their own feeling about themselves.

was a lasting breach in the college community whose counterpart—granting significant distinctions in formulation—could be roughly drawn for many years afterward.

The great exposé was unfurled by Fitzgerald in April, 1920, with the appearance of *This Side of Paradise*. Published shortly after his graduation from Princeton, it disclosed that petting, as an undergraduate institution, dated back to 1916, and was achieving new prominence, with embellishments in technique, among the post-war student body. "None of the Victorian mothers," he observed, "had any idea how casually their daughters were being kissed." The bearer of the revelation was heralded and damned for his frankness, his insolence, his perception and his vulgarity. But the thesis received vivid confirmation in an avalanche of similar studies—*Dancing in the Dark*, *The Plastic Age*, etc. All testified to the breakdown of the ancient code. And even as they emerged, there was more patent demonstration of their words. "Skirts climbed higher," * "nice girls" took up smoking and even an occasional nip was not to be sneered at; corsets, it was plain, had been relegated to the junk heap. At little Hobart College the editor of the student newspaper deplored the "syncopated embrace" which was sweeping the colleges.

This was a revolt "without benefit of Lenin," designed to overthrow every sanctity treasured by "the older generation," directing its fury against the modes and procedures which some blundering gray-beards had erected. It betrayed no concern for politics, politicians or the future destiny of mankind. Firmly convinced that the world was a maudlin, unhappy, oppressive place to inhabit, the lieutenants of the movement proposed to make the best—or the worst—of it. Many had been close to the scene of warfare, others had been under fire; to them, all those hours had offered was the fleeting opportunity for sensual relief—and, even when the

* See *Only Yesterday*.

24

danger was past, they could not shake off that feeling. But it was more than the impermanence of life which animated the uprising; it was the destruction of a deep, naive idealism to which all had been partner, even though they never reached the battleground. Nothing had been saved in the war to save everything. Confused, disappointed, duped, the "younger generation," or a substantial part of it, determined to set out for itself along those paths most repugnant to its elders. They did so deliberately, maliciously, but with an earnestness graphically descriptive of their plight. They had been cheated and deceived because they were credulous; now they proposed to be too sophisticated to permit of further deception.

It was a busy season for the soul-savers. Societies for the Protection of Seduced Youth sprang up everywhere to warn of doom. Although the image of hell was constantly placed before their eyes, the sinners remained unperturbed, suspecting that hell was on earth and that not even the preachers were angels. It was authoritatively reported that co-eds were carrying contraceptives in their vanity-cases.

That was the way of escape, a delirious, frantic retreat to an unnamed destiny. But there were others, moved by essentially the same circumstances, who refused to accept so tumultuous an emptiness. To them the war had been just as painful, chaotic and unsettling as to the defiant foes of all moral codes—but they were unwilling to acknowledge the death of hope, the drying up of idealism. In their denial of despair, they fashioned a new mirage. The Armistice was to signalize, not the arrival of static peace, but the onrush of even more cataclysmic events, driving men toward a better life and a more fruitful way of living. Humanity would not stand still in a dismal rut of massacre and misery; out of its sorrows was to come a more perfect order. True, the old men had blustered and blundered, swept the structure to the

25

brink of disaster—but there was still time for fresh hands to rescue that which had been so roughly misused.

This was the impelling conviction behind the growth of the Intercollegiate Liberal League: an unquenchable, passionate faith in the approach of a "New Day." It was a curious admixture of doctrine; there was an extravagant projection of Wilson's heralded vision, blended with the inspiration occasioned by the end of Tsarist darkness. For them the Russian revolution was not a remote, casual eruption; it was the omen of change in every realm, the fulfillment of at least one phase of the upheaval. Several years later one of the founders of the group, recalling its inception, wrote:

"Some of us—then students in a great Eastern University—had a feeling of the new era back in 1919. There were some among us who felt themselves filled with the truth—who thought they understood what was happening in the world and how events would shape themselves. . . . Others knew their own confusion but were eager to find an orientation to what they felt, that eventually they might know what parts to play in the new world." *

With the passage of months, their ranks extended into a score of colleges. Their mission assumed an importance far beyond their early expectations. For everywhere they were assured that the reconstruction of a disordered world was their job—and hardly anyone else's. President Hibben of Princeton was informing his students that "you are to be the builders of a new world"; similar sentiments were to be heard on every side. "The great changes ahead are to be engineered, in no small part, by the enlightened, far-sighted youth"; this was no time for an orgy of forgetfulness, for the flamboyant disregard of responsibility manifested by the moral rebels. Early in 1922 the League merged with the

* From *The New Student*, June 2, 1923.

National Student Committee for the Limitation of Armaments and its lively periodical, *The New Student*, came into existence. Its first issue boldly announced:

"Students hold within their careless, unmanicured fingers the preservation of our civilization. Our elders know it. They tremble at the casual way we grasp our inheritance."

In response to some nervous eye-brow lifting, this declaration of principle was somewhat modified the following week in an article called "No Need to Fear the Forum," but the timidity did not long survive. Soon afterward came "Youth to the Rescue":

"The world is calling upon its youth for aid and support. Up till now we have been merely sheltered, protected, trained. Now we are asked to serve. . . . The world is turning to youth and saying 'leave your shelter and seclusion and help us run the world.' "

This self-confidence, this unswerving expectation of vast readjustments to come was not diminished by the Harding "return to normalcy." These students did not believe that "normalcy" was to arrive without far more fundamental revisions than had yet been accomplished. The fervor was contagious. At Amherst a student editor pleaded for "college men of excellence" and "imbued with a passion for unselfish service" to solve "the turmoil and uncertainty of the present age." In the *Dartmouth Daily* an undergraduate berated his cohorts for "settling into a rut," calling upon them to recognize that "there is a race between education and catastrophe." Another campus journal, in Ohio, bemoaned the fact that "real discussion in the classroom" was popularly regarded as a "breach of etiquette." By March, 1923, *The New Student* could again proclaim:

"The power of the future is in our hands. We are almost the only section of the population which has the leisure and opportunity to study the controversial questions of the day without bias and to act accordingly."

This sense of their own prowess was understandable. To them social change followed no systematic pattern nor possessed any direct relationship to the hostility of social classes. The fact of change was ardently to be wished; but the formula by which it was to be achieved or the structure into which it would evolve was beyond their horizon. They dimly believed in some "evolution from above," by which men of enlightenment and enterprise would effect drastic revisions in the order. Naturally enough, they regarded themselves as the chief enigneers of the deed. With equal conviction, they envisaged the "older generation" as the major obstacle to be overcome. This combat with their elders was implicit in all their efforts. It was expressed thus by one leader of the German youth movement from which they borrowed much of their credo: "The struggle of the younger generation against the older is a never-ending happening necessarily attached to all spiritual development of the human race."

To which *The New Student* readily assented, declaring that "the students of this generation are called to be the emancipating leaders of tomorrow." And again, in October, 1923: "With all respect to the older generation, some of us become more and more certain that they cannot feel the chaos as we do."

And within their own immediate environment the conflict possessed a measure of truth. It was evident for example, that a segment of the "older generation," not students in knee-pants, had largely fomented the war—not because they were "old" but because they happened to be situated in seats of economic and political power. Neglecting that detail, however, *The New Student* generalized that all "old men" were the villains of the piece, rather than a particular group of

28

gray-beards in a particular setting. It was further deduced that all evil was the product of age and that youth was the obvious antidote. That was the crux of their belief. Stated in its most extreme form, it held that a man might be of some use to the community until he was thirty years old, but after that he was automatically aligned with the legions of darkness.

Nor was their image of the "New Society" any more clearly drawn than their choice of enemies. In fact, in awaiting the dawn of change, they seemed reluctant to do anything to hasten its arrival. Their hesitance was not due to insufficient energy; of that they had an abundance. The fact was that they were highly uncertain about the shape of these momentous things to come. When one insistent critic asked for a blueprint, or even a suggestion, of the goal, *The New Student* was compelled to confess:

> "All that we know is that as students we had certain dissatisfactions; that others seem to have similar ones. . . . We can't tell exactly what is coming. . . . When there is a common student consciousness which reaches across from campus to campus and includes a sufficient number of thinking students, any action will shape itself."

Of that, then, they were confident—and nothing more. With faith only in some undefined and abstruse kingdom, they waited for the realization of the fantasy. For a fleeting moment they thought they saw the explanation:

> "Spiritually this is an age of ruin—of nausea. We suspect that many of our elders retain the nineteenth century belief in science and knowledge. We cannot share it. We need a faith. . . . At least we know what must go. Mechanization must go."

29

But even that determination was soon ignored. When was the "New Day" to be ushered in? What was to be its form? Those were imponderables. Only the distant rumblings could be heard now, in Russia and throughout Eastern Europe. *The New Student* was not prepared to set the date or the manner of their arrival here.

With the birth of a new world still a stirring vision—but one about which nothing too precipitous could be done—there were more immediate and pressing considerations arising. Upton Sinclair's *Goose Step* came out in 1923; almost immediately a succession of events confirmed his exposé of the rigid financial domination imposed upon the thought of the college and the collegian. The issue had been sharply propelled into public notice late in 1922 when President Atwood of Clark University stormed into a lecture there by Scott Nearing; after listening for five minutes, the President could hear no more and abruptly ordered the session halted. Shortly afterward the Barnard Student Council protested censorship of the speakers' list of campus clubs, condemning the tendency to "quarantine students from ideas." The Administration replied that "questionable" lectures might react unfavorably on the endowment fund. At Denison University occurred the dismissal of Professor S. I. Kornhauser; he had been discovered to be a Jew and was consequently ineligible to teach at the institution. Dr. Arthur Slaten was removed from William Jewell College for "his failure to believe in the pre-existence and deity of Christ, the infallibility of His teachings, His vicarious death and bodily resurrection."

Following a long session of interferences with its policies, the staff of *The Michigan Daily* resigned in January, 1923 to dramatize the extent of the censorship. The ensuing days were enlivened by several notable disclosures: the music editor revealed that he had been criticized for asserting that he preferred opera to football; another student had been reprimanded for a tribute to the policies of *The Nation*; still a third made known that an article detailing these acts of suppression had been banned from the school literary magazine. And that spring witnessed the celebrated Meiklejohn affair at Amherst when thirteen seniors refused their diplomas because of his ouster.

It was in May, 1924, that a torrent of academic executions was unleashed. Suspected of atheism and liberalism, Frederick Nussbaum was dropped from Temple University. When Professor Bale of Parsons College was dismissed for similar heresies, one commentator remarked that he had been "too live for the cemetery." At Brown the axe fell on Percy Marks, author of *The Plastic Age;* President Faunce explained that there had been a "growing divergence in taste and ideals" between the writer and his University. Mercer University announced that it could function more tranquilly without the services of Dr. Fox, a professor of biology whose "attitude toward certain basic evangelic beliefs" prevented him "from presenting the facts of science in such a way as to strengthen the faith of the students in those doctrines which evangelic Christians hold to be most essential." There were two victims at James Milliken College in Illinois: Professors W. C. Casey and Watson Selvage sacrificed their jobs for their injudiciously liberal utterances.

There were a host of others uprooted in the foray, more frequently for their dissent from religious, rather than economic, orthodoxy. This emphasis was entirely logical; the entrenched citizenry was far more concerned in that era over the breakdown of its moral code than over the status of its price-system. The descent of man from the monkey transcended in vitality any conflict in political theory. It is illuminating to note that, just as the religious issue agitated the faculty and caused such frequent reprisals, so the campaign against compulsory chapel in particular and ritual religion in general occupied a large number of students. They, too, were more absorbed by the decline of God than any future debacle of capitalism. Each case provoked the resent-

31

ment of *The New Student*, arousing it to a pitch of critical thought and activity more realistic than any of its general hypotheses. Whatever clarity and decisiveness it lacked about the shape of a new social order was partially compensated for by its courageous, unrelenting fight for immediate academic freedom. And in this sphere it left a deep impression—peculiarly irritating to scores of administrators who found their acts under alarming scrutiny. The soft-voiced American Association of University Professors did not escape the counter-attack. Commenting on the apparent reluctance of the A.A. U.P. to defend the persecuted, *The New Student* observed: "The rout of the A.A.U.P. seems to be general. . . . Dismissals keep going on and the Association's committees inquire whether it has been done politely."

Even in the midst of the battle against repression, however, a new and more menacing foe was sighted on the horizon.

1924 had receded in the flurry of dismissals; educators rejoiced again after the gnawing uncertainty over contract renewals had passed. As the storm subsided, an unmistakable change could be perceived in the atmosphere, growing more pronounced with each succeeding day. A student on an average American campus, in the New Year of 1925, could not fail to sense the transformation in mood. In the pages of *The New Student* its reflection was inescapable, however much the editors were disturbed by the disclosure. The panorama was summarized by an undergraduate at Yale: "It is alarming to watch the spread of soundness in our universities."

That feeling was the essence of the day. It was becoming incongruous to herald the approach of world-wide detonations; least of all could an American undergraduate betray any enthusiasm over the summons of a New Era. There wasn't any—nor could the faintest inkling of its imminence be discerned. "Normalcy" had been ridiculed by *The New Stu-*

dent two years before; but, if economic vigor and expansion were barometers, "normalcy" was now even a gross understatement. Sadly, with ill-concealed chagrin, the Forum realized that its vision was receding further from view. In December, 1924, its editorial policy was set forth in four brief paragraphs, chiefly on the need for "fruitful reflection." Returning to England after a visit to American colleges, William Robson wrote of his journey:

"I found that drives for money were made on a vast scale and with a success undreamed of in England. . . . Although one meets students who obviously show promise of becoming great engineers, great doctors, captains of industry and so forth, one rarely, if ever, meets a student who seems destined to become a Darwin, a Beethoven, a Shelley."

The "success idea" was being nowhere more readily embraced, as it surged to the surface, than on the campus. Commensurate with the permeation of that magnetic credo into undergraduate consciousness, there was a perceptible shift in the strategy of *The New Student*—a shift which implied more than a revised array of tactics. It testified to an acceptance of the "economy of abundance" as an established, indisputable fact of lasting proportions. Equipped with no systematic understanding of the operation of the social order and the forces behind its upswing, *The New Student* came slowly to acknowledge the premises of its contemporaries: that capitalism, whether one liked it or not, was opening a new vista for industrial expansion and material plenty. Its own inconclusiveness about the nature or the method of inauguration of the "New World" of which it spoke augmented this self-delusion. It was becoming sheer wishful-thinking, the group reasoned, to herald a new order or to plead for a more rational, equitable scheme of relationships when precisely that

33

equity, that extension of opportunity was presumably being realized within the ancient modes.

The weight of these conclusions descended vehemently upon *The New Student*. Its rebellion was transferred abruptly to a different plane. The things of the spirit, the debasement of men's minds and surroundings, became of extraordinary importance. To an extent, of course, the members of the group had always been animated by a need to express emotional disequilibrium and spiritual nausea rather than by any deprivation of income or dinner-fare. Even in their most ardent salutations to the oncoming of "Social Justice" and its equally undefined accompaniments, they had been moved by what they felt to be the transient, helter-skelter foundation of their environment. Now the bulwarks were once more entrenched and 1925 became a landmark for the rebellion. The generals were abandoning the advance on Utopia to devote their attention to what seemed to be the only shortcomings in their immediate environment—the deficiencies in the mind, the habits and the ways of living of a materially-blessed country.

Of these enemies within the gates, "gigantism" was the first to be sighted. The nature of the conflict is best depicted in a favorite anecdote of the period, said to have been related by Professor George Santayana of Harvard. Walking through the corridors one day, he met the president of Harvard College, who asked him how his classes were "progressing."

"Most of the students are fairly intelligent," replied Professor Santayana.

The president seemed perplexed by the reply, then requested impatiently: "I meant, what is the number of students in your classes."

That conversation became the preamble of the movement, the *reductio ad absurdum* of the peril allegedly stalking the campus. It was reiterated endlessly in *The New Student* which, in January, 1925, indignantly demanded a suspension

34

of "quantitative and material expansion" in favor of "qualitative improvement." A special supplement entitled "Shells" was devoted almost exclusively to a study of the architecture of American colleges, professing to see in it "the building of glorified factories" adapted to "stupid mass haranguing" and enslaved to "masters of commerce and accumulation."

Earlier they had cried out against "mechanization" as the source of mankind's spiritual restlessness and discontent. Now the intruder was to be discovered in education's drive for "mass production." A typical manifestation of the trend they attacked was a headline in one newspaper: TIDE OF STUDENTS EVER RISING.

The New Student lamented that "like Ford cars and a certain brand of cigarettes, enrollment in the colleges is increasing." There was adequate confirmation for its fears. In October, 1925, registration in eighty-three leading colleges and universities had reached 245,000, an increase of 15,000 over the preceding year. An estimate of enrollment at the ten largest institutions of higher learning revealed an advance of 57,000 in fifteen years. Under the caption "Roll Your Own Diploma," Charles Merz portrayed "the spectacular growth of the collegiate system": "The wealth of the country has increased enormously in recent years and a college education, either on the spot, by mail or over the loud speaker, has become a possibility for thousands of people who never expected to have an alma mater."

With these thousands pounding at the doors of knowledge, the curriculum was naturally revised to provide some morsel for every member of the family. That weird hotbed of irrelevant information, the extension department, began to flourish simultaneously in a score of places. Southern California offered instruction in Advanced Tailoring, Traffic Management and Real Estate Advertising through such methods as "billboards," "trips to property" and the development of "golf links, country clubs and model homes." * At

* See Charles Merz, *The Great American Bandwagon.*

35

Virginia a course was offered in "Follow-Up Methods"; Indiana furnished lessons in "Renting and Leasing," while at Chicago students were tutored in "The Dedication and the Toast." If one preferred his learning by the fireside technique, there were limitless roads to culture—by mail. Chicago presented a choice of 396 correspondence courses; Columbia was even more extravagant in the disbursement of its pearls, with 745 courses available by post. The student of "radio communication" could find advanced guidance at Nebraska, the scholar in "Automobile Upkeep and Repair" was welcomed at California while Cornell sponsored researches in "The Administration of Hotels."

It was an incredible parade of which 1925 saw only the first detachment. The columns were to continue marching until the end of the decade, causing a wide series of "changed values" in halls of learning:

> "Business itself was regarded with a new veneration. Once it had been considered less dignified and distinguished than the learned professions. . . . Now college alumni, gathered at their annual banquets, fervently applauded banker Trustees who spoke of education as one of the great American industries and compared the president and the dean to business executives." *

Caught in the deluge, *The New Student* could only exhort its followers—steadily dwindling in number—to "look with disfavor on commercialized, wholesale education and the overburdening, all-absorbing mass of material . . . that goes with it." Its entreaty was applauded by a student journalist at Williams, who condemned the collegiate edifice for "teaching men how to make a living, not how to live." Another undergraduate noted bitterly that "the young American of this age is fathered by materialistic plenty and mothered by poverty of the spirit." Berating the current ideals of the stu-

* From *Only Yesterday.*

dent whirl, *The Ohio State Lantern* asked why there was only scorn for "men who love beauty," whose affection for "learning" surpasses their "love for the University" and who prefer "to think rather than to study." There were even intercollegiate conferences against "mass production."

The revolt was undergoing its most decided transition and one from which it never recovered. It was no longer solicitous of the social forms under which men lived or conscious of any impending modification of them. The question of the hour was the manner of men's living. This new pre-occupation was readily explicable. Prosperity, bigger, better, more convincing than ever, was the reason.

Meanwhile, from Cumberland University came a dramatic appeal for funds, despatched to citizens of property throughout the land:

> "God has given too much. If without children, make these children yours. If death took your own away, a Cumberland memorial will MAKE THE DEAD AND YOU LIVE ON together in blessed influence. . . . Send for me to guide your benevolence. . . . Put us in your will."

James Duke announced that he was prepared to donate six million dollars to Trinity University if it consented to be known henceforth as "Duke University." Within three weeks the Trustees solemnly convened to accept his benevolence.

Early in the same year—1925—a "Junior Kiwanis" was organized among Brown University students, declaring as its purpose a campaign to "boost the school."

In response to inquiry, the Dean of Columbia College asserted that he would feel justified in not recommending for a business post a student who failed to wear his freshman cap.

Commenting on Coolidge's decisive victory in the student straw vote of the previous Fall, Heywood Broun wanted to know where "all the imagination and vision of youth I've heard a lot about" had gone.

In an address full of acclaim for himself, his Trustees and the conduct of his University, President Lovett of Rice Institute pointed out that "Socrates, Plato and Aristotle would feel right at home among us." If he had pursued the notion further, he might have described their enthusiasm over the following apportionment of news in that day's edition of the student newspaper: 35 inches for sports, 18 for campus gossip, 6 for a B.V.D. parade, 3 for the account of an address, 3½ for an announcement of the humor publication—and editorials dealing with such controversial issues as "The Slime Nightshirt Parade."

A lone dissenter at Ohio Wesleyan deplored the sensitivity of the University to the whims of "outside opinion."

Incoming freshmen at Ohio State were admonished by President Thomson to heed one truth above all: "The best thing to do is to do what you are told."

"The American college," Alexander Meiklejohn was writing, "merely reflects the society of its time."

Slowly but irresistibly the creed of *The New Student* was veering into the camp of Henry L. Mencken. It was a surrender visible in every sphere where the embers of revolt could still be discerned, a retreat whose portents had been obvious elsewhere long before *The New Student* was willing to acknowledge Mencken's eminence. But when all hope of the new world had vanished, when smugness and complacence had become a national characteristic and Babbitt a national hero, Mencken's seizure of command was inevitable. The college, it was sorrowfully to be admitted, had become a "middle class paradise"—and Mencken was the apostle of middle-class self-criticism. As Lewis Browne later recalled, "the heavy wine of idealism had turned to vinegar, radicalism gave way to cynicism; H. L. Mencken supplanted H. G. Wells, Sinclair Lewis took the place of Upton Sinclair and the undergraduate intellectual ceased to frown and began to sneer."

The emergence of Mencken, I have said, was not a coup d'état abruptly carried out in 1925. His capture of the under-graduate dissenter had begun as far back as 1923 when Norman Thomas wrote that "the prophet of the minority of our youth is Mencken, not Marx" and another writer described the "supercilious young men bearing a green-covered maga-zine under their arms." These were omens of the deeper inroads which the sage of Baltimore was to make. Now Paul Blanshard was eminently convinced that the collegiate rebels were "closer to Mencken than Moscow." And it was plain that two factors had swung the battle: the ambiguous, grop-ing nature of the revolt itself—and the coming of material plenty, of unbounded economic opportunity for the student.

His security was obvious. Prosperity may never have en-compassed the lower depths; but for the middle class it was a revelation, a bearer of promise more glowing than ever before anticipated. The college student was a favorite son of the ascending economic cycle. The extent to which this belief was popularly accepted—and essentially true—was to be seen in the advertisements of a reputable insurance firm which maintained that "a college education is estimated to be worth $150,000 to the man who has one." That was no flamboyant fiction, nor a bait thrown out by extension departments. If the figure was somewhat premature, the meaning of the gesture was remarkably well substantiated.

To those dissatisfied with the internals of life there seemed only one struggle to be fought—against cultural barbarism, against the aggrandizement of fraudulent gods, against the shackles imposed by the "ideology of success." When Mencken denounced college students for their readiness to "consecrate themselves, on getting their degrees, to the mort-gage bond business and the development of refined suburbs," the intellectual fringe on the campus hailed him as its mouth-piece. He was recited as scripture, as the last virile voice in

39

a stagnant atmosphere. It was a campaign replete with the exultation of destruction. From the encounter with "gigant-ism" his disciples turned to the conquest of the "booboisie," a bitter, pointed foray against those whom abundance had made "fat, futile and intellectually vapid." On March 28, 1925, *The New Student* published a "Mencken issue"; there were journals arising everywhere whose pages teemed with the doctrine of the savior, the man who could express what the sensitive, unhappy undergraduate dissenter was thinking.

Only a fragment still adhered to the quest for a different set of economic relationships—and desertions from their ranks were occurring at every moment. The League for Industrial Democracy was pointing the way to a profitless, socialist society; but even to the undergraduate intellectual, the pros-pect was neither real nor particularly inviting. "The unignor-able fact stands out," wrote the editor of *The Daily Kansan*, "that students are a part of the bourgeoisie, which considers labor menial and labor organizations symptomatic of bolshev-ism." Another critic held that "college liberalism finds it so much easier to laugh at the booboisie than to understand or work with the proletariat, to criticize Main Street than to make an effort to recreate it." Even those who bestowed attention upon the problem of strife between capital and labor were eminently "objective," impersonal and academic in their approach:

> "Their (the college intellectuals') attitude is cynical, inquiring, distrustful, without loyalty to anything in par-ticular. . . . The ablest students on our campuses are convinced that capital has relatively too much power . . . but there are few who have any intense loyalty to the labor movement." *

The insurgents, rallied to the standard of Menckenism, were as caustic in their denunciations of the "masses" as of

* From an article by Paul Blanshard in *The Survey*, October 15, 1926.

the "booboisie." That was a logical culmination of their earlier self-aggrandizement; the earlier conviction that they, the "leisure, educated" class would single-handed effect social reorganization now prompted their firmer renunciation of alliances, their growing sense of isolation in the midst of a vulgarized, intellectually debauched civilization.

This was a war within the middle class and it never escaped from that confinement. For the insurgents themselves, whatever their dissatisfactions, could not bring themselves to a break with the economic ideals of their own environment. They never approached the conflict in those terms. Why should they have? Even the iconoclasts had to eat, and the existing capitalist order, despite its repulsive superstructure, seemed to assure them of that—if nothing more.

The ensuing two years witnessed the uninterrupted ascendancy of King Football and all the tendencies which became identified with his rule. If the dissenting segment of the campus was still carving weapons for the assault on Babbittry, the campaign evoked only scattered approval among the rank-and-file of the collegiate community. *The New Student* perceived its own retreat, its divorce from the main streams of undergraduate life. When it cited the two fateful alternatives confronting the student as "swimming with the current of our national life or struggling valiantly against it," two paragraphs later appeared the resentful admission: "unfortunately, most students aren't alive to the existence of the dilemma."

They weren't. Nor was there any outwardly compelling reason for such a pre-occupation. While they prepared themselves for lucrative posts in the industrial machine, there were other, more diverting themes of interest. Educators, far from seeking to inoculate their brood with a critical, sensitive understanding of events, preferred instead to solve "the dilemma of living" by ignoring it. Nowhere was this capitulation more manifest than in the unanimous homage paid to the gridiron. On November 10, 1926, *The Daily Californian* reported:

"Kindled by fiery challenges from the lips of Dean Paul F. Cadman addressed to his class in Economics 1B, a reminder of old-time California spirit burst forth when a room-full of students thundered out 'Fight for California' in support of California's varsity football team. . . . Cadman himself started the singing as he concluded a stirring talk."

Simultaneously students were answering the roll-call in Oklahoma Agricultural College classrooms with the phrase "Beat Washington." When a few professors objected to the procedure, the student newspaper mercilessly derided them, warning that "whether professors sanction it or not," the slogan would remain. President Knapp stood squarely behind his students in this challenge to the malcontents.

There was rejoicing at Howard Payne College. "This year," according to the student journal, "there were many difficulties to be overcome before the student body got the real Howard Payne spirit but when they did get it, it came like a cyclone."

And on the West Coast the presidents of two institutions agreed that the death of an undergraduate during a spirited football riot was not the fault of the student body of either school. The "incident" was dismissed as "unavoidably involved in the regrettable excitement of the game."

As the football fever spread, as housewives in the Bronx became vigorous partisans over the Yale-Harvard game and citizens whose education had ended in the fifth grade adopted the colors of Notre Dame, a handful of voices decried the spectacle. Terming the sport "a replica of bull-fighting," one Minnesota professor issued a bitter arraignment of its status—for which he was roundly rebuked by the editor of the undergraduate daily there. Alfred Dashiell, a Princeton alumnus, labelled the game "a national religion whose cathedrals are gigantic concrete stadia." The *Dartmouth Daily* denounced as "sentimental rot" the significance attached to Saturday's encounters.

But theirs were feeble protests, drowned out by the more numerous and loud-spoken apostles of a national institution. For football had ceased to be merely an extra-curricular amusement; it was hailed as the epitome of the "American love for sportsmanship," a reflection of "the soundness in body and mind of American youth," the "avenue to closer ties between the public and the college." William Roper, celebrated Princeton football mentor, stirred the applause of the W.C.T.U. when he cited the game as "a bulwark against Prohibition Repeal"—apparently unaware that more liquor was consumed in football stadia than in any other single gathering-place for thirsty men and women.

The antics of the major universities only incited more furious efforts by the backwoods educational centers. It had become established beyond dispute that the path to recognition for an aspiring college lay across the football goal-line. With thirty million people paying $50,000,000 every Fall to be uplifted by the art of pigskin-toting, no enterprising administrator could afford to resist the whirlwind. If a little college in Squedunk wanted to achieve the fame and fortune of its older brothers, the purchase of a triple-threat half-back seemed a far wiser investment than a professor of chemistry or a new wing for the library.

Early in 1927, one year after its founding, the University of Miami launched a drive for a $500,000 football stadium as a spring-board for its rise in the academic world. That its 200 freshmen were attending classes in a hotel whose facilities were borrowed for want of adequate instruction space did not deter the campaign. Nor was the student body in the least perturbed by this emphasis.

Out in the midwest Knute Rockne was advising professors who found students apathetic to their lectures to "make your classes as interesting as football."

43

What chance for the rebels? Their cries were relegated to obscure corners while the spokesmen of success bellowed more sonorously than ever. "The college radical," said Heywood Broun, "finds himself a lone and rather unpopular innovator surrounded entirely by Babbitts." To which Paul Blanshard added: "the great majority of our college students are like their parents, bent on making good in the highest social class they can clamber into; they reflect the philosophy of the hinterland." When one jittery soul lamented that college students were "going red," Dr. Glenn Hoover ridiculed the notion, pointing out that the average undergraduate was "the son of Babbitt" and was upholding the family tradition.

College enrollment was becoming so swollen that it seemed the walls of laboratories could no longer contain their multitude of inhabitants. Commenting on the trend, *The Daily Illini* cited "the unprecedented economic prosperity of thousands of families throughout the nation." It was everywhere reiterated that the college man had a wider stretch of opportunity ahead than any other section of the population. Addressing the students of Texas University, Governor Dan Moody declared that "many captains of industry have spent their years at the University; there is no acceptable reason why you shouldn't make an even greater contribution." President Burgstahler of Cornell College, Iowa, was more reverent than his contemporaries; he informed his undergraduates that "God has a great plan for your lives."

A whole generation was being moulded to the success pattern. The "rah-rah" boy was more than a popular image. He was a comfortable, inert, carefree specimen who knew that on the first of the month a check at least adequate to his needs would arrive from home. Certainly there were many not yet so fortunate; even the less well-to-do, however, could be comparatively untroubled about their futures and eminently convinced that the trek to success had begun. If they had to wait on tables to get there, the ultimate reward would be more than bountiful.

44

This limitless optimism was strikingly expressed by Bryan Hale, a student at the University of Southern California. When one dissenter murmured that "education costs too much," Hale heatedly ridiculed the notion, pointing out with some eloquence that "every day spent in college is worth a lot of money in return. We aren't on the short end."

The uprising was inevitably becoming sporadic, detached from its surroundings. "We are becalmed," confessed *The New Student* in 1927. "Only our dislikes are dynamic." One of its earliest leaders, Douglas Haskell, believed he understood what had happened. Regretfully he wrote, in May of that year:

> "The huge difference between 1927 and 1922, when *The New Student* was modestly incepted, is that there is no doubt of American prosperity and comfort. That changes the whole map and the whole enterprise. It occurred to me . . . that the whole effect we were after hung together with the idea that there were going to be grand changes in the country. There aren't. Therefore, reluctantly it must be admitted that nearly all the revolts we began fostering in colleges have degenerated into mean scuffles. . . . Where we used to dream of new faiths and new communities developing out of colleges and flowering through a thankful country, now the main hope is that students will be less bored by lecturing. . ."

The Purdue Dean of Men was urging freshmen to remember: "Everything has two sides; seek the explanation that promotes happiness and contentment . . . nobody cares for a grouch"; an editor at Washington and Jefferson was writing that "we wish the freshmen to acquire the spirit of loyalty if they gain nothing else from their campus life." A character in *Richard Kane Looks at Life* remarked: "At fifty, when I've made my pile, I'll go in for culture."

The only road for rebellion was the remorseless sniping

45

of the Menckenites. To them the scene was a half-ludicrous, wretchedly insane whirligig, a fertile ground for lampooning. It did not matter that no citadels were overthrown by their assaults.

There was one complacence-shattering disclosure in those months—and for a brief interval it agitated large circles of opinion in the academic world. A "suicide wave" was reported to be sweeping the colleges. In the period from January to May, 1927, twenty-six students in universities and secondary schools had taken their own lives. When the press stumbled upon the news, sixty-four point type was hauled out to blazon it forth. In the pulpit the revelation was greeted as long-awaited evidence that youth was reaching the hell which it had created for itself. A Methodist bishop intoned: "we must get back to vital religion and downright godliness or we are lost." The Catholic journal *America* exhorted parents to preserve their children from "the almost fatal dangers of the secular college." Joining piously in the post-mortems, Bernarr McFadden attributed the epidemic to "Too Much Brain, Not Enough Brawn." To Dr. John Watson, the founder of behaviorism "intolerable environmental conditions" had precipitated the outbreak; he recommended that those in similar surroundings be transported to other countries and there renew life under assumed names. A manager of athletics at one college refused to be dismayed by the circumstance, blithely urging "more and better athletics" as the solution.

When the furor had relaxed and the press turned to some other source for scandal, sober judgment revealed that the interlude had been extravagantly depicted—far beyond its own scope. It could not, however, be abruptly dismissed. Behind the black, screaching headlines resided some unpleasant, provocative facts. Primary was the high mental rating of almost all the victims, many of them distinguished students of philosophy; in only three cases could an immediate personal reason be discovered; the rest, apparently, were

46

moved by broader evaluations of their society and their own place in it. It was an unhappy thought. Why were some of the ablest, most talented minds on the campus dissatisfied with the magnificent edifice being wrought by "American initiative"? Could there be anything precarious, fraudulent, superficial about the structure? Was the scholar out of place in college, out of step with so promising a life?

The orgy of self-examination was brief and readily abandoned. Educators assured themselves, with some measure of justification, that the extent of the "wave" had been overdrawn, however real its causes. If one student writer was bemoaning the "gaseous world . . . without living significance," his was a lone reaction. The vice-president of the student body at Colgate was far more overwrought because "our 'long Colgate' cheer doesn't send that shiver-tingling up and down our spine as it once did."

At the University of California a student editor lamented that "13,500 out of 14,000 students came here only to make money." To them death was a remote, fanciful consideration.

There were still a few simmerings of mutiny. At the University of Georgia late in 1927 five students published *The Iconoclast* independently on the ground that the official college press was under rigid censorship. Pointing to the "low rating of the school," they charged that it was due to "the subservience of students" to "an official bouncer" who "promptly squelches any student who dares raise a protesting finger." To confirm their allegation, "the official bouncer" dismissed them from college, reinstating them only when they apologized for their "disrespectful language." Reviewing the case, *The Columbus Enquirer* observed that "the article was so packed with the truth that it irritated."

For violating a statute which banned "any criticism of the action or character of a student or officer of the University," an undergraduate journalist at the University of Arkansas was abruptly ousted from college. The remainder of the student body was advised to proceed warily in its discussions.

When *The Sacred Cow,* an independent periodical, appeared at Kansas City Junior College, its editors joined the ranks of departed academic spirits. The President of the college, in wielding the disciplinary axe, denounced their efforts as "part of a national Bolshevik program to wreck our schools."

Those were the last gasps of insurrection.

A survey by *School and Society* in January, 1928, reported that enrollment in the colleges had increased twenty-five per cent in the preceding five years. Dr. Marsten of Columbia was conducting tests to determine whether blondes or brunettes are more suspectible to excitement while watching love-scenes on the screen. Oppressed by the failures of the University of Colorado football team, students there blamed the "scholarship threat" for the inadequacy of material. To attract more versatile performers, the undergraduate journal suggested a school slogan to be widely broadcast: "the university is not flunking everyone out."

New Haven was still in an uproar over the appearance of Gene Tunney on a Yale lecture platform. The press was hailing another example of capitalist benevolence: Henry Fuller had offered a scholarship to Worcester Polytechnic Institute for the boy displaying "the most Yankee ingenuity."

Editorially *The New Student* was promising to "laugh at the assininities of the Rotarians," "continue to work for the heightening of student class consciousness" and "search for elements that will contribute to a satisfactory life in the modern world."

The thousands who strolled across America's college campuses appeared highly pleased by the present and future of things.

Toward the end of 1928 a morose silence descended upon the camp of the rebels. Their fireside was virtually deserted, their ardor gone, the remnants of their battalions weary and alone. The National Student Forum and the organ which had mirrored its life—*The New Student*—disappeared from the scene. It was a defeat noticeable on a far wider front. The whole temper of the intellectual movement had become one of despair—despair in its surroundings and in the insufficiency of its own efforts. On the campus, neither the "revolt in manners and morals," the romantic idealism of the early *New Student,* nor the bitter shafts of the Menckenites had provided any satisfactory answer to those who, for one reason or another, could find no adjustment in the world of boom. "What most distinguished the generation who have approached maturity since the debacle of idealism at the end of the war is not their rebellion . . . but their disillusionment with their own rebellion." *

iv. Depression Graduate

HERBERT HOOVER, the last living American to grant official recognition to economic decline, clambered effusively onto the platform of Drake University's Commencement Exercises early in June, 1935. Although time and circumstance had damaged his reputation for prophesy, Mr. Hoover was still irrepressible. Into this academic setting he came in his ancient rôle: gloom-chaser of the American Republic, antidote to depression nightmares, confounder of scepticism. Jubilantly, with the air of a man who has found the answers to the unfathomable, Mr. Hoover told the graduates:

> "I hear much lament over the outlook for graduating students. Did it ever occur to you that all the people who now live in these houses, who conduct this vast, complex life and civilization are going to die? And that just as sure as death you will take over their jobs?"

* Walter Lippmann's *A Preface to Morals.*

The audience stared, blinked incredulously and agreed that the thought had never before been adequately circulated. Someone whispered: "Nuts."

After six years of prayers, hopes and promises, death had become the only panacea which the most rugged of individualists could offer. It was a startling confession. The man who had ascended to office on the momentum of "Permanent Prosperity," the standard-bearer of the "Age of Abundance," was preaching bigger, better and more frequent funerals as the path to security for the student.

Almost simultaneously R. L. Duffus wrote his benediction for seniors in *The New York Times:* "About 150,000 students with baccalaureate or graduate degrees are emerging in the United States this month into a world which, as one college president said to a student assembly the other day, does not want them. . . ."

Summarizing the status of graduates in the nationwide search for jobs, W. Emerson Gentzler, secretary of appointments at Columbia, had admitted several months before that "the social order is unable to absorb those who are annually graduated from our colleges and professional schools." A man in a similar post at a leading Eastern Law School privately acknowledged that there were no places for even the highest-ranking men. *The New Yorker,* in the Winter of 1935, cynically suggested that the owners of the Burlington zephyr "hire a couple of college graduates to polish up the zephyr" which was becoming "terribly dirty." And their observations were dramatically borne out in an item in *The New York Post* of July 18, 1935: ". . . The United States Army is going collegiate. College graduates are trickling into the recruiting station at 30 Whitehall Street and joining up as privates. . . . Grub, prosaic grub is the impetus behind the rush."

These are recent and obvious manifestations of what has developed cumulatively through the era of crisis. The full impact of depression did not descend on the campus at once; one of the last centers to realize its effects, in their most devastating form, have been the schools of higher learning. Only within the past two years has this "loss of caste" been deeply impressed upon the consciousness of the undergraduate. There are multiple reasons for the "lag." Although colleges and universities experienced a sweeping expansion after the turn of the century, with enrollment advancing from 81,000 in 1890 to more than one million in 1930, only ten per cent of our youth of college age could—at the peak—attend these institutions.* John W. Studebaker, Commissioner of Education, recently declared that "there are 64,000,000 people in the country who have not finished high school, 32,000,000 have not finished the eighth grade and only 1,200,000 have finished college." The point does not need more elaborate documentation; even at the zenith of its growth, higher education in the United States was restricted to a definite economic segment of the population—the middle class and its immediate satellites. This, of course, included those in the top brackets whose wealth was an inheritance from our early expansion days; it also applied, and in thousands of cases, to that part of the lower middle class which had pulled itself up by its bootstraps in the boom decade. The favorite illusion of our democracy, that the workingman's son goes to college with the youthful Du Ponts, has long ago been exploded. Workers' children never comprised any substantial section of the collegiate population. Those who did come, in ever-increasing numbers throughout the 1920's, were the offspring of Babbitt, the sons of small business-men, shop-keepers, life insurance dealers and the like.

When the fraudulent bases of "prosperity" were exposed in the economic nose-dive of 1929, the first and most widespread devices of "contraction" were levelled at the lower strata. Their wages fell, employment channels dried up, evictions were not unknown; moreover, having never shared to

* Rex David's *Schools and the Crisis.*

any appreciable extent in the gains of the decade, these victims were least able to resist the avalanche. But this was not the immediate experience of those directly above them—the fathers of the college generation. Supported by a measure of savings from their brief flirtation with luxury, they were able to defend themselves, during what was expected to be only a transitory interlude, against the day of reckoning.

Thus, for varying periods of time, they carried on; optimism emanated from the White House, the sign-posts of recovery were allegedly discerned and the long Winter was soon to be over. With pathetic faith, the small investors, the John Smiths of boom-time achievements, desperately endeavored to keep their children in college. Their stubbornness was animated by "The Bread and Butter Purpose" with which college had become synonymous in the preceding years. In *College or Kindergarten,* Dean McConn of Lehigh had depicted what this meant: ". . . the social purpose of the college today, as conceived by the majority of the clientele . . . is . . . to afford special privilege and a differential advantage in the economic struggle."

Now, when the foundations of this doctrine were disappearing, John Smith still awaited fulfillment. Whatever privations the family might be compelled to endure, he determined to provide his son with an A.B. and start him on the uphill climb.

The illusion gripped the student. To him the dislocation in government was still a remote, impersonal phenomenon. It is not astonishing that, from 1929 to 1931, the average campus was almost devoid of social awareness or critical inquiry. "The brighter youths," one writer noted, "have rediscovered St. Thomas Acquinas and like to quote the French metaphysical poets. They recoil from naturalism . . . and prefer the sentimentality of a Willa Cather. In terror of the future, revolted by the present, they are trying to escape into the past."

The important fact is that they could still afford the retreat.

If checks from home had diminished in size, they still arrived in a regular stream. Propped up by the financial conquests of the years before, fathers were waging a valiant, last-ditch stand against the inroads of foreclosure and stock-somersaults. Out at college the intensity of the struggle was hardly perceived. In May, 1931, William Harlan Hale asserted: "Today . . . to be an Eastern college man is to be a collared conservative. . . . The average student in American colleges—and especially in the fashionable Eastern ones—scorns politics and public questions as beneath him." *

At Yale *The Harkness Hoot,* founded with the objective of revitalizing student thought, could make little headway against the "conventional ideal." Its numerous prototypes throughout the country were similarly rebuffed by the dominant mood of ivory-tower complacence. The undergraduate intellectual was more likely to be involved in a controversy over "Art for Art's sake" than in any conflict over economic laws. As for the vast majority of students, they were not "intellectuals," were loudly contemptuous of the term and could display no argumentative ardor over art, politics or educational principles.

Slowly but perceptibly, however, the fortress was being invaded. One of the most glaring aspects of the trend was the abrupt reversal of the enrollment curve. College registration, after its sensational spurt of the post-war decade, was at last declining. A survey conducted by the American Association of Registrars in April, 1935 discloses the following shifts:

> From 1929-30 to 30-31 increase of 2.3   per cent
> From 1930-31 to 31-32 increase of 0.10 per cent
> From 1931-32 to 32-33 decrease of 3.91 per cent
> From 1932-33 to 33-34 decrease of 3.15 per cent
> (From 1929-30 to 33-34 decrease of 4.32 per cent)†

* *The New Republic,* May, 1931.
† Recent figures, not yet tabulated in full, indicate a slight upturn for 1935 in certain sections of the country. The rise, admittedly meagre, is

It will be seen that, beginning in 1931, the crisis was being expressed in its most palpable form: students withdrawing from school to search for jobs, provide some revenue for their families and lift the burden of school expenses. Whereas, in 1927, Arthur Klein could assert in the Bureau of Education *Bulletin* that "under present conditions the costs are not the decisive factor in determining whether students shall or shall not attend college," now they were proving of real import to crisis-stricken homes.

Moreover, the solution of working a way through college was ceasing to be valid. By 1933 the Harvard catalogue was informing those who hoped to do so that "because of the temporary business depression, opportunities are at present greatly limited." To the graduating classes, the situation was even more acute: after four years of training, it was now far from certain that a job was waiting at the termination of the period. An ancient, carefully-nurtured truth was being shattered. College graduates were no longer a "privileged class." In 1932 H. M. Friend, writing in *Power*, maintained that sixty-two per cent of the graduating classes of 1931 were still in quest of employment. In New York H. M. Emery and Miss C. Haider reported that 3,324 professionals were on work relief rolls.*

While the undergraduate was beginning to perceive how tenuous was his status, his teachers were being stirred by similar circumstances. William Burl Thomas declared that "in 1932 the depression caught up with the universities"; supporting the assertion, he submitted a comprehensive chart of educational retrenchment throughout the country.† There were sharp slashes in the budget at Ohio State and Michigan, for example, causing "wholesale dismissals" of staff members. And if, in 1932 salary cuts could be regarded as "emergency

almost exclusively noticeable in free colleges; its causes appear to be despair at the possibility of finding employment and the emergence of F.E.R.A. jobs for students as a temporary stop-gap.

* *The New Republic,* May 17, 1933.
† *The Nation,* August 23, 1933.

measures," by the following year "all pretense at optimism had vanished . . . the faculty of the University of Iowa and the State College at Ames are wondering not how much of a salary cut they will take but whether they will get any salary at all next year."

That feeling was representative of universities, large and small, throughout the country. The boom in culture was over.

Despite these omens, the philosophy of the universities, as expressed in their curricula, pre-occupations and tenor of life, was remarkably unchanged. Although another rebel movement had begun,* college administrators were striving desperately to minimize the stability of its roots and to dispute its credo. And thousands of students, even in the face of these increasingly personal encounters with the crisis, were tutored in the old faiths and hopes. The extent to which they were shielded from the facts of life was admirably depicted recently by Professor Mark A. May of Yale. Citing the extraordinary unwillingness of the educational world to broadcast the truth, he contended that education itself was "geared to an economic theory that died October 29, 1929, the day that Santa Claus died." To every new testimony of havoc and disaster, educators were preaching that "somewhere there is a job for the man who can fill it."

But by 1934 even the most determined hotbed of optimism was finding scant ground for reassurance. It was estimated that one third of the previous graduating class could obtain no employment at all while another third was engaged in occupations for which it had neither interest nor talent. One college journal bade its seniors farewell with an editorial captioned "Into the Wasteland." And there were scores of others everywhere whom the homely platitudes of the academic cheer-leaders could not satisfy. The realities of existence were too imminent to be dispelled by either Willa

---

* The origins and growth of that movement will, of course, be discussed in detail later; here we are concerned with the general forces at work which provide the setting for the major events of this book.

Cather or Nicholas Murray Butler. A survey by Drs. Morgan and Remmers of Purdue University reported:

"There was a large and significant increase in liberal attitudes toward social problems among students in 1933-34 as compared with the early depression years of 1931-32. . . . College students are more radical because they realize they are facing a less secure world than in 1931." *

In the same month the man voted "most likely to succeed" by his classmates of 1933 at a large Eastern University was sealing envelopes at ten dollars a week in Wall Street. The former editor of the literary magazine at another institution was serving as a bell-boy in a downtown hotel. To these cases could have been added hundreds more, many of whom could not even boast any pay for their work. They were willing "to help around the office"—any office—in the hope that someone would find them indispensable. Usually nobody did.

The downfall of the graduate was not stemmed by Congressional legislation, pump-priming measures or a faint-hearted attempt by the press to ballyhoo "Recovery" out of hiding. If there were temporary, scattered gains, they made no significant impression on the ranks of the "surplus population." One recent graduate, commenting on Walter Pitkin's conviction that "Life Begins at Forty," remarked: "At the risk of being considered impertinent, I should like to ask what we who have taken a degree or perhaps a second or third degree are to do between now and that delectable age at which, he contends, life begins." †

The same writer cited a notable survey of the outlook for the 1935 graduating class at the college he attended. A questionnaire was submitted to the 243 graduates in which they were asked what they planned to do after Commencement.

* *The New York Post*, December 27, 1934.
† Wallace J. Cambell in *The Social Frontier*, May, 1935.

Only sixty-five—about one-fourth of the class—were sure of jobs of any description. Fifty-nine bluntly admitted that they didn't know. In forty-eight cases there was no reply at all; their silence was sufficient explanation. Twenty-two were holders of teaching certificates; they "hoped to teach" but had no idea where their services would be requested. Law schools had accepted eleven—and there are reputed to be 50,000 surplus lawyers turned out each year. Most eloquent was the reply of one lone, harassed individual who wrote "God only knows!" And finally there were twenty-seven able to postpone the "decision" by pursuing "advanced degrees." That was their last resort, as signified by the poem attached to the reply of one of the degree-hunters:

ODE TO HIGHER EDUCATION

I've always sung the praises
Of M.A.'s and Ph.D.'s,
But in pursuit of Pallas,
We are starving by degrees.

An identical questionnaire was distributed to fourteen graduate students at the same college, many of them holders of advanced degrees and clearly outstanding in their respective fields. The following answers were recorded:

"Will enter Medical School"; "hope to teach"; "probably teach"; "don't know"; "teaching assistant at Minnesota—$500 per year"; "hope to teach"; "work for advanced degree"; "question mark"; "coach, high school"; "keep house"; "prospects very indefinite"; "nothing"; no answer.

With calm understatement, Chancellor Chase of New York University recently urged the colleges to "abandon the idea that they are training all students for leadership." * One of

* The New York World-Telegram, April 30, 1935.

57

PANORAMA

his undergraduates paraphrased his utterance, imploring administrators "to recognize that they are training an appalling number of students for nothing."

"In many respects," one survey observes, "the post-1929 college graduate is the American tragedy. He is all dressed up with no place to go. . . . There were 50,000 young men studying engineering in 1920; 75,000 in 1930. . . . To what end? At the moment there are more than 50,000 unemployed engineers. The number of male college graduates for 1929-34 was between 1½ and 2 millions. During these years college appointment offices have generally placed the percentage of unemployment between 50 and 85 per cent. The actual figures, however, are appreciably higher." *

Only now are we beginning to visualize how drastic have been the changes wrought in these relationships of the student to society. They represent more than momentary deprivation. What has happened has been a large-scale development: the decline and fall of a large segment of the middle class. This factor has been amazingly neglected in popular discussion of student unrest. And yet, without these forces as a background, without an understanding of the scope of their influence the revolt itself is devoid of content. That transformation, from privilege to the brink of poverty, is the essence of the distinction between the undergraduate of 1925 and the young men to whom Herbert Hoover came last June with his cure-all for gloom—the inevitability of death. The extent and intensity of this descent down the economic ladder varies enormously from place to place; that, I hope, will become increasingly plain. Within the general definition of the student's origin—the middle class—there are a host of divisions and stages; these have been diversely affected by the crisis, depending upon their status before it took hold. Granting this reservation, however, the total impression remains. When, several years ago, *The New Republic* captioned an

* George Leighton and Richard Hellman, writing in *Harper's*, August, 1935.

58

article "Campus to Breadline," there was a tinge of melodrama in the phrase. Today the commentary has far more abundant justification—and more than one actual case history. It has been a steady, irresistible process; the best of men, the all-American halfback and the Phi Beta luminary, have shared of its devastation alike.

PART II

HAIL, ALMA MATER

1. The Legend

WHEN a young man first avowed his readiness to die for Rutgers, he was uttering more than conventional gridiron heroics. His cry embodied an illusion which has been painstakingly fostered in our higher learning: the ideal of loyalty, supreme and unqualified, to alma mater—whoever she happened to be. The concept was not merely a sentimental by-product of the "rah-rah" era; for, although its most glaring expression, the football mania, has partially subsided, it has been perpetuated in more fundamental form. No other notion is more fixed and deeply-rooted, and none has done more to preserve the provincialism of the American college and to guard its occupants against unorthodox, independent thought. To the extent that it has done so, and that it continues to be utilized on an increasing scale, it is crucial to the events and conflicts on the contemporary campus.

The theme is familiar; underlying it is the assumption of an everlasting identity of interest among the various segments of the university community. They are presumably bound together by one transcending aim: the "progress" of alma mater. Out of such achievements equal rewards will ostensibly flow. Reduced to its simplest statement, the doctrine posits a profound mutuality of interest between the chairman of the Board of Trustees and the student cafeteria worker. They are each, so the legend asserts, endowed with a similar share in the life of the university and each is expected to do a good job in the rôle which God has allegedly assigned him. The same, of course, applies to the remainder of the collegiate hierarchy: administrators, faculty, students and alumni and the citizens of the community in which the college is situated.

Every expression of student dissatisfaction in the present

63

crisis has been compelled to combat that illusion. It has been as assiduously resorted to by administrators in large universities as in more backward institutes. And the substance of their appeal inevitably flows from the same principle: that we are all, primarily, Siwash men and anything which injures her reputation with the better people is, per se, to be condemned. There is a further corollary to this: for, granting the precept of basic harmony, there should be no cause for grievances which divide the campus into contending groups. The Trustees, animated by the same ideals and aspirations as their underlings, can do no wrong. A graphic illustration of this credo was furnished by a student editor at the University of California in Los Angeles late in 1934; following a bitter dispute engendered by the suspension of five student leaders, he wrote:

"If some of the campus red-hots get down off their high horses long enough to see things as they are, they might realize that the University could use some of this energy that the Third International and the Constitution are getting. . . . When U.C.L.A. is an ideal university . . . then it will be time to take the weight of the world on our shoulders."

The writer was expressing a conviction with which he had been inoculated at any early age. It is an affliction common to his contemporaries, schooled in the same tradition. To deny that there is an unalterable bond between student and Trustee, to question the wisdom and benevolence of administrators is to court the fury of an ancient fixation. I am not suggesting that there is, or should be, eternal warfare over trivialities; but the issues over which this conflict has most frequently occurred are not minute. Their importance, far from diminishing, is becoming progressively greater in proportion to the increased tension of the outside world.

And that is the crux of the matter. For, although we have

been gradually admitting the interplay between the affairs of that world and the inhabitants of the college, we have not been so swift to realize that the campus mirrors the relationships and hostilities of outside society. We have come to regard the university as a unit, reacting uniformly to externals, each segment desiring the same resolution of outside conflicts. Specifically, we have been taught to believe that Trustee, teacher and student have the same stake in the happy disposal or resurrection of capitalism and its institutions. A host of similar examples relative to the theme could be cited.

How warranted is this assumption? Events in our colleges, particularly in recent years, seem to belie it; we have seen at least the surface manifestations of antagonism; the bulk of episodes which will hereafter be depicted testify to pronounced divergence on a wide span of issues. But what is not so clearly perceived is that these are part of a more far-flung battle with the destiny of civilization very likely in the balance.

Before proceeding to an examination of these events, we should have some conception of the personnel of the contending forces. The college is not a homogeneous body. Its constituents have a diverse background and present status. Once that is made plain, the nature of the ensuing strife will be more readily discernible, the likelihood of its future intensification realized. We have already analyzed the declining economic stature of the student and indicated its source and meaning; these are every-day facts with which the student is uncomfortably familiar. But he is not so keenly aware of their consequences in terms of his relationship to the other members of the university colony, those whose welfare is allegedly interwoven with his own. So absorbed is he by the task of creating a greater and more monumental Siwash that he seldom stops to inquire: why? what for? to what usage will the completed structure be put? Unless these first principles of university control, of the multiplying irreconcilabilities between those who rule and those who are ruled, are apprehended, neither the ensuing undergraduate revolt nor administrative reaction will be adequately evaluated.

II. The Hierarchy

"WHERE an institution is rapidly developing from a college of a few hundred to a university of ten thousand, where millions of dollars must be raised within three or four years . . . there is an imperative need for an executive of the captain of industry type. Under such conditions the president becomes a general manager responsible to a Board of Regents or Trustees as directors, the deans are managers and division superintendents, the department heads are foremen, the rank-and-file of the teaching staff are employees, the students are the raw material and the alumni 'the manufactured product' bearing the 'college stamp.' " *

The advent of a financial oligarchy into seats of educational power is not a latter-day phenomenon nor one attributable to the "business psychology" of the post-war decade. That period merely witnessed the extravagant culmination of a tendency. A large majority of American colleges and universities owe their earliest origin and growth to the funds of leading financiers. Of more than 900 existing institutions, more than 700 are private corporations with vast endowments administered by boards of trustees.† Seldom is the extent of the network realized. Students have been made repeatedly aware that they are indebted for their education to the benevolence of Wall Street; but the "supervisory" rôle which Wall Street has seized in return is not so widely explained.

* Slosson, *The Great Crusade and After.*
† Odegard, *The American Public Mind.*

66

A Trustee is an invisible, almost legendary figure to the average student. He appears on the campus only at stated intervals for the sessions of his board. His presence is rarely made known to the community; even faculty members are usually strangers to their overseers. If there is an acquaint-anceship, it is likely to be the result of a formalized university function at which they bow to each other over stuffed shirts. And yet a study of any college catalogue will disclose the virtual absolutism by which these men ultimately determine university policy. Their domination is not expressed by successive edicts or by incessant wire-pulling; I suspect that such direct intervention is far less frequent than the "rule of fear," a constant, ever-present recognition by their underlings of the Trustees' prejudices, wishes and ultimate authority.

Who are these Trustees? Most students are dimly aware that they are men of standing in the community, but the ramifications of that "standing" are not so clearly appreciated. At the outset it should be observed that certain definite groups are virtually excluded from these boards, groups representing millions of American men and women. To my knowledge—and this has been confirmed by numerous studies —there is no college Trustee who might be remotely regarded as a spokesman for organized labor. Perhaps even more extraordinary is the fact that the educational world has been almost as sweepingly barred from these ruling bodies; in these hundreds of posts of power in education, those who have devoted their lives, talents and energies to academic work are practically nowhere to be found. Nor does there seem to be any immediate possibility of their accession to such prominence. The selection of new Trustees has long since ceased to be of any major concern to educators; they know what to expect.

Those who defend the Trustee-system rationalize these exclusions on one traditional ground: that the function of a Trustee is financial, involving merely the supervision of funds and requiring long years of experience in the business world.

This defense, unfortunately, has been riddled by the Trustees themselves. Quick to boast of the eminence of their tasks, they have heatedly refuted the notion that their rôle is merely that of book-keeping. Of this there are manifold examples. J. H. Raymond, a Trustee of Northwestern University, stated the case quite explicitly many years ago:

"In social and political science, they (the professors) are only a little less qualified to be the final arbiters as to what shall be taught than they are concerning financial problems. In all things they should promptly and gracefully submit to the final determination of the Trustees. A professor must be an advocate but his advocacy must be in harmony with the conclusions of the powers that be."

The same view was voiced by the Trustees of Marietta College upon the dismissal of a professor there. In an official bulletin bearing upon the case they asserted that "it is the sacred duty of the trustees to administer the affairs of the institution according to their own judgment and the dictates of their own consciences." Perhaps the most revealing example was the ouster of Dr. J. E. Kirkpatrick from Olivet College in 1926, following the appearance of a book in which he decried the financial stewardship of our colleges; the Trustees explained that his removal was "not because of any inefficiency on your part but because your views of college administration . . . are not in harmony with the views of the Board of Trustees and of substantial friends of Olivet college who are giving financial support to the college."

The classic rebuttal, thus, loses much of its vigor. Trustees are far more than guardians of the treasury; they are the supervisors of the intellectual life of the university—and they do not hesitate to say so. Having seen the social groups which are not represented on the boards—labor, education and their associates—let us see who is. It has been suggested that "Big

68

Business" is the answer; and, granting sufficient latitude to include big business' spokesmen—corporation lawyers and the like—that is almost universally true. A study of the New York University board is illuminating: of its thirty members, thirteen are commercial or investment bankers and six are industrial executives; the rest are scattered through various adjuncts of these enterprises. Analysis of Columbia's overlords reveals that twenty per cent are associated with more than nineteen banks and trust companies, sixteen industrials, twelve insurance companies, four railroads and three public utilities. Similar results can be gleaned from a survey of any such board. To visualize the scope of the network, let us detail the connections of seven sample Trustees—understanding, of course, that they are drawn at random and can be duplicated in hundreds of cases:

Charles Francis Adams, Harvard Trustee: Director of the American Telephone and Telegraph Co., director of the John Hancock Mutual Life Insurance Co., director of Central Aguirre Sugar Corp. of Porto Rico, director of the Provident Institute for Savings, director of the Amoskeag Corporation, director of Edison Electric of Boston, director of Boston and Albany Railroad, director of Boston Consolidated Gas, director of Bigelow Hartford Carpet Co., director of General Electric.

Morris L. Clothier, U. of Pennsylvania Trustee: Director of United Gas Improvement, director of the Girard Trust, director of Philadelphia National Bank, director of Pennsylvania Fire Insurance, director of Union Passenger Railway, director of Lehigh Valley Railroad, director of General Refractories, director of Penn Mutual Life Insurance Co., director Baltimore and Ohio Railroad.

Edward Duffield, chairman of Princeton Trustees: President of Prudential Insurance Co., director American Telephone and Telegraph, director of Guaranty

69

Trust, director of United New Jersey Railroad and Canal Co., director of Hudson and Delaware Railroad.

Sewell W. Avery, University of Chicago Trustee: President of Montgomery Ward Co., chairman of the U. S. Gypsum, director U. S. Steel, director Armour and Co., director Northern Trust Co., director in the Chicago, Great Western Railroad, director in People's Light, Gas and Coke Co., director State Bank and Trust and director of The Chicago Daily News.

Newton D. Baker, Ohio State Trustee: Director of Cleveland Trust Co., director of Mutual Life Insurance Co., director Baltimore and Ohio Railroad, director of the Carnegie Corporation, director of Radio Corporation of America.

David F. Houston, Columbia Trustee: Director of U. S. Steel, director of American Telephone and Telegraph, director Guaranty Trust Co., president of the Mutual Life Insurance Co.

Ray Morris, Vassar Trustee: Director of Gold Dust Corp., director of SKF industries, director of American Woolen, director of Punta Allegre Steamship Corp., director of Munson Steamship line, director of W. A. Harriman Securities Corp., director of Continental Securities, director of Saltex Looms, director Selected Industries Investment Trust.*

Here are seven representative Trustees affiliated with corporations whose total wealth involves billions of dollars; and

---

* Much of this material was prepared by Mr. Norman Burnstine, the Labor Research Association and Pen and Hammer Society. I am here able to present only brief portions; it should be emphasized that the same results are found in a study of any university. Anyone sufficiently curious to ascertain the status of his own Trustees can do so by looking them up in *The Directory of Directors,* available at most libraries. It is true, of course, that in certain small colleges Trustees will not be found in that volume; only our leading magnates are listed. It is equally certain, however, that if they have not made the top rank, they are, in their own modest way, "affiliated with the dominant social and economic classes."

when the board of directors of these companies meet, each member will find himself surrounded by Trustees of other universities. For most significant is the concentration which can be traced through these seemingly diverse units. The twentieth century's consolidation of capital has created a monopoly even in the educational sphere. There is an "interlocking directorate" of finance and industry which cuts directly across the campus into the Trustees' chambers, leaving scarcely an institution untenanted by some vassal of the Morgan-Rockefeller-Mellon dynasty.* A noted survey by Scott Nearing in *School and Society* testified to essentially the same point; in every one of 243 institutions "business" dominated the school boards.

Endowments to universities have attained almost incredible dimensions. Logically enough, they emanate from the same source which provides the overlords of the college—and their influence is equally felt. Illustrations of this generosity are manifold: John D. Rockefeller Sr. donated $35,000,000 to the University of Chicago; another Standard Oil millionaire, Edward S. Harkness, has given nearly $4,500,000 to Harvard and a substantial sum to Yale; various colleges received sums of $15,000,000 from Andrew Carnegie and, when he died, Carnegie Tech. obtained $23,000,000 from his estate; Leland Stanford, California railroad magnate, furnished $30,000,000 to found the university which bears his name; the University of California has been the beneficiary of A. P. Giannini, banker, to the extent of $1,500,000; the late Phœbe Hearst, mother of the publisher, gave $2,000,000 to the same school.

These again are random examples. How sweeping is the total can be deduced from observation of the endowments of several leading universities: Harvard, $117,204,000; Yale, $95,000,000; Columbia, $84,000,000; University of Chicago, $59,475,000; University of Rochester, $33,800,000;

* For a detailed description of this "interlocking directorate," see *The Goose-Step*.

Stanford, $33,775,000; M.I.T., $32,000,000—and so on down to the smallest Jerkwater college aspiring to the grandeur of the mighty.

The universities have thus become a major agent in the business world, their returns often far outdistancing that of their competitors. While the total wealth of the country increased only three per cent in the decade 1920-30, the wealth of our colleges was augmented by 155 per cent; the nation's total income fell 4.7 per cent in the same interval but that of the colleges advanced by 200 per cent. In 1929-30 profits of $67,370,000 on investment were reported for 1078 institutions. According to a survey made in 1932, apportionment of investments was about as follows: 27 per cent in real estate, 24 per cent in public utilities, 18 per cent in railroads, 17 per cent in industrials and 7 per cent in government bonds.

These calculations must intimate the vast financial entanglements of our educational plant. A finance-chosen board of strategy has been named to direct the process. But the entanglement, it must be emphasized, has been more than one of dollar bills; its effect on ideas, on university procedure, on education's relation to the social order is only now being fully appreciated, when the status of vested interests and private property bears so directly upon the plight of the rest of humanity. For the Trustees and their hirelings are trespassing more than ever before beyond the realm of bill-collecting and investment.

Slosson has described our University presidents as "general managers," their assistants—deans and other administrative officers—as "division superintendents." The characterization is not unfair, with two modifications. The first is the existence of a handful of men who have refused to accept this rôle and have endeavored to make of their posts an honest, creative, progressive function. They are indeed unique and they seldom survive for any prolonged period. The most tragic illustration of their fate was the case of the

President of the Municipal University of Omaha, mentioned earlier, who committed suicide after reactionary groups had engineered his ouster. His death was startling testimony to the demands of an administrative position; those who cannot fulfill them should not, for their own sakes, accept the job— if that rare opportunity presents itself.

But the other exception to Slosson's depiction is even more important. For it should not be imagined that, in every instance, the administrator is merely echoing the desires of the higher-ups. He is very likely to be in utter agreement with them—so much so that the need for regular instructions or warnings is hardly evident. The fact is that in many places the president is more instrumental in the formulation of policy than his Trustees; they merely ratify his decisions, confident that he knows what is expected of him. And the same is observable of those categories below: the deans, assistant deans and other functionaries who have learned what is proper, what is orthodox and what is to be avoided. They, too, think in precisely the same terms, worship the same gods and combat the same menaces as their Trustees—and, by doing so, they decrease the burden of the Trustee's task.

This extraordinary accord in the administrative sphere is the result of present circumstance and past training. For administrators are well-paid; although their salaries are not normally made public, they seldom seem poverty-stricken. Numerous university presidents have corporation affiliations as impressive as the Trustees themselves; even a dean can hope for similar posts if he will lend distinction and atmosphere to some meat-packing firm. They live patently comfortable, secure lives; their tenure of office comes only rarely in danger as long as they behave. And, in turn, their major preoccupation is to prevent any "disturbance" to the smooth, tranquil, uncontroversial flow of university affairs; such controversies, whatever their merits, will inevitably require "explanations" to those who want academic peace at any price.

His own status fairly profitable and permanent, the admin-

73

istrator is not likely to be an unconventional, dissenting animal. And if the sparks of rebellion ever flared within him, by the time he reaches an administrative post they will almost certainly have disappeared. For the path to academic advancement is one demanding energetic self-discipline; he who sets out with his eye on an administrative chair must know that a long, wearisome stretch of boot-licking is before him. Once he has achieved the end of his endeavors, he can hardly be expected to sacrifice the goal by an inadvertent remark, or an insult to the sanctities. And he rarely does.

The "good" administrator is very likely to be a third-rate educator; education is his secondary function. He is essentially a drill-sergeant, dedicated to the assignment of keeping everyone, student or teacher, in step along the same paths which thousands of others have walked before. And for every official who is an exception to this rule, there will be a hundred to confirm it. Prexy is fondly pictured as a benign, friendly old man with the biggest heart in the world, devoted to his students and determined to protect them from harm. He probably is. But Prexy's definitions have been conditioned by the rigidities of his own rise to power. One of the precepts which he learned in that climb is to do nothing which will attract unfavorable glances from those who set the standards of society. He has also discovered that there are many rights a man must surrender to get anywhere in the educational structure. Among these, first and foremost, is the prerogative to think, and act, for himself.

I have said that at least administrators are well-paid for their subservience. The same cannot usually be said for the professor—and virtually never for the lesser lights around him. He is neither rewarded nor respected; the established citizenry's opinion of him was succinctly expressed by *The Banker's Magazine* in 1919: "We pay the day laborer more than the teacher because he is worth more—because he produces a service of greater value to society."

Indicative of the teacher's status was the conclusion reached by an alumni committee of Bowdoin University which reported, in 1927, that "college teachers are among the worst paid of school laborers." It is interesting to note that, on the day the report appeared, the University of Pennsylvania announced its intention to construct an indoor stadium involving expenditures of $1,500,000. Two years later the Yale chapter of the American Association of University Professors lamented that salaries in the teaching profession "are such as effectually to discourage many young men of high quality of intellect" from seeking academic posts.

Our faculties never reaped the dividends of the post-war expansion. Even when millions of dollars were being expended in the mad quest for culture, their status remained relatively fixed. "Although the average salary of all ranks of instruction in 302 liberal arts colleges rose from $1724 in 1914-15 to $2958 in 1926-27, buying power was only $100 more." * It is not astonishing that George Bernard Shaw regarded our college academicians as "overworked, underpaid school-masters." He said that nearly fifteen years ago, and ensuing boom and panic have only affirmed his judgment.

It might seem logical that such a profession, in which so vast a number of men are rewarded with a pittance for their efforts, would be teeming with revolt. But that has never been the case. Shortly after the onset of depression, Dean McBain of the Columbia Graduate Faculties observed, "It is manifestly cause for regret and, perhaps, for introspective inquiry that in the world's present emergencies so little of light and leading has come out of the world's universities. . . ." †

This "reticence" in the face of so crucial an exigency is not new, nor is it attributable to excessive modesty. Our fac-

* *The New York Times,* December 29, 1928.
† It is noteworthy that shortly after he made this statement, Dean McBain signed a statement "explaining" the dismissal of Donald Henderson, outspoken economics instructor, from Columbia.

ulties long ago surrendered the right, and with it the desire, to speak out on controversial issues. And they did so, not because they were without opinions or wanted them to flourish unseen, but because of an age-old, oppressive fear—loss of job, diminished prestige and, for the younger men particularly, curtailment of the possibility of advancement. Their acquiescence is an ancient heritage, derived from the bitter experience of those who, upon entering the teaching profession, refused to surrender the rights of ordinary citizens. Only a valiant handful have been willing to make the sacrifice entailed by defiance of the status quo. The remainder have learned the supreme requisite of university life—to conform, to adhere to the rigidities, prejudices and habits of their surroundings, to accept without a grimace the "eternal truths." That is their function, as frankly expressed by one of the most prominent figures in the educational world, Dean Paul Klapper of the C. C. N. Y. School of Education: ". . . education has ever been a product of the existing social order, charged with the function of rationalizing and perpetuating the society that supports it. However progressive the teacher and however unfettered the school, they nevertheless seek to justify what is."

Out of that realization has been nourished the conservatism, the flight from critical obligations of the American faculty. But it should not be imagined that this is produced only by overt discipline. Often that is not required. The fear-complex is as much the result of implied authority as of outright punishments. Even in that handful of universities where a measure of academic freedom prevails, the professor understands the nature of the university, the "sensitivity" of the Trustees and the need for endowments. He knows that there are limits to the scholarly quest—whether those limits have been demonstrated by local dismissals or not. And that acknowledgment is almost universal, whatever the relative merits of one school over another. It is deeply embedded in the consciousness of those in academic posts;

they realize how perilous is their position, how transient is the favor of their superiors, how abrupt may be the end of the great struggle for a secure place in the world.

These accusations are, I have said, not unknown; to reiterate them may seem to be an unwarranted attack on men who have been down, and nearly out, for decades. But the matter is not quite so simple. If these conditions were admitted by the faculties themselves, if teacher and professor alike stepped forward without sham to grant the "limitations" of their rôles, then the need for repetition would be gone. They have done just the reverse. With years of enslavement have grown up elaborate rationales to justify the conduct of the academician; his "explanations" have flowered into a full-fledged body of doctrine, the credo of the "academic mind." Even these avowals might be inconsequential if they were restricted to the faculty club where men meet to share, and justify, their misery; but they do more than that. They have sought to exonerate themselves, with remarkable persuasiveness, before thousands of students. They have spread their gospel of self-vindication as widely as their efforts permitted. And, in turn, many of their students, captivated by the illusion, have defended their own inertia on the same grounds.

The postulates of this "academic mind" are eminently familiar. What student has not heard of the need for "objectivity," for "an impartial weighing of the facts," for "mature contemplation"—for anything but a meaningful, decisive gesture? Each time that undergraduates have proposed to deal with one of the manifold evils of their time, the soothing hand of this doctrine has been placed upon them by their professors. The essence of their academic position is the traditional dichotomy between thought and action, the desperate attempt to prove that "thinking" is, per se, negated by practice. And the result of this principle is inevitable: the way is left clear for those who promote catastrophe to do so without any interference, without a semblance of resistance from those who should be in the front line of defense. Years of servility have proved to the professor that "contemplation" is an ideal and a necessity. To ease his conscience, he has erected this vast philosophic barrier which enables him to keep his job, his comfort and his mental assurance. Ironically, many of those who most vigorously denounce the student anti-war movement because it is "unscholarly" and an "unscientific approach" were the bulwark of the army propaganda machine less than twenty years ago. I am not suggesting their affinity for vain bloodshed of one sort or another; it does seem evident, however, that they were willing to break their own rules when circumstance and pressure so dictated. Many of them have repented, but continue to retain the principles which were instrumental in their earlier downfall. They vow that they will never be duped again, nevertheless refusing to sanction any course of conduct which might prevent the recurrence of that situation.

Even more ardently have they championed the notion of the "unbiased search for truth" as opposed to the "propaganda" of the unorthodox. They have almost convinced themselves that so arbitrary a division exists. They should know better. They must have some suspicion that "truth" lies on the side of the established order and that "propaganda" is anything which tends to undermine that order. I say that they should be conscious of this because they are the best practitioners of the axiom. Their rejection of "politics," their hostility to "propaganda," is directed against only one aspect of it—against those spheres of effort which challenge the status quo. Even while they are brandishing their swords toward such "distortion of educational values," they are openly and actively "propagandizing" for existing institutions, and being paid to do so. The advocates of individualism, laissez-faire and private ownership of public utilities are granted every facility for carrying out their endeavors. They have every "right" to defend existing institutions in any way they see fit. No one will hamper them in this line of duty.

Indeed it is entirely likely that their efforts will be greeted with the enthusiasm of their superiors.

The fact is that orthodoxy can advance unchecked into any channels without a suggestion of administrative disapproval. Perhaps the most startling disclosure of how vast and unimpeded is this "search for truth" was furnished by the investigation of the Federal Trade Commission into the propaganda campaigns of the public utility corporations.

At the outset the utilities realized the possibilities of the field. Dr. C. E. Eaton, in an address to the National Electric Light Association in 1924, described professors as members of the "starveling profession". Continuing, he said:

> "Here is a professor in a college who gets $2,500 a year and has to spend $3,000 to keep from starving to death, who walks up to his classroom in an old pair of shoes, and some idiot of a boy drives up and parks a $5,000 automobile outside and comes in and gets plucked. Then because that professor teaches that boy that there is something wrong with the social system, we call him a Bolshevik, and throw him out. What I would like to suggest to you intelligent gentlemen is that while you are dealing with the pupils to give a thought to the teachers and when their vacation comes to pay them a salary to come into your plants and into your factories and learn the public utility business at first hand, and then they will go back and you needn't fuss—they can teach better than you can."

The same admonition had been given by M. H. Aylesworth, then managing director of the N.E.L.A., at a conference of the Middle West utilities company in 1923:

> "I would advise any manager who lives in a community where there is a college to get the professor of economics, let us say, interested in your problems. Have

79

him lecture on your subject to his classes. Once in a while it will pay you to take such men, getting five or six hundred or a thousand dollars a year, and give him a retainer of one or two hundred dollars per year for the privilege of letting you study and consult with them. For how in heaven's name can we do anything in the schools of this country . . . if we have not first sold the idea of education to the college professor."

Achievements were soon registered in the campaign to spread the "truth" about the utility corporations. For instance, in 1924, George E. Lewis, executive manager of the Rocky Mountain Committee on Public Information, could boast that "We now have every university and college in the State of Colorado utilizing our speakers."

There were six mediums through which the "starveling" professors could be rewarded by the utilities for services rendered. As cited by the federal inquiry, they were:

"1. Salaried—whole or in part. 2. Professional employments. 3. Fellowships and special employments. 4. Special studies. 5. Addresses and attendance at utility conferences and conventions. 6. Books and textbooks."

How these various rôles were played is copiously documented in the committee's report; there was virtually no institution which did not have in its midst a faithful follower of the utilities gospel.

Dr. Hugh M. Blain, while professor of Journalism at Tulane University, also served as director of the Louisiana-Mississippi Committee on Public Utility Information from 1923-25. He proved highly useful because of his "intimate acquaintance with the faculties of Louisiana State University and Tulane University."

Professor Theodore Grayson of the University of Pennsylvania was another esteemed torch-bearer for the corporations. While teaching at the Wharton division of the University and directing the evening and extension schools of the institution, he had served for thirteen years as treasurer of the New Jersey Utilities Association and later as secretary and treasurer of the New Jersey Public Utility Information Committee. In his testimony at the probe Professor Grayson frankly admitted that he was "earnestly against government participation in business" and received $250 for each address in which he said so.

For "expenses and services" from March, 1924 to June, 1928, Dean John T. Madden of the New York University school of commerce received a total of $1,340.88 from the N.E.L.A. In the year 1929-30 the same group paid him $2,000 for a study of the holding company business.

Shortly after the Rocky Mountain committee on Public Utility Information established a fellowship at the University of Colorado, the committee took elaborate steps toward "imparting to Mr. Wolfe (the fellowship recipient) a practical utility viewpoint." Mr. Wolfe performed to the utmost delight of the utilities as evidenced by this generous letter he received from Mr. Lewis:

"My Dear Hub:
You will recall that a short time ago I assured you that Santa Claus might be prevailed upon to visit your squalid hut. That I succeeded in convincing the boy is evidenced by the check herewith.
This check is in accordance with the arrangements mentioned some time ago for stepping up your income a bit."

From 1927 to 1932 Dr. H. M. Diamond, while head of the department of economics at Lehigh University, was busily occupied preparing a "historical research bearing on economic policies of government with special reference to public operations and the relations of government to business." For this he was rewarded with $10,460.23 by the N.E.L.A. The minutes of the N.E.L.A. executive committee, June, 1921, reveal the existence of a "technical advisory committee" consisting of Professor A. E. Kennelly of Harvard and M.I.T., Professor C. F. Scott of Yale and a third man, each of whom received $5,000 for his efforts. When the Missouri Committee on Public Utility Information determined to have "a carefully selected college professor address teachers attending the Summer schools . . . upon the economics of public utility operation," Dr. E. J. McCaustland, dean of the college of Engineering at Missouri University was chosen. He received $75 for each talk and expenses, a total of about $270. In February, 1928, Mr. W. Griffin Gribbel, chairman of the Committee on Cooperation, wrote to the Secretary of the American Gas Association:

"I have a letter today from Moore who is working on Cornell and Swarthmore. It is interesting to learn that Professor Fressell spent his vacation year in the employ of the United Gas Improvement Co. This ought to make him a 'cash customer.'"

From 1924 to 1929 The Dixie Construction Co. had, at one time or another, the following men on its payroll:

Professor Maxwell of Alabama U.	$ 519.16
Professor Patterson of Mississippi A. & M.	584.27
Professor Tarboux of Cornell	1,695.33
Professor Switzer of Cornell	2,456.50
Professor Lloyd of Alabama U.	2,631.79
Professor Allen of Worcester Polytechnic Institute	7,151.62

Not content with subsidizing spokesmen, the utilities maintained close scrutiny of any one whose work remotely related to the field. An instructor of the University of Pennsylvania

82

testified before the state legislature; a utilities' spy reported that he had voiced "radical sentiments" and "wandered off into general channels and lauded 'giant power' from its public ownership angle." The matter was referred to the previously discussed Dr. Grayson who conducted a thorough investigation and then communicated his findings to the University authorities.

The commission found that large sums were spent by the utility industry in the support and maintenance of endowments for research, scholarships and fellowships, since the utilities were thereby "offered a broad avenue for employing the facilities of a university with all the dignity and prestige that an institution enjoyed." Among these payments was one made by the N.E.L.A. to Northwestern University—$25,000 a year from 1925 to 1928 to be "devoted to consideration of government ownership of every character." It need hardly be added that throughout the country strict attention was given to textbooks, as borne out in the response of the Kansas director to a survey sent out by Director Blain: "National Electric Light Association headquarters informed us months ago that textbook of right kind was in course of preparation."

I have cited substantial sections of the F.T.C. revelations because they are the most comprehensive yet uncovered. But the same results could be obtained—and have been on a lesser scale—in regard to such issues as the status of Soviet Russia, the settlement of labor disputes, social and economic reform and countless other questions in which privilege finds it necessary to rationalize and perpetuate poverty. The professor can serve and serve well on the side of vested interest; but let him raise his voice against social injustice and he will quickly discover the fate of the "propagandist." He will find that he has transgressed the sanctities to which the academic mind must remain ever faithful.

Let it not be believed that all professors and their underlings are paid for this prostitution. Some have learned to love

83

the occupation or at least inured themselves to it without monetary reward. These are the most pitiful specimens, deprived of even the external comfort of an improved living standard but still clinging tenaciously to the ideal of "contemplation." It is among the younger men that the conflict is probably most severe; they come with honest convictions about the responsibility of a teacher, they regard themselves as dispensers of genuine knowledge—and slowly the process of corruption begins. They must either abandon their aspirations or attune themselves to the laws of their environment. They must heed such warnings as that recently delivered by Silas Strawn, former president of the American Bar Association:

"I am unable to sympathize with the elastic consciences of those who inveigh against the capitalistic system while in the pay of a college or university whose payroll, or whose budget, is due to the philanthropic generosity of those whose industry and frugality have enabled them to make an endowment." *

This is at least a frank and unashamed statement of the case in sharp contrast to those who still proclaim that "academic freedom" is a divine right of American teaching. It isn't, and never has been. In certain large universities there is comparatively little restriction on what a professor says in the classroom; but, beyond that, he is constantly reminded of his place, admonished to bear in mind the source of the university's income. There are exceptions, men who have entrenched themselves in university posts and whose dismissal would arouse too great a furor, and who, consequently, are allowed to say what they think. There are occasional university presidents who are seriously devoted to the preservation of their professors' integrity, but they too are a unique, rapidly diminishing tribe. And the teachers themselves hardly

* See *The New York Times*, June 11, 1935.

merit the efforts. They have made their peace, a peace of slavery; and they almost resent the suggestion that their status might be improved.

The epitome of this attitude is manifested in their unwillingness to organize themselves into any militant, determined body aligned with broad groups of people outside the university. The idea is repugnant to their Olympianism. It would expose the fact that they are not creatures of special privilege, citizens set off from the rank-and-file of the community. It would be a confession of the weakness of the academic mind. Their existing organizations are indicative of the temper of their approach. Of these the most widely known is the American Association of University Professors whose policies have long been a source of dismay to those who are honestly concerned over the teacher's plight. The A.A.U.P. has conducted several notable campaigns in behalf of dismissed professors, but its reluctance to do so, its timidity and its desperate attempt to offend no one are an inevitable accompaniment of such campaigns. The Bulletin of the American Association of American Colleges carried a significant judgment of the A.A.U.P. in March, 1935:

"We are impressed with the fact that the A.A.U.P. strives vigorously to settle misunderstandings wherever possible without recourse to printed findings. The number of cases settled annually by official notification that the committee will not investigate because it believes the question can be settled internally or the evidence is inconclusive or no useful purpose will be served or that the teacher is mistaken exceeds the number in which there is a printed report criticizing the college."

This "judiciousness" in the selection of cases is not mere ordinary concern over the validity of the victim's charge; it has become almost a standing rule that a man below the rank of professor cannot expect aid from the A.A.U.P., that only a small proportion of professors dismissed can hope for its support, and that the conduct of even these more fortunate professors' defense will invariably be apologetic, unobtrusive, soft-spoken and abject. This may serve some good result in individual instances; but it does not constitute a bulwark against further reprisals nor does it throw light on the basic, general issues involved. The policy of the A.A.U.P. is steeped in gentle reformism, in isolation and in avoidance of tactics which would inspire concerted, far-flung action by teachers in defense of their colleagues. For every victory which it gains, there will be ten other victims whose plight is ignored; for every temporary concession it wins, there will be countless retreats invoked. And it need hardly be added that the organization has always shied away from the prospect of union with labor and its allies who are essentially battling the same foe. To the A.A.U.P. dismissals are "misunderstandings." Publicity, which might focus public attention on the state of our colleges, is to be eluded wherever possible, united and outspoken activity is to be deplored. Nor is there any reason to believe that these policies are being revised in the face of current attacks on the profession.

Occasionally one finds an energetic local group ready to act more vigorously and without the all-consuming passion for timidity. There is promise of such work, for example, in the Anti-Fascist association formed by nearly one-third of the City College faculty. There are teachers and professors, a handful of them in each college, seeking to organize defense of their integrity and their scholarship, and willing to fight militantly in organized bodies. Their numbers are growing. But they are still an infinitesimal part of the teaching system.

The plight of the faculties, it should be emphasized, is much of their own making. More than a decade ago a cartoonist in *The New York World* pictured the professor trading his name for that of a wealthy contributor, just as Trinity University became Duke. The comparison is not too far-fetched. Professors have stood by silently while their researches were mutilated lest they reflect unfavorably on the business of a financial friend of the school. Curricula have been distorted to satisfy an endowment-provider; and the professor does not speak out. These things do happen, frequently and in every place, and the professors know it. But "pure thought," "detachment" and "impartiality" are still the sales-talk of American learning.

It is written in the Talmud that "Jerusalem fell because her teachers were not respected." If the parallel were enacted on our own shores, this society would long ago have vanished and the country been restored to the Indians. And yet the professor's life is not an unhappy one. He has come to enjoy subservience or maintain calm indifference to it. If he can pick up a few dollars on the side, his contentment is usually complete.

That is the "happy family" within the university, a hierarchy with thousands of young men and women at the bottom. To render the picture more complete, we must not forget that unique, ageless specimen, the ardent alumnus. He was quite vividly described by President Angell of Yale: "As I meet American college graduates, nothing is more depressing than to remark the astonishing number who give absolutely no suggestion of intelligent acquaintanceship with anything whatever outside the range of business and sport. Indeed, did they not assure that they were sons of Dear Old Siwash, you would never on your own initiative have made that inference."

Or, as Professor J. M. Cattell once noted, "the average University club in America could more easily dispense with its library than with its bar." Certainly men of intelligence, awareness and sensitivity have gone forth from our universities in the past decades. But that number—unfortunately small—is invariably the group which maintains no further contact with the university. Nor are any strenuous efforts made to reach them. The Alumni Associations, regulated by

87

staunch administrative partners, offer them no place; the football season has not created the sentimental ties felt by more enthusiastic citizens; collections for funds are conducted most vigorously among the "success" graduates, the men who went from Plato to Wall Street without sensing any discomfort. And it is they who, in turn, exert influence on university procedure, since they may leave a stipend for the old school in their wills. They are the alumni "who matter," the men whose presence is felt long after they received their degrees.

PART III
REVOLT

1. Pilgrimage to Kentucky

WHEN, late in the Spring of 1931, William Harlan Hale lamented the "conservatism" of the American student, there was scarcely a murmur stirred by his indictment. No one dissented—and few betrayed more than fleeting interest in the circumstance. For this condition, however extraordinary, was an accepted fact; if educators were perplexed by it, if critics of the educational system regarded it as the vindication of their views, the vast proportion of the populace was utterly unmoved. The collegians themselves were in the front lines of apathy; having heard the wailing and the weeping so long, they had by now cultivated a nonchalant resistance to it.

Less than two months afterward a celebrated Englishman recounted his own impression of the same spectacle. That was in July. The campus had been deserted by its regular occupants, the Brain Trust migration to Washington was still a distant vision, the business "slump" was being solved by the orthodox economists and the American undergraduate was being assured that the "dislocation" would pass by the time the universities reopened. In an article in *Harper's* Professor Harold Laski inquired: "Why Don't Your Young Men Care?"

His thesis was formulated in fairly conventional terms. To Professor Laski the most startling and widespread attitude which he had encountered while visiting and lecturing at several leading universities was the bored, detached response of the student toward "politics." And by "politics" he meant the issues of public life as espoused by the traditional political parties. He was writing not in terms of long-time economic reform but of the immediate, day-to-day affairs of established government. "He (the student) studies

politics as he studies biology or the fine arts. It is a unit in
the taking of a degree. It has no connection with the prospect
of citizenship." And further: ". . . To improve his economic
or social position has been the purpose of university life
rather than a desire to enrich the community by disinterested
service."

He had discovered that, after two years of uncertainty and
decline, the "Bread and Butter Purpose" still dominated the
residents of our higher learning. But that was only one phase
of his enlightenment; the other was more significant and
lasting. For he found that even in the small, isolated groups
of alert students, those to whom education was more than a
"success prerequisite," the same hostility to "politics," in its
traditional sense, prevailed. Thus, among them "the situation is the more curious because it cannot be traced to absence
of knowledge"; they were at least cognizant of the conflicts
and controversies of customary political life; many were
earnest students of them. And their very familiarity with the
sphere had bred an even more bitter contempt. They would
have none of it; if ultimately they desired a medium to express their convictions, that medium would not be the Republican and Democratic parties. On every side he met with the
same response; the American student was usually an uncon-
cerned, tranquil specimen with neither interest in nor even
awareness of the realm of "politics"; he was eminently un-
shaken by anything the least fundamental to government
and social order. The scattered groups whose pre-occupations transcended football and Fraternity Row were most
likely to be absorbed by literary disputes, fanciful concepts of
Utopia and other more abstruse discussions. They shared
only one feeling with their contemporaries—the flight from
"politics." Commenting on Professor Laski's judgment, *The
Outlook* remarked:

"It may be so. It was so in our college days. . . . In
the future, as in the past, America will have to struggle

along and solve her problems without the aid of her college students. If political change is necessary, no student bodies will do the voting. If revolution comes, there will be no Harvard or Columbia students on the barricades. Russia, Spain, England, France, China, Germany— these are lands where college students feel themselves charged with responsibility for the future of their country. But the land of the free and the brave is not yet on the list."

In the ensuing months several college journals endeavored to explain the breach between the campus and the ancient political entities, to ascertain why Young Republicans and Young Democrats were that by inheritance, if at all, rather than by inclination. Yale's answer was succinct: "The best men stay out of politics because it is just too dirty." The Dartmouth editor enlarged upon the point:

"The dozen odd years which lie between graduation and the age at which a man is considered ripe enough for political plums must be spent ward-heeling, vote-getting, packing baseball bats and May-poles for Farley-for-Sheriff associations and in general ingratiation."

This was certainly part of the explanation, granting at the outset that among thousands there was comparatively no thought at all bestowed upon the matter. To those who did manifest any interest, the popular image of "politics" was a repelling prospect—a merry-go-round of grafters, ward-healers, do-nothings, a way out for people who couldn't earn an honest living, a sham battle between parasites. It offered neither opportunity nor appeal; it was a three-ring circus with a disproportionate number of clowns.

That impression was fixed and of long standing. Others had stumbled upon it long before Professor Laski recorded his dismay. The point is of prime importance, however, in relation to what was to follow; for, when a ferment was at last discernible in our universities, when the transformation in mood and activity was projected to the surface, it was in no way associated with the established political agencies. They never aroused any considerable enthusiasm or participation among university students. And that condition has persisted despite the overwhelming changes which have occurred since Professor Laski's visit. Were he to return today to the scene of his earlier observations, he would find one attitude substantially the same. There is no real appetite for traditional "politics"—Republican and Democratic model—on the American campus. Not even the tom-tom beaters of the Old or New Deal have been able to fill that vacancy in their ranks.

At about the time that Professor Laski issued his critique of the American student, there was a sharp dispute crystallizing within the League for Industrial Democracy. It was traceable to many factors which cannot be comprehensively detailed here.* One was the indisputable fact that the L.I.D. was making no headway on the campus commensurate with the impact of social forces; if, in the post-war era this had been an understandable reflection of an era in which the idea of social change seemed utterly remote to the average student, that explanation was no longer tenable; the insurgents believed that the time was now ripe for a fresh beginning. They argued that the L.I.D. was not devoting sufficient attention to the problems of students as such; they charged that its ap-

* In view of the imminent possibility of amalgamation between the L.I.D. and the National Student League—which arose out of it—I do not believe that any exhaustive discussion of the earlier conflict and ensuing distinctions is necessary. The amalgamation will be discussed in the concluding chapter; here I am simply setting forth the bare outlines of the original dispute. In the past two years the organizations have worked almost as a unit; much of the bitterness of the original divergence has been overcome by a realization that, divided, the two groups cannot survive the growth of reaction—one of whose primary aims is their extermination.

94

proach was too generalized, divorced from the increasingly acute issues of the campus, a lack most plainly visible in the fact that the L.I.D. had no program of action or interpretation on the specific problems of the undergraduate within the university. It was a bitter dispute and one which, to an extent, reflected the hostility then so prevalent among left-wing groups. For many of the insurgents were communists, nettled by what they felt to be the failures and impotence of the Socialist party; they envisaged a broader student movement which would not be merely a subsidiary of that party. In this view the communists were not alone; when the departure from the ranks of the L.I.D. occurred, they were joined by liberals and certain socialists alike who accepted the essential premise of the break—the need for an unattached, independent student group to act on the specific issues confronting the student in his relation to society. The result of that exodus was the formation of the National Student League; that its origins were in New York was plainly logical since, at that time, New York was almost the sole center of student revolt, centering around the city colleges.*

The program of the new group was inescapably an outgrowth of the developing economic storm. It was probably most distinguished for what conservatives called "undue pessimism" and was ultimately to prove extraordinary foresight. Those who were instrumental in the promulgation of its policies were neither utopians nor Bohemians; it was neither the undefined idealism of *The New Student* nor the spiritual dissatisfaction of the Menckenites which animated their efforts. They were alert and talented young men and women who had begun to perceive the devastation which economic disorder was bringing not merely to "humanity" or some other vague quantity but to themselves, as students. That was their premise; from it flowed their conception of a student movement. For, they argued, this was to be no transitory

---

* I think the reasons for this will become evident when we discuss the status of the city colleges.

95

crisis; it was to mark the beginning of the end of a whole system of economic relationships—capitalism. Before it died that system was to destroy—had already begun to destroy—the "privilege" illusion of the student. He was to return to the ranks of ordinary citizens, increasingly subject to the ills of an order whose decline would accelerate an ancient conflict between those who own and those who work. And in that struggle the vast majority of students, the sons of a sinking middle class, would find themselves steadily propelled into the camp of the dispossessed.

This was the foundation. On the dormant American campus of late 1931 it had no horde of followers. But the insurgents proposed that, whether their cohorts accepted this general assumption or not, some structure for unity on specific fronts should be erected. There were immediate local problems—retrenchment, discrimination, the status of academic liberty and opposition to the Reserve Officers Training Corps on which such joint efforts could be waged. These were to be viewed, not as fragmentary, isolated disputes, but as reflections of the external world. Perhaps even more important, indeed a prerequisite at the moment, was an inquiry into that world. It had been almost forgotten by the campus. Conventional education approached it in terms of fixed, eternal truths, even at an hour when the "eternals" were being thrown into appalling confusion. The average undergraduate, it must be emphasized, was incredibly ignorant of what was going on beyond his own horizon, of either the nature or complexion of outside society. He boasted of his seclusion. He was snug and lethargic. His curiosity had never been incited, and his educators, as a rule, were content to leave him as he was.

If there was to be a student upsurge, the educative process would have to begin; and that, combined with the intimate hardships of depression soon to be experienced, would demolish complacence. Nothing else would. It was in those terms that the student delegation to Harlan, Kentucky, was conceived.

The educational world for many years before had produced numerous exponents of experimentalism. They were men who argued that student apathy could be routed only by contact with "real life." They wanted their undergraduates to learn about society and its operation by first-hand study. That concept was one of the impelling convictions behind the sponsors of the journey.

But before it was over most of the experimentalists—and this school included many college presidents—had suddenly retreated. The explanation seemed fairly plain. To them "real life" meant dabbling in Republican party politics, interviews with celebrated individualists, journeys to "centers of scientific management." It did not mean an expedition into such critical sectors as the land of the impoverished and oppressed—the coal country of Kentucky.

Experimentalism, when it finally evoked a wide response from American undergraduates, assumed very different patterns from those anticipated. It cut through the pretense and careerism of established political groups. It meant, not safe and "healthy" back-slapping in neighboring Republican clubs, but involvement in the broad economic struggles of a whole people. It was inevitable that this groping exploration should ultimately become partisan and calculated. For, on his own campus, the student ran headlong into the same antagonists he had encountered in his field-work. And those who had most feverishly espoused the doctrine he was practicing had strangely fled to the opposing camp.

Any student of the social sciences searching for a field of investigation in the Spring of 1932 would inevitably have focussed his attention on Harlan and Bell counties, Kentucky. Even the sporadic, censored reports emanating from the territory confirmed the impression of one writer that "Kentucky is again a dark and bloody ground." Strife in the mine area had proceeded intermittently for years; now it was being renewed on an even more bitter scale. And others than the local

97

operators had stakes in the conflict. The network of leading financial moguls could be readily observed. According to Anna Rochester:

"Morgan, Insull, Mellon and Ford are strongly entrenched in Harlan county; Rockefeller and Mellon companies are important producers in the mountains northeast of Harlan. The Morgan empire includes the railroads that carry out the coal. Morgan and Insull utilities between them supply the light and power for Eastern Kentucky."

Only one in a series of cumulative grievances, the wage-cut of February, 1931, had proved the breaking-point. Miners were being compelled to sell their furniture, or, if installments were still to be met, to return it to the stores. Pellagra and "flux"—the afflictions most dreaded by the inhabitants—had spread so rapidly that in one camp, where 125 families lived, seven children a week died of these diseases. Pay-checks, even before the actual slash, had steadily fallen to the point where miners often found no more than one dollar in their envelopes after "services" had been deducted—the "services" which in any company town so mysteriously devour the earnings of the residents. If economic crisis was driving thousands of workers throughout the country below subsistence levels, in Harlan and Bell counties misery was merely more acute; depression only accentuated those conditions which had never even dimly resembled the "prosperity" of certain sections of the country. When in March, 1931, a decentralized strike flared up among the Harlan miners, it symbolized the growing restlessness, a conviction that "we have nothing to lose" and the surge toward union organization in a land where, according to one commentator, "even company unions are regarded as bolshevism by the operators." Troops patrolled the area, augmented by spies, thugs and "supervisors" of every description. Yet the daily routine of their lives was so oppressive that the miners could no longer be held in check. On May 5 of that year occurred the Battle of Evarts in which seven men were killed, machine guns and rifle bullets flew for half an hour and, as an aftermath, thirty-four miners were rounded up and charged with murder. Determined to quell dissatisfaction, the operators did not hesitate to introduce "evidence" of an admittedly specious form.

Throughout that summer and fall hostility increased steadily; the strife-torn counties became images of the most corrupt and degenerate economic tyranny in America. These instances are only hints of the feudal subjugation imposed upon 15,000 miners and their families in the land of King Coal.

It was entirely logical that students whose eyes were being shifted to more basic quantities in human affairs should have chosen, as the itinerary of their first exploration the tense mine-country of Kentucky.

The call for the Kentucky delegation was answered by the most heterogeneous group conceivable. There were many with radical sympathies of various degree and color; there were others who were merely curious, whose imagination had been stirred by the "horror-tales" of Kentucky. The one common denominator was their curiosity and their courage. They proposed to discover what was taking place and they were willing to undergo manifold risks to do so. Describing the composition of the delegates, Professor Joseph D. McGoldrick wrote: "Fundamentally, they wanted to see for themselves what was going on in the Harlan coal regions. They wanted to see how the miners were living; they wanted to discover, if they could, the hardships they were suffering and the degree of unemployment. They could hardly have been said to disbelieve these or to have been in doubt as to their general truth but they did want to see for themselves."

It was, however, more than an investigatory mission. The miners desperately needed aid. A year before, the Red Cross had absolved itself of any obligation until the striking men "went back to work and showed that they can't make a living"—although everyone who had ever probed the region had testified to that.* There was urgent need of food, money, clothes, and the bare necessities of existence. These the students collected before they started on the trip; several days were spent in the task.

On March 23rd, 1932, the first bus left from the Columbia University campus and headed for Kentucky. If they had been football warriors leaving for a major game, there would have been cheering hundreds to bid the group farewell. This pilgrimage set out almost unnoticed. It comprised about eighty students, drawn from all the New York colleges, from Harvard, Smith, Cincinnati and Tennessee Universities. It was, as I have said, a thoroughly diverse group; there were those who were quite confident of what to expect and others prepared to be surprised; there were the ardent, the curious and the detached; there were those who viewed the enterprise as a memorable cross-roads in student life and others who were frankly searching for sociological data—and nothing more.

The first two days were relatively uneventful. The cavalcade proceeded without interruption to Knoxville, Tennessee, twenty miles from the Kentucky border, arriving there on the second night of the journey to rest until dawn. It was in Knoxville that they received the first intimation of impending conflict. They hadn't long to wait before the "reception committee" was set in motion. The students found themselves barred from the hotel where they had planned to stay; they were closely scrutinized by detectives; hordes of reporters besieged them. Recalling the brutal treatment which had been accorded to a delegation of writers led by Theodore Dreiser

* For a graphic description of these conditions, see *Harlan Miners Speak,* the published report of a writers' investigating committee headed by Theodore Dreiser.

a few weeks before, they immediately wired the governor of Kentucky for an injunction to insure their safety in the ensuing days. They never received it. In Kentucky, it appeared, a "foreigner," like a union organizer, proceeds at his own risk. Meanwhile, two emissaries of the National Miners Union had travelled over the border to lead them back into the mining camps—a sharp refutation of subsequent statements by Kentucky officials that the students were not wanted even by the miners.

Early the next day the caravan started off again. As it approached the Kentucky border, the meaning of the manifestos issued previously by the coal operators was becoming disconcertingly plain. And at Cumberland Gap, the mountain pass into Kentucky, the full impact of Kentucky law and order descended. The road was almost dark when the bus turned the corner over the boundary; out of the approaching night the scowling faces of a mob of more than 200 people greeted the visitors. Cars drove up and surrounded the bus; most of the throng were armed, wearing the badges of deputy sheriffs. District Attorney Smith and Attorney Cleon Calvert strode into the bus and proceeded to fire provocative questions without waiting for answers. When a student sought to address the crowd to explain the peaceful purpose of the delegation, he found that his auditors had been incited too intensely before the arrival to heed any reason. There were derisive cat-calls, then the ominous lynch-cry: "String 'em up."

At this point District Attorney Smith delivered a speech which inflamed the mob further and dramatically revealed the mentality of a ranking official of Kentucky. He announced that the students were "Yankees, aliens and agitators," then reversed himself and proclaimed that they were not students at all but revolutionists in disguise. With a final flourish, he demanded that they turn around and start back North. Taken aback when they declared they intended to remain, Smith packed the bus with armed deputies and led the students to the courthouse of Middlesboro.

"Let's investigate the investigators," he shouted.

What transpired then was a revelation which no college text book had ever carried. The "prisoners" were crammed into a courthouse packed by agents of the coal operators, men half-hysterical from drink and carrying guns which stuck out of their pockets. With the aid of Judge van Beber, Smith launched his probe, which had the double virtue of being both informal and illegal. A spokesman for the students asked if they were under arrest; if they were, they wanted a lawyer; if not, they did not feel obligated to answer questions. Smith replied that "you can wait for your lawyer in jail." Having settled that technicality, he turned to the drunken crowd with new incitements dealing with the semitic sound of some of the prisoners' names; when the students dared to mention "constitutional rights," Smith flung back his most cherished paragraph:

"You have sounded your trumpets on the specious claim of liberty of free speech and free press. Your self-constituted, uninvited commission comes here on your claim of right and protection to wield your alien propaganda. We interpose our rights, vested in our property, churches and sacred institutions."

The speech electrified the mob. There were angry murmurings, sullen, derisive shouts toward the bench where the students sat. Women and men pressed around the terrorized group, screaming "String 'em up."

A Southern newspaperman who had covered countless Negro lynchings said afterward that "Judge Lynch" was never more nearly satisfied than at that moment.

Any reference to "constitutional rights" only brought forth another roar from Smith and his followers—many of them the hired gangsters of Kentucky coal barons, a handful of them miners who did not dare protest.

When the inquisition neared its end, Smith repeated his

order: leave Kentucky at once. "Obey the law," he boomed, then confessing that the law, in this instance, was whatever he chose it to be.

The students had come equipped with questionnaires and plans to interview miners, coal operators, representatives of the Red Cross, local officials and the townspeople. But Kentucky would not tolerate investigation; District Attorney Smith wrote his own Constitution. With the crowd inflamed to the point of mob action, the students were driven out of the courthouse, pushed into their bus and forcibly propelled down the road whence they had come. They were admittedly fortunate to escape.

The return journey was accompanied by an enforced escort of two attorneys and three armed deputies; one of the deputies twisted a girl's arm until it almost broke for "disobeying orders"; when another student sought to intercede, he was knocked down by another guardian of order—who drew a revolver. A third official—dead drunk—stood in the back, waving a pistol around and declaiming:

"What I say goes in Kentucky. I would as soon shoot now a United States marshal between the eyes as I shot Germans in the war."

Inadvertently he dropped three dum dum bullets while toying with his weapon. They were later produced in evidence.

Despite repeated protests, the deputies forced the driver to advance over the boundary for six miles into Tennessee. Not only had they violated the students' ostensible right to enter Kentucky as free citizens but they had also extended their power illegally beyond their own state line.

The next step was an appeal to higher authorities. After sending word of the developments to the second bus, which was proceeding to Kentucky by another route, the students journeyed to Nashville and Frankfort to lay their cases before the governors of Tennessee and Kentucky. Both offered them no assistance except their assurance that they were powerless in the situation. Governor Laffoon of Kentucky, to demonstrate his sympathy, posed with the students for newspaper cameras. Each governor had been apprised of the facts, of the violation of constitutional rights, of summary terrorization, of the denial of free passage to American citizens. But the dictatorship of the coal barons extended beyond the local officialdom. The governors, even had they wanted to act, evidently had not the courage to do so.

With this rebuff, the students issued to the miners, through the press, a document which, in the history of the student movement, is of major importance. It was the first declaration broadly circulated—newspapers throughout the South published it—in which students voiced a realization of common interests with workers as a social entity. It is notable because it represented the first decisive break with the "humanitarianism," condescension and self-sufficiency which had characterized much of the student radicalism of previous years.

Having appealed in vain to the highest officials of the two states involved, the students turned to Washington as their last and presumably most hopeful resort. For the first time on the trip, a government official greeted them cordially. He was Senator Edward J. Costigan. A hearing was arranged before him, Senator Royal S. Copeland of New York and Senator Logan—of Kentucky. Although a large number of the students were from New York, Senator Copeland could spare only a few minutes for the interview and Senator Logan followed him out shortly afterward. Only Costigan remained to hear the testimony of the delegation, accompanied by a plea for a Federal investigation of conditions.

"In preventing us from entering the mining district," the chairman of the group said, "the operators have clearly shown that they are desperately trying to keep from the outside world the knowledge of living and working conditions of thousands of miners, citizens of the United States and entitled to federal protection where county and state officials have so ruthlessly violated their rights."

While he spoke, Herbert Robbins of Harvard and Margaret Bailey of New York University sat in an anteroom of President Hoover's office, awaiting an opportunity to present an official petition for a Federal probe. After some time had elapsed, the secretary of the secretary of the secretary of Mr. Hoover accepted the petition, adding that it would be placed in the hands of the Department of Labor.

Reverberations of the Kentucky trip were felt most acutely by students in Chicago and Philadelphia. In the first city, where Samuel Insull made his home, students from colleges and high schools there marched to his residence bearing signs with pointed slogans about his stake in Kentucky oppression. They were seized by the Chicago police, arrested and thrown into jail. Some of them were roughly handled by the energetic officers.

Almost simultaneously, a group led by Maynard Kreuger, an instructor in economics at the University of Pennsylvania, rallied outside the offices of Drexel and Company, a Morgan affiliate and owners of extensive mining property. They carried signs referring to the close connection between such financial leaders as Morgan, Henry Ford and Mellon, and the bitter plight of the miners. Philadelphia's police duplicated the performance of Chicago's. They broke up the demonstration and threw the participants into jail. They were summoned before a patronizing judge who warned them against the evil paths of radicalism, emphasized the sanctity of the home and American institutions and, when the students seemed unconvinced, finally released them, holding only Krueger on a charge of inciting to riot.

At this point President Gates of Pennsylvania stepped valiantly into the picture. His students had been denied the right to peaceable assembly; an instructor was being railroaded for daring to join with them in the protest. But President Gates ignored those details, issuing a statement in which he absolved the university of any responsibility for the deeds of the "minority."

His action was only characteristic of the response of the whole academic officialdom. The educators had not enjoyed the interlude; they could not refrain from expressing their displeasure. To the students, particularly to those whose opinions on the issues roused on the journey were still being shaped, this was an instructive development and one which made a lasting impression. And the hostility of their administrators was widespread. A writer in *The Nation* observed: "University authorities did little to help their students. Officials of one university so far betrayed their own teachings as effectively to deliver their students into the hands of a Bell County mob by informing 'I'm the Law Smith' that these students did not represent their institutions 'officially.' Since their return the students have been criticized by some university authorities and old grads."

The students had embarked upon a mission fraught with peril and hardship; they had upheld what they felt to be elementary principles of a civilized order. Now, upon their return, they found their educators peeved, intolerant, aloof.

The Mellons, the Rockefellers, the Morgans, the Insulls ruled in Harlan, Kentucky. To an extraordinary number of undergraduates, their power seemed now to extend far beyond the realm of the coal fields. The surrender was equally complete among the most lucid advocates of the "experimental" educational technique which stresses the "importance of group activity in relation to real life."

Administrative disapproval was only one phase of the discovery made by the participants in the expedition. That their unlawful ejection did not arouse the protest of the teachers was, of course, a bitter disappointment. But even more profound was the shock incurred by the more general aspects of the journey. Writing in *The New Republic*, one student summarized his observations thus: "We found the press corrupted, the county government controlled by the coal operators, the governors evasive. We saw the inefficiency of the liberal nostrums of public opinion and gradualism."

Another commentator succinctly noted that the students had begun to use quotation marks around the term rights. Still a third, one of the leaders of the delegation, saw that "with our disillusionment began our education."

It remained for an English youth to depict most vividly the broader implications of the episode. Certainly the students had, as individuals, experienced memorable contact with the institutions of their land. Their future thinking and perspective could not fail to be conditioned by what they had seen. But of far wider import was the momentum for student awareness which the journey provided. If only eighty had been eye-witnesses, hundreds more in colleges everywhere had felt some of the repercussions and had become receptive to the reports of those who had done the "field-work." The event attracted nationwide attention, and however antagonistic much of that attention was in the press and in administrative chambers, it could not hide the real disclosures of the journey. Thus it was that Gabriel Carrett, an English student then studying at Columbia University, wrote to *The New Statesman and Nation*: "Now for the first time American students have come out of their shell and realized themselves as a social force."

Not long afterwards seven students in midwestern universities tried to conduct a survey of conditions in the coal fields there—and were promptly arrested. Undaunted, more than 150 students and teachers in the same area convened at the University of Chicago and set out for a tour of the Illinois coal belt. Hardly had the delegation penetrated the coal district than Sheriff Robinson of Browning County confronted them, demanding that they leave at once. His performance almost equalled that of Kentucky's Smith. His hand gripping a menacing shot-gun, he announced that "no agitation is

needed in Franklin county just now." Most of the delegation was compelled to turn back; five who managed to elude
the "law" were seized soon afterward. They learned, for the
first time in their lives, what the inside of a backwoods jail
is like.

Nothing in undergraduate life through the preceding decade had provoked more authentic and widespread interest
than the "sociological expedition" to Kentucky; this was only
confirmed by the later pilgrimages in Ohio and Illinois. Two
things were happening simultaneously: a large number of
students were becoming aware of some of the more palpable
evils of their society; they were also sensing, however dimly,
an identity between their own status and that of the people
whom they had come to study. That was the root of the insurgents' prophecy, the belief out of which the National Student League had arisen less than twelve months before. Its
realization was begun.

The expedition, though not an unqualified success, was certainly not a failure; but it cannot be understood in those
terms. Its ramifications were so diverse, its aftermath so turbulent and its influence exerted in so many places that too
precise an evaluation is futile. In the light of the years to
follow, the eighty who went to Kentucky were an "historic
vanguard"—and all the condemnation of their administrators
could not alter their prestige.

ii. Columbia Strikes

IF Kentucky had captured the imagination of thousands of
American students, the expulsion of Reed Harris from Columbia University set free even more sweeping currents. It
may have been less of a spectacle than the invasion into the
land of Bourbon rule; yet the Harris case, localized, with a
single Campus for background, indicated trouble close enough

to home to atone for its conventional setting. Terror in the Kentucky coal regions was, to some extent at least, a remote consideration even to those aroused by the reports. However much they may have been astonished or chagrined by the fate of the student investigators, however intensely they might have become aware, for the first time, of such conditions, there were many who did not sense any genuine relation to the Campus.

But Harris was an American undergraduate, a member (in not very good standing) of the Phi Gamma Delta fraternity, the editor of a student newspaper at a major University. These were familiar items to any student, whatever his institution. Moreover, Harris was hardly unknown; a series of incidents prior to his expulsion had established his repute beyond the Columbia Campus. And finally, coming directly in the wake of the celebrated Kentucky furor, this episode found the Campus world already partially sensitized to the conflict of which it was a stormy symptom.

When the affair had at last subsided, Dr. John P. Neal, a Columbia alumnus of Knoxville, Tennessee, wrote that "this was the most significant event which has occurred in the colleges in a decade. . . . The students of Columbia have fired a shot which will be heard around the college world."

When Harris assumed the editorship of *The Spectator* in April, 1931, his unobtrusive arrival seemed no excuse for jubilation. The paper had always behaved in the best tradition of American college journalism: unhesitant pandering to the Administration, only intermittent and usually uninformed comment on affairs outside the realm of the University, devout catering to the institutions made sacred by Trustees, Alumni and their subordinates. The most illuminating example of this heritage has been furnished by Nicholas McD. McKnight, now associate dean of Columbia College but in 1920 a crusading editor of *The Spectator*. His ardor was directed most frequently against those who insisted upon witnessing football games from their dormitory rooms over-looking the field, rather than taking their places in the cheering section.

On October 28, 1920, he turned his virile pen upon these iconoclasts and wrote: "We also take the attitude that those dormites . . . are showing very poor college spirit. A man who comes to college should put something into it for what it gives him. And it certainly is not too much to ask him if he cannot play himself to at least lend his full support to the men who represent Columbia on the field of play.

"No matter how hard a man may exhort from Livingston or Hartley (dormitories), the team cannot hear him and he cannot help them. Where his cheer will help, is in the cheering section of South stand. And that is where he belongs if he is to call himself a Columbia man."

Whatever may have been the troubled state of the world two years after the war, no matter how infinite were the changes being wrought in certain patterns of civilization, the problem of indolent football rooters remained uppermost in the minds of the editorial department of *The Spectator*. But Mr. McKnight was not alone; he set the standard for a decade and his own prodigious efforts were equalled and often excelled by ensuing editors. The college press through-out the country was, on the whole, absorbed by topics of similar weight.

The background is important if we are to contemplate the outcries which greeted Harris' declarations. Mr. McKnight may have been apoplectic at the desecration of pages he once edited; there were hundreds of others accustomed to his treatises who must have been startled into confusion by these first rays of light.

In November, 1931, Harris questioned the eternal verities of high-pressure football, intimating that certain more valiant gridmen were receiving more than honor as their reward; whereupon Ralph Hewitt, quarterback par excellence, loudly offered to sock Mr. Harris in the eye. But when Harris asked for publication of the books of the Athletic Association to prove his charges, there was concerted silence in the camp of the enemy. (Now, four years later, despite efforts by every ensuing editor to achieve the same end, the books are still firmly shut.) From football Harris proceeded to evaluate critically the sacrosanct senior society, Nacoms, of which he was a member. Nacoms is a secret "honorary" body, addicted to all the mumbo-jumbo of such institutions and dedicated to the ideals of the better people. This attack was no small irritation to those Alumni whose very life was dependent on mumbo-jumbo. Anti-semitism, rife in almost every quarter of the University, was not, presumably a topic for public discussion; Harris discussed it fully and comprehensively. Although several high administrators were known to be in opposition to the Kentucky trip, Harris gave his editorial support and substantial news space. The awarding of jobs by the Appointments office, still an operation shrouded in considerable mystery, was probed for the first time. Nicholas Murray Butler, the highest monarch of all, was not immune to criticism. Nor did Harris confine himself to an estimate of institutions at Columbia. The world which his predecessors had so conveniently ignored was introduced as a subject of editorial analysis; the existence of R.O.T.C. units at other colleges was mercilessly attacked; repression in education became a field of inquiry. Finally, Harris approached more forbidden territory—the administration of the college dining halls, which had been mildly scrutinized the previous year. He merely reprinted the charge that the halls, ostensibly run for the service of students, were actually being manipulated for profit, and that student waiters were receiving far less than benevolent treatment. Citing these allegations, Harris demanded an investigation; and with this demand went his editorship of the paper. It becomes obvious, however, that his expulsion did not arise from that isolated incident but climaxed a series of Administrative grievances.

For Harris had broken the shell. Many of his writings—

and those of Donald Ross, the editorial associate—might today be regarded as groping and undefined in terms of objectives; in 1931 he was speaking out amidst a dead silence.
No wonder that one irate alumnus snapped: "Harris is too
grown-up." His words summarized the view of the whole
network of Columbia administrators. Accustomed to deal
with the subservient and the credulous, who took what was
offered without examining the contents, they were appalled
by a critic who resisted them. Harris was marked for departure.

Dean Herbert E. Hawkes did not know, to his everlasting
sorrow, that the Friday he expelled Reed Harris was the day
of the election of Harris' successor. Had he been aware of
this, he would hardly have taken such drastic action; he would
have placed his faith in the board which was to come into
office the following Monday. But this sad lack of information
about the affairs of his college was to plague him for the rest
of his life. In the words of a prominent faculty man, he
committed a bull.

On the last three days of March, 1932, *The Spectator*
republished articles criticizing the preparation and serving of
food in the John Jay dining hall, condemning the treatment
of the student waiters and summarizing the results of previous investigations of the dining-room. On March 31 Harris
was summoned to the Dean's office and substantiation of the
charges was demanded—within the next twenty-four hours.
Harris then wrote a letter of explanation to the Dean pre-
ceded by an expression of surprise at the Dean's dictatorial
attitude. He said:

"Before submitting the explanation regarding a statement made in *The Spectator*, I want to protest against
the manner in which I was 'demanded' to produce an
explanation. You have repeatedly said to me that my
mode of presentation in my editorial column has been

unmannerly. Surely the dictatorial tone you adopted yesterday was not an example for me to follow in changing the tone of that column. In spite of the fact that we have had, almost constantly, major differences of opinion, I believe that I have acted in a gentlemanly fashion while in your office during my term as editor of *The Spectator*. That you should have adopted a tone suited only to a sergeant in the Marine Corps surprises me."

The letter then outlined the basis of the accusations against the dining hall. Its contents should be observed because subsequently this document was used by the University as a last, desperate excuse for the ouster of Harris.

The following day, Harris, suddenly called to the Dean's office, was informed that he had been expelled. Startled by the abruptness of the pronouncement, he asked for a reason. Whereupon the Dean read him a statement prepared for the press, the substance of which was:

"Material published in *The Spectator* during the last few days is a climax to a long series of discourtesies, innuendos and misrepresentations which have appeared in this paper during the current academic year and calls for disciplinary action."

Having explicitly informed Harris of his dismissal, Dean Hawkes then took him before the Committee on Instruction for a "hearing," although that committee had no authority to veto or modify the expulsion order. This was later explained by Harris, who quoted Dean Hawkes as saying that he had conferred with President Butler and the latter had cautioned him to give Harris "the pretense of a hearing." It was obvious, at any rate, despite Dean Hawkes' later repudiation of this statement, that there was to be no genuine hearing for the dissenting editor. And when the news appeared in the afternoon papers, Alumni, Trustee and administration rejoiced that the rebel was at last gone.

But his departure did not bring peace and quiet to the University. By the next morning the case had become a nationwide issue; any hope that Harris' ouster would still the waters he had troubled must have fled swiftly from Columbia's administrative halls.

So instantaneous and pronounced was the protest against the University's action that it became evident that her original defense would not suffice. The Dean had already admitted that more than a single editorial was involved in the expulsion, that Harris' whole editorial policy was the source of his discharge. Confronted with the dissatisfaction this explanation had caused, he reversed himself in mid-field—very likely after consultation with more authoritative groups. He informed a delegation of conservative students that Harris' "personal misconduct" prompted the ouster. To another delegation he gave the publication in *The Spectator* of the following paragraph as his reason:

"Waiters asserted that the personnel in charge of the dining room evidently were working only for profit, serving poor food, attracting organizations not strictly student in character and otherwise changing the character of the organization from one of student service to one of personal profit."

This was a tragic blunder which the Dean will not soon forget—and which was carelessly repeated by President Butler in an interview with another group. They had apparently been very negligent in preparing their alibis, for precisely that paragraph had been published in *The Spectator* a year before under a different editor and without any reprisals against him. The republication occurred in the course of an historical survey on previous inquiries into the dining-halls.

Neither Dean Hawkes nor Dr. Butler was ever able to explain why, if a previous editor could make this statement without punishment, Harris would have to be expelled for it. If all the other testimony could be forgotten, this phase alone would have demonstrated beyond dispute the real motivation behind the dismissal.

That was Dr. Butler's only direct statement on the case— his reference to "slanders" against the dining hall management. After that had proved a boomerang, he retired behind the scenes, resuming the attitude he had adopted on April 3, when interviewed by *The Herald-Tribune:*

"Would you make a statement on the expulsion of Harris," Dr. Butler was asked.

"Of whom?" he queried.

"Harris, Reed Harris, editor of *The Spectator*."

"Oh," said Dr. Butler, "I don't know anything about that. That hasn't come to me at all."

He was, by Dean Hawkes' earlier statement, not telling the truth. He had been consulted. Moreover, the event had been broadcast over the radio and spread over the newspapers; only a recluse could fail to have heard of it three days later.

Student indignation crystallized on the Monday after the expulsion, when a mass meeting was held on the Library Steps with more than 4,000 students present. Columbia had never witnessed—since the war years when R.O.T.C. men had held their review in exactly the same place—so impressive an outpouring of serious and determined students. And there, a University strike of major proportions was voted, to take place on Wednesday.

Since that time students in other colleges, faced with similar situations, have adopted the procedure of those thousands who massed on the Steps in the warm April afternoon. In 1931 that was a bold and almost unprecedented move.

Simultaneously the first hint of opposition developed. Its origin, tactics and appeal is worthy of note because, in subsequent years, almost every college has been visited by a similar bloc. At Columbia in 1931 the group styled itself "The Spartans"; later we are to see them as "Vigilantes" and even as "Silver Shirts." It was perhaps too early to comprehend their full meaning; yet some intimation of their later nature could be discerned.

Part of this opposition did not follow the action of "The Spartans" on the day of the strike when a meeting "to uphold the Dean" was held in front of his office under the auspices of that group. The "loyalists" preferred to attend the strike meeting, to hurl eggs, provoke fist-fights and attempt to disperse the assemblage. When one of their number was urged to express his sentiments verbally to the crowd, he rose and shouted: "I think it's a lot of boloney," then fled before the disgust of the audience. Another rose up to defend him, crying, "We all know what Harris said was true. But he didn't have to say it in public."

With these two eloquent contributions, the invaders, recruited primarily from the football team and Fraternity Row, then returned to their egg-throwing. At the meeting of "The Spartans," equally eloquent orators swore their fealty to the Dean and then devoted most of their time to a valiant assault on "communism." One of them later admitted the essence of his feeling on the matter: "The only way to run a corporation or a university or a government is to have discipline or authority vested in one person." He also confessed that, like most of his fellow-supporters of the Administration, he was an athlete, residing at the Manor House and otherwise enjoying a remunerative college career.

"The Spartans" and their sympathizers were plainly outnumbered. If a few hundred followed their leadership, close to seventy-five per cent of the 1800 students in the college, augmented by hundreds from other schools of the University, went on strike. The Dean's loyal lackeys could not carry the day despite the red menace, eggs and a substantial number of powerful football players.

On the steps of the Library several thousand students were demanding the reinstatement of Harris and a probe of the dining-halls.

The appearance and methods of the opposition was nevertheless ominous. It is equally significant that those who sought to break up the strike and provoke a riot were never censured by the Administration. They were its handmaidens and, if their tactics were crude, their intentions were noble. No sentimental Dean could have penalized such boyish devotion. They came from what we shall discover to be the accustomed seats of reaction—from Fraternity houses, from the athletic field and from that group which, in return for its willing and unquestioning loyalty, receives the numerous favors an Administration can afford to dispense.

Two days after the strike Dean Hawkes departed for a "long planned" trip to England. He told reporters at the boat that there was no possibility of Harris' reinstatement.

But the pressure did not cease. As one periodical wrote at the time, "This issue agitated the student body of the country for almost two weeks. From Maine to Texas, literally, letters and telegrams of protest came pouring into Columbia."

On April 20th prolonged negotiations between the Civil Liberties Union, representing Harris, and the University came to an end. Harris was reinstated. As he had originally intended, he immediately submitted his resignation to the University. In addition, he had previously sent a note of apology to the Dean for any personal injury the Dean may have experienced.

But, as the Civil Liberties Union commented in reviewing the case: "Columbia University's reinstatement of Reed Harris is a plain confession of error despite its face-saving conditions."

Student editors had been disciplined before; in the five preceding years, however, no case of expulsion had been reported.

The severity of the reprisal unquestionably served to project it into public notice. There were, however, more basic aspects to the protest. For Harris had become the standard-bearer of incipient student revolt, of a campus awakening from its stupor. His editorial policies had declared what others everywhere, in increasing numbers, were beginning to think. The restlessness caused by the perceptible inroads of economic uncertainty, the news of the Kentucky delegation—these had launched the downfall of "isolationism." Now there arose an unceasing uproar over Harris' expulsion. The event, moreover, served to dramatize the need for organized student force to combat similar moves, an emphasis continually set forth by the National Student League members who capably and energetically led the strike. They warned that this was the beginning of a crisis in students' rights—in the course of which students would be compelled to realize that their rights existed only so long as they defended them.

In the aftermath of the controversy its full significance was profoundly appreciated. One commentator remarked: "Teachers and others familiar with American student life agreed that the Columbia strike was the most militant student demonstration of recent years. It was noted far and wide that at last American college students were becoming excited over something more important than football and crew."

Its effects were visible in the amount of space which college journals in every community devoted to it. Thousands in eating-clubs and fraternity houses hundreds of miles from New York discoursed upon the issues involved. The sessions of undergraduate liberal clubs were occupied by similar discussion.

Perhaps more important than the mere fact of undergraduate thought—however extraordinary—was a conviction of power which the triumph of the strike engendered. When the resort to this weapon was first proposed, students ridiculed it, contending that it would be a lame, "undignified" gesture and nothing more. Now the move was vindicated. Faculty members had urged undergraduates to "bide your time" and "allow us to talk it over quietly with the administration." Their reticence was something which the strike participants will never forget. Only one man, Donald Henderson, gave unhesitant and vigorous public support to the walkout. When John Dewey was approached for aid, he said that he "knew nothing about it"—a rebuff which some of his disciples bitterly remembered. This was an hour, it was felt, when the faculty should have recognized an identity between its own welfare and that of the students in the face of so outright an invasion of an allegedly cherished principle. Instead there was almost hushed silence; some deplored "hasty action"; others cited their "loyalty to the Dean." Throughout the whole university only sixteen men, mostly young instructors, consented to sign a petition for Harris' reinstatement.

The reluctance of the teaching staff only enhanced the victory of the students. With the entire administrative machinery mobilized to affirm the expulsion, the University was eventually forced to surrender. Certainly the threat of legal action accelerated its retreat. On the other hand, without the pressure of nationwide opinion and the attendant glare of publicity, it is highly doubtful that Columbia's capitulation would have been so sweeping and swift. At the outset there were those who sought to "keep the affair among ourselves"; they resented the intrusion of "outsiders"—students and teachers from other schools who readily avowed their support. But the hostility slowly evaporated; in its stead was the acknowledgment that precisely such joint agitation had been effective and that, moreover, the disagreement could not be isolated from the academic scene as a whole. The outcome of the Columbia conflict, it was admitted, would condition activities of administrators everywhere.

These were broad truths; the extent to which they were

accepted, of course, varied with individual cases. What was uniform and of prime consequence was the crystallization of opinion. The Columbia strike of April, 1932, was an inspiration and a model for the rest of the country and one which was to have its counterparts in the months to come. It established the place of the student movement and the paths of procedure for it to follow, arousing students in other areas to the imminence of parallels on their own campuses and outlining the strategy of counter-attack.

When Dean Hawkes blundered on that Friday in April, he served a far more distinguished purpose than was then supposed. The revolt was penetrating the "intellectuals" and the "collegians" alike.

III. "Pre-War Generation"

IN an atmosphere attuned to lethargy, these had been unsettling events. Even while the campus was feeling their impact, however, a foreign observer was pointing to another alarming symptom of instability. Almost imperceptibly, he noted, the world had completed its evolution from a post-war to a pre-war condition.

The disclosure could not escape the notice of a maturing undergraduate, become conscious for the first time that all was not serene in his or anybody else's domain. Economic upheaval was an established, ineffaceable fact; to its distress were added now the omens of a Second World War. If less than a decade before the nations had solemnly renounced arms, their pledges were being belied by the roar of munitions factories. When or how the boiling point would be reached, no one could be sure; but steadily and remorselessly the prerequisites for conflict were being fulfilled.

The issue of war and peace was not unknown on the campus; to a limited extent it had agitated the colleges of the 1920's. But beyond the general theme, the parallel is slight.

In scope, in program, in analysis and in technique the two movements are utterly distinct. In 1925 one writer summarized the status of peace endeavors thus:

> "The truth is that between the horror of the next war and our disgust for the last, most of us have come not to think about war at all. Most boys at college accept the general thesis that war is an abomination, that they detest it and that they will fight only when desperately necessary; beyond that they do not go." *

Those who did bestow more than private hatred on the "enemy of mankind" were relatively few; their efforts were dedicated to one transcending aim—American participation in the League of Nations. To create popular sentiment in behalf of this agency, scores of clubs and societies were formed; conferences of students from representative colleges reaffirmed the objective. It was ardently believed that our entrance into the League and the cementing of some of its more gaping loop-holes would guarantee everlasting goodwill. Years before the seizure of Manchoukuo, prolonged hostilities in the Gran Chaco and Hitler's repudiation of the Versailles Treaty, hundreds of students had been captivated by Woodrow Wilson's dream. They set about, through the League of Nations Association, the National Student Federation and similar groups to effect its realization.

Underlying their labors were the tenets of pure pacifism. Although they did countenance lobbies on certain legislation, recurrent campaigns over local intrusions of the War Department, their perspective was essentially that of "individual conscience." At conclaves summoned by Christian Associations, young men stood up to vow that they would have nothing to do with war. That was just the point. So abhorred and overwhelmed were they, so distasteful of the prospect of destruction that they were hardly willing to do anything

* Oliver La Farge, writing in *Scribner's* for July, 1925.

about it. Their deeds were animated by high purpose and deep feeling; but they were based on personal fervor rather than scientific analysis—on what they wanted rather than what they thought. It was the approach of liberal, acquiescent non-participation in any future war, without any immediate program for averting it or resisting it save by martyrdom at Leavenworth once it broke out. The doctrine was the mirror of a comparatively placid, less truculent era when statesmen talked of preserving eternal peace, not postponing an inevitable war. The earlier conflict was still fresh in men's minds; they could not genuinely believe that it would be repeated. And the League of Nations seemed a promising safeguard against such a disaster.

Sentiment on the issue never attained any notable organized proportions. Europe was far away; there were manifold assurances from high places that the United States had "learned its lesson"; even the more earnest undergraduate groups found other problems more absorbing and immediate. While this apathetic confidence gripped our centers of learning, however, the War Department was entrenching itself firmly in the educational sphere. Its instrument was the Reserve Officers Training Corps. For every handful of students registering their conviction that the United States should join the international peace body, there were thousands who marched across our campuses in their military colors, accepting preparedness and national honor as gospel. The pacifists took up the challenge, but they were pitifully outnumbered. They could not combat the alliance between the government's military agency, the local R.O.T.C. officialdom, university administrators and the "patriotic" horde led by the American Legion.

When, in 1932, students again and in larger numbers awoke to the war danger, they were confronted on their own campuses with this powerful impediment to anti-war action. The R.O.T.C. was an established factor, abetted by educators and Legionnaires alike. How the corps had achieved this prestige and prominence merits exploration; the circumstances of its rise to supremacy provide the setting for December, 1932, the month of the momentous Chicago student congress against war.

With the passage of the Morrill Act in 1862, military training was injected into the curriculum of land-grant colleges. Many fictions grew up around the statute, principally the assertion that all schools in that category were legally required to conduct compulsory drill. Not until 1923, when Wisconsin made the course optional, was this illusion challenged. Since that time a former Secretary of the Interior, a Secretary of War and the U. S. Attorney General under Hoover have supported Wisconsin's interpretation.

On the impetus of the statute, fifty-seven colleges had, by 1912, instituted military training. With the passage of the National Defense Act, drill was introduced on an unprecedented scale into our educational halls. In the first year, the number of schools offering training spurted upward from fifty-seven to 115; there was a marked slump in the early post-war period but by 1927 there were 280 colleges in which the R.O.T.C. had gained a foothold. The figure had reached 313 in 1931. Commensurate with this advance were the vast funds expended by the government for support of the corps. From 1921 to 1931 $106,965,041 was disbursed; in 1932 alone $6,000,000 was appropriated for R.O.T.C. and C.M.T.C. upkeep, exclusive of the salaries of commissioned officers and enlisted men in charge of the work. Three years later the largest appropriation in the history of the corps, designed to enable the introduction of new units, was voted by the Roosevelt government.

Throughout the expansion process, one ancient and vehement defense has been delivered by those susceptible to the voice of criticism. Whenever the corps is under fire as a citadel of militarism, its administrators assume a pose of offended innocence, pointing to the physical and healthful accomplish-

123

ments wrought by the training. This fraud has been adequately disproved by a man whose broader sympathies were unquestionably on the side of the institution. He, the late Lieutenant Colonel Herman J. Koehler, founder of the West Point System of Physical Training, declared many years ago:

> "The use of the musket as a means to physical development of anyone, be he man or boy, is worse than worthless; it is in my opinion positively injurious. . . . The army, in fact, uses calisthenics, not drill, for physical training." *

A similar view was expressed more recently by Dr. Jesse F. Williams, former President of the American Physical Education Association:

> "Military training in the colleges never has provided and in my opinion never can provide the kind of developmental activity essential to the organic development of young men."

Abundant testimony to the same point could be gathered. Still the health slogan is revived at regular intervals to justify education's homage to the corps. And meanwhile the drillmasters mobilize an impressive conscript army on the campus. The headway they have made is demonstrated by the increasing numbers enrolled since 1912:

$$
\begin{array}{ll}
1912 \ldots \ldots & 29{,}979 \\
1923 \ldots \ldots & 103{,}894 \\
1930 \ldots \ldots & 145{,}902 \\
1931 \ldots \ldots & 147{,}009 \\
\end{array}
$$

In the years directly following the war, the army moguls were dismayed by a sharp decline in the prestige and num-

* Quoted from the *American Physical Education Review.*

bers of the units. Desertions were frequent; students were drifting away from the military regime or bitterly rebelling against it. Confronted with this emergency, the officialdom drafted one of the most fantastic and extravagant ballyhoo campaigns ever conceived. Its central themes were women, and horses. To the accompaniment of winsome smiles and pounding hoofs, the circus was engineered, while educators sat in the grandstand and vociferously applauded. Beginning in 1925, the fanfare steadily progressed until the R.O.T.C. had charmed the hearts and the minds of thousands of American students.

In an item which appeared on April 4, 1928, in *The Schenectady Gazette,* the technique was briefly exemplified:

"Oh, it's great to be a soldier when the officers are as nice-looking as El Delle Johnson, nineteen-year-old Kansas girl. Miss Johnson has been made honorary colonel of the Kansas State Agricultural School R.O.T.C."

From *The Binghamton Press* of November 20, 1928:

"The custom of appointing leading co-eds as sponsors of the local Syracuse University unit of the R.O.T.C. was established two years ago to further favorable sentiment toward the unit among the student body."

The Omaha Bee-News of November 27, 1928, disclosed:

"With so pretty a Colonel, it is no wonder that the Creighton R.O.T.C. is so well-drilled a unit, said Major-General Charles P. Summerall, Chief of Staff of the United States Army as he reviewed the cadets of the Omaha school."

One of these attractive sponsors freely admitted, at a congressional hearing in 1929, the nature of her assignment. According to *The Baltimore Sun:*

"Charges made in the House of Representatives by Representative Ross A. Collins that sex appeal and social aspirations are capitalized in the nationwide development of the military idea were declared true here last night by the regimental sponsor of the R.O.T.C. at the university of Maryland. . . . Miss Leighton added that she thought the sponsors were instrumental in getting more students to take the advanced course in military training which is optional at the university. . . ."

Sex-appeal was destined for new laurels under the tender guidance of the military hierarchy. There was equal solicitude for the horses. Where women failed, or were unavailable, the animal might prove even more magnetic. The *Princeton Alumni Weekly* observed in January, 1929: "In April, 1903, Princeton put the first college polo team on the field. . . . Its present renaissance at Princeton and other colleges is due to the establishment of the R.O.T.C. . . ."

The *Congressional Record* reveals the following testimony obtained during a debate on military appropriations in 1930:

"The young ladies are not the only agencies used in the R.O.T.C. for the purpose of popularizing military training. There are certain schools that would probably not have an R.O.T.C. were it not for the riding horses provided. . . . So you can see that we now add to the saying 'Join the Army and Become a Man,' 'Join the R.O.T.C. and ride.' "

And at Cornell University, *The Albany Times-Union* reported, "2500 students have been given instruction during the past ten years." Colonel Joseph Beacham, commandant of the Cornell R.O.T.C., boasted that the school was "horse-conscious."

But even these two stellar appeals have often proved inadequate; consequently, when the great campus military

126

boom got under way, all the tumult of martial ceremonies was added. There is no ceremony now in most colleges equivalent to the military parade—and the officials know it. All the trappings and frenzy synonymous with the incitement of war fever have been introduced onto the campus. The following headlines, chosen at random, indicate how lavish the enterprise has been:

R.O.T.C. UNITS STRUT STUFF IN ANNUAL
REVIEW

PRETTY SPONSORS SPUR BOYS IN R.O.T.C.
FIELD DAY

THEY DID THEMSELVES PROUD, THOSE
CADETS

PRETTY CO-EDS SHARE HONORS WITH R.O.T.C.
UNIT AND BAND AT SEMI-ANNUAL REVIEW
HELD IN STADIUM

A whole series of rewards were devised to encourage the academic troops. *The New York Herald-Tribune* of June 12, 1927, ran the following picture-caption: "Miss Sarah Marshall handing the cup to Frederick Mills for having the best all-round company in the Drexel R.O.T.C." From *The Syracuse Journal*, May 10, 1928: "For service to his country, senior cadet officer is presented the Rotary Club sabre by president of the Rotarians for outstanding work in the student army corps."

Despite this myriad of embellishments, the corps did not fare well when unaided by compulsion; that was demonstrated at Wisconsin where, in the five years after drill was made optional, enrollment fell sixty-three per cent.

There was, however, one underlying phase of the military spectacle which served to preserve the units where membership was not mandatory. Perhaps no single element contributed more to their maintenance than the moral suasion surrounding their efforts. This was dramatically illustrated at a Business High School in Washington in 1928 where a slogan was posted, in large black letters:

DON'T BE A SLACKER, BE A CADET.

That brief warning is integral to the whole existence of the corps. In the post-war decade it flourished precisely because there were only a handful of students interested and courageous enough to resist these weapons. Combatting the military officialdom meant the condemnation of fair "sponsors," their coterie of admirers, the "best people" in the university. There were those prepared to risk this hostility; occasional conferences and meetings were held at which this opposition was reaffirmed; but it was almost always a small, isolated group which defied the sanctities—and the R.O.T.C. was not severely hampered by their moves.

This liaison between militarism and education was frequently minimized even by those unsympathetic to it. If the students wanted to show off for their co-eds or march the goose-step for army functionaries or capture some of the shiny medals doled out so generously or, more prosaically, obtain a portion of the funds paid to students in advanced courses, let them, it was argued, have their hour of splendid stupidity.

But others maintained that the matter could not be so easily waved away, that, aside from the inherent militarism of the corps, there was an even more ominous aspect to the training. Beneath all the glamor and insanity in which drill was shrouded, there were being cultivated the two twin menaces of the age—war and reaction. And this was being done under the guise of "citizenship."

Only a scattered chorus perceived how appalling this trend was to become in later years. If today the R.O.T.C. is being utilized as the stepping-stone for a fascist youth movement,* the seeds of that development were planted long before. That was taking place, I have said, in the name of "citizenship" which, next to the claims of "body-building," was hailed as the alleged raison-d'être of the campus military machine. It is therefore important to inquire what form of "citizenship" was, and is, being inculcated in those whom the War Department's emissaries are allowed to guide for a substantial part of their college lives. The obvious source of investigation should be the *R.O.T.C. Manual*, in which "Citizenship" is discussed from the point of view of the cadet officers.† The findings can roughly be divided into two categories: the fundamental militarist doctrine espoused and the reactionary, intolerant, chauvinist credo accompanying it. One of the earliest passages we encounter reads: "This inherent desire to fight and kill must be carefully watched for and encouraged by the student. . . ." Further: "To finish an opponent who hangs on or attempts to pull you to the ground, always try to break his hold by driving the knee or foot to his crotch and gouging his eyes with your thumbs."

And to the ballyhoo of "good citizenship" the army indiscreetly gave its own answer. In *The Army and Navy Register* for July 25, 1925, when controversy over the manual was still being waged, an army officer wrote:

> "Good citizenship is an excellent thing. . . . But . . . an army exists to kill men, when ordered, in the nation's quarrel irrespective of its justice. . . . We should not tell lies about its (the army) being a school for citizenship or manual training."

* For elaboration and documentation of this charge, see the chapter on "Students in Uniform."

† This manual was withdrawn from public use in 1925 after concerted protest by City College undergraduates. It should not be believed that the withdrawal implied a surrender of principle or that the policies of the military clique have been altered. An official communiqué issued at the time the manual was "abandoned" quite frankly admitted: "young officers will be relieved as it gives them a chance to teach citizenship on their own initiative *without expert advice or restriction.*" The emphasis is mine.

That the R.O.T.C. recognizes war as a necessary, not undesirable and eminently just thing whenever our own government is involved should be plain. Thus Major McNair, commandant of the Purdue University Corps, wrote in *The Purdue Alumnus* in 1926: "If a pacifist is one who believes that war is unnecessary and preventable, then pacificism becomes a menace."

There is also, however, the other side of the militaristic credo of the corps. It is the philosophic root of fascism. On the one hand the manual in describing democracy states that "a government of the masses . . . results in mobocracy . . . results in demagogism, license, discontent, anarchy"; on the other it preaches an extreme, intemperate nationalism whose counterpart can be found most fully expressed in German and Italian fascism. Compare the following section on "Destructive Idealism" in the citizenship *Manual* with the more vibrant passages of Hitler's *Mein Kampf:*

"An impractical and destructive idealism called internationalism is being propagated by certain foreign agitators and is being echoed and re-echoed by many of the nation's 'intellectuals.' Its efforts are to combat the spirit of patriotism, to destroy that spirit of nationalism without which no people can long endure. . . ."

From these "theoretical" considerations it has been only a short distance to the overt manifestations of reaction—a concerted, deliberate attempt to silence liberal thinking by means seldom fair and usually foul. Today that tendency has reached more decisive stages as later evidence will demonstrate; even in a less critical era, however, the organization of repression was vigorously carried on. There are scores of examples of the disconcerting link between "patriotism" and intolerance; the following are illustrative.

Donald Timmerman, student pastor of the Methodist Church and Reserve Chaplain, was recommended for discharge by the R.O.T.C. commandant at Ohio State University in February, 1927, for publicly condemning compulsory military training. Scabbard and Blade, the military honor society, denounced his stand as "traitorous to the society, disrespectful to the country and unfitting as a member of the Officers' Reserve Corps."

A year before at the University of Nebraska a Citizens' Committee of One Hundred was organized to advocate the abolition of compulsory drill at the school. Rev. Harry Huntington, Methodist student pastor at the University, was chairman; two other student pastors and Arthur Jorgensen, Y.M.C.A. secretary, were active members. In the midst of the campaign, the Board of Regents suddenly issued a public rebuke to "the attitude of certain religious and welfare workers assigned to the university who do not seem to realize the gross impropriety of accepting the good will and hospitality of the institution and conducting, from offices given them by the Regents, a campaign against the traditional policies of the institution and against the authority of the governing body." Shortly afterward Mr. Jorgensen "resigned."

At about the same time Mrs. Lucia Ames Mead was preparing to deliver an address in the Chapel of Agnes Scott college, Decatur, Georgia. Without warning she received word that her talk had been cancelled. The action, she later learned, had been taken in deference to the protest of Asa Warren Candler, President of the Argonne Post of the American Legion. Citing the insidious nature of the "youth movement for peace" and labelling Mrs. Mead a "Red and a Bolshevik," Mr. Candler had compelled the administration to intervene.

Meanwhile out at West Chester Normal College in Pennsylvania the officials of the Legion were boasting that they had brought about the dismissals of Professors Kerlin and Kinneman—because they had dared to support the right of the student liberal club to criticize the jaunts of American imperialism into Mexico and Nicaragua.

In 1926 Oklahoma University proved fertile soil for another assault on free speech by the innocent upholders of the academic army. Writing to President Buzzell at the University, Lieutenant Colonel George Chase Lewis urged him to prevent a lecture that was being planned by foes of compulsory drill at which the Reverend John Nevin Sayre, noted pacifist, was to speak. "I trust that you will be able to curtail pernicious activities at Norman (the university town)," declared the indignant colonel. President Buzzell was quick to comply. Mr. Sayre was barred from the University grounds and only the offer of facilities by a neighboring church enabled him to appear in the region.

On the same tour Mr. Sayre was able to gather additional data on the united front between the military department, the Legion and college administrations. On December 2 he had been denied permission to address students at the University of Missouri Y.M.C.A. Anxious to secure the War Department's "Distinguished Service" rating, the local R.O.T.C. had felt constrained to preserve "good morale" by "stepping on peace agitators."

At the University of Indiana he was informed that prospective speakers at the "Y" must first run the gauntlet of an advisory committee led by Paul McNutt, dean of the law school and State Commander of the American Legion. Even greater precautions were being taken at the University of Wyoming, he disclosed; a speaker needed the rubber stamp of the R. O. T. C. administrators before he could hope to appear on a university platform.

In the same year Kirby Page was greeted with similar treatment in his efforts to place the pacifist philosophy before undergraduate audiences. Acceding to the request of military officials, the President of West Virginia University ordered Page to stay away from the Campus. At Oregon State President Kerr assigned the convocation committee to handle the situation—with the same outcome.

It was the same everywhere. Students were being compelled to dance to the tunes of the military department—and not to question why. Captain Harmon, commandant at Norwich University, expressed the prevailing notion with admirable brevity: "To be successful with the commandant, cadets have but one simple thing to do—obey orders."

There were heroic, but usually isolated, protests. Numerous cases of conscientious objectors risking academic discipline were reported. For refusal to submit to drill, thirty-eight students were ousted from the University of Minnesota, causing one editor to inquire:

> "Is Minnesota under martial law? It is impossible to maintain a healthy morale among faculty and students where the military department has such an influence with the office of the Dean of student affairs that drill must be given precedence over all else in the program of every first and second year student."

But the revolts were almost uniformly sporadic and short-lived, save for occasional risings such as that which occurred at City College.* A Syracuse student declared he would prefer to sacrifice his diploma rather than enlist in the corps; and his action was typical of the valiant but single-handed gestures of his contemporaries.

Scabbard and Blade is the honorary fraternity of the R.O.T.C. Its members are ostensibly the cream of the corps, men whose work has far outdistanced their competitors. To obtain a picture of the workings of this society's collective mind—after it has been subjected to the zealous manipulation of the military officialdom—we have only to turn to the bulletins launched by the organization in 1926. The avowed purpose of the bulletins is to disseminate information about "dangerous individuals" and in its first editorial we find:

* See the chapter on City College.

133

"It is our earnest hope that you will retain this document for future reference and publicity use, if speakers appear in your city to orate against national defense. . . . Americans should be on guard against any propaganda from any source whatsoever belittling and deriding the benefits obtainable through our present R.O.T.C. and C.M.T.C. systems."

Who are these "dangerous individuals" whom the cadets have been taught to fear? We might at least expect to be warned against the Executive committee of the Communist International. But the zealots are not too discriminating in their fury. The selection of acts, utterances or affiliations made by the drafters of the black-list is a revealing mirror of hysteria:

William E. Sweet—"In 1922 Mr. Sweet was a subscriber to the pamphlet service of the American Civil Liberties Union and also was in England studying workers education and industrial relationships."

J. Henry Scattergood—"In an address before a peace luncheon, he declared in effect that the people must drop hate and work for peace."

William E. Borah—"R. M. Whitney in *Reds in America* indicates connection with American Civil Liberties Union."

Jane Addams—". . . For the past twenty years her efforts have been directed to international and subversive channels until today she stands out as the most dangerous woman in America."

George Foster Peabody—"He is interested in Negro schools, being a trustee of the American Church Institute for Negroes and the Hampton Normal and Agricultural Institute. The latter is said to be a hotbed of race equality."

134

This is the product of the military caste system in American colleges. On December 2, 1926, *The New York Times* carried a headline:

DRILL HELPS MORONS

and went on to describe the effective use of military training at the New York State Institute for Defective Delinquents. Without meaning to be unduly facetious, one cannot ignore the incongruity that in the same year the University of Wyoming should be devoting nearly two thirds of the first-year course to drill.

However ludicrous or inane its practices may seem, the growth and expansion of the R.O.T.C. has not been a source of humor. By the end of the post-war decade its influence was openly acknowledged as supreme on scores of Campuses; on others the link, if less glaring, was equally strong. While administrators were hounding peace advocates in the mildest of activity, the War Department was authorized to do as it pleased with thousands under its command. Deliberately and viciously, the process of instilling "patriotism" was paving the way for the more sinister technique of 1935—the resort to violence on a national scale. The transformation in method will become highly understandable as we trace the emergence of an anti-war movement, the potentialities of which are only now becoming evident.

From campuses as widely separated as New York and California there began a long, wearying procession to Chicago late in December, 1932. It was the most bitterly cold interval of the year. To appreciate the solemnity and determination in which the event was to be conducted, one need only visualize the difficulties under which the gathering came together. That year the government was expending its customary millions for the erection of an academic war battalion; no such sum had been appropriated for the peace advocates.

The students traveled by any conveyance in sight—and, if there was none, they walked for drab, chill miles until another vehicle consented to bear them further along. From Arkansas a group of delegates rode the rails, half-frozen, hungry, barely able to reach their destination. The New York delegation was more fortunate; it rode by bus for almost two days and nights, without more than brief stop-overs for meals. And the bus possessed utterly inadequate heating equipment.

In the closing days of 1932 more than 600 delegates from schools and colleges in every part of the country assembled in Mandel Hall at Chicago University. Although the congress had been conceived by the National Student League, the summons to it had been issued by a large, heterogeneous group. The response was eminently diverse. There were Republicans, Democrats, Socialists, Communists, pacifists of every shade, spokesmen for campus liberal groups and literary societies, and a host of others who had been aroused by the increasingly precarious state of international relations.

It was an impressive array and one whose deeds are often neglected in the more spectacular stage which the anti-war movement has attained. Yet, if any single enterprise can be viewed as the origin of so vast an awakening, such was the Chicago Congress. It was significant for more than the fact of its existence—although even that was of singular proportions in an undergraduate world still weighing the meaning of its first major struggles. Even more notable was the mixture of opinion at the conclave and the mutually acceptable program adopted after two days of debate, study and interpretation. At Chicago the guiding principles of the student movement against war were established.

The results of the deliberations can be conveniently divided into two phases—analysis and strategy. Both constituted a sharp, permanent break with the formulae of the early pacifist blocs. This charting of new paths, moreover, was accepted by the pacifists themselves, cognizant of the failures and

inadequacies of their previous endeavors. They did not surrender any of their basic convictions nor did anyone ask them
to do so; they did accept a series of broad revisions dictated by
the exigencies of the period. And they declared their willingness, confirmed in later efforts, to accept the offer of cooperation on specific fronts with the left wing at the congress.
That accord was a prerequisite to discussion and it was
patiently woven.

At the outset the assemblage could not fail to set forth a
fundamental assumption arising from the evidence of the
previous war and the approach of a new one: international
conflict is primarily an outgrowth of the profit system, inherent in the status and politics of imperialism. A decade
before, some credence might have been attached to the notion
that war was an instinctive desire of men to which governments acceded; by 1932, there had been sufficient revelations
to demonstrate that Morgan was more guilty than mankind.
It was a realization common to all segments of the congress;
whether one liked this social order or not, one had to admit
that war was one of its most flagrant deficiencies. Even the
once-fervid advocates of the League of Nations assented to
this premise; they had seen their vision evaporate in each
major trial. They perceived, with little to deny the perception, that the most convincing pact could not swerve the
course of the quest for markets and the placement of capital,
especially at a time of enduring internal distress. The League
of Nations, as a permanent bulwark against war, was not to
be trusted, whatever tentative impediments it might provide.

The conclusions which flowed from this groundwork were
inevitable. Effective opposition to the menace of imperialism
demanded more than a clash with diplomats or an erring
State Department; it would require vigorous combat with
the essence of imperialism and the vested interests involved.
One might still conceivably hold faith in a "benevolent capitalism" as many of the delegates did; they were nevertheless
compelled to grant that capitalism, unless swept from the

natural course of its development and decline, was destined to precipitate another war for its own salvation—without benefit of benevolence. "Preparedness" was a symbol of that inevitability; those who raised the prospect of invasion as a defense of the military machine were invoking a bogey-man to disguise more basic truths—the implicit war-like character of the social system, of which arms and armies were the manifestations.

There were obvious corollaries in strategy derived from these suppositions. Isolated, passive opposition to the war machine, whatever its value as a spiritual catharsis, was doomed to failure in terms of objectives. Every preceding effort along these lines had negated that procedure. It was fruitless, unwarranted heroism to stand up alone in the face of the War Department; one might gallantly prepare for a journey to Leavenworth—but it would be of no avail. If there was to be an effectual blockade of impending disaster, it would have to assume an active, dynamic quality, on a prepossessing scale and consolidated into organizational form. In this framework, the student could neither be the lone nor leading element—an admission which his predecessors were seldom willing to make. Whatever his brains—and of these he might be quite confident—his numbers and his situation mitigated against the rôle of leadership. An alliance would have to be forged with those whose power and energies were dedicated to the same aim, and whose labors were exerted in more strategic places. It was quite plain that the financial barons would lend neither their talent nor their resources to an endeavor which threatened their prestige and their policies. Whatever their individual propensity for peace, their investments could usually be expected to be closer to their hearts. There were, on the other hand, millions of human beings whose stake in these events approximated the student's; they fought the wars, they and their families were the victims of it; the only dividends which they obtained from the rise in war-stocks were the sham tears of professional mourners. It was with these men and women—workers on the docks, in the factories, on the farms and in the mines—that the student's search for peace would have to be aligned. That was neither romanticism nor self-sacrificing submersion of the undergraduate's identity; it was dictated by the commonplace logic of the situation.

In Kentucky the first proclamation of union had been issued; at Chicago its potentialities were even more clearly realized. Ten years before, round-table discussions in secluded classrooms might seem an adequate antidote to warfare; now their pitiful insufficiency was only too plain. When the undergraduate accepted the concrete hegemony of those employed in the crucial areas of war production and related industries, his whole tactical concept was altered. He could no longer be repelled by "mass action"; he could no longer heed the restraining hand of those who lamented that "war is too big a problem for human understanding." It was a "big problem" but one which had tangible, real accompaniments. Certainly discussion, debate and controversy were intrinsic to the movement; but beyond them was the need for agitation, rallies, demonstrations, public avowals and pressure-moves of every sort; and later, militant protest strikes on the campus held in unison with groups in every sphere. These were rigorous devices; they would inevitably encounter the fierce hostility of those inured to the "academic tradition"; Trustees would illegalize and damn them, invoking every instrument to divert the movement. But—and this is the feeling which has grown and been strengthened ever since—the "stakes are high, so high that caution is an incongruity."

Those were the outlines and purposes of Chicago. It was, as I have said, a beginning whose import not even the delegates may have fully appreciated. There was formulated at that conclave an approach utterly different from anything which broad groups of American students had ever before embraced. "Pure pacifism" was dying; self-conscious heroics were no longer to be heralded. There was, moreover, one

immediate challenge to be taken up: the existence of the
R.O.T.C. One might argue that optional drill was preferable
to compulsory; but the ultimate drive of the insurgents, as
distinct from their precursors, was for the abolition of what
they viewed as the rule of the war machine on the campus.
This conviction was intensified by the inroads of depression;
with thousands of students being forced to curtail their education, with whole schools being shut down as "economy"
measures, the appropriation for the corps was rising. Transfer
of these funds to education was the demand to be incessantly
placed before the government. Several months before more
than fifty students representing ten colleges had borne such
a petition to Washington. One month after the Chicago Congress a student from Cornell and another from Penn State
testified in the House against appropriations for the R.O.T.C.
The commandants did not rejoice in the Chicago assemblage.
And they seemed to sense what was to follow.

Among the 600 delegates at the convention were, we have
seen, students from colleges throughout the nation. So large
and widely distributed a gathering had within its range thousands of undergraduates who, if only dimly aware that this
congress was taking place, proved eager to hear reports of
the delegates. Rallies were held at scores of schools for the
returning spokesmen and at these the theme of the congress
was re-echoed. Its decisions and plans aroused a significant
measure of enthusiasm. And even while this was happening,
as local anti-war bodies were being set up on various campuses,
word came of an event destined to give profound impetus to
the aspirations of the congress.

In the opening weeks of 1933, England's country gentlemen awoke to a ghastly and distressing disclosure. After a
stormy session in the halls of the celebrated Oxford Union,
the undergraduate assemblage had voted 275 to 153 that
"this House will not fight for King and country in any war."
The die-hard press pointed to the resolution as further cause

for enactment of stringent sedition laws. Shortly after being apprised of the vote, a group of respectable, old and terror-stricken ladies sent white feathers to leaders of the Union. From all the best people and all the King's vassals came ugly references to the cowardice and treason of the young men who were the hope of the kingdom. There was an incessant outcry on every side. Faced with the clamor its resolution had precipitated, the Union reconvened. Repudiation or modification of its stand was promptly expected and, in the interim, the din subsided. But the Union did not retreat; its declaration was upheld by an even larger majority when submitted to another vote. While its stand was being reaffirmed, students at the Manchester Union endorsed the pledge by 371 to 196 and there were similar avowals at Glasgow, Nottingham and Leicester Universities.

The effect of these reports was instantaneous at colleges throughout the United States. Undergraduate journals devoted columns to the resolution. Even more conservative editors admitted the importance of the episode; a few pleaded hysterically for American undergraduates to reject any similar proposals.

It was more than a dramatic, momentary inspiration. The implications of the resolution were manifold and lasting. There was, first, the concrete international aspect which it provided for the student movement against war—a sense of international union without which no such principles could have made any headway. The people of one country do not stop war; the peoples of all countries, aligned together against their common enemies, may. The Oxford vote was a vivid prelude to what might be hoped for on an ever wider scale.

Perhaps of even greater consequence was the formulation of the resolution "not to support King or country in any war." This was a declaration to which communists and conservatives alike could adhere; the former could maintain that class conflict was an historic necessity to social change; the

141

latter could deny it—and still could join hands in common resistance to imperialism. The Oxford pledge was an enduring and distinguished concept of the "united front" translated into meaningful terms. That this accord had been established at Oxford served to spur similar endeavors in this country.

Among the first to act was the Brown *Daily Herald* which launched a poll of students to determine their willingness to endorse the Oxford pledge and to verify their opinions on related issues. It was a gesture of supreme importance because it projected the controversy directly onto the American campus. As the deeds of the Chicago congress were being circulated, this survey helped to arouse and coordinate undergraduate sentiment.

Almost at once the poll was taken up by students throughout the nation; shortly after it had begun more than ninety colleges, situated in about thirty states, were involved. The attitude of administrators and their cohorts outside was an ominous forecast of their later behavior. Tabulation of the results, which indicated overwhelming opposition to any war waged by the government, intensified the dispute. In Providence, William Needham, an attorney, led the onslaught against the students, describing the survey as "immature, false, pernicious and dishonorable, positively vicious." Moreover, he added, "I know the horrors of war better than they do—those immature minds which do not know the smell of powder nor the sound of an enemy shot." His ranting went on for days, until someone stumbled upon an unfortunate disclosure; upon scrutinizing Mr. Needham's war record, it was discovered that his contact with the "horrors of war" was definitely limited, since he had never been closer to action than the Boston Navy Yard. After his downfall, Mrs. Paul Fitz Simons, from her post as president of the Newport Women's Republican Club, took up the cause. No doubt recalling her own service under fire, she had "no words to express my scorn and contempt for those who would

corrupt the youth of the nation to treason and cowardice."
The State Legislature voted to investigate the affair and
only retreated in the face of a storm of liberal protest.
In Pennsylvania an even more menacing resolution was introduced into the legislature, proposing that the holders of Sena-
torial Scholarships be penalized if they had announced their
refusal to bear arms for the government. The scholarships,
the resolution recommended, should be revoked and transferred to more deserving students.

Nor did administrators champion the right of their students to speak out on peace. The first attempts to halt the
campaign occurred at the University of Nebraska, causing
the student editor there to write: "It is unfortunate that a
university must be so subservient to mass opinion on account
of the necessity for support from state resources."

The poll had revealed an extraordinary amount of incipient anti-war feeling; but that was important only as a barometer of thought and interest. To reenforce these declarations,
a series of local anti-war conferences was summoned. By the
fall of 1933 such gatherings had been held in almost every
territory, at large, densely-populated universities and small,
secluded institutions. With few exceptions they adopted the
programmatic outlines of the Chicago congress, augmented
by acceptance of the Oxford pledge. Representatives of seven
colleges in the San Francisco Bay Region convened to draft
plans for future activity and sent greetings to the Oxford
Union. At Northwestern, Chicago, Columbia, Syracuse, New
York University and a score of other places there were similar
conferences. What was most impressive about them was the
composition of the participants. Even at such conservative
schools as M.I.T., students from every segment of the undergraduate body elected representatives to the congresses. In
almost every instance they came from groups as diverse as
Fraternity Row and the Young Communist League. There
were bitter, prolonged disputes, and yet each dispute was
noteworthy because of the surrounding discussion, because of

143

the absorption displayed by the "collegiate" members of the community in heretofore unknown issues. These conferences were the result of patient, arduous preparation; it required indomitable persistence to convince such entities as Greek-letter row that war was worth pondering. And yet the ventures achieved remarkable success. The spectacle of football players, house leaders and communists meeting together and charting joint activity was bewildering to many; it was an incredible departure from the ancient tradition. But it was even more notable for what it presaged, as *The Nation* pointed out in March, 1933:

> "Conservatives find it difficult to comprehend that American students are extending their interests beyond football, liquor and sex. Even today the average college man does not read a newspaper regularly but the great interest aroused by the peace campaign augurs well for the future. The American college student may be finally emerging from his mental lethargy."

It was to be anticipated that the patriots would undergo continual convulsions. They did. The most encouraging evidences of student thinking in American academic life were swiftly branded "Moscow"—and that, presumably was to suffice. One of the major concerns of the flag-wavers were praiseworthy references at these conferences to Soviet Russia's peace policy; so many lies and distortions about socialism had been customarily accepted by students that their overseers could not fathom this seeming reversal—and hence proceeded to distort it. Acknowledgment of the peace influence of the Soviets did not constitute, as the Hearst press sought to prove, widespread endorsement for communism; it merely implied realization that a country engaged in creating a new system of society was not likely to desire interruption by a devastating war; and that, moreover, the essential causes which were impelling crisis-ridden nations toward conflict did not exist

144

in the U.S.S.R. Whether one believed in communism or not was irrelevant, except to the Hearstlings and to an appalling number of college administrators.

Yet a casual inquiry into the press reports of the day might have banished the perplexity of those unnerved by the spread of peace agitation. Its success was not—could not have been—the work of some peculiarly sinister, alien force playing upon virtuous innocence. Those who initiated the movement were students precisely the same in origin and aspiration as their colleagues. If they were more alert to the danger, then they fulfilled the provocative rôle which education found too hot to handle. Their actions aroused sympathy and support because the common, every day facts of world politics and economics had become too perilous, too pressing in their imminence, to be evaded. That, in this task, students met the indifference or outright hostility of administrators was something to which they were becoming accustomed; the lessons of Kentucky and of Columbia were still fresh in their minds. "I am for peace too, but . . ." was becoming a familiar stereotype in the weekly lectures of soft-voiced college presidents.

We have seen the controversies engendered by "conscientious objection" to military drill in the 1920's. Parallel with the new advances of the peace movement, these disputes continued to break out on numerous fronts. A series of circumstances, however, had shifted the emphasis and forced a revaluation of the whole form of such resistance. The incidents served both to clarify the undergraduate approach to the problem and to center even more pronounced attention on related issues.

Late in 1932, Ennis Coale, a sophomore at the University of Maryland, voiced his unwillingness to participate in drill because it "is a preparation for war, which is contrary to my religious convictions." In his stand he was joined by Wayne Lee, an "A" student in the same class. Apparently seeking to curry favor with the right people by playing a loud patriotic rôle, the Administration rushed into print with long-winded statements about "foreign influences"—several days before the boys received the notices of their suspension. The editor of the student newspaper was prevailed upon to write a bitter denunciation of the two dissenters, declaring that "we hesitate to claim these men as Marylanders." When the cases went before the Maryland Supreme Court the University was staunchly upheld; and upon appeal to the U. S. Supreme Court it was held that no "federal question" was involved. At Ohio State the axe was wielded even more vigorously, resulting in the dismissal of seven undergraduates who defied the University's right to make drill-puppets out of them.

There were numerous other cases arising over the same issue; most noteworthy, however, was California's, because, for the first time, it evoked a decisive enunciation of principle from the United States Supreme Court. Albert Hamilton and Alonzo Reynolds, Jr., had been dismissed for conscientious objection to drill and the California courts, citing the Maryland precedent, had upheld the authorities. This time the highest court in the land consented to judge the merits of the dispute. Its decision was awaited throughout the country because on it hinged a score of questions of strategy and analysis confronting the undergraduate revolt against the military department.

The Supreme Court sustained the University and plainly reenforced the "right" of land-grant colleges to dismiss any student who rejected drill. Its decision came as a stunning blow to those who had placed their faith in the judicial method of combatting the R.O.T.C. For years this test had been looked for as a coup de grâce against the emissaries of the war office; now that it had come, it only strengthened the military, removing one more obstacle from its undisputed rule.

An inescapable conclusion grew out of the verdict for

146

those who had adhered to the strategy of legal procedure. Single-handed resistance to drill, accompanied only by reliance upon the courts, could serve no purpose. Hamilton, commenting on the case, wrote:

> "With this latest and unanimous decision of the highest court in the land to the position that religious freedom and conscience are subject to the domination of the state, the church may well begin to realize its position. . . . It means that the struggle for peace and freedom must be realized outside the arena of the courts."

The verdict established an even closer harmony in the anti-war movement. It confirmed the conviction of those who had mapped the Chicago program that extra-legal pressure methods would have to take the place of faith in the traditional instruments of "justice and rectitude." The disciplined pacifists at Ohio State had rejected any organized action on their behalf, preferring to transfer silently to other colleges. But the futility of such conduct was becoming manifest. Either one resolved to take organized, determined and unrelenting steps against the R.O.T.C. or else one might just as well forego isolated penalties and march with the corps.

At the University of Minnesota the first technique was most consciously translated. On the day of the annual R.O.T.C. review, "Jingo Day," a demonstration was called by the continuations committee of the anti-war conference. The Administration sought desperately to curb the move. It denounced the meeting as "discourteous" to the military department. It threatened reprisals against the participants. When the student newspaper expressed sympathy for the project, its news and editorial columns were censored for a week by a special committee of the Board of Publications. In reply *The Daily* published two satirical editorials advocating a square sprinkler-system to water campus ground and calling upon students to keep off the grass to protect it from "tender shoots." But on "Jingo Day" six thousand handbills were circulated throughout the university, announcing a protest meeting in the Union. Several days before, the military officialdom had proclaimed drill "a dead issue"; now 1500 students thronged the Union to refute the assertion. So large and enthusiastic was the gathering that a rumored invasion by local "patriots" did not materialise. And two weeks after the demonstration, the Board of Regents declared drill optional at the University of Minnesota. That was one of the first major accomplishments of the anti-war movement and an unprecedentedly bitter reversal for the commandant.

The lesson was keenly felt. On the one hand there had been, at California, Ohio State and elsewhere, vain, if courageous, "conscientious objection"; at Minnesota the concerted protests of hundreds had crippled an entrenched force—and not even the Supreme Court could alter the verdict. Incidents such as these confirmed the judgment of the Chicago congress. Neither administrators, the courts nor lone martyrdom would budge the R.O.T.C. Mass action was dispelling academic timidity by the weight of its own palpable power.

Throughout the nation undergraduate peace groups were affiliating to the American League Against War and Fascism as a link between their own efforts and those of a vast body of people in the heart of industry and other sectors.* Commensurate with these moves, panic was afoot in the higher learning. From coast to coast the great Red Scare was being prepared. All these discouragements did not avail. They only consolidated the efforts of those who were to be intimidated. Repression was failing—and its failure had only begun—because, with the relentless approach of war, the bombastic threats of college presidents seemed utterly puny.

---

* The American League is an organization of men and women of all strata—workers, farmers, professionals and students—and all political and religious beliefs who are willing to act together on these specific issues. It has branches in almost every territory.

iv. On Picket Lines

"SCABBING" is an ancient art and students were among its earliest practitioners. "One of the greatest obstacles to the progress of an organized labor movement," a writer noted several years ago, "has been the facility with which employers have obtained help from the universities." That condition was widely disclosed in the bitter labor upheavals of 1919; in almost every area where unrest assumed its coherent, decisive form, the colleges were summoned to perform their accustomed rôle. And they responded as they always had. Detachments of strike-breakers literally streamed from the campus. Bureaus of Appointments within the universities operated overtime to fulfill their "quotas." Students, with relatively few, although noteworthy, exceptions, accepted their mission as defenders of the "public welfare" and where they seemed reluctant to do so, remuneration adequate to their consciences was usually effective.

When labor dissatisfaction attained large-scale dimensions in the early years of the present crisis, the call for undergraduate volunteers became increasingly frequent. This appeal has not diminished; more recent developments have accentuated the need for national scholarship in the ranks of the scabs. I hasten to add that scabbing is not the conventional term; the universities are again salvaging the "common good."

To the dismay of industry and its Trustee-spokesmen and friends of enlightenment everywhere, however, the behavior of undergraduates has veered sharply from its earlier course. Recruiting of strike-breakers has proved a disconcertingly arduous task. Even more menacing has been the tendency of a significant number of undergraduates to abandon all the tenets of learning, decency and objectivity. They have joined hands with the striking men and women on America's picket line.

This has been one of the pronounced and extraordinary

149

phases of the insurgent movement, embracing far more than a narrow segment of the campus. In these steps are dramatized the whole formulation and perspective of the dissenting student. For the change in loyalties from employer to employee has been motivated not merely by a revised system of ethics and morality, however prominent these considerations may be, but by a drastic revision of the student's self-estimate. The process of revaluation was suggested, at the outset, in the migration to Kentucky; the issue was squarely faced at the Chicago congress; in day-to-day alignment with labor's struggles, its meaning is most plainly detailed. That "identity of interest" between the student and the working populace, posited in the infancy of the student upsurge, has been dramatically realized in the realm of industrial conflict.

There are numerous qualifications to the trend, depending upon specific localities and circumstances; an overestimation of the extent to which this sense of mutuality is accepted can be easily made. There are many whose participation in labor's endeavors is due primarily to an abstract passion for social justice; others are moved only by sympathy for the underdog when his rights are flagrantly invaded; still a third group is impelled by a desire to see life as the other half lives it. But a growing segment has perceived far more intimate factors at stake. Its members come from homes already depicted where "middle class pride" is often the only survival of vanishing middle class affluence; they find themselves threatened by the advance of impoverishment and insecurity; where they are realistic enough to acknowledge the import of these events, alignment with labor becomes a logical outgrowth of their own debacle, the only apparent solution to their plight. This has not, as the well-mannered apologists for the status quo like to assert, resulted in a deification of the working-class and all its constituents; that is essentially irrelevant. Fundamentally the realignment has been brought about by an insight into social forces, a conviction that the economically dispossessed constitute the only dynamic challenge to a decadent system in which not the better half, but a bare one per cent, are supreme. And the matter is not solely one of economic disorder but of parallel cultural sterility. The man who was once the campus intellectual is repelled by the barrenness and retrogression of the cultural superstructure. Ten years ago his prototype retreated from that condition into the fantasies of escapism; but escapism has proved neither satisfactory nor permanent. Now the intellectual and the aesthete, whether their incomes have substantially fallen or not, are appalled by the void, by the lack of purpose, by the confusion and disintegration of the order in which they live. They have come to look upon the quest for social change as an impetus and inspiration which is nowhere else to be found—and that quest is inevitably linked with the image of a working-class commonwealth.

There have been several conspicuous consequences of this shift in allegiances. The first has been an acute awareness of the bias of the university structure. Precisely those administrators who so impartially assented to undergraduate strike-breaking have resented—and impeded—student deeds on the other side of the fence. They have not hesitated to express this animosity. Even more revelatory, however, have been the actual episodes of industrial warfare. Conventional academic stereotypes speak of the "orderly processes of justice"; but justice, it is found, is often tempered with economic pressure. The traditional sanctities of democratic procedure are belied by the blunt conclusivenesss of a policeman's night-stick. These are aspects of an educative process beyond the curriculum; the young men and women who have been involved in them testify to the effectiveness of the schooling.

These gestures had their precedents. In 1925 Justine Wise led a delegation of five students on an investigation of the Passaic textile strike, returning with indignant descriptions of spy-systems, intimidations and hunger. There were other groups of that nature organized throughout the period. Contemporary expeditions are enormously distinct in tone, scope and frequency. No longer is it merely a group of high-principled, usually well-fed but sensitive iconoclasts bringing solace to the oppressed while the rest of the campus remains inert or unaware of what is taking place; those who stand on picket lines today are more likely to be responding to the first intimation of their new place in society, one which is neither as exalted nor assured as heretofore conceived.

Within the Kirschner Foundry at New Haven there had been incessant omens of restlessness throughout the closing months of 1933. A series of "economies" had driven the moulders to desperation; formerly accustomed to receive from thirty to forty dollars a week, their incomes had been repeatedly slashed until the average was reduced to about fourteen. Augmenting this was an intense speed-up arrangement and the refusal of the employers even to indicate how much the piece-rates of the workers were. After persistent attempts to negotiate for improvements, the men laid down their tools and strode from the plant. That was in November, 1933.

No swift victory ensued—nor even the prospect of concessions. But for eight weeks, despite unceasing attempts to stampede them back to their jobs, the pickets held firm. Having exhausted gentler coercion, the employers decided to resort to their most effective weapon, ordering thugs to swoop down on the plant and attack the unarmed picket lines. It was not an inspiring spectacle—and the men realized that they could not long persevere against that technique. Warned that it would be repeated until they surrendered, the workers issued an appeal for outside aid. A mass picket line was to be prepared for the following day.

The Kirschner Foundry is in New Haven and so is Yale University—and the sons of Eli had served in labor strife many times before. Their most celebrated accomplishment was scabbing in a teamster strike of several years before, a rôle from which they desisted only after widespread protest to the institution. On this occasion they—or rather a group of them—responded to the plea of the striking moulders. On Thursday morning there were four Yale men on the picket line at six o'clock preliminary to further detachments later in the day. They were greeted effusively by the employees and their ranks were enlarged by the arrival of citizens from throughout the city.

The employers failed to enjoy the scene. They had one opportunity to end the strike, and to do it quickly before this support grew even more formidable. With a mass meeting scheduled for the afternoon, there seemed every reason to believe that the situation was critical and demanded prompt attention. That attention was furnished with eminent thoroughness by the police force of New Haven.

There was an impressive crowd gathered as the rally outside the plant got under way. There was also a business-like contingent of police beginning to descend upon the scene. Supervising their activities was an official of the foundry, designated to point out those whose incarceration would best serve the community welfare.

Shortly after the meeting began, a girl speaker was abruptly seized and arrested at the instigation of the foundry official. While she was being dragged away, Lawrence Hill, a Yale student, was suggested as a subject for forcible investigation. A policeman headed for him at once; seeing four other officers advancing up the street, he apparently decided to enact a lesson in police method. Without warning,* he proceeded to club Hill on the head until the boy fell helplessly to the ground. As he lay there the other officers gathered around, adding their own vociferous trimmings to the assault.

Hill, stunned, arose slowly and started to leave. Before he could do so, he was loudly commanded to stand still; he was to be held in police custody for "resisting arrest," "general breach of the peace," and "obstructing the sidewalk."

* These facts were substantiated by later court testimony.

A few moments later a worker in another foundry, prominent in union activity, walked over to the plant to ascertain what was happening. He was immediately arrested at the direction of Mr. Hancock, alertly supervising for the Kirschner employers.

Word of these events was quickly relayed to the Yale campus. On Saturday a delegation of students from all parts of the university trooped to the offices of Chief of Police Smith and Mayor Murphy to demand punishment for the officers. The Mayor declined to see them. Two days later an even larger delegation was organized and the Mayor finally granted it a "hearing." But his behavior was remarkable. He was not interested in the details of the complaint; he became impatient when it was mentioned. This servant of the people spent thirty minutes recounting the evils of communism, local and international.

Meanwhile William Gordon, another student, had returned to the scene of the outbreak to obtain the badge number of Patrolman Enright, Hill's assailant. He was doing so at the request of the police officials who had been appraised of the complaint. As he approached the street, Enright confronted him. First the patrolman sought to ease him away, suggesting that "if you stay the hell out of this neighborhood and keep the students away, I'll let you go." When Gordon informed him of why he had come, Enright's demeanor changed. The student was immediately arrested.

Gordon's trial, set for the following morning, had aroused more undergraduate concern than anything since the previous Yale-Harvard game. Scores of students filled the courtroom, and, if two out of three had come primarily out of curiosity, their detachment was quickly dispelled by what they saw. Gordon was innocent; that was so plain that any possibility of conviction was hardly discussed. And yet the presiding judge, with virtually no semblance of a legitimate trial, passed a sentence of twenty-five dollars or twenty-five days and costs. There could be no doubt that the verdict had

154

nothing to do with the merits of the case; it was based upon Gordon's earlier picketing at the foundry. He was denied all but the barest fragments of a defense: he was refused permission to examine his own witnesses; Hill was not allowed to testify that, previous to the arrest, the patrolman had threatened "to clip you guys on the head" when they passed him on the street; nor was he even allowed to make clear that the chief of police had requested Enright's number. So outrageous was the conviction that, upon appeal, the case was dropped. But the memory of that courtroom scene was not easily shed by those who witnessed it.

At nine o'clock on Friday of that week the cases of Hill and the two workers were to come up. Although it was the coldest day of the year, more than one hundred students braved a blinding sleetstorm to reach the courtroom. Not until an hour later were the trials even mentioned; an attendant announced that they had been postponed until 11:45. Hoping that the audience would diminish by then, the magistrate was to be painfully disappointed. There were fifty more present at the appointed hour. This time he did not even appear; the spectators were informed that the trial had been delayed until 2 o'clock—and that only witnesses would be admitted.

A hundred carefully-nurtured text-book illusions vanished as the students realized what was taking place. Outside the courtroom a spontaneous demonstration was staged; delegations were immediately despatched to the judge and the mayor to demand revocation of the ban on spectators. By 2 o'clock the crowd had doubled. Unnerved by the turnout, the judge sought to adopt a new protection. He announced that he had changed his mind; outsiders would be permitted at the trial; but since the large courtroom was "in use," the case would have to be shifted to a smaller one which only seated twenty-five people.

The court found Hill guilty on all three counts, offering him the alternative of a sixty-dollar fine or sixty days in jail.

155

The two workers received sentences ranging from ten to twenty-five days or fines of an equivalent amount. It is interesting to note that the witnesses for the prosecution were four policemen, two strike-breakers and four officials of the foundry. As the Civil Liberties Union pointed out, the only witnesses who might have been regarded as utterly unrelated to either side unequivocally came to the defense of the accused. Their testimony did not avail.

Even while the judgment was being pronounced Dean Mendel of Yale declared in a statement to the press:

"Yale college authorities are entirely out of sympathy with the interference of students in New Haven affairs about which they are uninformed. The college will not encourage the students in any extra-legal attempts to determine the right or wrong of any problem."

The Dean's reference to "extra-legal" activity was noteworthy. As *The Nation* pointed out for his benefit, picketing was still presumably a lawful prerogative in the United States.

Gordon's case had been dismissed upon appeal; the others were to be held as "examples." Appearing before Judge Pickett in the Court of Common Pleas in January, Hill, with an irrefutable mass of evidence at his command, was cleared of the only serious charge against him—"resisting an officer." But his fine was reduced only ten dollars. The trial constituted the second chapter in the extra-curricular enlightenment of Yale students. They heard the judge persistently evade the merits of the case to deliver long-winded harangues on "Moscow influence"; they listened angrily to his denunciations of Hill as an "outsider" who had no place in a labor dispute. One of the students present—who had never before interested himself in such affairs—later wrote: "All through Pickett's performance, I had the feeling that if Hill had been a strike-breaker, the community would have hailed him as a public hero, Pickett would have saluted him as an example for youth and nobody would have called him an 'outsider' who did not belong in a labor controversy."

That impression was widespread. One year later a large contingent of Yale students was to be aiding the strikers at the Colt Munitions Plant and Lawrence Clendenin was to receive a fifteen day jail-sentence for his efforts, accompanied by this judicial spanking: "This man is evidently a person on whom a great deal of education has been wasted. To me his actions are most reprehensible."

But the wire of Corliss Lamont, leader of Harvard's rebel undergraduate bloc in 1924, probably mirrored university sentiment more accurately:

> "Congratulations on being found guilty of helping American workers to secure a decent existence and on coming out of your college study to share concretely their struggles with them. There are many Harvard men always ready to abet Yale men in the performance of such high crimes and misdemeanors."

And in 1935, when Yale launched an "economy" program at the expense of campus employees, there was a considerable outcry among undergraduate groups. The university proposed to slash the wages of janitors, maintenance workers, campus police and gate porters rather than reduce the incomes of high-bracket faculty men or administrators. The resistance which its plan encountered among students was indicative of the undermining of what William Randolph Hearst has called "a good university for Americans to send their sons to be educated."

Yale is one of the "Big Three." Its students are comparatively well-to-do, recruited from the nation's better families; and, again comparatively, not profoundly affected, in their personal habits, by the inroads of depression. The ferment occasioned by these episodes has not attained any vast overt proportions. Their influence has been primarily exerted on the thinking and prejudices of those involved. Such disclosures prevent reaction from gaining a firm foothold; they solidify undergraduate sentiment against the more palpable evils of present-day society; they breed curious citizens. That is all that has happened thus far; but, if the revolt does achieve more decisive advances at Yale, if the descent of crisis shakes the complacence of the "Yale man" more visibly, the judicial agencies of New Haven will have amply contributed to that eventuality. The stigma of Mr. Hearst's acclaim may yet be vanquished.

Shortly after the arrests at New Haven, three students at the Massachusetts Institute of Technology set out on a tour of inspection through the Cambridge Rubber Co. Their visit was inspired by the report that several girl employees there had contracted industrial tuberculosis and were suing the company for compensation. The plant was a notorious one; there was a report that a sanitorium had written the officials a warning against the conditions which prevailed.

The students' inquiry justified the most critical rumors. It was found that the factory had been set up in a building never designed for its purpose; ventilation was grievously inadequate as were facilities for dust control; virtually the only relief was furnished by fans scattered on the walls. Dust from pigments and rubber preservatives was abundant; particularly acute were the ammonia fumes emerging from vulcanizers which were built in the same room where shoes are assembled. Every two hours the vulcanizers were opened, ammonia immediately filling the plant.

There were other equally hazardous and repelling discoveries made during the investigatory mission, to the distress of the company officials. That was not the end of their discomfort. Angered by their findings, the students decided to designate one of their number to testify in behalf of the girls whose service had resulted so tragically—and whom the company was not anxious to remunerate. The student sub-

158

mitted the results of the probe which he and his two companions had conducted, to be placed in evidence by the employees' lawyers.

The Cambridge Rubber Company was highly nettled at this "intrusion." Hardly had the testimony been brought to light than the company communicated with officials of the Institute, denouncing the behavior of its students.

M.I.T. did not defend its sons. There was no administrative applause for the young men who had challenged the right of the Cambridge Rubber Company to impose the most merciless working conditions upon its employees. When the three students who had caused such displeasure in the executive offices of the Cambridge company later applied for assistance from the M.I.T. loan fund, they were firmly rejected.

The Loan Fund Board does not customarily explain the basis for its refusal of undergraduate applications for aid. But Dean Lobdell did not adhere to that practice in the case of these students. Interviewed by one of them, he declared that they had been denied loans because their activities made them "poor risks"; by intervening in such unmentionables as the fate of the Cambridge employees, they severely diminished their own possibilities of future employment—and hence their ability to return the loan. That was M.I.T.'s fulfillment of the ideals of "industrial justice" when those devoted to it became lamentably specific in their endeavors.*

A hundred years of a liberal tradition were celebrated at little Oberlin College in Ohio in 1933. If any American institution could justifiably hold such a ceremony, Oberlin was probably most fitted to do so. It was the first college to open its doors to women and Negroes; in the famous Wellington rescue its students protected a fugitive slave from the pursuit of a sheriff; throughout the Civil War the college was a cen-

* More detailed discussion of M.I.T. will appear in the chapter on "Students in Uniform."

ter of Abolitionist sentiment, serving as a station on the "underground railway" to help slaves escape over the border into Canada.

These are unique attributes. I doubt that any college in the country has an heritage equivalent to that of Oberlin. Precisely because of that, the fate of the magazine *Progress* is noteworthy far beyond the existence of that little journal. It is significant, both as another barometer of the altered preoccupations of the American student and as at least a partial answer to the question: how liberal can "liberalism" be?

Toward the end of 1933, *Progress,* the organ of the "Radical Club" at Oberlin, published an article entitled "The Aluminum Company of America and the N.R.A." The substance of the material was based upon a series of exposures originally printed in *The Nation,* bearing upon the labor policy of the Aluminum Company. Outstanding among the revelations was the fact that, under the "code" established by the company, girls were being paid sixty-three cents a day in the factories where aluminum bronze was made; other employees fared only slightly better in the weekly pay-envelopes. Few more shocking examples of exploitation could have been found anywhere.

Now it is probably true that *Progress* would have been aided and encouraged in a general plea for "economic justice." But this was getting close to home. Oberlin College owned $4,002,500 of stock in the Aluminum Company of America.

Citing these conditions in the Aluminum plant and Oberlin's relationship to it, *Progress* wrote:

"From the slavery of the many workers comes the peace and comfort of the few students and faculty members. Out of the chaos of barbarism, represented in the code, out of the suffering and starvation of the workers, comes peaceful Oberlin. . . .

"Of course, Oberlin college itself can do nothing about

this. However, the students of Oberlin college can and should do something. As long as they live, they should remember that any advancement they have made has been helped by girls working for sixty-three cents a day and men supporting families on $455 a year—less than it costs one student to stay at Oberlin for nine months."

And the editorial concluded:

"Perhaps the best use the professed Christians of Oberlin could make of their religious chapels would be to pray that their God would not hold their aggrandizement at the expense of the workers against them. Even the red roof of Finney chapel might be held symbolic of the workers who help make this institution of learning possible."

President Wilkins could not conceal his distaste for such bald language. Hardly had he recovered when another jolt awaited him. He received an open letter from the Radical Club, a copy of which was published on the front page of *Progress*. It read:

"In the second issue of *Progress* there appeared an article dealing with one of the numerous ways in which Oberlin receives its funds. It was intended that the article on the Aluminum Company should be followed by an article on conditions around the Campus, especially in regard to economic issues.

"However, we were balked in our investigation. No matter what employees we asked, we could find absolutely nothing in regard to the working conditions at Oberlin College. . . . Therefore we are asking your aid. . . . Why is it that workers in Oberlin refuse to make known their salaries or hours of work? Are they afraid and, if so, what do they fear?

161

"We would like, Mr. Wilkins, to ask you to dispel these rumors and impressions which have reached us— we hope erroneously—by permitting us to print the official salary scale of Oberlin chefs, maids, janitors and other manual laborers."

About three months after its denunciation of the "sweat tactics" of the Aluminum Company and its inquiry into the wages of campus employees, *Progress* was banned. President Wilkins said that he did not enjoy either its tone or manner.

In response to inquiry, a professor at Oberlin gave what seems to be a convincing statement of the case, the cause of the reprisal and its implications. As he saw it:

"The boys are radicals. They have broken through the smug veneer of Oberlin complacency and have touched it to the raw. They have irritated the president. They have really had the best of him in controversy in the college press. They have driven him from the position of a liberal (and I believe that he prides himself on his liberalism) to the conservative stand which really represents his position. Faculty committees have prevented him from taking more drastic action."

They had touched the "untouchables," those unpleasant aspects of American academic life which liberalism would rather forget than reconcile. One might dwell in the realm of social issues at Oberlin; the Administration was one of the few to encourage the student peace movement; it has a record and a tradition of long standing behind its devotion to liberal principle. But even where this maximum of freedom prevails, there are certain fields barred to exploration. The Aluminum company is an invisible power in Oberlin. Campus employees are employees of a business—and the same principles govern them as their brothers elsewhere. When undergraduates joined hands with these people, they courted

162

the enmity of a network far more sweeping than they realized. President Wilkins, whether he enjoyed his rôle or not, was forced to behave as a "captain of erudition."

Meanwhile, Amherst and Smith students were participating for the first time in a labor struggle. In the college town of Northampton the employees of College Weavers Inc. had gone on strike to protest a forty per cent wage cut. To organize strike relief, a mass meeting was held at Smith attended by more than 500 students and faculty members. Funds were raised and a systematic program of aid outlined.

At Baltimore undergraduates of Goucher college came to the side of the Amalgamated Clothing workers, risking police attempts to rout the picket lines and holding their ranks in the face of continual intimidation.

Several months afterward, girls from Vassar college rallied to the support of striking workers at Beacon, N. Y. Their participation attracted widespread attention in the press, giving rise to reports that President McCracken was preparing to curb their activities. A delegation was named to ascertain his stand; it returned with a statement that "any prolonged absence from college will be considered a violation of the spirit in which fellowships and scholarships are granted." That was a blunt warning and it was followed almost immediately by the calling of a college assembly. The president began by saying: "Of course you have the right to picket . . . but," and then resorted to the traditional arguments of his colleagues. The girls were allegedly endangering the life of the college; their first duty was to their school-work; they could be "of greater service to the labor movement later." To which the girls replied that their picketing occupied less academic time than did the bridge-parties and other social functions of "the average Vassar girl." They also pointed out that, of the twenty who picketed, four were members of Phi Beta Kappa, one-third of the group was on the Dean's honor list and almost all had scholarship rating. It

163

should be stated in fairness that no disciplinary action has been taken; I have cited President McCracken's remarks as indicative of a vanishing enthusiasm for "student participation in politics"—the wrong kind of politics.

Students at the University of Michigan—including a group of fraternity men—took part in the annual May Day parade at Detroit in 1934. Along with the workers of Detroit, they were attacked by city police and beaten up, only to find their university administration entirely indifferent to the assault and irate because the students had become involved in so "controversial" an incident.

In Brooklyn, New York, students from neighboring colleges were instrumental in the victorious strike of local cafeteria workers. They led a boycott movement and joined actively on picket lines.

And now, as I write (in the fall of 1935) a despatch from Terre Haute, in the midst of a general strike, reveals that several college professors and students at Indiana State Teachers College have been seized and thrown into jail for aiding the strikers. "God only knows what will happen next," murmurs one professor. Simultaneously two students at the University of Chicago have been arrested for participation in a demonstration of unemployed men and women who were requesting the right to two meals a day.

These are characteristic episodes whose counterparts have been enacted in every area. It should not be assumed that the rôle of strike-breaking has been utterly abandoned. A deep and bitter cleavage has penetrated our student bodies for precisely that reason. While increasing numbers have decided that the "public good" may occasionally rest on the side of labor, there is still a formidable array of servants for the distraught employer. In the course of the longshoremen's strike on the West Coast in 1934, this conflict was, as we shall see, long and fierce. A student investigator at the University of Washington issued the following report:

"The first place employers went to obtain strike-breakers was the University of Washington. All fraternity houses were contacted. . . . Employers guaranteed them board and room and wages higher than those offered longshoremen. Students were provided free taxi service to work. . . . Out on the waterfront, student strike-breakers were housed in boats tied to the docks. Excellent food, brand new sheets and first-class Negro valet service convinced many that the life of the longshoreman was not so bad as they had believed."

The academic community has provided its moral salve for the task of strike-breaking. Thus, from Hamline University, Minnesota, a student writes to me of widespread undergraduate hostility against the recent truck-drivers' strike. Why? Because they had been taught to regard "labor disturbances" as offenses against law and order, unwarranted interference with the public, invariably the nefarious work of agitators. They have been warned against sympathy for the inciters of disorder. But their education has not so lucidly informed them of such gruesome details as hired gunmen used to intimidate strikers, of unwarranted police attacks against pickets, of the summoning of militia to defend the public by hurling tear-gas into throngs of innocent people. A recent survey indicated that less than fifty per cent of the nation's teachers favor even the closed shop. It is not astonishing that a large number of students are still eager to obey the dictates of industry.

The controversy is rooted in the recurrent bogey of impartiality. While professors are busily writing apologia for corporations and their students are learning that the life of a longshoreman is not so bad after all, those whose efforts are aligned on the other side become "biased," disturbers of "academic routine" and "immature martyrs out to get their names in the papers." They are, further, guilty of injuring the "good name of the college." What this good name means,

I hope we are beginning to understand. It is curious that selling oneself to the utilities or replacing a striking longshoreman is never an affront to the reputation of the college. It is more likely to merit a varsity letter or an honorary degree.

But steadily and valiantly, from 1932 on, an ever-larger number have penetrated the sham. In doing so they have learned more about the processes of the social order than in any classroom function. One need not argue that such activity alone should constitute education; it does serve as a useful testing-ground for the conventional curriculum. That was the experience of Hill at Yale, of the M.I.T. insurgents, of the editors of *Progress* and of similar groups in scores of institutions. And these ventures into the outside world did more to accelerate the growth of student awareness than a vast proportion of systematic training.

v. April 13, 1934—April 12, 1935

WHERE was this insurgence to lead? We had become accustomed, by the end of 1933, to popular clamor against the revolt, certifying more plainly than anything else its penetration into new areas. For two years now the campus had witnessed a series of outbreaks, reverberations of which were often louder than the original sound. But most of these were momentary; hardly had they subsided than the peace of apathy and ignorance was restored. At first glance it did not seem that any great headway had been made; certainly, in terms of numbers or sustained activity, that was true. Although there had been a host of changes engendered in undergraduate attitudes—in their interests, their enthusiasms, their perspective—the trends were slow to assume organizational form.

A multitude of reasons could be cited for the lag. To an extent it was the fault of the rebels themselves; confident of their own position, supremely certain of their own analysis, they often lacked understanding of the web of student delusions, inertia and prejudice first to be undermined; they became impatient at lethargy and, instead of nursing it, denounced it; they could not fathom why others were not as swift as they to see. If this circumstance was partially responsible, it was far from the crux of the matter. The truth is that the American student was not, by education, by environment or by background, non-conformist. His training had developed just the reverse instinct. Whatever transient disturbances shook the world, he believed that they could not forever endure, and that he would once again be restored to a place of eminence in society. Although there was manifold data to indicate how precarious was his status, he preferred to regard it as a temporary phenomenon. A great illusion had been carefully nourished; why should it not survive? He had been taught to expect rewards from the world; he had seen his brothers before him carried along on the tide of boom-time dividends. To envisage for himself a similar life of comfort, of security, of advantage was a day-dream not easily shattered. Nor, as we have seen, did his education seek to rid him of the delusion. If the success formula might seem temporarily overturned, soon "inexorable forces"—the panacea of orthodox economics—would resurrect it. The vision was encouraged on every side—the same false hope and aspiration which animated the whole middle class. The student could not avoid its enticing conclusions. Like his father, he sought to embrace a mirage rather than face the readjustments entailed by the situation. Through two distressing years, his left-wing contemporaries had urged him to acknowledge that the vision was dead beyond recapture. Although he betrayed increasing concern over the issues of the day, although he might respond to a specific problem with fervor, his zeal was usually transient.

Why, in the face of all these difficulties and discouragements, did the insurgents not surrender? There was ever-increasing academic pressure, abetted from the outside, to stem the movement at its source, which augmented the obsta-

167

cles of original preference. The student who was almost ready to involve himself in the revolt, after a long grapple with instinct and prejudice, was often restrained by the overt hand of his administrator. What kept the upsurge alive and gradually transformed it into a large-scale element? The answer is not to be found simply in the innate stubbornness of its constituents, although of brave persistence there was plenty. It can more readily be traced to the everyday facts of the world.

For by the dawn of 1934, had come the vindication of those predictions once derided as radical inventions or false-alarms. That is the primary clue to what was about to take place. Three years before, a small group in Eastern colleges had joined together in the conviction that this crisis was emphatically distinct from those which had gone before. Pointing to the progressive severity of each depression, they held that the existing one would be the most intense yet experienced. They were derided for their "pessimism"; economics professors heatedly disputed their view, upholding the formulæ of automatic "readjustment" and minimizing any singular aspects to the latest disorder. But by 1934 the "systematic laws" of capitalist economy had still failed to assert themselves. At Chicago in 1932 the insurgents had foreseen the reckless advance of the forces leading to war; the two succeeding years had amply confirmed their judgment—to the consternation of those who had vowed it could never happen again. When, with Hitler's seizure of power, the dissenters had prophesied the onrush of reaction throughout the crisis-ridden world, their forebodings were ridiculed; but within twelve months repressive authority was being invoked on our own shores to stifle hunger-inspired discontent.

This substantiation of their judgment was of wide import. It vastly altered the relations of the student rebels with the other inhabitants of the academic community. They could no longer be confounded by orthodox professorial assurances; continued singing of revival was far more incongruous than warning of doom. The average undergraduate, it must be emphasized, did not enjoy the revelation; he clung valiantly to every hint that things would again right themselves. That faith endured for a disproportionate amount of time. Perhaps no circumstance was more influential in its undoing than the debacle of the New Deal. For Roosevelt's accession to office was, for several months, a cause of jubilation on the campus as elsewhere; he was to furnish the easy, unruffled way out of despair without any basic realignment of the social order. The undergraduate was to regain his "privilege" status in a nation tempered by "social justice" and "planned economy." While his place was solidified without "loss of caste," the "New Era" was to be ushered in without strife or confusion. But the great transformation never occurred. Rooseveltism was little more than the insurgents had declared it to be—a determined but futile attempt to "patch up" an outworn structure without touching its foundations. When the Brain Trust went to Washington, a bright, eager coterie of young college graduates went with it; there were syndicated articles about the "young man in politics" and the emergence of idealism in government. The trek homeward was a sorrowful one; in unhappy procession, the talented Bachelors of Arts departed from Washington after a brief flirtation. Only a handful remained to "reason with big business."

Those were discomforting disclosures in the academic world. Out of them arose the prestige of the student insurgent. What he said commanded attention and, as often as not, respect. What he did was likely to be looked upon with more than cynicism or suspicion. What he thought ceased to be so alien an importation. It was not, of course, so simple a process. The rebels did not stand still and allow their predictions to be fulfilled. There were a hundred dramatic and animated phases of the revolt, some of which have been cited; there was the other side, less colorful to detail and less spectacular in conduct, but of equally great influence. I refer to the scores of discussion groups, conferences, symposia carried on by the National Student League and the League for Industrial Democracy throughout the country. The trend was manifesting itself in unobtrusive items; professors found their classrooms alive with at least a modicum of curiosity; often, to their uneasiness, they found that the stereotypes by which human disaster was customarily explained were no longer adequate. These were the background of such events as the strike of several thousand New York University students against the censorship of their press. And the background was of transcending importance, providing the prerequisites for broader activity.

In December of 1933 Henry A. Wallace, Secretary of Agriculture, was deploring the absence here of any "youth movement" comparable to those of other nations. His utterance was made at a conference of the "Student in Politics" in Washington, D. C.—a conclave at which the traditional entreaties to the student were made. He was being urged to join with all good Democrats and Republicans for the salvation of the Republic. But if Secretary Wallace had remained for the duration of the congress, he would have seen the startling beginnings of a youth movement—in terms vastly different from his own formulation. For that week the National Student League and the League for Industrial Democracy were holding their own conventions in Washington and many of their representatives sat in on the "Politics" assemblage. When they proposed certain resolutions for discussion, the controversial result was indicative of the leftward drift of the heretofore unorganized, detached throng of students whose emissaries had come to the conference. The possibility of a far broader, more concerted upsurge was visible.

For now, in the close of 1933, the point had arrived when a large number of American undergraduates were prepared to articulate their own dissatisfaction. The ferment which had begun nearly three years before was about to shift from passive to active form, from sympathetic interest to direct cooperation. The transformation would not occur overnight. But its inauguration was at least entirely conceivable. Its fulfillment was to depend on the clarity, vigor and adaptability of the left wing.

The most impressive, if perhaps incomplete, barometer for appraising the onrush of events in the fifteen months after the Washington congress, resides in two sets of figures. They do not signify the full and enduring importance of the period; they emphasize primarily how swift and far-reaching was the general upheaval in the ranks of American undergraduates.

In response to a call for a nationwide strike against the war preparations of the United States government, 25,000 students left their classrooms on April 13, 1934. That demonstration was unprecedented; nothing in the history of American undergraduate life was equivalent to it. Twelve months later, on April 12, 1935, there were 175,000 participants in similar demonstrations throughout the country. So startling and unique was the development that now, when it is still fresh in our minds, its dimensions are hardly appreciated. One leader of the national strike committee admitted that "we did not know our own strength." That impression was inescapable. Perhaps the outstanding aspect of the event was the fact that it had occurred. It was so sharp a departure from the "academic tradition," so tumultuous a contrast to the dead silence of inertia, that even the most detached could not fail to be shaken by it.

The scope of the walkout was literally nationwide.* There were at least 10,000 on strike in each of five major cities: Philadelphia, Boston, Chicago, Washington, D. C. and Los Angeles. New York City alone saw 30,000 students surge

* In discussing the nature and meaning of the strike, I shall use as my general reference the walkout of 1935. The strike in 1934 was of vast importance in paving the way for the following year's response; it was, however, only a pale image of the succeeding effort. In 1935 more students struck in New York alone than throughout the nation on the previous occasion.

171

from the classrooms in dramatic unison. But the movement was not restricted to these centers. In small, out-of-the-way hamlets where an official emissary of the strike committee had never penetrated, there were spontaneous strikes. At little Phillips College in Oklahoma, 200 students—half the college—staged their own rally. In Oregon the entire student body of Reed College took part. More than 1000 students from three small institutions in Jackson, Tennessee— Union University, Lambuth and Lane colleges—streamed from their classrooms at 11 A.M. and marched through the streets. These were characteristic of the response in the minor, almost unknown colleges. While at large institutions like Chicago, Columbia and Minnesota there were thousands joining the strike, they were, it must be emphasized, not alone; overshadowing their importance was the sudden, unrivalled awareness which seized the schools in the backwoods, heretofore so assiduously sheltered from any such activity.

Those who responded to the summons were as divergent as the whole student population of the country. In 1934 the National Student League and the League for Industrial Democracy had sponsored and carried on the strike almost single-handed; one year later they were being immeasurably helped by such national groups as the National Council of Methodist Youth, the Middle Atlantic Division of the interseminary movement, two divisions of the National Student Federation, the American Youth Congress and others.* The mixed opinion represented on this committee was even more vividly evident among the students participating. We have seen how, in earlier conferences and meetings, broad strata of undergraduates were betraying increased interest in affairs

---

* These groups have, since that event, organized a permanent "Vigilance Committee" to insure the continuance of joint activity and to combat the concerted effort to outlaw the student anti-war movement as well as all insurgent movements. The presence of the American Youth Congress in that committee is notable; the Congress is the broadest, most heterogeneous youth group in this country today and serves as an excellent link between students and young people generally.

beyond their own locality. But those were merely preludes; they indicated a shift in pre-occupations, a willingness to deal with controversial questions, a growing curiosity—and often nothing more. To engage in them was to display one's consciousness; it constituted no commitment beyond that. The strike, I think it will be evident, was a profoundly different matter. And yet, in the dominant proportion of schools, it was endorsed by campus groups of every allegiance. The chairman of the meeting at Columbia, for example, was a leading fraternity man. Nor was he an exceptional figure; there were others everywhere with precisely the same affiliations who gave freely of their energies and their enthusiasm. Five years before, they would have ridiculed such a project; now they found themselves actively supporting it. No wonder that a lone standard-bearer of preparedness at Mercer was almost in tears, weeping that "everybody has gone communistic." He could not fathom what was taking place—and so he accepted the most convenient label for it.

The conduct of the strike varied from place to place. In some schools, "peace meetings" were held later in the day under administrative guidance; in others classes were cancelled and convocations called; at a little Kansas college a prayer-meeting sufficed. But the implications of the strike, whether it was such in actuality or not, were felt almost everywhere: the solemnity, militance and determination associated with the term prevailed. It would be gross distortion to contend that every student, or even a large percentage, of those who participated were radicals. They were not; many of them were entirely unsympathetic to or ignorant of left-wing doctrine. To believe that the 175,000 who joined hands from coast-to-coast were declaring their hostility to the existing order is a grave delusion. Many of them still believed in it and others did not think much about it. Almost uniformly, however, they were manifesting their opposition to one palpable procedure of that order—imperialistic war. The radicals contended that imperialism was an essential, historical outgrowth of capitalism, not a specific "policy" to be accepted or rejected. The conservatives did not adhere to this view—or to the conclusions arising out of it. But whatever the disagreement on this point, there was accord on the problem in hand: resistance to imperialism as represented by the war budget of the Roosevelt goverment and the brewing conflict in Europe. In impressive unanimity students throughout the nation enunciated the Oxford pledge: "We pledge not to support the government of the United States in any war it may conduct." It was uttered in California and in New York and throughout the intervening territory. No one who heard it spoken could ignore the seriousness of the occasion and the deep-seated solidity which had been welded.

The strikers were drawn from every segment of the student community; that should be plainly understood. On the other hand, their action, in terms of traditional academic habit, was "radical." It was radical as a departure from the sanctified formulæ by which war was allegedly to be averted; it did not fly the dove of peace nor did it place faith in the divine benevolence of statesmen. The "strike" is a solemn weapon; directed against government policy it assumes even broader connotations. Those who endorsed the move, representing every political faith, did not do so because they were "out for trouble" or because they desired to "precipitate violence." They did so in acknowledgment of the immediacy of the issue and the incessant, overt pressure which the war danger demanded. No sinister hand forced the tactic upon innocent undergraduates; the American government, by adopting a program of arms expenditures unparalleled in peace-time, was responsible for the vehement form which this protest took. One conservative student, addressing a strike rally, stated this case admirably:

"I don't know whether it's radical to strike or not. I don't care. I do know that the government will listen to a strike a good deal sooner than it will heed a peace-picnic. And I'm not afraid of being called a communist or of working with communists. I'm a hell of a lot more afraid of the bankers and business men who make wars."

Even more noteworthy was the anti-fascist sentiment accompanying the protest. It was important because it signified an awareness of the roots of war and its present-day carriers. There was widespread recognition that the peril of conflict was inseparably linked with the existence of fascism abroad; and that, moreover, American involvement in such a war would be accentuated by the development of fascist tendencies in our own government. For fascism was nationalism epitomized; its leading exponents have not hesitated to say so, and if they had, the impending Italian invasion of Ethiopia would have adequately disproved their assertions. Mussolini believes that "imperialism is the eternal and immutable law of life" and cries "three cheers also for war in general." Hitler has echoed him, proclaiming that "an alliance whose aim does not include the intention of war is worthless nonsense" and that on his assumption of power "Germany struck out the word pacifism from its vocabulary." * These things were felt by the striking students; it was folly to oppose imperialist warfare without taking cognizance of its most ardent practitioners. And that was an understanding common to conservatives and radicals alike. Its most immediate meaning was the realization that the emergence of an American fascist régime would, in its first official legislation, illegalize any concerted protest against war. The omens of such measures were most acutely experienced by students at the hands of their administrators on April 12th; the details of this tendency will be recounted later, but its bearing cannot be omitted here. One of the prime convictions of the strike was this growing sense that fascism and war were inseparables, that they .aggravated those international economic rivalries and local disorders which were the preliminaries to armed strife.

* These quotations are from John Strachey's *Menace of Fascism*.

175

Virtually every strike assemblage expressed this belief: fascism is the most extravagant, pronounced and pernicious phase of imperialism.

These were general assumptions underlying the event. Their specific relation to the campus was most concretely voiced by opposition to the Reserve Officers Training Corps. The hostility was based upon more than preparedness questions; there was, further, the intolerant, repressive credo of the R.O.T.C., and, of even more intimate concern, the vast funds which the corps required for its upkeep. At countless universities, there was organized on April 12th a determined campaign to end the rule of the military department—where such a campaign was not already in existence. It was an unhappy day for the generals.

The strikes were the expression of an idea, or of a set of ideas; yet their spectacular, colorful and dynamic qualities will not soon be forgotten. In 1934 undergraduates at Springfield planted white crosses on the campus on the eve of the walkout to commemorate the betrayal of 1917. At Vassar a throng of girls marched behind impressive placards declaring, not some illusion-tinged ode to peace, but "We Fight Imperialist War." Several weeks before the demonstration, students at the University of Washington hired a truck, draped it with appropriate jingoist placards and joined the Army Day parade sponsored by the American Legion. As the procession reached the center of Seattle, the students suddenly reversed their placards; on the other side were appeals to "Fight Against War." Legionnaires attacked the students, hurling them from the trucks; police arrived to arrest the victims of the attack. But the episode had served its purpose.

One year later 450 students jammed a room at the Carnegie Institute of Technology for a demonstration unequalled in the history of the institution. In the South, Negro students from Morgan College joined with whites at Johns Hopkins

176

and Goucher, resisting the attempts of an R.O.T.C. band to disrupt their ranks. At little Dakota Wesleyan every church in the town and every campus organization joined together to prepare the strike; there were scores of townspeople at the actual meeting. That alignment between students and working-people in neighboring communities was repeated elsewhere; it testified to the solidification of those bonds essential to the movement. Thirty-five hundred students, assembled in the Columbia University Gymnasium, listened to a rendition of "Taps," and the chairman quietly declared that "these notes are in memory of those who died in the last war and in solemn determination that we shall not repeat their mistake." To an audience which overflowed the meeting-hall at Virginia, a speaker asserted: "If those who profit from war insist upon bringing it on again, then we, with the mass of American people, must take power into our own hands and force peace upon the war-makers."

At Emory University in Georgia, where membership in the League for Industrial Democracy is considered treason, 250 students braved outside pressure to gather in a chapel peace meeting. And at New Hampshire University 1000 of the 1300 undergraduates left their classes at 11 o'clock to support the strike.

In every sector the move had gripped the imagination of American students. The Cornell *Daily Sun* commented: "The Cornell undergraduate seems to have finally cast aside his usual cloak of apathy toward world problems." The *Daily Princetonian* wrote: "The thinking and far-sighted youths of this country will no longer be restrained but will shout their defiance of war so that all may hear it." Virginia's student editor added: "Pro Patria Mori Is Bunk." According to the *Dartmouth Daily:* "When war comes, an editorial like this achieves nothing but an indefinite prison sentence for its writers. It is in time of peace that we must build up anti-war sentiment to the point where it will be able to fight cooperatively against the emotional hysteria of war-time." The *Idaho*

177

Bengal: "The cumulative effect of many of these moves is bound to be great."

The strike was a militant gesture; the term itself was borrowed from years of struggle against oppression by people of all creeds and countries. But it was more than a momentary flare-up or one whose effects would swiftly fade. Those demonstrations were a "dress rehearsal" for the immediate stand which students had vowed to take should the government declare war. That point was reiterated on every side. "Passive resistance" was not the prevailing tone; these young men and women, as one speaker shouted to an earnest crowd of thousands of students, "do not propose to be a lost generation—and we are ready to fight for our lives."

On the same afternoon, a delegation of students visited the White House to present a message from that nationwide assemblage. It was addressed to Mr. Roosevelt and set forth the refusal of 175,000 American students to support the government of the United States in any war it might conduct.

In the Spring of 1924 three conspicuous and celebrated feats agitated the American campus:

NEW HAVEN, CONN., March 9, 1924—A new record has been set for Old Eli. H. Howitzer and C. Souris took part in a marathon needle-work contest last week beginning at noon Tuesday and ending at 9.30 Friday.

IOWA CITY, IA., March 10, 1924—Two students of the University of Iowa, Dan Gilson and Judson Large, established an endurance record here when they played bridge for twenty-five hours consecutively.

MINNEAPOLIS, MINN., March 10, 1924—Swan Swenson of the University of Minnesota has for the past week been rolling a peanut around the campus, finishing last night at 10:30. He worked for 150 hours, making 90 circuits of the campus, a distance of 217 miles.

Eleven years afterward, a tabulation of the participants in the student strike against war disclosed the following totals, arranged by regions and with reports from certain sectors still incomplete: *

NEW ENGLAND

Amherst	250
Bennington	200
Brown	1,300
Clark	100
Colby	500
Conn. College for Women	400
Dartmouth	500
Emerson	250
Harvard	600
M. I. T.	150
Mass. State	43
Mt. Holyoke	100
New Hampshire	1,000
Radcliffe	300
Simmons	700
Smith	800
Tufts	300
Wesleyan	400
Yale	500

MIDDLE ATLANTIC

American U.	500
Barnard	400
Brooklyn College (with Long Island U. and Seth Low)	6,000
Bryn Mawr	500
Buffalo	400
Carnegie Tech.	450
C. C. N. Y.	3,500
Colgate	1,000
Columbia	3,500
Cornell	2,500
George Washington U.	1,200
Goucher (with Johns Hopkins and Morgan)	2,000
Haverford	150
Howard	600
Hunter	2,200
Lafayette	1,000
New Jersey Coll. (with Rutgers)	1,000
New York University	2,000
Penn State	1,500
U. of Penn.	3,000
Pittsburgh	800
Princeton	1,000
St. Lawrence	400
Swarthmore	500
Syracuse	1,000
Temple	2,500
Vassar	entire student body
Wilson	500

SOUTH

Berea	1,500
Chattanooga	200
College of the Ozarks	800
Emory	250
Florida State (with Rollins and Tampa)	1,000
Louisville	350
Mercer	100
Morehouse	100
Vanderbilt (with Peabody, Fisk and Scarritt)	250
North Carolina	1,000
Southwestern	200
Tennessee	100
Texas U.	1,500
Texas Christian U.	1,600
Tulane, Louisiana	500
Virginia	1,000
West Virginia	90

* These figures are obtained from *The Student Outlook* which made the most exhaustive survey available of the strike total.

MIDDLE WEST

Butler	200
Central	500
Chicago	3,500
De Pauw	1,000
Drake	300
Eden	100
Hamline	500
Illinois	300
Iowa	250
Illinois Wesleyan	500
Lewis Institute	500
Michigan State	50
Michigan	1,000
Milwaukee State (with Wisconsin Extension)	2,500
Minnesota	3,000
Missouri	800
Northwestern	1,200
People's Junior College	750
Washington U.	400
Wayne	500
Wisconsin	2,000
Wright Junior College	50

OHIO

Akron	250
Antioch	350
Denison	600
Fenn	200
Marietta	175
Miami	500
Muskingum	500
Oberlin	1,200
Ohio State	400
Ohio	1,200
Toledo	600
Western Reserve	2,000
Wittenberg	700

ROCKY MOUNTAINS

Baker	38
Colorado U.	500
Dakota Wesleyan	400
Denver	800
Friends University	300
Idaho U. (Southern and Moscow branches)	1,100
Kansas State	500
Kansas University	1,000
Montana	500
Nebraska	500
North Dakota State Teachers College	400
North Dakota U.	No estimate
Phillips	200
Salina	300
Wyoming U.	750

PACIFIC COAST

California Tech.	400
U. of California (Berkeley)	4,000
U. C. L. A.	1,000
Linfield	200
Los Angeles J. C.	3,000
Pacific College	600
Oregon U.	1,000
Pasadena Junior College	500
Reed	300
San Diego State	500
San Jose	500
San Mateo	800
Stanford	1,500
Washington U.	500
Whittier	500

The strike had grown seven-fold in one year. Dr. Stephen Duggan, writing in the *News Bulletin* of the Institute of International Education, predicted that by 1936 "the movement will be almost universally observed." How is this sweeping growth to be explained? Certainly the first year's demonstrations were part of the answer; they had attained a maximum of discipline and effectiveness despite the attempt of rowdies to disperse them. Even more important, they had broken an entrenched set of prejudices against precisely such action, paving the way for more decisive inroads. But this alone does not account for the increase. It was primarily due to the gathering of external forces, the ominous tempo of world events. Implicit in the student's response was the fear that the depression was to be "solved" by another international war and that he, as part of the "surplus population" was to be sacrificed for it. The signs of catastrophe were visible on every side. Growing out of this apprehension was his abandonment of traditional antipathies; he could not be dissuaded by appeals for "scholarliness"; the time had come when the organized might of mass opinion throughout the world would have to make itself heard. That had been, we have seen, the contention of the insurgents since 1932. By the spring of 1935, whether he liked the admission or not, the aware student had to grant their judgment. It was too late to contemplate the virtues of "restrained objectivity." It was hardly feasible to remain aloof from so intimate a peril. If the American undergraduate on April 12th was a changed, revitalized human being, that was because the world had changed from its post-war to its pre-war attire.

PART IV
REACTION

1. Panic

SHORTLY after the strike of April, 1934, William Randolph Hearst's press recommended the firing-squad for those who had inspired the move. Despite the more notable demonstrations of the following year, no formal executions have occurred; but of academic beheadings, of terrorization, of unbridled violence and discreet intervention, we have seen an incessant parade. These reached their peak in the days immediately preceding and following April 12, 1935.

The American administrative hierarchy, with a few distinguished exceptions, bestowed neither aid nor enthusiasm on the deeds of its students. Repression was not a sudden, spontaneous policy; its growth will be traced through the remainder of this work; the strike interval merely provided the climactic phase to the retreat of the "experimentalists"—a flight which began with the student pilgrimage to Kentucky. April 12th was the day on which a large segment of undergraduate thinking attained a maximum of soberness and clarity; in the same interlude, education made its most deliberate, intense attempt to restore the nostrums of childhood. The strike was an unwanted intrusion.

There were several main roads which the course of administrative interference travelled. Perhaps most ingenious were the numerous attempts to take over the proceedings and project them along lines which no sensitive Trustee could have resented. Thus, at St. Lawrence University, the administration sent a note to the faculty announcing a revision of recitation hours on the day scheduled for the strike. Accompanying these instructions was this explanation: "This will give students an opportunity for a meeting in commemoration of our entrance into the World War."

With this agile manipulation of phrases, the student body of St. Lawrence discovered that an anti-imperialistic strike had been converted into a "respectable" sob-fest over the great crusade. Instead of condemning wars and those who make them, the undergraduates were to "commemorate" the exploits of General Pershing and his cohorts. At De Pauw University President Oxnam was even more solicitous; he personally paid for a visit by Frances Lederer who addressed the assemblage and later condemned the whole concept of the strike. At the same meeting the students were requested to sing "America the Beautiful." A special convocation was held at Lafayette College at which President Lewis defended the R.O.T.C., relieved himself of several generalizations on preparedness and saved the day. The administrators of Western Reserve University made a conspicuously energetic effort to distort the event. After preliminary negotiations between other officials and the students, Dean Trautman took command of the scene. He emphasized humanity's need for "dignity"; he derided the committee's plan to conduct a parade on the day of the walkout because it would be too "emotional" a gesture. In its stead he advocated a "dynamic silence," one so noiseless, presumably, that the community would not be aware that a demonstration was taking place. When the students rejected his proposals, he became imperious, declaring as administrative edicts three prerequisites to any peace activity on the scheduled day: that no resolutions be passed without official approval; that the meeting could condemn war as "a means of settling international disputes" without any more specific assertions; and, finally, Newton D. Baker would have to be present in some capacity, whether as chairman or speaker.

Newton D. Baker was the Secretary of War under Wilson; he is a staunch advocate of preparedness; his corporation affiliations include the most established sections of American finance. His place in any anti-war assemblage was as incongruous as the appearance of the munitions ring would have been. And for precisely those reasons Dean Trautman regarded him as a reliable antidote to any more militant phases of the protest. The maneuver failed; student indignation, in a notoriously conservative college, was too overwhelming, especially when backed by liberal journals and organizations throughout the city. Two days before the strike, the administration retreated. At the rally, attended by 2,000 students, Mr. Baker was one of the major targets of attack.

The Minnesota functionaries were equally captivated by the idea of Mr. Baker's presence. They urged the students to postpone their demonstration until late in the afternoon, so that this bearer of the message of peace could be the principal speaker. Again the students rebelled; although the college press monotonously echoed the voice of its superiors, more than 3,000 undergraduates responded to the call for a genuine, outspoken meeting. At little Emerson College the president likewise sought to divert students from the nation-wide movement, conducting his own session and denouncing the outside protest as "red."

Such were the more elaborate and restrained moves, but their design was plain. Confronted with student pressure for a strike, these administrators aimed to destroy the content and direction of the day. They decided to "supervise" undergraduate activity. They wanted it to be as innocuous and inoffensive as an Armistice Day Chapel service.

More frequent was the abrupt denial of facilities for any strike meeting. At the University of Colorado, for example, the Administration barred the use of the Memorial Building, although it was regularly placed at the disposal of the National Guard. The case of the University of Washington merits more detailed examination.

For several weeks before the strike, the President of the University occupied the front page of the student newspaper with repeated denunciations of the move. In this he had the admiring support of the undergraduate editor and together they waged a determined campaign. They did not succeed.

About 300 students proceeded with their plans for a demonstration. At this juncture the administration, despite a petition of protest from twenty instructors, announced that no university facilities would be granted for the conduct of the meeting since that would constitute an intolerable "interruption of classes." The students were driven to the edge of the campus where the scheduled assemblage took place. Shortly afterward, a group of undergraduates formed a Student League Against War and Fascism to carry on the program begun in April. At first they were granted the use of a hall in the school; two days before their first important session was to be held, however, the President again intervened, withdrawing the permit to the meeting-room and declaring that there was "no need for such an organization" at the University of Washington. That much is generally known; what is more revealing, however, is the fact that one year before, an organization called The Pathfinders was formed at Washington with the secret sponsorship of President Seig. It was an allegedly non-partisan group, with an impressive front of fraternity men—and no independents. For two months it commanded the front page of the student daily. On Armistice Day in 1934, it was this array which violently dispersed a student anti-war rally, without any subsequent administrative punishment or warning. The bulk of the Pathfinders were members of Scabbard and Blade. Although the bloc has not recently been in evidence, the administrative sanction with which it operated is illuminating. It was at this institution that Bernard Stern, distinguished sociologist, was dismissed in 1931 for his non-conformist views; two years later nine students were suspended for inviting a communist to address a luncheon group; now, in April, 1935, the University of Washington banned the anti-war movement from its halls because it challenged the R.O.T.C.-ridden, subservient routine of campus life.

At Hunter College in New York the girls were compelled to hold their meeting in a mid-town hall; no campus room

was open to them. One of the most extraordinary performances, however, was that of the President of George Washington University in Washington, D. C. Many of the students
there are government employees; President Marvin threatened them with the loss of their posts. When this failed to intimidate them, he discoursed more abstractly on the general
perils of communism. On the day of the strike, however, he
resorted to his most contemptible gesture. When the students
gathered for their strike meeting, they waited in vain for
Congressmen Maverick, Sisson and Amlie, the scheduled
speakers, to appear. In the interim President Marvin had
communicated with the congressmen, misrepresented the nature of the event to them and prevailed upon them to remain
away. The congressmen later learned of his duplicity; Representative Sisson read an open letter in the House denouncing
Marvin for allying himself "with the Army and Navy lobby
here in Washington, the munitions and armament makers,
the Shearers and other provocateurs of war."

Dean Taylor of the College of Engineering at Texas University was more succinct in his disapproval of the strike:
"The whole thing was started by a bunch of Russians from
the East Side of New York."

While universities denied their facilities to the peace advocates—the same structures, of course, which were so readily
transferred to the War Department in 1917—their "supervision" was often more drastic. The case of a student editor
at Santa Clara University is outstanding. His set-to with the
authorities occurred several months before the actual strike,
at a time when the Santa Clara authorities were apparently
striving to prevent the movement from getting a foothold
there. In an editorial this student had asserted that "students
have nothing to gain from war," a fairly simple and elementary statement and one which, I suggest, should not be out-
lawed from our universities. But at Santa Clara that was an
impudent, intolerable affront to the sanctities. The faculty
sought to impress more conventional sentiments upon him.

189

Ultimately he was expelled from school, without even the customary attempt to conceal the reasons behind his ouster. The academic career of this young man was ended because he had written that "students have nothing to gain from war" and had subsequently refused "to print what the faculty wanted him to." Following his ouster, the student tried to gain admission to the University of California, but the verdict of Santa Clara was staunchly upheld by this supposedly more cosmopolitan and erudite citadel. There was no place for an undergraduate who refused to acknowledge the inspirational and human qualities implicit in international conflict.

The University of Michigan is a leading member of "The Big Ten"; it is no primitive institute in the recesses of American civilization; there are 10,000 young men and women in its undergraduate population. I cite these items to indicate that hostility to the anti-war strike was far from restricted to the more backward entities. Two days after the nationwide walkout had taken place, Alexander Ruthven, president of this University, issued the following pronouncement:

"University work has been interfered with and the reputation of the institution has been called into question recently by perversive activities of a few professional agitators. . . . The continuance of activities will not be tolerated. . . . The university has no desire to curtail freedom of speech but as a state-supported institution, devoted to education, it proposes to fulfill to the utmost its obligations to the state and to the cause of genuine education. . . . Students who are known to have interfered with the proper conduct of university affairs are being investigated and action will be taken promptly. Students guilty of such misconduct in the future may expect disciplinary action."

Several months before, the University of Michigan had barred its halls to John Strachey, noted writer and lecturer, because his opinions did not coincide with those of the solid citizens of the community. Now a blunt warning had been served upon those who would agitate in behalf of peace. Shortly after President Ruthven's statement had been made public, a Michigan alumnus and a teacher in a neighboring school both wrote letters to *The Michigan Daily* protesting the utterance as a threat to any independent thought at the school. To confirm their apprehension, these letters were immediately censored by a "Board of Control" whose function was to provide "advice" and "suggestion" to the editor. And the censorship, involving removal of the letters from the edition, was done without even a consultation with the editor. Dr. Ruthven and his aides had vividly testified to the accusations in the letters—by forbidding their appearance.

It was confidently expected that the reprisals against the anti-war leaders would not be carried through. One student, in fact, told me at the time that he believed Dr. Ruthven's statement was merely a maneuver to assuage the Board of Regents and the legislature. But this was an unwarranted flattery to administrative moderation. On August 1, 1935, Alexander Ruthven paid his debt "to the state" by denying readmission to four undergraduates prominent in anti-war activity at the school. The reason stated was: "It has proved to be impossible to persuade you to refrain from interfering with the work of the university and the work of other students."

Dr. Ruthven steadfastly refused to make any more specific allegations; but there can be no one in Ann Arbor who is unaware of the cause of the expulsions. An undergraduate cynically suggested, privately, that, were administrators to state their motivations frankly, the letters of dismissal would have read:

"It has proved to be impossible for me, although I am an ardent lover of Peace, to satisfy my conscience and the Board of Regents simultaneously. A university whose Regents are all affiliated with the auto industry

(study the profits of that industry during the last war)
must not concern itself with the causes and symptoms
of so profitable a venture. The Board of Regents loves
Peace, too. But its members feel they may soon have to
take up the cudgels of Righteousness again. In such a
project they must be assured of universal cooperation; I
must therefore dismiss you for interfering with the som-
nolence in which several thousand Michigan men must
be preserved. Yours for education, free thought and international good-will.

(Signed) ALEXANDER G. RUTHVEN."

That letter was never written. But its implications are perfectly plain in the Michigan community. Four students were
sacrificed there to save the "good name" of the university and
to safeguard against the repetition of any organized undergraduate expression of opinion.

There were other penalties, threats and impediments placed
in the way of the strike; * no one man served more valiantly
in that campaign than the energetic, irrepressible head of Los
Angeles Junior College, Director Ingalls. I recount this episode as indicative of the scholarliness and profundity with
which the educational world sought to combat the expression
of student opinion. Director Ingalls is a temperamental, ex-
citable man; on April 12, 1935, he was experiencing peculiarly acute prostration. He did not want to hear about peace
nor was he remotely interested in discussing it. On the other
hand, hundreds of his students were; they gathered on the
campus shortly before eleven o'clock to demonstrate that interest. Infuriated by their appearance, alternately panic-
stricken and overcome by rage, Director Ingalls ordered loud-
speakers placed around the crowd, with his aides blaring into

* Here I am citing only a limited number of incidents to reveal the general setting; in later chapters numerous other events will be described under
specific headings. The nationwide organization of violence, in connection
with this and other student actions, will be discussed under "Students in
Uniform."

192

them to drown out the speeches of his students. The strikers continued to make themselves heard, denouncing the crudity of their Director's exhibition. He did not enjoy that; in fact, he almost fell over himself in an effort to devise another weapon. Suddenly it came upon him; he would toot a whistle until the meeting dispersed. And so, in his best academic manner, his face reddening and his eyes bulging menacingly out of their sockets, Doctor Ingalls tooted. When his lungs were exhausted, when his mental processes were shaken by so laborious an exertion, this good man of learning discovered that the strike assemblage was still in progress. There was only one remaining alternative. Flanked by a burly detachment from the "Red squad," the high-strung Doctor Ingalls advanced upon the throng, determined to wipe it individually and collectively out of sight. The students did not retreat. Whereupon peace-loving, devout, church-going Director Ingalls stood by while the police mercilessly clubbed two girl students into unconsciousness. Her colleagues fought back; they refused to be driven from their own campus by imported police and Director Ingalls decided that the time had arrived for the final gesture. He ordered the campus sprinkler-system turned full speed on the crowd until it had departed. Two weeks later, four students were suspended.

That was an edifying exhibition; no more so, however, than that of Dr. T. W. McQuarrie, president of San Jose State Teachers College who, on the eve of the strike, suspended two students and encouraged "Vigilantes" to disrupt the assemblage. He accompanied these steps with this declaration:

"Don't make any mistake about it. I'm not in favor of war myself and I don't know of anyone who is. It's a silly, disturbing, wasteful and unsatisfactory method of settling disputes. I'm thoroughly in sympathy with any move that will avert wars and I gladly pledge myself to use any influence I have to that end. However, I'm not going to take the program of a disloyal group of vicious and partly demented people and state beforehand that I will not support my country if war should be declared."

It is hardly astonishing that the strike meeting at San Jose ended when Dr. McQuarrie's more loyal subjects unleashed a torrent of missiles on the throng.

I cannot hope to detail adequately the status of similar events in American high schools; the unrestrained viciousness and brutality of administrative figures on April 12th, however, must be briefly mentioned. Out on the West Coast, and particularly in Los Angeles, hordes of police surrounded every school to prevent students from leaving their classrooms. Two students—one at John Marshall High School and the other at Fairfax—were suspended. There were 200 policemen jammed around Belmont to prevent any exodus from the building; students milled around in the halls, seeking to reach the streets but finding themselves prisoners in an academic setting. Nothing on that day, however, was equivalent to the situation at Crane Technical high school in Chicago. Lester Schlossberg, a student there, was one of the leaders in an attempt to organize a strike committee at the school. He was seized by school authorities and turned over to a group of "patriotic" students who took him down to the cellar and, in the dark, beat him until he was half-unconscious. At that point a rope was placed around his neck in a mock-lynching ceremony. After several more attacks, Dean Quick came in and proceeded to give him a lecture on allegiance to the flag.* That was not a single episode. At De Witt Clinton High School in New York, for example, youthful R.O.T.C. boys attacked peace demonstrators with the full sanction of educational authorities. It was a day of terror throughout the city. Superintendent Campbell had declared his opposition to the strike; his edict was carried out by the barring of doors,

* This incident is testified to in an affidavit made out by the student.

assignment of strong-arm squads in various schools and, later, the disclosure that those who participated in the strike were being hampered in their efforts to gain entrance to colleges. And the colleges—Penn State and Cornell specifically—readily agreed that a student whose record showed affiliation with the strike against war and fascism was not worthy of admission. The victims of this device were students of Abraham Lincoln High School.

Violence figured prominently in the secondary schools; but, as has been indicated, the colleges were hardly free from similar outbreaks. Hundreds of students in Michigan State were incited to an assault on speakers at the peace meeting, culminating in a "ducking" in the neighboring river. At Louisville, on the day following the walkout, high-minded undergraduates formed a Student League for National Defense "to preserve the sacred traditions on which our country is founded." A parade at the University of Chicago was greeted by a barrage of rotten eggs hurled by R.O.T.C. members and their assistants. And in the same city police forcibly halted a march by undergraduates at the Lewis Institute, driving the participants from the street.

That was the mood in which the academic overlords responded to the second strike against war: fantastic maneuvers to blunt its meaning, denial of university facilities, dismissals and expulsions, accompanied by what was usually administration-sponsored violence. I have indicated here the outlines of their behavior; one significant conclusion arises most readily from it. When the strike was originally planned, a number of administrators shed anguished tears because, they alleged, "it is a move directed against the university." They were only partially correct. The demonstration was against the university rulers only in so far as they wanted to make it such. They were urged to join with their students in the protest. The students earnestly asked for such aid. It was not, with a few important exceptions such as North Carolina, Vassar, Oberlin and a handful of others, forthcoming; elsewhere, if aid was offered, it was either after attempts to curb the demonstrations had failed or where the terms of such cooperation could minimize the strength of the protest. But there was a more basic aspect to the question. The university system, Trustee-dominated as it is, was on trial; conservatives argued that "all people are against war and there is no reason why our administrators will not help us combat it." They were wrong. I am not suggesting that administrators are inherently blood-thirsty or constitutionally addicted to warfare; neither are Trustees, per se, agents of death. But the anti-war movement, once it assumed a concrete, anti-imperialist character, was an economic struggle in which permanent alignments took shape. It was directed against the roots and by-products of a system —because it could not help being so. Again I emphasize that the vast numbers of students who participated in it were not prepared to renounce that system; they were approaching that point, however, where they would be prepared to say that, if war is the destiny of capitalism, then let us search for a more rational order. The strike was a serious gesture; it was symptomatic of a profound alteration in thought and perspective. And those who are the standard-bearers of the status quo, those who live by it, and off it, could not avoid that realization. Mr. Morgan did not stamp into the administrative chambers and demand that the strike be halted; he didn't have to. American education fought this strike more vigorously and tenaciously than any other battle in its history; and, by doing so, it confirmed the suspicion of the insurgents. To the extent that this opposition was manifest, then, the strike was against the university—not as an affront to university routine but as a challenge to a finance-dominated structure. Less than twenty years ago the higher learning went to war; now its constituents were declaring that they would resist a repetition of the performance. An independent handful of administrators aligned themselves with their students; the remainder stuck by their posts as last-ditch upholders of the status quo—whether that status quo was to mean war and destruction or not.

That day saw the far-flung emergence of fascistic technique on the American campus. I say fascism because it possessed all the incipient characteristics of that credo—repression of minorities, forcible cracking-down on the anti-war movement, the rise of hysterical jingoism and, above all, an unwavering defense of the existing order against any prospect of reform or overhauling. It was not a sudden, mysterious arrival; the path of its coming had been adequately prepared. It is that process with which we shall now be primarily concerned. There are certain stages in the development which can be plainly perceived. The first is the long and entrenched rule of administrative orthodoxy; that has been evident since the first American student sensed that all was not fixed and divinely-wrought in the world; it is predicated upon what Dean Klapper called the inevitable tendency of education "to rationalize the existing order." The second stage is the attack on professors launched from outside the university but linked by pressure-finance to forces within it. That is followed by an inquisition into the thought and activity of professors and students alike, a heresy-hunt aimed to banish any hint of dissension or critical inquiry. But perhaps the most ominous and highly-developed barometer of reaction is the organization of terror-bands among the student body to smash the undergraduate insurgence. Administrative reaction, in this era, becomes fascistic in intensity and tone; the outbreak of Vigilantism mirrors that spirit which has begun to pervade the academic sphere. The student revolt was born and advanced in spite of the educational structure; undergraduate reaction is a direct and cherished offspring of it. That is the essential and tragic paradox of our university edifice: a movement based upon an intellectual awareness and appraisal of social phenomena, an upsurge in which reason was the motivating impulse, was hounded from our academic halls; but the counter-attack, premised upon violence and bigotry and prejudice, was received with outright acclaim or silent approval.

11. Preludes

PANIC seized the academic barons in 1935; but long before there was any excuse for concern, they were betraying symptoms of delirium. They have never been at rest. Even when the average undergraduate was steeped in the vacuum which he so readily accepted, devoid of concern for anything but "the moment of living," the lone dissenters were being hunted out. The fact is that nowhere in the world can there be found more alert and sensitive watch-dogs than in the American university; only now are we beginning to perceive the real consequences of their vigilance. The following case histories are not unique. Although the tendency will, perhaps, be more eloquently revealed in these than in others, the foundations are fundamentally the same. No two universities are identical in detail; but the control of the educational system can be traced to a single source. With the first inklings of student inquisitiveness, the control became steadily more direct. It is with this in mind that these early cases are set forth; for they were the prelude to the appearance of deliberate, present-day reaction. Nurtured in this tradition, it has not been difficult for administrators to meet the more rigorous demands of the contemporary scene.

Chancellor John Bowman of the University of Pittsburgh looks upon himself as an "idealist" whose vision is tinged with the sound, homely matter of "practical sense." The self-estimate may be granted. Out of that curiously blended personality there emerged the most persistent fixation which has ever gripped the academic mind. Dr. Bowman stated its origins quite simply, with inadvertent irony: he aimed to make Pittsburgh a city of "achievement just as great in education as in manufacturing." That was not to be achieved by the importation of scholars, the revitalizing of the curriculum or any more prosaic devices. Dr. Bowman's idea was one of magnitude, of stature, of steel—a "Cathedral of Learning" which would rise higher than any tower in the educational world. The edifice could not be built on the ephemeral groundwork of a Great Idea. According to early estimates, at least ten million dollars would have to be fused with the dynamic, guiding power of the spirit. Dr. Bowman was not dismayed. Pittsburgh has produced more millionaires this century than any other city. On his own Board of Trustees are Ernest T. Weir, steel magnate; George Clapp of Mellon's Aluminum Co., Andrew Mellon himself and all his available bank officers. These were reassuring figures, men who would help to realize the dream. The task did not seem overwhelming nor did it have to be engineered single-handed.

The revelation occurred in 1926. From that time on, Dr. Bowman has never lost sight of the fulfillment; the idea has been embedded in his brain almost to the exclusion of anything else. And at the outset he seemed to be making distinguished headway. His ardor never subsided, his enthusiasm overwhelmed temporary frustrations—and the monument steadily arose over the streets of Pittsburgh. If the pains and difficulties of his labors were manifold, Dr. Bowman could at least be comforted by the rising structure of stone, mortar, steel and glass. There was only one incessant torment: the fear that a misstep, a deviation from the beaten academic path, a whispered affront might cut off the source of his subsidy. Dr. Bowman understood the requirements of the situation; he knew the sensitivities and preferences of the men on whom his plans depended; he was aware that they could demolish his hope. His dual personality harbored a conflict, for in him there was a quaint admixture of high aspiration and blunt realism. And so a compromise was effected; as the cathedral mounted upward, ideas were remorselessly banished from the university, a maximum of thinking was sacrificed for the lasting testimonial to Dr. Bowman's ability as a bill-collector. When the job was finished, it was remarked, Pittsburgh would have the largest citadel in the educational system—and it would be barren and empty inside. That was how idealism was to merge with the demands of the practical, drab world.

When the coal strike broke out in 1929, Dr. Colston Warne was a teacher at the University of Pittsburgh. That was the year in which Andrew Mellon's coal company severed its contract with the United Mine Workers of America, restored the open shop and drastically slashed wages. In those months the miners who struck in protest found themselves black-listed, evicted from their homes and attacked by hired company police.

Following a visit to the coal-fields in the midst of these developments, Dr. Warne was invited to address a forum in Pittsburgh at which contemporary issues were discussed. In response to the request, he recited his impressions of the scene, emphasizing the need for collective bargaining and government intervention to stem the unchecked rule of the coal barons. Shortly afterward Dr. Warne was summoned to the offices of Chancellor Bowman, who informed him that the Board of Trustees had "reacted very violently" to his address. About a week later *The Pittsburgh Press*, a Scripps-Howard publication, urged him to prepare an article containing his own judgments on the coal strike. Casually mentioning the proposals to the head of his department, he received a prompt verdict:

> "The university has an unfinished cathedral of learning. If we were to go seriously into opposition to the Mellon interests, who are counted on to help the university substantially, and other large groups, we would be imperilling the situation of the university."

Dr. Warne abandoned the project; but he could not avoid another encounter. In the course of an address to a church group, he criticized the labor policies of the Weirton Steel company. His remarks were quickly sped to Mr. Weir and Mr. Weir, in turn, brought the matter forcibly to Dr. Bowman's notice. Again Dr. Warne was called to administrative headquarters, where he was ordered to abandon any further speech-making or resign his post. He assented. But he did not sever his affiliations with the Civil Liberties Union, joining in a petition of that body to the governor which urged an investigation of terror against the coal-miners. Dr. Warne did not wait to be dismissed; he obtained a position in another university and retired from the Pittsburgh campus. The exodus had begun.

At about the same time Frederick E. Woltman prepared an article for *The American Mercury* in which he denounced the "Cossacks" employed by the coal companies to stifle labor organizations. Several hours after the indictment appeared, Dr. Woltman was engaged in an animated conference with university officials who apprised him of his crime: he had offended the better people. His ouster, it was suggested, was not too remote a possibility. Following the interview, Dr. Woltman related the incident to the press as an illustration of the sweeping power of the coal dynasty. That was the end of his academic career; he was loudly directed to "get off the campus and not come back."

Dr. F. E. Beutel was a conspicuously dangerous figure. When the United States Senate launched an investigation into the campaign of Senator-elect Vare, one of the most powerful men in the state, Dr. Beutel was called to testify. It was an unfortunate step. The professor submitted evidence exposing "the effect of the political activity of the Mellon machine in Pittsburgh, the amount of money they spent on that election and the long lines of employees that got paid off at their headquarters after the election was over." Such revelations were not hailed as a public service in the bailiwick of Andrew

Mellon. Within a brief interval Dr. Beutel was informed that he had "no future" at the university. The class to which he had devoted most of his thought and energy was taken from him and he was simultaneously advised, "in all friendliness," to resign. The advice could not be misconstrued; Dr. Beutel joined the procession out of Pittsburgh.

Dr. Ralph Turner's execution was delayed by a peculiarly significant accident. One of the first complaints about his liberal activity resulted in the customary summons to administrative chambers. When he arrived there, a university official who was awaiting him suggested that they look up the status of the complainant in the *Directory of Directors*. This inquiry disclosed that the man was, in the descriptive language of the university functionary, "small potatoes." "We shall not pay much attention to the complaint," he added.

In March, 1933, Dr. Turner assumed a prominent post in the Pennsylvania Security League, an organization pressing for the enactment of various forms of social legislation. It was an able, energetic group which swiftly drew the fire of the financial caste against whose rule the legislation was directed. Dr. Turner was soon informed that the university did not want "so able a man to divide his energies." At this admonition Dr. Turner resigned his post in the League—but that did not suffice. Early in his career at the school, Dr. Turner had been ordered to "soft-pedal" his discussions of evolution. Now he was warned that his beliefs about social betterment were even more offensive; the university frankly informed him that "the Union Trust Co. kept a constant check on your activities in the spring of 1933." And J. Steele Gow, then executive secretary of the university, told him to choose "between a political career and a scholarly career."

An address he delivered before the Western Pennsylvania Historical Society, in which he denounced the policies of the Mellon interests, assured his doom. That summer in which he was apprised of his dismissal, he received almost identical letters from Dr. John Oliver, head of the History Department and Dean Seig; they both quoted Dr. Bowman as saying that his campaign for funds had been injured by the conduct of "certain faculty members"; Dr. Turner was earmarked to go. When he learned of his ouster, he went to Dr. Bowman for an explanation; the latter was evasive, almost mystical, but one sentence was meaningful: "The Board of Trustees is a group of business men and among them you will find a great deal of discontent."

Dr. Turner is admittedly one of the foremost historians in the country; Dr. Bowman had acknowledged that he was "one of the ten best men in the university." Now he was departing from Pittsburgh without the blessings of his overseers.

While the faculty was being mercilessly mowed down, the student body could hope for no better things. In the spring of 1929 the student Liberal Club invited Dr. Harry Elmer Barnes to deliver an address on the status of the Mooney-Billings case. On the eve of his arrival, the club was ordered to cancel the session, the permit for its meeting-room being withdrawn. Dr. Barnes spoke to a group of Pittsburgh students from the running-board of a car.

Three days later the chancellor moved to prevent the possibility of any further undergraduate extra-curricular thought. Ordering the Liberal Club disbanded, he arbitrarily expelled two of its leaders to reenforce the verdict. In protest against his action, twenty faculty men signed a petition of protest— and virtually every one of those twenty has subsequently "disappeared" from Pittsburgh.

A few years afterward a group of undergraduates sponsored a peace meeting on the campus designed to inaugurate a local anti-war committee. At the instigation of the university, three of the leaders of the move were arrested and fined. When they later won a sweeping reversal of the verdict, the administration instituted a "loyalty pledge" for all students, accompanied by the declaration of John Weber, business manager of the school: "We want right-minded students here. We wanted to have an understanding."

1934 saw another insurgence and it was combatted with equal vigor. When students organized a League for Social Justice on the campus, their request for a university charter to legalize their activities was firmly rejected. The University of Pittsburgh will harbor no successor to the Liberal Club nor is there any place for undergraduate dissenters in the community. When a chapter of the National Student League was being formed, Leon Falk, a leading Jewish philanthropist and war-profits millionaire, strode into the meeting and immediately called a caucus of Jewish students present. He told them that, if they persisted in joining liberal activity, a Jewish quota would have to be imposed at the University. It will be seen that Mr. Falk's philanthropy was as judicious as Mr. Mellon's. Deprived of its outstanding faculty men and barred from any inquiry on their own initiative, the student body is receiving what is commonly described as an education.

There was a political upheaval in the city of Pittsburgh in 1934; the Democrats were returned to office after a prolonged absence. Spurred by a series of facts and innuendoes, they voted a probe into the "status of academic freedom" at the University of Pittsburgh. These are only random items of the testimony which was submitted to them, constituting probably the worst scandal in American academic life. Witnesses paraded to the stand in monotonous succession to detail the circumstances of their leavetaking from the university. The reports were briefly summarized by one commentator: "No one knows who else is being watched. Everyone is afraid. Student activities even remotely concerned with social or economic problems are barred." *

But the investigation, although it provided an opportunity for bringing to light the full nightmare through which the

* See *The Nation,* July 24, 1935.

Pittsburgh community of learning lives, failed to accomplish much more. It was conducted by men who were genuinely aroused over the situation; even they feared, however, to allow National Student League members to testify lest the probe become too offensive to the interests involved. And the legislature proceeded to grant the university its usual subsidy without reference to the recommendations of the committee. What will happen next no one dares to predict. "For a while perhaps calm will reign. No one knows however when Pittsburgh's steel and coal and glass and aluminum workers may find it necessary to stage a fight against oppressive conditions. The teachers will again forget they have to eat, and speak out." *

During the past five years twenty-five men have been dismissed from the university; fifty-nine have resigned and their ranks will continue to grow. Meanwhile the 12,000 students are betraying signs of restlessness; the same motivation which impells Mellon's employees to defy him is beginning to make itself felt among them. They know what will happen. Chancellor Bowman's Cathedral is still unfinished, desperately in need of funds to carry the project through. One of his staff members told a committee of the American Association of University Professors: "Chancellor Bowman's one objective is the securing of money with which to complete the Cathedral of Learning and . . . he subordinates every other interest to that objective."

But Chancellor Bowman is not alone nor is his Cathedral the only obstacle to independent thought within the university. In every one of his gestures he has had the sympathetic accord of his Trustees. His reign has only exaggerated the rule which they have imposed, and which, with the increasing severity of the depression, has become more meaningful and more intense. Chancellor Bowman, or someone else, will have to remember how precarious is the university's financial

* See *The Nation*, July 24, 1935.

status. The Cathedral has become a symbol of that degradation.

One cannot depart from Pittsburgh, however, without studying Chancellor Bowman's most celebrated exercise in mysticism. In the course of the dispute over Professor Turner's dismissal, he penned the following epistle of explanation to Congressman Ellenberger:

> "The right explanation is not simple. The university deals with facts and the meaning of facts, as they may illuminate a path toward a happy, useful and good life. The material of the university is boys and girls. They come many of them vague in purpose, but with a fine earnestness. For them the world is new. Days are all days of discovery. Just around the corner is fresh and wider vision. Surprised by what seems an escape from all that is ordinary, they are fair and open-minded. They are quick about taking up new ideas. Now the point of this is that a teacher, if he even half realizes his responsibilities to these impressionable students, will feel himself exceedingly humble before God. . . ."

And God, in Pittsburgh, walks under the pseudonym of Andrew Mellon. Ernest T. Weir is Gabriel.

Commencement time is a season of flourishes and at Syracuse University, Chancellor Flint annually gives himself to the spirit of the occasion. Addressing the seniors of the class of 1935, he burst forth:

> "The supreme, all-inclusive duty of a university is to seek to know the truth, the whole truth and nothing but the truth; a search, full, free, thorough; for every side, every factor, every angle of every phase of the truth; a search wholly untrammeled, no area verboten, no suspicion of financial inducement or tenure-incentive to color findings or to warp honest interpretation."

206

If there was incredulity in his audience, if there were those who guffawed gently at his neatly-turned phrases, then they must be forgiven, for they must have encountered Chancellor Flint at other times. He is a man of moods; while on Commencement Day he regularly attains heights of pedagogical idealism, on other occasions he has been known to recognize the limitations of his credo. More often than not, in fact. the Chancellor has his ear to the ground and hears the rumblings of his contributors—and to him that sound is the echo of Truth.

About ten years ago a group of undergraduates at Syracuse announced their intention to form a Peace League. The disclosure caused no minor flurry among their associates and among the administrators of the University. Chancellor Flint literally quaked; but soon he recovered himself sufficiently to invent a decisive antidote. If there was sedition in the ranks, he would, in person and without restraint, serve as the torch-bearer of enlightenment. Logically enough, he proceeded to have himself sworn in as a colonel in the Reserve Officers Training Corps. Perhaps uncertain as to the weight carried by this gesture, he augmented it with a lively declaration:

> "I have felt it fitting that the head of an institution with an R.O.T.C. should himself be a member of the reserve corps. . . . For that reason I place myself at the disposal of our government and am proud to be in this position of potential service. . . .
> "I am an apostle of peace. . . . But if, in this, I working humbly with all others, with them also fail, then I am ready to render any services within my power in the only way left for service. . . ."

Not that there was any immediate cause for panic. But the chancellor believed in caution. Seven years passed, prosperity hurtled into decline and another segment of undergraduates decided to expand their vision beyond the placid confines of Syracuse. The chancellor was prepared.

In the fall of 1931 a group of liberal and radical students, together with some professors, formulated the idea of a Liberal Club. They proposed to utilize it as a medium for focussing student attention on those problems which were rapidly absorbing the world. Similar ventures were springing up elsewhere; this one was modest in aim and program without any grandiose visions of its own immediate future. Its aim, above all, was to shake the shell of indolence in which the campus was so appallingly gripped.

Chancellor Flint halted the project in its infancy. In response to an appeal for university recognition of the club, the members received the following reply, allegedly a prescription for the conduct of all student societies:

"When any organization is openly affiliated, or still more, if it is covertly affiliated, with the milder inspiration or more militant lash of paid secretaries, and in some cases of persistent and occasionally fanatical propagandists, the University has a further duty in the matter of approvals and encouragements."

In his enthusiasm for the crusade, Chancellor Flint neglected one pressing detail. There were on the Syracuse campus at the moment he wrote a series of organizations "openly affiliated" under the "militant lash of paid secretaries." Among these were a host of fraternities, the Newman Club, the Y. W. C. A. and the International Relations Club, an offspring of the respectable, weak-kneed Carnegie Foundation. The target of his attack, of course, was the fact that several members of the Liberal Club were affiliated with the League for Industrial Democracy.

Undaunted by his interference, the Liberal Club moved off the campus, held its meetings in the vicinity and continued to attract a substantial number of followers. Its next project was the organization of a Peace Council. Chancellor Flint was wary about his steps. There was a definite amount of liberal pressure on the campus and in the city, so he launched that second strategy of higher education—guerilla warfare against the leaders of the group. Thus, the Chairman of the Peace Council was a woman student and she soon received an invitation to discuss her status with the Dean of Women. During the interview, she was "persuaded" to renounce her post. These subtleties did not achieve the anticipated effect. The Peace Council held a conference attended by delegates from fifteen colleges. It passed a spirited resolution against the R.O.T.C. and outlined a comprehensive analysis of the profit-drive behind warfare. At the conclave a prominent Syracuse clergyman delivered a bitter indictment of the R.O.T.C.; the editors of the student newspaper were "persuaded" not to publish his remarks.

Late in April, 1932—the month following the student delegation to Kentucky, the month of Reed Harris' expulsion from Columbia—the administration of Syracuse University abolished the Peace Council. Even this did not quell the activity. On Jingo Day—on which the R.O.T.C. holds its annual review—students gathered on the campus in protest and denounced the administration's ban on the council. Of this ban the Chancellor suddenly betrayed pathetic innocence; he had one of the council's former faculty advisers issue a public denial that such a step had been taken. But the other adviser, then travelling in England, could not be "persuaded" to forget so easily. Apprised of his colleague's statement, this man, Professor Johnson, cabled that the Administration had inspired the dissolution of the group. He added the interesting item that the Chancellor had urged him to conceal the source of the "inspiration." It was Professor Johnson himself who had made the formal announcement of the council's dissolution; his explanation was pointed.

Having, so he believed, routed two attempts by students to form their own organizations on the campus, the chancellor proceeded, or was prodded into, an attack upon "314 Waverley," woman's living center and one of the few havens of liberalism in Syracuse. It was a privately-endowed institution, not comparable to the other university cottages, and conducted by people interested in the house as an educational experiment. Every Sunday evening meetings were held; scores of prominent American liberals can recall a fireside meeting at "314." Chancellor Flint didn't like this and he was joined in this cordial hatred by propertied citizens throughout the city. Late in May of that year an executive order closed the doors of the institution, on the pretext of a "revision" in women's living quarters at the university.

Faculty members had no better fortune. Herbert Abraham, an instructor in 1931-32, was indignant over what he regarded as repeated evidence of prejudice against Negroes in the University. (Negro women are not allowed in the women's dormitories, Negro men are barred from crew, etc.) He expressed his feelings in a well-documented report. For this service he was rewarded with the loss of his job shortly afterward on the ground that he was a "poor teacher."

Four professors who co-signed a list of suggestions to the chancellor on possible retrenchment moves which would not impair the university's educational facilities were asked to resign—and only by bitter efforts did they keep their posts. Dr. Louis Hickernell, in charge of hygiene instruction, was suddenly informed that his course was to be terminated for reasons of "economy." The actual reason was that the course included material on sex hygiene and a study of marital relations. (It should be noted that the "economy" excuse did not affect any other courses in the department; apparently the facts of life, sexual and economic, could be dispensed with most easily at Syracuse.)

To accompany this setting, one cannot ignore the flagrant symptoms of race prejudice which Mr. Abraham, to his misfortune, opposed. One of its leading exponents was the Dean of Women. It is customary each year for the girls to elect senior guides for the incoming freshmen. On one lamentable occasion, however, an Italian girl and a Jewess were chosen for the posts—whereupon the Dean gently relieved them of their tasks.

When all else failed, there was devised at Syracuse one seemingly invulnerable weapon for the suppression of dissenters. This weapon has been accurately described by students as a yellow-dog contract; under its provisions every student is forced to agree to accept dismissal without submission of charges or a hearing in his defense.*

In 1934-35 *The Syracuse Daily Orange* was edited by an outspoken, courageous student, Marvin Wahl. Previously it had been readily controlled by the university and subservient to all dictates from above. Apparently unwilling to risk the furor of a dismissal, the university launched a program which should prevent such a situation in the future. An electoral board for Campus publications was set up, composed of five students and three faculty members; it was stipulated, however, that a majority of each group was necessary for election. Wahl wrote to me: "This has been aptly termed 'polite censorship'—but it's not so polite at that. There is an unmistakable trend to censor all published matter on the campus and it will not be long before it has taken complete hold."

The Administration has its allies. When, in April, 1934, the Social Problems Club, as the Liberal Club had done three years before, appealed for recognition from the Men's Student Senate, the plea was voted down, 5-2. Leading the fight against recognition was Benjamin Moses, who repeatedly announced that the vice-chancellor did not favor the club. The others gave equal evidence of the source of their decision. As the student newspaper pointed out, the Senate was now ready to do the unpleasant work for the chancellor's office, to serve as "the agent to repress radicalism" on the campus.

---

* This statute was upheld by the courts in the case of Syracuse vs. Anthony.

Somewhere there is a reward for such devout loyalty to the men upstairs.

The Trustees have manifested no uneasiness over this history of repression. Comprised exclusively of financiers, industrialists, manufacturers and corporation lawyers—including Nathan Miller, general counsel for U. S. Steel—the board has beamed with approval at the antics of its chancellor. "Controversial questions" are better left unspoken, they ardently believe—and the chancellor is a practical man.

The anti-war strike of 1935 found Dr. Flint in a quandary. A year before he had no uncertainty of his stand; the student newspaper was prevented from publishing any news about the meeting and a few other devices of a similar nature were introduced. On the eve of the second walkout, however, his church expressed sympathy for the event; the struggle between conscience and repression must have been long and painful. It was finally resolved by a statement of personal disagreement with the strike, but by abstention from any direct interference.

Writing of his Alma Mater, one student observes: "The continuous duress, tacit and direct, under which student and faculty live, the breaches of faith and contract, the discriminations, especially on the part of the Dean of Women against 'non-Aryans,' non-sorority women, etc., and the spy-system of student stool-pigeons, all take their toll of academic freedom. . . . The Trustees call the tune, the Administrative officials are the fiddles and it now remains to be answered—will the students dance?"

Surrounded by these souvenirs of the past, having given adequate warning for the future, Dr. Flint strode to the rostrum on Commencement Day in 1935 to speak of the untrammeled quest for Truth. In distant corners of the land there were hundreds of men and women, victims of his regime, who read the text of his address and pondered the eternal art of self-deception. Others, less charitable, used more descriptive epithets. The students who sat before him that day must have remarked that the old boy had an infinite capacity for invention.

When the Ku Klux Klan was at the height of its power, Ohio was one of the major centers of its exploits. The Klan has dwindled, its adherents have fled, but within the halls of Ohio State University certain of its basic precepts have gone marching on.

In 1926 the state legislature scented radicalism at the university and since that time there has been a deep "legislature-consciousness" on the campus. Everyone treads lightly; a misstep may offend the president, or it may injure the Trustees or it may rouse the state capitol where funds are dispersed. About ten years ago, Dr. W. O. Thompson, President Rightmire's predecessor in the stewardship at the institution, set forth its philosophy without adornment. Addressing the incoming freshmen, he admonished them: "The best thing to do is to do what you are told."

Wesley Maurer was a member of the Ohio State faculty in 1928; he wrote an article for a local paper in which he dwelt favorably upon the strike of coal miners. With the appearance of the article, Mr. Maurer had terminated his usefulness to the school.

It was not until about two years later, however, that a rapid sequence of events demonstrated even more plainly the fear which gripped the university. Over a long period of time, student resentment against compulsory military training had been growing; the proportions which this feeling had attained were indicated in a poll of the undergraduate body where the unpopularity of the colonels reached new levels. Finally, in 1931, the matter came to a head; there were rumblings of a strike in the drill corps, student protest meetings and a host of other symptoms of unrest. At this juncture the Trustees convened to renew their faith in military training of the compulsory brand. Simultaneously a meeting of the faculty was held at which President Rightmire made his own

213

position equally clear. He indicated that anyone, student or faculty member, was free to depart if he didn't like the conduct of the university.

But the discontent did not evaporate. So, on May 22, 1931, we find him lashing out against the dissenters in a lengthy statement to *The Columbus Despatch*, conservative journal linked by financial ties to the Board of Trustees:

". . . The University through its sixty years of existence has been remarkably free from ill-considered or socially destructive agitation with which the world outside has sometimes been disturbed. . . . The University has been a wholesome, socially constructive and sound educational force in the life of the state. . . . Recently, however, certain students have come forth as critics of University policies and departments and various members of its personnel; this they have done . . . with an enthusiasm born of half-knowledge, adolescent judgment, lack of experience. . . . It is current report over the state that some members of the teaching staff have encouraged students to give expression to their hastily formed views and have failed to exert the sane and wholesome influence on students which members of the faculty have a right to exercise."

Three days later an Associated Press despatch from Columbus carried the brief announcement:

"Professor Herbert A Miller will be dropped from the Faculty of Ohio State University next year. The University announced failure to renew his contract today."

At first it appeared that Professor Miller's ardent championing of the student campaign against drill had called forth his ouster. This was unquestionably part of the reason. But there were other fields, too, in which he had violated the tenets of Ku Kluxism. Three matters seemed to have accelerated his downfall.

1. Professor Miller was a sociologist—and an eminently distinguished one. On various occasions he examined critically the origins and effects of race prejudice, particularly in regard to Jews and Negroes, and severely questioned the espousal of race purity shibboleths. This phase of his teaching was obviously and avowedly a source of dissatisfaction to the Trustees, who announced that their feelings were based upon the complaints of the public.

2. In the course of a world tour, Professor Miller visited Korea, a conquered nation held in subjugation by Japan. There he was invited to deliver an address before a group of Ohio State graduates and other Americans. It was first necessary to obtain permission from the Japanese police for the meeting; they granted it and also despatched five of their representatives to sit in on his remarks. His lecture was devoted to a review of conditions in Europe; when he remarked that "Czecho-slovakia is now a republic and doing well," the police abruptly halted him and adjourned the meeting. They had decided that the reference was seditious—and in Korea that was probably true!

3. The Bombay incident was almost equally fantastic, although his Trustees were later to approach it with dread seriousness. On the same trip Professor Miller attended a meeting at which Gandhi was present. After repeated invitations to speak, he felt that it would have been impolite for him to refuse—and he thereupon delivered an address of one hundred words. It was for this speech that the Trustees accused him of "inciting the natives to civil disobedience." Fortunately, he had preserved a copy of his remarks—which were somewhat, but not seriously, garbled by the press. He had told the audience:

"I do not think it is appropriate for an American to speak at this time. I am simply the sort of professor who

215

is interested in learning how people try to solve their problems. India has been experimenting with religion for five thousand years and all the world is watching to see how she applies religion to the solution of her internal and external problems."

And this highly inflammatory address was one of the reasons tendered by the Ohio State Trustees for the dismissal of one of the country's leading sociologists.

But there can be no question that the race question was of even greater import. The Trustees had asserted their own position before by denying fellowship status to Negro students whose stipend was offered by the Urban League. Once Professor Miller took his classes to visit a Negro college, causing a Trustee to observe: "He made his students dance with niggers." *

Added to his defense of the student position on drill, these episodes had branded him an enemy to the Ku-Kluxers on Ohio's Board of Trustees. Among these Julius F. Stone is the dominant figure, and the A.A.U.P. furnishes the following description of him: "Notable for his interest in, and support of the natural and physical sciences; and equally notable for his prejudices in social matters."

In answer to their critics, the Trustees have inadvertently disclosed just how supreme is their domination over the university. On one occasion, speaking of their responsibilities to the people of the state, the Board said that "the final determination of these responsibilities is imposed by statute upon the Board of Trustees." During the dispute over military training, its manifestos were even more vehement. To those who cherish the illusion of democratic control in our universities, the following paragraph should be enlightening:

"The Board feels that the University should not be subjected to emotional criticism because of the unripe

* From the findings of the American Association of University Professors.

vociferations of a small group of students and a very few members of the faculty who were under no compulsion to come here and are under none to remain unless they can subscribe to the fundamental purposes of the University."

Further, the Board has clearly set forth its own views about the freedom of teaching. "Members of the faculty of Ohio State University have enjoyed and now enjoy wide latitude in expressing their opinions *in the classroom.*" (Emphasis mine.)

Despite their resentment at outside activity, there is no record that the Trustees ever penalized or admonished Dean C. O. Ruggles of their own School of Commerce for his valiant service to the public utility corporations. He received the modest sum of $15,000 a year for conducting the celebrated "Ruggles Survey" to determine the treatment which the utilities were receiving in text-books and class instruction. To perform this task he took a year's leave of absence from the university.

Considering the pre-eminence which Mr. Stone assumed among his colleagues in the resolution of these affairs, his affiliations are worth exploring. They are: President, Columbus-McKinnon Chain Co.; Chairman of the Seagrave Corporation; Director of the Ohio National Bank; Director of Mahoning Coal Railroad. The assets of these corporate entities come to about one hundred million dollars—and they are interlocked with scores of even more important companies.

Professor Miller's departure had precipitated a storm of protest; but, with the blunt threats of the Administration, even that subsided. It was not until 1934 that another flagrant expression of reaction emerged when, as cited elsewhere, seven pacifists were ousted from the university for refusing compulsory drill.

And in 1935 President Rightmire threatened expulsion against students who took part in a meeting in behalf of the

217

imprisoned Scottsboro boys. A few hours before the assemblage he had withdrawn the permit for the demonstration; it is a tragic irony that this was done on the anniversary of the birth of Abraham Lincoln.

Despite his orders, more than 500 undergraduates gathered on the steps of the Commerce Building to carry through their plans. It was a notable lesson in united action. Confronted by so large a throng, not even Dr. George W. Rightmire could wield the traditional axe. He knew, as did Mr. Stone, that you can't expel 500 students.

To visualize the conditions which prevail there, one need only read the moderate, subdued report of the A.A.U.P. in the case of Dr. Miller:

> "The location of Ohio State at Columbus is a material handicap. . . . The city does not exhibit true metropolitan toleration, or perhaps indifference, toward the University, and within it there seems to occur rather rapid growth and strong expression of group opinion. With trustees appointed by the governor, with three trustees out of seven resident in the city, constantly under the eye of the legislature to which it must apply for its support, the University experiences difficulty in maintaining . . . detachment from political influences. . . ."

Upon his dismissal, Professor Miller wrote that he could see no other explanation than the "animosity" of Mr. Stone "related to the political and financial interests with which he is connected." That reign has not been broken. Only recently the Alumni secretary has been crying for the removal of the remaining liberal professors and student groups. If the Trustees have their way, and if they are able to forget the wrath engendered throughout the nation by their earlier moves, his wishes may be heeded.

Down in the little town of Berea, Kentucky, there is a college whose fame has certainly never transcended the borders of the state. In a hundred places scattered throughout the country its replicas can be found, serene and untroubled to the casual observer, yet always conscious of the overhanging fist of conformism.

The college is proud of itself. In their expansive advertisements, the overseers depict Berea with phrases such as "the silent, resistless appeal of thousands of mountain girls and boys." When a financial drive is being carried on, the institution heralds its Christianity—and Christianity at Berea means: 1. No smoking. 2. No drinking. 3. No meeting of the opposite sexes in private places.

About 650 students are enrolled there, few of whom are wealthy, most having chosen Berea for their education solely because they cannot afford to go elsewhere. Whatever else one may say about it, Berea is inexpensive. A student can attend there at a cost of never more than $160 a year—and that includes everything from board to instruction to incidental expenditures.

What hope has there ever been for student curiosity? What rights as a citizen and as a person does the teacher or student possess? The answer, almost without reservation, is, none. And it has always been that way. In all the letters which I received from undergraduates, I obtained no more unequivocal reply than from a young man at Berea in regard to the status of freedom. Quite simply he said, "There certainly has never been any student freedom or liberty in Berea." His charge continues:

"Visitors staying half a day at Boone Tavern write home about the venerable holiness of the place; visitors staying half a week might give their blessings to the school if supervised by the proper representatives. But those who poke around the Campus for more than half a year find things strangely different from the Berea of which they read in the advertising news stories."

President Hutchins has quite unequivocally stated his position. There is no place in the institution for a Communist. But the taboos cover far more than the extreme left wing. What happened to Berea's Christianity when a strike broke out in the neighborhood?

Under the terms of codes formulated for the industry, coal miners at Sand Gap had conducted an election of check-weighmen because they felt that they were being viciously cheated of their returns. Hardly had the election taken place when the operator fired all the men who had voted—virtually all of the seventy miners employed. To complete his revenge, the operator drafted a black-list and sent it around the district, thus insuring that the men would not obtain other posts.

These miners were unorganized; they were unskilled in tactics and procedure; they knew only that they were being robbed and sought to rectify the situation. When they suddenly found themselves without jobs, they realized that they had nowhere to turn, for the local code administrator, who was in charge of the code which they believed would be their salvation, proved to be the same Mr. Scrivner who was co-operator of the plant! And to add to their plight, the mine inspector was a man named Daniels, who was generally known to be in the pay of the owner of the mine. Election of a check-weighman would hardly appear an inexcusable crime; it was, in fact, nothing more than the exercise of a legal right; considering that Ronald Scrivner, a son of the operator, had been weighing up till then with the weights running from 100 to 500 pounds short on a load of coal of 2,800, their attempt would appear eminently justified. To which Mr. Moore, the other operator, quietly replied: "I've got my money in this mine and I'm going to run it as I please." He accompanied this declaration with recommendations to the neighboring grocers not to give the men any food on credit. The network was complete.

Apprised of these developments, a group of students at

Berea interested themselves in the case. An article containing the essential facts outlined above was submitted to the college paper—without any results. An editorial on the same theme was prepared. Again it did not appear. Letters, news items, a barrage of material were sent in—to no avail. The student newspaper at Berea never stirred from beneath President Hutchins' thumb. And from his sanctum had come the decree that no data relating to the strike was to be published. Why? Partly because the coal operators were influential in the community; further because the coal company did too much business with the heat and power plant of the college and, indirectly, with the Boone Tavern Garage, which is owned by the college. Had the college wanted to, it could have compelled a showdown, since its contracts were, theoretically, broken by the operators' violation of the codes. Berea preferred to ignore the incident. So acute was the fear of the Administration that faculty members and college workers did not dare to take students to the mines to study the situation and to provide aid.

Such was Christianity, 1935 model, in the little college of Berea, Kentucky.

In the same year a group of students formed The Vanguards, including several followers of the League for Industrial Democracy, one follower of the National Student League and a group of independents. It narrowly survived and now lives a half-legal existence through some unexpected support from a few faculty and administrative members. Three days after its formation, the Dean of Men, T. A. Hendricks, revived an old statute barring political organizations from the campus. He may yet succeed in disbanding The Vanguards.

One might anticipate that a Christian institution would have granted full freedom to the peace strike. Instead, it converted the strike into a "protest assembly"; the program was strictly subject to the veto of the president, and an outdoor demonstration was banned because it would be "futile, noisy, and would ruin the grass." The Dean said that if he had been on the campus at the time, no "fool demonstration" would have been held at all. An undergraduate comments:

"Berea is, candidly, a fraud. It flings such phrases as 'the glorious ideals of goodness' before the faces of men with fortunes or of women with a few extra dollars. . . . And they, to expiate their souls, give to bring the mountains into the Kingdom of God. Meanwhile the college uses 'tolerance' and 'freedom' and 'Christianity' in speeches in other states or in press releases. They are never applied to the students; they exist only for public consumption."

Before a speaker can appear at Berea, he must have the approval of the administration; before a club can be formed a similar sanction must be obtained. And this, I have said, is no recent application of Christian principles, but has always prevailed since the first Berea man began to inquire about the world beyond. Thus has the college fortified itself against those who might favor literal adaptation of the Sermon on the Mount to the conduct of the coal operators in Sand Gap— or anywhere else.

If you travel across the country, you will run into scores of such hamlets, standing at the wayside and warning outside ideas to keep their distance. They have long been guarding the fortress at Berea and their vigilance will only intensify in the coming months. For the student body, almost uniformly oppressed by economic crisis, struggling desperately to remain above the surface, is becoming increasingly conscious of its plight. It will be a bitter test for the apostles of Christianity when they are again called to intervene.

III. "Red Scare"

TRUSTEE-ADMINISTRATIVE domination has been of long duration, merely varying in intensity. It is equally evident that this domination became more pronounced as world-wide disorder projected basic issues of social organization into the range of men's thoughts. In 1934 the reign of orthodoxy was reenforced by the determined intervention of pressure-groups possessing no official affiliation to the universities. Of these the Hearst Press, the American Legion and the Daughters of the American Revolution were the vanguard. Certainly their presence had been felt before. They have never been content to leave education to educators—any more than have the Trustees. No phase of their efforts, however, was equivalent to the Red Scare which began on a large plane late in 1934 and has grown progressively more acute since then.

Their antics cannot be disassociated from the setting in which they occur. In the past six years an increasing number of human beings have started to question a social system fraught with palpable distress and incongruity; the possibility of deep-seated reform has ceased to be a whimsical speculation. This loss of faith in the present structure could not have failed to be discernible to those steadfastly attached to things exactly as they are. To prevent the maturation of any critical inquiry, the defenders of the system invoke a method common to every era of impending social change. When the issue of slavery agitated this country, Benjamin Hedrick was a professor at the University of North Carolina. Fremont announced his candidacy on an anti-slavery program in 1856; Hedrick was one of that handful of Southerners to support him. Whereupon *The North Carolina Standard*, edited by W. W. Holden, a leader of the pro-slavery interests, began to campaign for his ouster from the university, declaring: "Let our schools and seminaries of learning be scrutinized; and if Black Republicans be found in them, let them be driven out. That man is neither a safe nor a fit instructor of our young men who even inclines to Fremont and Republicanism."

An alumnus of the University exclaimed: "Upon what

ground can a Southern instructor, relying for his support upon Southern money, selected to impart healthy instruction to the sons of slave-owners and indebted for his education to a Southern State, excuse his support of Fremont?"

The Trustees of the institution denounced Hedrick as a "stirrer-up of the poor against the rich," and throughout the South the cry for his dismissal spread. Despite a vigorous and uncompromising defense, the youthful professor was dismissed. The Trustees explained that he "had violated the established usage of the university" by "becoming an agitator in the existing politics of the day"; they did not reveal why hundreds of other professors throughout the territory could write apologies for the slavery system without any reprisals for partisan politics.

That is a model for the Red Scare of 1935. When one realizes how assiduously the universities themselves have resisted the idea of social realignment, when one contemplates the rigid rule of a Trustee-ridden set-up, the need for external aid seems remote.

But our Bourbons do not propose to assume any risks. There is no secret about the origin and design of their onslaught, nor can its weight be minimized. The Red Scare directed against the faculties was the first major stride of a deliberate, nationwide campaign.

It was at Syracuse University, in November, 1934, that the attack was first visible. Recalling the adept, ironclad régime of Chancellor Flint, the aid of the patriots would hardly have seemed imperative. Yet a beginning had to be made, and Syracuse seemed as strategic a place as any other.

The Syracuse Journal, on November 22, 1934, carried scare headlines:

DRIVE ALL RADICAL PROFESSORS AND STUDENTS FROM THE UNIVERSITY

Under this appeared a two-column editorial:

"The great champion of genuine Americanism, Mr. W. R. Hearst, recently wired the editor of this paper as follows:

"Please support the actions of the universities in throwing out those communists and say, furthermore, that they ought to be thrown out of the country."

Continuing in this vein, the editorial revealed how a Hearst reporter had "exposed" Professor John Washburne, head of the educational psychology department at Syracuse. Lest Professor Washburne be "shy of making direct statement," Mr. Hearst had resorted to an expedient. Two young reporters were told to represent themselves as students and, in that guise, to interview the Professor. They were to tell him that they were communists planning to visit Russia the following Summer; that in the meanwhile they wanted to take a course "along communist lines" at Syracuse, and that they were "extreme radicals" with an irresistible desire to overthrow the government. To pave the way for an interview, the following letter was despatched to Professor Washburne:

"Dear Professor Washburne:

"I have been thinking about going to Columbia but a friend of mine in Syracuse says Syracuse is nearer and I can get good courses in sociology at Syracuse.

"Down at Columbia they give you the real stuff about capitalism and socialism but my friend says I can get the same thing at Syracuse, that you are a liberal and not afraid to give the liberal side that the university here does not give.

"Please tell me when I could come to Syracuse and see you about attending college there. Also, do they have any liberal clubs there where students can get the truth about things and can students get into the communist clubs. . . .

Respectfully yours,
(signed) Dick Smith."

And in its editorial *The Journal* published the alleged text of the subsequent conversation between Professor Washburne and the two supposed students. Among the statements attributed to him were:

". . . Here is another course, Political Science III. THESE WOULD BE GOOD AND ONE CONDUCTED BY PROFESSOR BEYLE WHO IS VERY LIBERAL INDEED, WOULD BE OF ESPECIAL VALUE. . . .
OH YES, SYRACUSE HAS FOR YEARS BEEN ONE OF THE MOST LIBERAL COLLEGES IN THE COUNTRY. . . .
(Asked about his political beliefs, Professor Washburne was then alleged to have said—
I AM A LEFT-WING SOCIALIST. . . .
I WAS VERY ACTIVE ON THE PACIFIC COAST WITH THE I.W.W. DURING THE WAR. . . .
(Finally, in reference to governmental change, the following dialogue was published):
SMITH: DO YOU THINK THERE COULD BE A REVOLUTION IN THIS COUNTRY WITHOUT BLOODSHED?
WASHBURNE: NO. WE ARE NOT READY FOR A REVOLUTION NOW. WE MUST FIRST HAVE PEOPLE WHO WILL ACT AND NOT SIT BACK AND WAIT FOR THINGS TO HAPPEN. . ." *

The report, which wended its way through several columns, studded with large letters and exclamation points, was almost exclusively the fabrication of the writers. Hearst had stooped to falsehood before—and this was falsehood on the grand scale. Two witnesses to the conversations later made out the following affidavit:

* Capitalization is as in original.

I was present during all of the interview. . . . Nothing was said about the overthrow of the U. S. government. . . .

The rest of the account was equally mythical. It had quoted the Professor as saying that he was closely affiliated with the I.W.W. on the Pacific coast during the world war; the fact is that he had not the remotest connection with that organization, and during the entire period of the war, was thousands of miles away from the Coast serving the army. He was described as stating the Constitution was "meaningless"; in reality he had said he wished it were more strictly enforced—especially the Bill of Rights. The story claimed that he had refrained from joining the Communist party only through "caution"; actually he had told the reporter he was unsympathetic to the communist position on several crucial issues. These were only three outstanding items on which the report was made of utter lies or distortions. The same could be said of almost every sentence which appeared. The object was to put Professor Washburne "on the spot"; if that could not be done by truth, then the underlings of Hearst's battalion would have to invent. They did—and *The Journal* spread their delusions over the front page as an exposé.

Nor was Professor Washburne alone the victim. Other professors were interviewed, and similar innuendoes were transmitted to the scare headlines of the newspaper. In this they had the plaudits of the patriots. On November 24th *The Journal* carried this item:

"Keen interest aroused throughout central New York by frank discussion in *The Journal* of communistic tendencies among Syracuse University students and faculty members brought wide approval today from leaders of various Syracuse patriotic societies."

It quoted statements from the commander of the American Legion post and from a member of the local American Legion Auxiliary. Two days later the paper urged the Trustees to examine eight professors at the institution for "Red" leanings.

Finally, Hearst emissaries invoked another weapon of 100 per-centism—old-fashioned bribery. The editor of the student newspaper was offered remuneration if he would publish an article favorable to *The Journal*. He replied by vigorously condemning the whole campaign.

Meanwhile, Hearst's hired men in New York were inaugurating the drive in their own territory.

In his mail on December 14th, Professor George S. Counts of Teachers College received the following letter:

Dear Dr. Counts:

I am thinking of entering Teachers College at the next term.

Several friends and former instructors have told me that I can get the real stuff about Capitalism, socialism and communism there. They tell me that you and several of your associates are real liberals and not afraid to give the liberal side on subjects in your classes.

That is something I have not been able to get in State universities.

I hope you can give me a few minutes time soon to outline a study program and help me decide what instructors and classes to seek.

Also are there any liberal, or even forthright communist organizations or clubs at the college that I might join for open discussion?

Sincerely yours,

———

(The reporter preferred not to have his name used and is hereafter referred to as Mr. X.)

228

Sensing that this was a replica of the Syracuse affair, of which he had been apprised, Dr. Counts replied that he would not be able to grant an interview until after the Christmas vacation. In the interim two reporters visited Clyde Miller, head of the Bureau of Educational Service at the institution. Despatched by the local Hearst press, they did not endeavor to conceal their mission. They wanted to know about so-called liberal and radical activities. In the course of the interview Mr. Miller ascertained that one of them had written the letter to Dr. Counts; he thereupon arranged for Dr. Counts to see him the following morning.

Their meeting took place as scheduled. It was an extraordinary revelation of the degradation imposed upon Hearst employees and, more pertinent to this inquiry, the real nature and aim of the Hearst campaign. For the reporter did not seek to hide anything; he hated his job, he despised the man he worked for and scorned the assignment he had received. The conversation was taken down verbatim by a stenographer, present throughout the interview. From her notes the following dialogue is gleaned:

"Mr. X. began by apologizing for his letter . . . written in compliance with instructions from the city desk. Said he was a newspaperman and that this was his way of earning a livelihood. Decided after writing the letter, however, to call on Dr. Counts as a newspaperman rather than under false pretenses. He went on to explain the reason for the above instructions from the city desk. 'Mr. Hearst,' he said, 'is engaged at present in conducting a Red Scare.' Said the idea of extricating information from alleged liberal and radical institutions, organizations and individuals, by means of a letter similar to the one written, belongs to Mr. Hearst."

After discussing Dr. Counts' opinions on social change and related matters, the conversation shifted to student activities:

"Mr. X.: . . . How about social and political demonstrations on the part of students in universities?

Dr. Counts: I think such demonstrations are desirable.

Mr. X.: So do I.

Dr. Counts: I favor permitting students to participate in any demonstration they wish. I think one of the hopeful things is that college students are beginning to think about something besides football and fraternities. Although Mr. Hearst need not be alarmed; college students for the most part are still engrossed in these childish interests. . . . It is unfortunate that there are not more student demonstrations with regard to social and political matters. If the students will not become interested in these matters, the country is certain to drift into catastrophe."

Following a few brief references to conditions in the Soviet Union, Dr. Counts asked:

"When will you prepare your article?

Mr. X.: It will probably be a series of articles, beginning next Monday, taking different institutions in turn.

Dr. Counts: I suppose it would be violating Mr. Hearst's standards of ethics if you let me see a copy of your article before it is printed.

Mr. X.: Yes, it would be, but I will see what I can do.

Dr. Counts: I have no objection to a statement appearing in the press, provided it is a truthful one, or at least relatively truthful.

Mr. X.: You realize of course that because of my assignment, I will have to select the most sensational statements from the interview in order to make out a good case. That is what Mr. Hearst is expecting."

Having concluded the interview, the reporter then went to see Professor William Kilpatrick, another celebrated liberal. They discussed the same matters, on which Professor Kilpatrick, too, had often expressed himself publicly. Then the Professor assumed the offensive.

"Dr. Kilpatrick: . . . Don't you feel ashamed to come and talk to me this way?

Mr. X.: I'm not ashamed for myself but for the situation that makes it necessary for me to do this in order to keep alive.

Dr. Kilpatrick: Wouldn't it be a tremendous relief to you if that whole situation could be got rid of?

Mr. X.: . . . I know it. But after all I have had periods of being out of work. . . . I wouldn't like working in a slaughter-house either, but if that was the only work open, I would probably do it. There's very little choice.

Dr. Kilpatrick: I could do that with a clear conscience."

Shortly afterwards the reporters admitted to Mr. Miller that a host of similar "investigations" were to be waged at colleges throughout the country with a series of about a dozen articles in prospect on the outcome of the "research."

The previous Thanksgiving Day, Sidney Hook, a philosophy professor at New York University, had received a visit from another hireling of *The New York American*. Having been a former student in the professor's classes, the reporter did not conceal his intent. He told him that a drive against radicalism of every hue was in progress and that, as a member of a small, left-wing group Professor Hook seemed a notable exhibit. Expressing similar sentiments to those which Professor Counts had heard, the reporter confessed his dislike for the assignment and warned that the published story would be replete with distortions. It was. One week later *The American* carried a "sensational exposé" about the

231

"merger of two groups, so radical that even the communists have always refused to have anything at all to do with them." Again the material was abundant with lies. It invented a special post of national organizer in the party for Professor Hook. It "revealed" that another N.Y.U. professor, James Burnham, had been elected to a post of equal prominence. It deliberately misquoted what Professor Hook had said about the aims and procedure of the party. And on December 25th an inflammatory editorial appeared, declaring:

"Well! Gentlemen of the faculty of New York University, trustees, alumni, students and everyone else who is a friend of New York University and proud of its history—if the alleged actions of these two professors have been correctly reported, what do you say about it? WHAT DO YOU PROPOSE TO DO ABOUT IT? Is this old and respected institution of learning to be classified hereafter as a seeding-ground for disloyalty to America and its cherished institutions—as an active center of treasonable plotting for the overthrow of the American government?

But Mr. Hearst's "exposé" of Teachers College did not appear. Two days before the date on which, as the reporter told Dr. Counts, the material was to be published, a vigorous counter-blast emerged from leaders of the progressive educational world. Led by Professors Counts, Kilpatrick and, among others, Charles A. Beard and John Dewey, a statement was issued outlining the conversation with the reporters and details of the "frame-up." Accompanying the disclosure was an appeal to the Dickstein-McCormack committee, allegedly investigating un-American activities, to probe Mr. Hearst's attempt to "Hitlerize education." *

* It should be noted that the committee, arduous in its pursuit of "Reds," ignored the appeal.

Although the Teachers College "revelations" were, for obvious reasons, never published, the hysteria did not relax. Headlines screamed over editorials: "Communist Professors Tell It to Congress." Most frequent target of the assault was Professor Counts, menacingly described as "Red Russia's apostle." Seldom did a day pass without a tid-bit, ranging from the personal vituperations of Mr. Hearst to commendatory agreement from that other great crusader, Billy Sunday.

Out at Chicago Professor Frederick L. Schumann became the next object of pursuit by the enterprising subordinates of the San Simeon monarch. Dr. Schumann's troubles were of long standing, tracing back to that day in November, 1934, when he had dared to address an assemblage of the Student Union Against War and Fascism at the University of Chicago. Attending the session was an agile reporter who knew what the office wanted. Without any zealous regard for accuracy or truth, he proceeded to pound out his own version of the Professor's remarks.

When Dr. Schumann picked up Hearst's *Herald-Examiner* on November 14, he encountered the full force of the distortion. He was quoted as saying things which he had never said; he was reported, with equal facility, as implying things which he had never contemplated. Bewildered and angered, he proceeded to write a letter to the local editor protesting the mistreatment of his remarks. He also decided to utilize the letter for what he knew to be another grievous inaccuracy in the paper—and this act, he was to discover, was a declaration of war.

For many weeks the Hearst press had been publishing, at the top of its editorial page, a series of alleged quotations from the works of Lenin. These selections, of course, were to illustrate the sadism, insanity and perversion of the communists and their doctrine. Sensing that the quotations were fantastic distortions, Professor Schumann had looked them

233

up in the pages to which they were attributed. They could not be found anywhere in Lenin. A Hearst editorial writer had written them.

Professor Schumann suggested this suspicion in his letter, recommending that the editor check up on the documents. For this solicitude he was soon rewarded with a visit from Charles Wheeler of the *Herald-Examiner*, sent by his chief to "investigate." Received, in the presence of a third person, he immediately drew forth a profusion of notes to prove that Professor Schumann had been "accidentally" misquoted— and succeeded in proving quite the reverse. He finally conceded the point. The discussion then shifted to the origin of the quotations from Lenin, and Mr. Wheeler again graciously acknowledged that they were pure fiction. Elaborating upon his confession—he seemed to be warming up to the task —Mr. Wheeler added:

"We just do what the old man orders. One week he orders a campaign against rats. The next week he orders a campaign against dope-peddlers. Pretty soon he's going to campaign against college professors. It's all the bunk, but orders are orders."

Meanwhile, the Hearst press had been carrying a series of Sunday features by Hitler's lieutenant Goering—blatant and unabashed eulogies of the Nazi regime. Shortly after this interview, Professor Schumann received a request from an anti-Nazi group in New York to prepare a series of answers to Goering's fabrications; the group had been told by a Hearst syndicate that such refutations would very likely be published. An authority on the history and policies of the Nazi government, Professor Schumann wrote two articles and submitted them. Both were rejected. They did not augment his prestige with the Hearst office.

In February, 1935, the opportunity for which the flag-wavers had been waiting arrived. In an address before the

234

Cook County League of Women Voters, Professor Schumann discussed "Communism and Liberalism," quoted with approval the Declaration of Independence and appealed for a new liberalism adequate to current exigencies. Seated prominently at the lecture was Mr. Charles Wheeler. And the next day *The Herald-Examiner* announced:

HOPE LIES IN SOVIETS, U. OF C. TEACHER SAYS

The article was filled with statements allegedly taken from his lecture—and actually the product of Mr. Wheeler's latest flight from reality. It is interesting to note that in the same issue there appeared a bitter editorial attack on a group of educators in which they were branded as "advisers to Moscow"; the victims of this denunciation were all men who had publicly criticized the Nazi regime.

One month later the Hearst press called for the dismissal of Professor Schumann from his post at Chicago, calling him one of "these American panderers and trap-baiters for the Moscow mafia." Its assertions were based upon two of Mr. Wheeler's misquotations and the claim that Professor Schumann had just written a book on Russia, which, incidentally, he hadn't. (Seven years before he had prepared a doctoral dissertation on "American Policy Toward Russia Since 1917.")

It was this clamor which helped to set the stage for a legislative inquiry into radicalism at the University of Chicago.*

The drive on professors wound its way around scores of campuses. Its effects, of course, were not instantaneous; they never are. And, as we have already indicated, the attack was so indiscriminate, often without any foundation at all, that administrative reprisals could hardly have been expected at once.

* The investigation will be discussed in the next chapter.

On the campus of Rensselaer Polytechnic Institute at Troy, N. Y., however, there was a real, live, communist professor. He had never concealed his sympathies. He wrote literary criticism for *The New Masses;* he supported communist candidates at election time; he did not hesitate to voice in print the convictions he had adopted. That man, Granville Hicks, was the first to be dismissed as a direct outcome of the Red Scare of 1935.

It was natural that he should be the first to go. His opinions could not be misconstrued; if, at Syracuse and Teachers College and Chicago, the red-hunters had been over-zealous, here was an open-and-shut case. They didn't have to "frame" him, they needed no reporters disguised as students to draw his opinions out, there were no fiery distortions required. Hicks was one of that ever-diminishing group—a Communist, open and avowed, on an American faculty.

Rensselaer is proud of its tradition: "The oldest institution of higher learning in any English-speaking country that has devoted itself continuously to instruction and research in engineering." Herbert Hoover is one of the more celebrated recipients of an honorary degree from the institution—and there has been a long, concerted attempt to secure his services as president of the Institute. Thus far he has held out.

This is a school of "practical learning" and it has never gone in for culture in a big way. Its graduates are supposed to march steadily and relentlessly from the campus into posts of eminence in large corporations; there, as one writer remarked, they bring glory to R.P.I. by utilizing "engineering methods tempered by sound business practice." Six years ago, however, the Trustees were prevailed upon to provide a measure of literacy with instruction in engineering. One of the departments formed as a result of this break with the past was in English, and to it was appointed Granville Hicks, a young Harvard graduate.

Nor was the step soon lamented. For Hicks did bring prominence to the Institute. He became esteemed throughout

236

the country as a literary critic; he wrote *The Great Tradition,* which received wide plaudits among his contemporaries; he swiftly won national repute as a scholar. These were accomplishments in a field heretofore barred to the advances of the Institute. Hicks was a bright boy, a credit to the school, a boon to the reputation of his head of department, Dr. Baker, for, after all, it was Dr. Baker who had "discovered" him.

Slowly, however, this scene began to change. Not that his classroom work differed; as Hicks later noted with some regret, only a handful of his students knew that he was a communist. Although he taught literature from a Marxist point of view, he steadfastly avoided Marxist terminology. He did not raise political issues and, if the students did, he treated them briefly. Moreover, he was a highly competent, distinguished teacher; with that there could be no question. At the end of the first year there he received a raise in salary; later he was prevailed upon to refuse an attractive offer from another college. But in 1932 he made the first public avowal of his position: he supported the communist candidate for president. From that time on his stand could not be mistaken.

Even this did not precipitate any difficulties for the next two years. Then one day he received an invitation from an anti-war committee at a neighboring high school to deliver an address; the principal had challenged the students to produce a speaker to present their views. He accepted. Whereupon the principal wrote the Board of Trustees charging that Hicks had tried to organize a communist society at the school and ought to be dismissed. When the latter explained the matter to the Trustees, they indicated that his position was satisfactory and agreed to drop the dispute.

The second incident occurred in the fall of 1935. Hicks had written a comprehensive article condemning the "Book Review" section of *The New York Times* for its flagrant anti-Soviet bias, describing in detail the methods which this had assumed. One morning he was summoned to the office of his head of department who told him that an influential alumnus had written to him protesting the article. Dr. Baker assured him that no censorship was implied; he merely wanted to indicate that a dissent had been registered. But the same afternoon he was called in again, this time for a conference in which Dr. Baker was joined by the late Palmer Ricketts, then head of the Institute. Director Ricketts did not mention the influential alumnus. He began by asking Hicks whether he felt a responsibility to the Institute. To which Hicks assented with two qualifications: first, that his responsibility ended when he left the campus; second, that he had certain obligations to himself as a critic. The interview was quite amiable. It ended with the following dialogue:

Director Ricketts asked Hicks about his political beliefs:

HICKS: I am a Communist.

DR. RICKETTS: What is a Communist?

Hicks tried briefly to explain.

DR. RICKETTS: You used to be a Socialist.

HICKS: Yes.

DR. RICKETTS: What is a Socialist?

Hicks again went into an explanation.

DR. RICKETTS: Do you think you'll ever become an anarchist?

HICKS: That's most unlikely.

DR. RICKETTS (smiling): Well, if you were to become an anarchist, would you throw a bomb at Dr. Baker?

Hicks promised immunity for Dr. Baker.

The same winter John Strachey had been threatened with deportation by red-hunting immigration officials; Hicks, along with professors at other schools, circulated petitions of protest. Two other faculty men signed them along with him and their names were released to the press. No direct mention of the incident was made to Hicks; but it was known that the other two had been reminded of their place in the world.

Rensselaer's stated policy is that men of the rank of assistant professors who have served three years or more are to be given a year's notice of non-renewal. But on May 13, 1935, Hicks received the following information:

"Facing the necessity for immediate retrenchment in the expenditures of the institute, the Prudential committee has decided not to renew your contract."

"Economy" is an age-old screen for the elimination of dissenters; R.P.I. did not have the courage to admit at once the real reason for the dismissal. Not until later did Acting President Jarrett break down and tell all.

It was absurdly clear, however, that "retrenchment" had not the remotest connection with the case. Under the terms of the dismissal, Hicks was to be paid half of his next year's salary; further, an instructor has been appointed to take his place. Together these two disbursements equalled $500 more than Hicks regular salary! Moreover, although economy was supposed to be the order of the day, Hicks was the only assistant professor ousted; as Dr. Jarrett later remarked, he could be sacrificed "most easily." In an interview * with a reporter, Dr. Jarrett was asked:

Has there been any other retrenchment?
DR. JARRETT: Of course.
REPORTER: Any other professors?
DR. JARRETT: Yes, professors.
REPORTER: Could you tell me who the other professors were?
MR. JARRETT (blinking): I don't know offhand. I'm sure there were other professors.

Meanwhile, the student newspaper at the Institute had spoken out boldly—too boldly for the quiet shades of R.P.I.

* An interview with Bruce Minton in *The New Masses*.

It had labelled the dismissal for what it was, a flagrant evidence of the "limitations" on academic freedom at the school:

"The administration's claim of retrenchment is an arrant smoke screen. Why pay Professor Hicks a half year advance salary as conscience money? If the necessity to decrease the teaching staff exists, why discharge the only really outstanding individual in the English department. . . . ?

"The students would much rather be stimulated by contact with him (Hicks) than to be put to sleep by the stupefying drivel so many of his colleagues hand out. Why penalize a man for having ideas? . . . This discrimination against Professor Hicks is a manifestation of the narrow conservatism that dictates the school policy. . . . The student at Rensselaer is being defrauded by being given a narrow and one-sided education."

Mr. Jarrett held his ground for a month; he declined any further explanation; he rejected repeated attempts by a committee of the American Civil Liberties Union to interview him. To every protest which poured into his office, to every demand for reinstatement of Hicks, Mr. Jarrett murmured the same words: "We must retrench."

But early in June hundreds of alumni returned for Commencement Exercises. They were well-to-do men from all over the country, products of the R.P.I. tradition, staunch advocates of individualism and "sound business practice." With them to bolster him, with their enthusiastic assent to soothe his feelings, Mr. Jarrett decided to drop the security of his previous position. He would fight the case on another ground—and make himself a hero in doing so.

It was a fortuitous occasion. The exercises marked the centennial observance of the conferring by R.P.I. of the first American college degrees in engineering and science. Bursting with the spirit of the day, Mr. Jarrett declaimed at a meeting of the Alumni Association, just prior to Commencement:

"The excess of academic freedom must be stigmatized as academic license. We adhere to an unwritten regulation of long standing that there shall be excluded from our classrooms all controversial discussion about politics, religion and sociology. Time devoted to such subjects when used to arouse or incite is, if we are to cling to our functions as an engineering school, lost time."

This was, of course, sheer irrelevance however revealing; no one had suggested that at any time did Hicks usurp classroom time for discussion outside the curriculum; students had willingly testified to Hicks' avoidance of extraneous issues. But the alumni applauded wildly. Mr. Jarrett beamed and continued:

"We were founded by a capitalist of the old days. We have developed under the capitalistic régime. The men we have sent forth and who have become industrial leaders have, in their generosity, and for the benefit of the youth of the country, richly endowed us. We have trained men eager to work under that system, full of confidence that the doctrine of rugged individualism is the doctrine which, supported by strong self-effort and self-sacrifice, fighting bravely the battle of legitimate competition will bring to them financial independence and protection from adversity. We are proud of those alumni and we are proud of their adherence to inexorable human laws. I think we should stand four-square to the world and declare our faith. . . ."

And, with a final, sweeping, overpowering flourish:

"If we are condemned as the last resort of conservatism, let us glory in it."

Roused by his address, the alumni, drawn from industrial and utility corporation boards throughout the country, passed

241

a resolution "endorsing emphatically the position of the Institute authorities."

Outside the Alumni meeting, a disconsolate and unhappy young man was distributing copies of a letter to the crowd as it emerged from the harmonious conclave. He was the editor of the student newspaper; the letter was an apology for the editorial defending Granville Hicks. It stated:

"The article was contributed, not by the Board of *Polytechnic*, but by a student completing his fellowship course who was not connected with the paper. The article should have appeared, if at all, under the caption, 'Letters to the Editor.' The *Polytechnic* has no desire to oppose the policies of the institute."

To insure that no such "accident" should again occur, the editor announced, according to *The Troy Times-Record* that, "with the assistance of Acting President Jarrett 'we have formulated a plan for making *The Polytechnic* what it should be.' The letter adds that the board has been reorganized."

R.P.I. had flirted with culture and now the honeymoon was over. As one writer observed, freedom of speech could again prevail within her secluded halls—because the only man with anything to say had been silenced.

IV. The Inquisition

THE witch-hunt was not confined to the editorial pages of the Hearst press or the isolated yelpings of American Legionnaires. It travelled swiftly to even more crucial centers: the state legislatures. The college administrator hangs upon the words of the law-makers, especially in state universities. On their decisions hinges the fate of his budget and the continued expansion of the educational apparatus. Let them begin to hack away at his funds and the disintegration of his institution is near.

The patriots knew it. They also knew that they had their friends in the State capitols, men who would bend to their dictates. Their next guns boomed in the legislative chambers, where earlier in the year a flood of loyalty-oath statutes had been enacted in half a dozen states. Under these laws students and professors were compelled to pledge their allegiance to the constitution. The intent was plain: the moment a man deviates from hundred-per-centism, out he goes for breaking his word. A similar drive had taken place immediately after the World War and its most typical results had been the Lusk laws in New York state. In the Lusk report of 1920, we find the classic statement of the purpose behind such legislation:

"No person who is not eager to combat the theories of social change should be entrusted with the task of fitting the young and old of this state for the responsibilities of citizenship."

In other words, a man must be not merely an ally of the status quo; he must be "eager to combat" any idea of revision. That was the ancient formula. And in 1934 it was revived on a nationwide scale. In state after state the Americanism lobby brought forth a loyalty bill; in many they were enacted by the legislature and signed by the governor, except where liberal pressure proved equal to the counter-attack. One of the most distinguished examples of this resistance was furnished in New York by students from colleges throughout the state. The previous summer the Ives law for teachers had been passed; now a bill providing a similar pledge for students was introduced. While the legislature was going through the motions of discussing it, however, a delegation of seventy-five Vassar girls appeared on the scene. They did not come for a "sociological investigation." They came to

243

protest the bill. Unaccustomed to such an intrusion, the senators were startled; they soon regained their composure sufficiently to pose for the cameramen. A few, of course, hit the front pages of the Hearst newspapers by denouncing the Bolshevik invaders. This delegation was not the end. Shortly afterward nearly 200 students from widely separated colleges convened at Albany for the same purpose. The senators ceased to laugh. They were, above all, politicians; they did what the Legion wanted because the Legion meant votes and so did Hearst. They liked their jobs, whatever they had to do to keep them. But here was a concerted demonstration from the other side; the students had families, friends; they represented a cross-section of the citizenry. With the tact to which a life of servility had so well nurtured them, the legislators shifted their ground. They killed the Nunan bill a few days later.

Although this was a decisive victory for the progressives, they did not fare so well elsewhere. By the spring of 1935, the patriots were clamoring for even more drastic measures. Having jammed through their loyalty bills, they now proceeded to press for direct investigations into specific schools. Thus began a remorseless inquisition whose ludicrousness and absurdities were matched only by the serious implications behind them. It found staunch advocates; throughout the country commissions sprang up to wage the war of righteousness. On April 21 the Associated Press could report:

"New steps to smoke out and turn back the alleged 'red menace' among college students were in the making today.

"Arguments by patriotic and civic groups . . . have attracted attention of legislators in half a dozen states.

"In Illinois a committee of five to investigate alleged Red activities in the State's schools of higher learning, is scheduled to be named tomorrow.

"Texas solons have before them a measure calling for

244

a similar inquiry. In Iowa and California anti-red bills centering around instruction in radical doctrines have been offered.

"Wisconsin's inquiry, already under way, will begin its third week tomorrow."

Down in Arkansas the State legislature had already concluded its performance, providing a dramatic preview for the more far-flung snooping.

Twelve miles from the diminutive community of Mena, Arkansas, stands a college which the interlocking directorate of American finance has never endowed. Even the respectable citizenry of Mena long ago repudiated any connection with it. Here you will be unable to find either over-zealous Trustees, keeping the vigil over the students' minds, or adolescent alumni, pining away for a triple-threat half-back. A man who assumes a teaching post at the institution does not automatically surrender his rights as a citizen; he is allowed, and expected, to speak his mind and to act when conviction so impels him. If the familiar hierarchy of careerists is strangely absent, so is the military caste disguised behind the letters R.O.T.C. and the superstructure of snobbery known as Fraternity Row.

Commonwealth is America's outstanding labor college. It has led an embattled, precarious existence for twelve years, confronted alternately by the spectres of reaction and bankruptcy. For the moment the former has the upper hand. Visiting the campus you will fail to discover anything comparable to Chancellor Bowman's Cathedral of Pittsburgh or the host of other monuments erected in our educational plants. All that awaits you is a drab series of twenty-seven wooden buildings. They are painful in their simplicity, unadorned with the conveniences of the modern country club. If you intend to stay in them, the school warns you to beware of rainy nights—the roofs leak! Whatever grandeur there is in this setting has been endowed by nature, not by Morgan.

245

There has been a cynical lament in our universities in recent years; its theme is that professors, for the first time in their lives, should be forced to go out and work for a living. At Commonwealth this has been literally realized. Situated on a 320-acre farm, the college raises virtually all of its own food; students and teachers work side by side at diverse industrial and communal tasks, the former contributing fifteen hours of labor per week and the latter, twenty. To augment their efforts, a group of resident workers is housed on the campus, giving its services in return for maintenance. Commonwealth today is almost exclusively the product of these people; they have built, preserved and extended its facilities by their own unpaid labor. To this have been added the small donations of people outside who are sympathetic to its endeavors. Contrast the 120-million-dollar endowment of Harvard University with the annual income of Commonwealth from its supporters—five thousand dollars. To the weary bursars of our established universities, this would be a restful retreat, a college whose most recent budget showed receipts of $9,537 and expenditures of $7,487.

If you are searching for Olympian impartiality, for self-styled pure learning, Commonwealth is not your destination. Its essential difference from established colleges in this respect is that its bias is avowed and unashamed, while theirs is shrouded in the platitudes earlier explored. There is, of course, another fundamental distinction. For Commonwealth's partisanship is not on the side of Wall Street-born-and-made Trustees. In its own announcement the nature of the school is set forth: "The training of young men and women for active service in some militant organization in the labor movement. . . . Its courses are taught from a point of view partisan to the working-class."

To the paid servants of the public utilities, of course, this will sound like propaganda of the most vicious form. They must at least acknowledge its simplicity. It is a far more frank declaration than our orthodox centers of culture will ever make.

Behind the inspiration of those who have founded and preserved Commonwealth has been one guiding conviction: that somewhere in this land there should be a college independent of the bountiful providers of endowments, free from the pandering required by those who donate the upkeep for education. Its founders envisaged a citadel where criticism of the status quo, piercing and bold insight into its machinery, might flourish. But more than that, they wanted one school where the sons and daughters of the underprivileged, those whose lives and interests are interwoven with the American labor movement, might receive preparation for the strenuous tasks of their time. Commonwealth's undergraduates did not train at Groton; some of them come from other colleges; many come direct from factories and farms and mines with not more than a public school diploma for their credentials. All that is required is some knowledge of and concern for the multiple events of this era—a requirement, incidentally, which hundreds of our venerated alumni could not fulfill. No extension system, with its horde of courses in advanced etiquette, has been built to reap the dollars of innocent culture-hunters. The curriculum deals primarily with the historical growth and expansion of the labor movement, its present-day ramifications in theory and tactics, its relationship to dynamic social forces. Upon graduation one does not head for a post in a banking firm; Commonwealth alumni return to a score of posts in the labor movement, organizing, writing, acting, editing labor journals, teaching and the host of other occupations so desperately in need of applicants.

Long ago was the shibboleth of equal opportunity in American higher learning destroyed. Commonwealth is one of the diminishing handful of places where a son of the working-class can obtain a measure of information so long the exclusive property of a limited number. Commonwealth has not easily survived. That it has gone on, in the face of adversity should

247

conceivably have aroused the admiration of those who hail courage, resourcefulness, persistence and believe that workers are entitled to some of the privileges now so grossly restricted. But the patriots and their stool-pigeons, the snoopers of the American Legion and the intricate financial network behind them pay only lip-service to the credo. They become particularly distraught when students and teachers emerge from the classroom to take a hand in the struggle of human beings for a decent life. That was the inspiration behind the witch-hunt at Commonwealth.

In the last months of 1934 the Southern Tenant Farmers Union began to make startling headway among the sharecroppers in Arkansas. To visualize its progress one must understand the history of serfdom which had gone before. For the people of the territory, those who work the fields for absentee owners, are among the most oppressed of the earth. They have lived for years on bare subsistence, without hope, without certainty, racked by disease and hunger and the thousand other ills which such men and women are heir to. Every description of the scene draws the same parallel—China; nowhere else, it is claimed, can equal degradation be found.

The share-croppers had one hour of revival, one interval in which they believed the Messiah, of whom they had heard so much, seemed to have come. That was the time of the advent of Roosevelt and the Agricultural Adjustment Administration. They were assured of salvation—or the closest to it for which they dared hope. But there was rapid disillusion awaiting. Where were the funds doled out by the A.A.A.? Where were the payments for crop-reduction? To the share-croppers' dismay, these sums trickled miraculously into the usual channels, toward the pocketbooks of the planters. There could be no mistake about it. If they still retained faith, the launching of evictions dispelled the final remnants. For with each passing day scores of them were unceremoniously dumped out of their homes, left to wander the countryside. Mementos of the period were graphically displayed on the roads—the half-starved shadows of men, women and children.

But give a man hope, just one moment of hope, and much of the lethargy and the quiet acceptance disappears even when that hope has faded. It happened in Arkansas. With increasing swiftness, unrest spread throughout the territory, crystallizing in the Southern Tenant Farmers Union, and the absentee rulers did not fail to observe what was taking place. In this growing, fearless union Negroes and whites stood side by side, bound together by the ties of misery and slavery. The planters were quick to sense the danger. They saw unemployed workers spontaneously rallying together—workers who for years had gnawed upon their discontent in silence. A struggle was brewing and the planters prepared to head it off.

It was in January, 1935, that Ward Rogers, an organizer for the Union, was seized by police and thrown into jail. The crime: advocating, in effect, that the planters be compelled to obey the law and restore to the share-croppers the funds to which they were legally entitled; he had also quoted from the Declaration of Independence! The young Methodist preacher, a Vanderbilt University graduate, was sentenced to six months in jail and a five-hundred-dollar fine.

Apprised of these developments and other indications of terror throughout the state, the students and faculty at Commonwealth gathered to plan aid for the Union. The first step, upon the receipt of an urgent appeal from one of the Union men, was the departure of Lucien Koch, director of the school, Bob Reed and Atley Delaney, students, for the scene of the strife.

Meanwhile meetings were being held throughout the sector; it was to these that they immediately sped, Koch and Reed starting for Gilmore while Delaney went to Marked Tree. The Gilmore expedition was most crucial because Crittenden County, in which it was situated, had not yet been

249

penetrated by the Union. Arriving at the church house, site of the meeting, Koch and Reed found about 200 people crowded into the building. Sprinkled among them were spies, planters and their agents, providing a setting of acute tension. It was not until Koch had finished speaking that the real outbreak occurred. Then, as he later wrote:

> "It was obvious to almost everyone that something was bound to break. . . . Whites and officers were herded outside the doorway. Five men filed into the room, walked toward me, headed by the riding boss. They ordered me to 'come along.' I refused. They brandished their revolvers, dragged me from the seat and kicked me from the room. . . . Outstanding brutality was handled by two chiefly, Jake Lewis and Benton Moore (ex-justice of the peace, currently deputy sheriff and recently released from the insane asylum at Little Rock!). Both were violently drunk. . . .
>
> "I was hustled to a car on the road. Bob was too loyal to see me go alone. He came out to inquire where they were taking me. They started beating him and forced him into a car with me. . . . They poked guns in our bellies and faces, they kicked us, punched us—Bob's presence dividing the blows. We were both bloody about the face and head. . . .
>
> "Our lives weren't worth a penny in the hands of those drunk, frothing madmen. . . ."

Then they were driven down the road where two other deputies boarded the car and the procession headed for the sheriff's office at Marion. After a lengthy interview, the sheriff announced that he would not prefer charges and that they were to be set free. Returning to the church for their coats, they suddenly encountered a rope in the corner. One of the deputies who had been assigned to guide them back willingly informed them that the rope was there in readiness for a lynching.

The following Saturday Delaney and Koch entered the town of Lepanto at four o'clock in the afternoon, planning to participate in another meeting. Walking through the streets, they were abruptly seized by a sheriff on a charge of disturbing the peace. The accusation was later shifted to obstructing the streets and another charge, barratry, added. Barratry was an ancient statute and the offense meant spreading rumors. It seemed that the rumors, in this case, were the mistreatment of the share-croppers.

They were tried on Monday, "framed, kangarooed and railroaded." The defendants were fined fifty dollars each for coming to Lepanto.

Several days later the trio returned to Commonwealth to rest before another venture into the terror-stricken area. But in the interim the planters had reached the state legislature. Unnerved and angered by the intrusion of the college, equally upset by the tide of discontent throughout the state, they demanded that their underlings intervene. To augment their distress, word had just come from Fort Smith that another group from Commonwealth had been discovered aiding the organization of the unemployed.

Spurred by these disclosures, Representative Marcus Miller of Polk County, introduced a resolution into the Arkansas legislature calling for an investigation of Commonwealth. *The Fort Smith Times-Record* quoted Miller as declaring:

> "It is evident that the college is fostering ideas which strike at the very foundations of American government, as things are taught by them that will in time tear down the home and when that is done, it would be only a question of a few years when our citizenship would be affected.
>
> "Lucien Koch, head of the college, recently became one of the leaders in the movement to organize share-croppers in Eastern Arkansas and others reputedly con-

nected with the school were arrested in Fort Smith Tuesday in connection with an agitation for a general strike among relief workers."

Simultaneously Representative Gooch introduced an infamous sedition bill whose provisions were accurately described by one liberal Southern journal:

". . . Under this (measure) the death penalty could be inflicted upon almost anybody connected with a labor dispute if a death occurred in a strike. Under the terms of the proposed law, Abraham Lincoln and Thomas Jefferson could have been sent to the penitentiary for twenty years for some of their public utterances."

With only fragmentary debate, the bill was enacted in the House and prepared for submission to the Senate. Meanwhile, a group of buffoons, disguised as investigators, started for Commonwealth College to get the lowdown.

In the expedition were three senators, two representatives and a coterie of armed sheriffs, newspapermen and flunkeys. Arriving at the college, they were welcomed by officials there and urged to make themselves at home. They were somewhat startled by the greeting; it did not take them long to get back into their routine. The first object of attention was a class in history presided over by Koch. Alert, scenting sedition, the investigators trooped in, sat themselves down and prepared to listen. But then a disconcerting thing happened: they discovered that they didn't know what Koch was talking about. Occasionally a sentence gripped their attention but they were soon bewildered again by the complexity of the material. They yawned. They squirmed in their seats. They made a few desperate attempts to understand, then lapsed into coma. Although they were certain that words of great and sinister magnitude were being spoken, they were sadly unable to keep their minds on the treason.

Baffled, annoyed, the party decided to look elsewhere. Two

of the senators had a deep and overwhelming suspicion that free love was the clue to the scene and they proceeded in search of evidence. By now they were, it must be admitted, somewhat higher in spirits because of the effects of several healthy swills; they hunted out every woman on the campus, demanding of each, "When does the petting begin?" It was gravely hinted that they had more than an investigatory interest in the subject; but they were firmly rebuffed. The United Press generously took up the crusade, leading virtually all its stories with a reference to the wide symptoms of free love on the campus. To which Koch replied that there was probably more of it at Vassar than at Commonwealth.

Meanwhile the others were sniffing around the campus. Representative Miller maintained the unhappiest expression, glowering at everyone, preserving a mysterious and knowing air to hide his own confusion. When Koch urged him to insure an impartial and objective inquiry, Miller shot back a devastating reply: "I am not impartial and objective because I have nothing against the college."

The highlights of the hippodrome, however, were to be delayed until the hearing at Mena. It was there that the committee barricaded itself behind closed doors, summoning before it a series of witnesses from the college. Koch was kept at the inquisition for six hours; among the significant questions flung at him in that period were: Do you believe in the American flag? Do you believe in God? Is there any foreign country superior to the United States? Do you believe in free love? The energetic legislators hung on his replies, waited breathlessly for some scandalous morsel but only succeeded in augmenting their own bewilderment. In despair they decided to call Henry Black in whom they were profoundly interested because he gave a course in Fascism and Social Revolution. The dialogue began:

Senator Shaver: Do you believe in marriage?
Black: Yes.

253

Shaver: Do you believe in free love?

Black: No.

Shaver: Has free love been practiced on your campus to your knowledge?

Black: The question is hypothetical.

"Hypothetical" was an unfortunate word. To Black's amazement he found his interrogators were completely unaware of its meaning. And as this confusion incited their fury, they then proceeded to become uncomfortably tangled in the subject of fascism.

Shaver: Is the Italian government superior to the American government?

Black: No.

Shaver: Then why do you teach a course in it?

Slowly, painfully, at some length, Black sought to explain why fascism was studied, and to ease their distress, he could assure them that he was opposed to it. But they persisted, demanded to know if there was a fascist unit on the campus. Again Black sought to enlighten them, but with little success. The hearing was abruptly interrupted by the stenographer who was uncertain about the spelling of "fascism." Then the scholar of the probe, a man with an L.L.B. degree, which he flourished, launched the first offensive. Wasn't it true, he demanded, that all the political doctrines studied at Commonwealth originated in foreign countries? Black replied that the question was ambiguous and again threw the hearing into turmoil by the use of so alien a word.

The inquisition wound through the testimony of five teachers and two students. One of these was a mystic. When the committee asked him whether he believed in God, he replied: "What do you gentlemen mean by God?"

They wrote him down in the little black book as a heretic, a man to be watched. And so it went on, a fantastic burlesque which the legislators too often could not enjoy.

254

If farce lightened the tension, the interlude was ended by the ominous warnings of violence. Four days after the committee's visit, the following item appeared in *The Arkansas Gazette:*

". . . A life-long resident of the city of Mena, a large owner of real estate and interested in several business firms, admitted to members of the press late last night that there had been some discussion of the organization of a secret group of Polk County residents to warn Koch and his faculty and students to leave this section of the state voluntarily or take what might follow."

And *The Mena Star* issued an inflammatory plea for the citizens to "take matters into their own hands." It was a rare opportunity for the almost defunct Ku Klux Klan to revive its prestige by the tactics which had once brought it fame. Under its auspices a pamphlet was issued, featuring the free love allegation, and joining in the incitement for direct action.

Faced with this danger, Koch immediately wired the governor of the state for protection. There was no response. Again he appealed, as reports of impending invasion grew. But still from the legislative chambers came no reply, not even a warning to the carriers of violence to desist.

It was clear that Commonwealth would have to defend itself. It did. Barricades were thrown up on the roads, sentries were placed at strategic posts, two students stood at the gate to the school, ready to toll the alarm bell at the approach of an attack. For three nights the inhabitants of the school kept the vigil, in momentary fear of destruction. For they knew the mob, if it came, would not be mild. Under the incitement of "large owners of real estate" and "spokesmen for business firms," these marauders would not leave until irreparable damage were done.

The defense forestalled the attack. Word of the barricades, of the intense precautions which had been taken, trickled back to the town. Without benefit of the governor or any of the agencies of law and order, Commonwealth protected itself. Through the long, soundless nights, the students and teachers waited, side by side, prepared to resist any intrusion. They won by default.

In that crisis were discernible the real need and possibilities of a united front. Commonwealth's population represents almost every point of view in the labor movement, factions which have been warring with each other for generations. There are socialists, communists, progressives, liberals, every shade of labor opinion. Confronted with the imminence of attack, all differences suddenly seemed secondary. The foe was a mutual one, powerful, equipped with every weapon. Out of that common peril arose a unity for which enemies of reaction everywhere might well strive. And today it is stronger, more enduring and firm than ever before.

For Commonwealth had allies outside, in every state of the Union. When the first news of the concerted drive to close down the school was despatched, there were hundreds who rallied to the side of the victims. Immediately a campaign of protest was launched. From educators, the clergy, students, liberals everywhere came telegrams denouncing the move and demanding that the legislature withdraw the sedition bill and the investigation. It was an unprecedented experience for the Arkansas law-makers. They had never encountered mass pressure before. They had never been deluged with letters, with telegrams and resolutions of such wide proportions. One of the attendants at the State capitol remarked: "I wish they'd lay off Commonwealth. . . . I'm tired of delivering telegrams every half hour."

At a hearing on the measure in the State Capitol, even hosts of Arkansas citizens, aroused for the first time, came to voice their convictions. The planters and their lobbyists could not stem the onrush. The sedition bill was defeated.

Those who sponsor reaction do not surrender easily. Less

256

than two weeks after the rout of the Gooch statute, a brand-
new bill was introduced hurriedly at a night session of the
House, avowedly aimed at the destruction of Commonwealth.
Under its provisions any five citizens could band together and
condemn an institution as a nuisance, thus securing an injunction against the continued operation of the school. Sponsored
by the same Mr. Miller, the statute would have enabled any
five planters to destroy what to them was unquestionably a
nuisance—Commonwealth College. Again a thunder of protest descended from everywhere. Again the volume of disagreement dimmed the ardor of the legislators. They wanted
to please the planters but they could not forget about votes.
Moreover, they feared that they were going too far; their
anticipated support had not come forward; their own constituents were deserting them. When the investigating committee finally published its report, the recommendations were
tacit acknowledgment of the protest. It contented itself with
the admonition to the legislature to keep a close check on the
future conduct of the school.

Commonwealth had temporarily been saved. Of course, its
outlook is hardly placid. Share-croppers are still restless; the
S.T.F.U. is leading them to new struggles for bread and
land; throughout the state dire poverty is at last provoking
the rebellion so long in coming. And at the side of these half-
starved human beings are the students and faculty of Commonwealth. The planters will not cease their efforts. They
are not interested in dispelling the causes of misery; they are
seeking to smash its symptoms. One of the centers of their
attack will be the school whose president has aligned himself
with the impoverished, while the Nicholas Murray Butlers
dine with the directors of U. S. Steel. Commonwealth will
not be allowed to pursue its way untroubled.

Another inquisition will be launched; another set of buffoons will start out for Commonwealth. And their antics will
seem less humorous, less fraught with innocent comedy, each
time.

257

Charles Walgreen is a man of righteousness, of staunch views, of determination. He also happens to head one of the largest drugstore chains in the country. So, you see, Mr. Walgreen is both a citizen of property, a magnate of no small dimensions, and a symbol of civic virtue. Occasionally he slips, totters from his throne; but the press has always been kind to Mr. Walgreen and dealt lightly with his missteps because they were so overshadowed by his deeds of charity and his sense of the true and beautiful. Thus, for example, amidst all Mr. Walgreen's exploits the press never mentioned the case of the United States vs. Walgreen company, case no. 22585. The charge was: adulteration of Elixir Iron, Quinine, Strychnine and Milk of Bismuth. The Walgreen company pleaded guilty.

But such incidents are the unmentionables and they must not be allowed to dim the halo around his head.

Examine what he did for his niece, Lucille Norton. When Lucille was graduated from Lincoln High School in Seattle, Washington, Mr. Walgreen stepped in to carve her destiny. Prevailing upon her widowed mother to allow him jurisdiction over the girl's education, he selected the University of Chicago as the scene for her quest. Now Mr. Walgreen is one of those bountiful men who endow scholarships for universities and Chicago had been one of the recipients. What more natural, then, that Miss Norton, wide-eyed and innocent, entered the university on a Walgreen scholarship. For the duration of her college course, moreover, Lucille moved into the home of Uncle Charley.

I have said she was innocent; of that there can be no question. And naïveté was her undoing in the badlands of the Windy City. Even Uncle Charley did not immediately realize what was in store for her.

That was the month when the patriots were moving ahead on all fronts, when the drive on professors was being succeeded by a series of inquisitions throughout the country. It was the month of the student strike against war which sent one hundred per centers into a new orgy of trembling. And on April 11, 1935, the day before the walkout, the flag-wavers discovered a new hero, Uncle Charley Walgreen.

For that day the press carried the disclosure that Uncle Charley had withdrawn niece Lucille from the University of Chicago. According to Hearst's *New York American,* Mr. Walgreen explained:

"It was the result of serious and, I believe, moderate thinking, after my niece had told me about the new ideas she was acquiring. When it comes to communism and advocating of violence in overthrowing the government, I am dead set against it. That she was learning such things was revealed to me in frequent arguments on the subject."

The story concluded with the following morsel:

"Friends of Mr. Walgreen, who rose to his present position from humble beginnings, said he feels strongly that America is still the land of opportunity."

The situation was a natural for the witch-hunters. They packed their bags and headed for Chicago, cameramen, reporters, and patrioteers of every order.

Nor did they lack cooperation from the State legislature. If John Smith had withdrawn his daughter from Chicago because he could no longer support her, there would not have been a line in the public print. But Uncle Charley had taken his niece away because there was treason in the air and the Hearsts, big and little, were ready to act. Thus Senator Baker was declaiming at the state capitol:

"It's time something is done about this situation. If the Board of Trustees and the heads of the university are unwilling to prevent the use of the school by communist sympathizers, the state government should protect the students from the assaults of insidious propaganda."

The campaign fittingly coincided with the Red Scare. A few months before there had been a concerted attempt to oust Professor Schumann; now Uncle Charley provided the signal for an even more drastic clean-up. With significant rapidity, the demands of Mr. Walgreen and Mr. Hearst and the bee-hive of red-hunters around them were translated into action by the legislature. A committee of five was appointed to investigate Chicago, and any other schools in the state where the flags were not waving vigorously enough.

The room was crowded to the doors as the inquiry got under way. On one side were the university officials; on the other the D. A. R., the Legionnaires, a host of major and minor figures in the great war on sedition. There were others, liberals and radicals come to protest the drive on independent students and teachers. On the rostrum sat the judicial body, the five senators named to wage the probe.

Into this setting strode Uncle Charley, first witness for the prosecution. He enjoyed his rôle, took himself very seriously, bowed slightly to acquaintances and proceeded to the stand. It was a tragic tale he unfolded. To paraphrase it would be unfair, an assault on an historic work. Let Uncle Charley speak for himself, as he did that afternoon in Chicago:

". . . After attending the University of Chicago for a time her (Lucille's) thoughts as disclosed by her conversation turned to communism. . . . During her first quarter at the university social science was a compulsory subject. Among the selected reading it required the Communist Manifesto by Karl Marx and F. Engels, in which the institution of the family, as we know it, is belittled and criticized and its alleged sacredness ridi-

culed. . . . It was during this period that she told me
the family as an institution was disappearing."

One can understand how that had jolted Uncle Charley.
When he sought to ascertain the cause of her deviation, a
new shock was forthcoming:

"I asked where she got that idea and she answered
'At School'. She told me at a lecture marriage was described as an institution that was not universal and that
there were varying standards of morals and that she was
at a group at which both sexes were present and moral
questions were discussed. After the discussion the leader
was asked why such subjects were brought up and treated
so thoroughly and the class leader answered: 'Who shall
say that our system is the best?' . . ."

As Uncle Charley told the committee, these revelations
were a source of no minor discomfort to him. He tried to
fight the menace single-handed: "I cautioned her not to take
these subjects too seriously and to retain her faith in the
standard of morals as taught by her mother."

His admonition was in vain. Even more devastating
exposures were at hand:

". . . We were discussing communism and capitalism
and I lightly said to Lucille: 'You are getting to be a
communist.' And she said: 'I am not the only one—
there are a lot more on the campus.' I said to Lucille:
'Do you realize that this means the abolition of the
family, the abolition of the church, and especially do
you realize it means the overthrow of our government?'
And she said, 'Yes, I think I do; but doesn't the end
ever justify the means?' "

Whereupon Uncle Charley had implored her to recognize
that "this means bloodshed." And Lucille, with surprising

discernment, replied: "Yes, but how did we get our independence—wasn't it by revolution?"

The testimony of Lucille's downfall was long and detailed
and fraught with successive sensations. Perhaps the climax
was Uncle Charley's discovery that in one of the courses she
was studying, the following quotation from Stuart Chase had
been assigned as a topic for discussion: "It must be more than
a little of a bore to be a business man dedicated to a life of
unrelenting greed."

So fantastic a statement, of course, did not merit controversy, Mr. Walgreen averred. And there it was, being
mulled over in a classroom at Chicago. All these things had
accumulated until the very pillars of the Walgreen home
were shaking. Hence, Uncle Charley concluded before the
attentive senators, he could see no alternative short of withdrawing his niece from the university and instituting a campaign of redress. The legislators bowed in solemn approval,
the D. A. R. ladies clapped, and the more dour-faced Legionnaires just frowned at the whole frightful tale.

Not until the second session did the faint-voiced, child-
like Lucille Norton enter the scene. Her coming created
another stir, auguring new sensations. A few days before, a
reporter had interviewed her to ascertain her own views as
to whether she had been indoctrinated. To which Miss Norton
had replied with a firm "no." When she took the stand, she
asserted quite definitely that she had been. Reminded of her
denial to the reporter, she seemed somewhat flustered—and
then the truth emerged. When first questioned, Miss Norton
did not know what indoctrination meant, but she had vaguely
suspected that it implied immoral sexual relations! Upon investigation, her suspicion had been confounded; she could
now assure the legislators with full conscience that she had
been a victim of indoctrination. Let it not be feared that she
did not recover from the effects. Following her withdrawal
from the university, she told the committee, her beliefs had

undergone sharp revision. Uncle Charley, she now was compelled to admit, had always been right.

There was one other matter upon which she was full of information. That was free love. After a symposium, Professor Schumann had said, within her hearing, "I believe in religion for some people and free love for myself." Professor Gideonse then proceeded to explain that the remark had been made ironically in his presence, in an effort to turn away an irrelevant and trivial question. To which Miss Norton piped up: "It never occurred to me that Professor Schumann might be insincere."

The pathetic ignorance in her voice could not arouse even the hero-worshipping D. A. R. There were badly-concealed snickers in the room.

The fireworks were reserved for the third session. They were inaugurated by Mrs. Albert W. Dilling, resident of the exclusive North Shore, author of *The Red Network*, a volume in which everyone from Mrs. Roosevelt down is meticulously proved to be an agent of The Third International.

For an hour and a half Mrs. Dilling pounded away, gesticulating wildly, her eyes burning with fervor. No one was immune from her attack.

". . . Yes, they are all affiliated with the communists. Professor Robert Morss Lovett, Professor Schumann, Dean Gilkey. The whole university is filled with them. Jane Addams was on many of their committees. So is Mary McDowell. . . . Judge Brandeis is one of the biggest contributors to that filthy, lousy little communist college down in Arkansas."

A well-groomed gentleman murmured: "A wonderful woman—a remarkable book, that book of hers." The Legionnaire next to him assented.

Finally, when her stack of evidence had been exhausted,

when her voice threatened to break down after so uninterrupted a strain, when her shrill screeches were unnerving
even her cohorts, Mrs. Dilling abruptly sat down. The old
ladies and their husbands pattered out applause, smiled at
each other in approval and awaited the next exposé.

Harry Jung stepped to the stand, a man notorious as a
red-baiter and anti-semite, head of the American Vigilant
Intelligence Association. Boisterously, defiantly, he described
his own rôle in the struggle against communism. With equal
vehemence he slashed at the university.

Then suddenly the scene shifted. Mrs. Dilling had been
popping up and down, interjecting remarks, murmuring to
her neighbors. In the midst of her antics, a small, spectacled
man turned to the listener in an adjoining seat to comment:
"Her name ought to be Mrs. Dillinger."

Whereupon pandemonium broke loose. A big fellow in
gray flannels went for the little man, sent him reeling against
the wall with a resounding blow accompanied by the cry,
"You dirty little Jew." The little man slipped out as fast as
he could. The assailant was Mrs. Dilling's husband.

In the front of the room, the chairman was banging
heavily with his gavel to restore order, the uproar persisted
throughout the room and the session was abruptly adjourned.

It was a comic opera without benefit of music. And yet all
the ludicrous gyrations of the patriots could not obscure its
sinister purpose. Mrs. Dilling ranted, Jung echoed her outbursts, Uncle Charley maintained a grim, stolid exterior and
Lucille piped feebly; but behind them were arrayed a powerful battalion which reached into thousands of homes, offices
and government quarters. It was no sham battle. It represented another decisive phase of the campaign to preserve
the goose-step in academic life.

In the face of this assault, the university's stand was dis-
appointing. If anywhere we might have anticipated a frank,
courageous counter-attack, it should have occurred at Chicago.

President Hutchins is hailed by liberals as one of the few independent men in American education, far outranking any of his contemporaries. Certainly he sensed the danger implicit in the probe and he said so. But instead of challenging the investigators, instead of flinging their charges back at them, instead of proclaiming the right of students and teachers to say what they wanted, whether radical or not, the dominant note was a defensive one. Virtually every faculty member up to President Hutchins sought to "acquit" the school, to "prove" that there was no radicalism existent there; they catered and pandered to a tribunal of scandal-hunters lest their appropriations be impaired. When Walgreen's denunciations had first been issued, Professor Ogburn commented: "There are some radicals among the student body of every college. After five years of depression, why shouldn't there be?"

Yet in the actual hearings Professor Lovett was almost alone in confessing his crimes—his vigorous opposition to war, his willingness to address meetings of the National Student League and other sins of equal proportions. When they asked him whether he would advise his son to bear arms if Germany declared war on the United States, Professor Lovett replied that he would give him no advice at all; he would hope that his son knew what he was fighting for— and proceeded to embarrass the committee by informing it that his oldest son had been killed at Belleau Wood.

This was a straightforward stand and one which was made even more distinguished by its uniqueness. One must acknowledge the pressure on Hutchins and his colleagues to clear the name of the university; they did so, but by retreating, by granting the essential premise of the investigation. That does not alter the fact that Chicago today under Hutchins is one of the most liberal universities in the country; it only serves to foreshadow how increasingly difficult it will be to preserve that liberalism in the face of the Dillings, the Jungs and the interests which, however crudely, they represent. Further, whatever may be the personal courage and independence of Hutchins, the time is drawing near when he will have to face the issue far more squarely than he did in this probe. For the real issues, obscured by the turmoil of the inquiry and the attempts of Chicago to vindicate itself, were far more fundamental. Do Chicago students have the right to be radical? Have their professors a similar privilege? Or are they to be hounded ruthlessly at the first sign of awakening?

Perhaps the most illuminating indication of the character of the university's defense was furnished by the report of the investigating committee several months later. It cleared everyone but Lovett of whom the Associated Press reported:

"The majority report declared that Professor Lovett had 'pursued an unpatriotic course of conduct for a period of eight or ten years.' He has been known as a liberal and has been interested in labor difficulties and freedom of speech movements."

Commonwealth survived the Red Scare; but another school devoted to workers' education was sacrificed to the rabid onslaught of the finance-backed flag-wavers. Since 1921, Bryn Mawr College had turned over its campus during the summer months to a group of girls drawn from factories throughout the country. It was a notable enterprise and one which attracted the sympathy of friends of the underprivileged throughout the nation. Each summer scores of working girls partook of facilities always denied to them. They came from uniformly impoverished homes, determined to equip themselves for the pursuit of a better life, and the living of it.

But in 1935 Bryn Mawr College launched a campaign for a million-dollar endowment fund for the regular operation of the school. Almost simultaneously an announcement disclosed that the school for working girls had been transferred to Pomona, New York. In explanation, it was stated that the new site would provide better vacation facilities for the girls.

266

Sceptical of this assertion, a group of Bryn Mawr alumnæ selected a committee to make further inquiries into the situation. Their findings might have been anticipated. In the summer of 1934 girls from the school had aided the strikers of Seabrook Farms in New Jersey; they had given freely of their aid and, in doing so, attracted the attention of the owners of the land. Their efforts had received publicity—publicity of a kind which often discomforts conservative alumnæ and supporters of the school. It had also offended the board of directors of Bryn Mawr College. Activity in other strikes of a similar nature intensified the breach.

When the one million-dollar endowment campaign was inaugurated in 1935, Bryn Mawr realized the peril. Throughout the nation the Red Scare was advancing on all fronts; entrenched groups were threatening to boycott institutions suspected of radicalism. Confronted with the demands of expediency, the board of directors decided to move the school for working girls safely out of the way lest it interfere with these ambitious plans.

The alumnæ committee, headed by Mary Van Kleeck, of the Russell Sage Foundation and Dr. Dorothy Douglas, Smith professor, reported:

"Here is the familiar issue as to whether those who are intrusted with the holding of the property of an institution are also to control teaching and student activities. In workers' education this is sharply brought to the front by the fact that, on the whole, members of boards of directors include representatives of employers and therefore the issue involved is not between workers and a liberal college, but between the claims that workers have upon educational institutions in opposition to control of those educational institutions by employers of labor."

267

The girls of the regular session at Bryn Mawr—the daughters of those who can still afford to send their daughters to a first-class college—may well ponder the episode. An endowment of one million dollars is being prepared for them at the expense of a group of young girls whom philanthropic Bryn Mawr so readily disinherited. The patriots may assume credit for the triumph, and with them the established citizens on Bryn Mawr's board of directors.

v. Vigilantes in California

THE jitters seized California's vested interests late in the spring of 1934—from the day that several hundred longshoremen strode from their jobs and took up their stand on picket lines. It was a disquieting development, to be followed by even more ominous storm-signals. For, with startling rapidity, West Coast labor came to the side of the longshoremen. As the summer approached, San Francisco found itself in the grip of a general strike which the most frantic insistence of the industrialists could not shake off.

That was a crisis in which, as we earlier observed, the citadels of education were expected to perform their accustomed rôle—the recruiting of strike-breakers. And the West Coast institutions knew their job. It was estimated that nine-tenths of the scabs whom the Industrial Association could find were from the universities and schools of the state. A large number came directly from the regular school employment bureaus. Nor was this function restricted to the students. Professor D. P. Barrows of the University of California stepped gallantly into an even more public-spirited task: he became one of the chief commanders of the National Guard which Governor Merriam had summoned to quell the strike. Meanwhile, John Francis Neylan, regent of the University of California, chief counsel for Hearst's *San Francisco Exam-*

iner, prevailed upon General Hugh S. Johnson to speak at the Greek Theatre on the California campus in Berkeley; it was there that General Johnson, while receiving a Phi Beta Kappa key from the university for his spirited explorations into learning, delivered his famous incitement to violence. He urged the citizenry of California to put down the "Reds" by force—and by "Reds" General Johnson admitted that he meant every man on a West Coast picket line. "Crush them like rats," bellowed the general.

Such was the setting when a group of undergraduates in the Coast universities sought to intervene in behalf of the strikers. They knew what their universities were doing. They understood that scores of their colleagues had already been enrolled as strike-breakers. And so they intensified their own efforts on the side of the strikers—efforts which had begun at the start of the walkout with collections of food and clothing for the longshoremen. At the University of Southern California a leaflet had been issued in May declaring:

"The strikers' struggle is our struggle. In their victory or failure our future is involved. They are laying the foundation for resistance to future war, against fascist advances in America and for a higher standard of living for all Americans who toil."

Similar documents were published in the ensuing months, testifying to the number who were unwilling to perform their traditional "public service." The universities didn't like it. Particularly were the overseers of the University of California—and its southern branch at Los Angeles—outraged by these incidents. Such steps, it was felt, weren't cricket; they were communism.

And so, shortly after General Johnson's incitement, *The Daily Californian* carried the following echo of his remarks:

"Just as there are Vigilantes in the East Bay community, there will be Vigilantes in the university com-

269

munity designed to blot out university communists. Just as action and force are being employed outside the campus to quell red radicalism, Social Problems Club members will face action and force when the regular session starts in August. That action and force will be generated by student Vigilantes with the approval of the university community."

This manifesto is worth careful study as an indication of the source of the subsequent violence, usually to be described in the die-hard press as "Red rioting."

The prediction was quickly realized. According to one writer, "vigilante groups of students were formed with the knowledge and tacit sanction of prominent members of the university faculty." They merely furnished a preview of performances to come. On the momentum of a frenzied Red Scare, the San Francisco strike was broken and students and their universities could feel secure in the knowledge that, despite the energies of a more enlightened band, they had done their part.* Among the heroes was Homer Griffith, one of the best ends ever to don a headgear on the coast.

The termination of the strike did not bring peace to the state or to the campus. Hardly had the Industrial Association, composed of the leading open-shop, red-hunting Coast employers, conquered that spectre by force, lies and distortion, than a new enemy walked the streets in the person of Upton Sinclair. Sinclair had announced his candidacy for governor, challenging the rule of Frank P. Merriam, friend of business. Even Sinclair's diluted and moderate EPIC brand of social reform was a living menace to the barons of the coast. They

* It is notable that, although students were widely utilized in breaking the strike, there were many places in which they were forced to abandon their efforts by the determined counter-action of other undergraduates. The National Student League and the League for Industrial Democracy did mobilize aid for the strikers which,' in numerous sectors, overcame the influence of the "scabs"—and often won them over to the strikers' side.

hated him, they feared him and they were out to stop him at all costs. They were well-equipped for the attack, having just concluded their spectacular feats of the general strike which left the populace in a state bordering on anti-Red prostration. Fresh from the triumph, Big Business went after its second coup, with Sinclair—and anyone else suspected of a high "I.Q."—as the object of their wrath.

Merriam's candidacy had the support of every big interest on the coast; among them must be remembered the Regents of the University of California and U.C.L.A., many of whom contributed heavily to the campaign. Why not? They are the men who control the largest banks, corporations, utilities, power companies and industries throughout the state. They include the previously-discussed Mr. Neylan, who is a frequent spokesman for the Industrial Association, Mortimer Fleischacker, chairman of the Board of the Anglo-California National Bank; William H. Crocker, president of the First National Bank and a director of the Pacific Gas and Electric Company; Chester Rowell, editor of the reactionary *San Francisco Chronicle* and a host of others of equal stature in the community. These gave freely to Merriam, the man of the (better) people. And Merriam, their man, was running on the slogan "Save California from Communism." The cue was obvious.

Back in April of 1934, a debate between U.C.L.A. and the Berkeley division of the university had been scheduled for the Los Angeles campus, at which the proposition: "Communism Is Fit for America," was to be argued. On the eve of the debate, the manager of the Berkeley team wired ahead:

"Rumored that Jingo press is making efforts to call off Monday's debate. We intend to debate and uphold communism. We are not being financed by Moscow nor very much by anybody. We have yet to be propositioned by a Russian."

271

An immediate reply came from Los Angeles debate officials:

"Telegram very indiscreet. Communism cannot now be discussed. We must debate: Resolved, that the power of the president shall be substantially increased as a settled policy, or cancel debate altogether."

The Berkeley men declined the substitute. To ascertain what had happened, the manager went down to Los Angeles and there interviewed responsible parties. His most enlightening discussion was with Provost Ernest C. Moore from whom he learned that a university must not antagonize the Better American Federation, the American Legion or any of their cohorts. The Provost did not hesitate to assure him that "free speech is not being challenged."

That was not the Provost's first symptom of nervousness. As far back as 1928 he was making his presence felt, to the supreme comfort of his overseers. That year Kirby Page was touring the colleges speaking in behalf of pacifism; when he neared California, the Provost delivered himself of an ultimatum: "It may be necessary to take some action if Mr. Page should belittle military training."

His behavior since that time has justified the judgments which were made. To find his counterpart, one must retrace one's steps all the way back to New York to the office of Dr. Frederick B. Robinson, whom we shall later encounter. Dr. Moore is a high-strung man, afraid of his own shadow, so inured to the idea of subservience that he would feel ill at ease if some one were not ordering him around. When the ghost of Moscow came to the Coast late in 1934, Dr. Moore was in the front line of defense. Like his colleague in New York, he is a blunderer; he has never developed the academic habit of suppressing without appearing to suppress; one must acknowledge that he has never hesitated to say out loud what other people have taught him to think. Hence, it was to be anticipated that in the great war on sedition, he would abandon the scholarly veneer; he was, to put it mildly, indiscreet. In the tense California atmosphere, however, his indiscretions were hardly unique; and if some administrators later wished they could subdue him, it is safe to say that at the time praise enough to satisfy his vanity was heaped upon him.

The Provost had been worried ever since the fall term began. There was, first, the election of a Student Council, three of whose members had been ardent EPIC campaigners. The Council had proceeded, for probably the first time, to inject an element of thought into the usually innocuous proceedings of student governing bodies. In doing so it had offended precisely those groups to which the Provost, and the University, were most deeply bound. Early in October the Navy League (whose last president was Charles Schwab of Bethlehem Steel) proposed to Dr. Moore that U.C.L.A. sponsor an essay contest throughout southern California high schools on "Our Navy." The League generously agreed to finance the move. When it was presented to the Student Council, however, there was disconcerting opposition. The students contended that they were unwilling to serve as propaganda instruments for a League which had been dominant in pushing through the extravagant Navy budget of 1933; they further pointed out that it was hardly equitable to keep the National Student League an illegal organization and simultaneously throw the doors wide open to the munitions patrioteers. Dr. Moore was stunned; he remonstrated with them; he tried every cajolery to push through the plan. But the council was adamant. Dr. Moore had to run back to the Navy League with the doleful news.

There was another shock to his balance soon forthcoming. It was customary for the American Legion to act as co-sponsor of U.C.L.A.'s Armistice Day football game; the receipts were divided, the Legion and the R.O.T.C. paraded together and a good flag-waving time was enjoyed. But again the council interceded, declaring that this year there was to be no university partnership with the Legion. Again Dr. Moore was compelled to face the patriots with so impudent a rebuff from the students of his own university. He was an unhappy, nervous man.

When, on October 10th, the Student Council voted to launch plans for a student-controlled open forum, Dr. Moore became convinced that alien forces were at work. Such a forum may seem an altogether innocent project; to Dr. Moore, however, discussion was anathema. Twelve days after the proposal to petition the university for the forum had been voted, Dr. Moore summoned John Burnside, the president of the student body, to his office. He instructed Burnside to halt any further agitation for the forum. If Dr. Moore believed that the Council could be gently coerced, he was quickly relieved of the hope. On October 24th the group reconvened, determined to exercise what it regarded as an elementary right. Under the terms of its constitution, students are entitled to petition for a referendum vote on such questions and the council proceeded to prepare the survey. A diverse group of students, representing all sections of campus opinion, was called together to organize the campaign. In the midst of their deliberations, a self-styled unofficial representative of Dr. Moore appeared to inform the body that, if the initiative clause were invoked, it would be summarily removed from the constitution.

It was during this week that the Merriam campaign had entered its final phase with the cry "Run out the Reds." The American Legion was conducting an Education Week, in which school children were treated to an extraordinary display of war propaganda. At Berkeley, Provost Deutsch was declaiming: "Any teacher who misuses his or her position to preach to pupils the overthrow of our government by force should not be permitted to teach a single day after this charge has been substantiated."

Simultaneously a student editor was being expelled from Santa Clara for daring to write that "students have nothing to gain from war" and because he "refused to print what the faculty wanted him to." And the president of San José State Teachers College was inciting violence among his students without even a thin disguise to his efforts. Upon the issuance of a left-wing leaflet on the campus, these were his words:

> "I hope every true citizen on this campus, every one who loves the United States of America as well as his college, will assist in the eradication of this festering sore. Will all loyal groups, clubs, classes and societies act immediately. Make plans to get the necessary information. If you know members of the group, *please feel quite free to take them to the edge of the campus and drop them off.*" (Italics mine.)

The day after the appearance of his "unofficial" spokesman, Dr. Moore moved ahead more vigorously. Another gathering of sponsors of the forum was abruptly halted by the arrival of police who "understood that a communistic meeting is being held." The students were told that "if such a meeting takes place," they would be arrested at once, and they were also warned that no petitions were to be circulated.

Meanwhile, the Merriam forces were pressing onward with their anti-Red convulsions, sounding the tocsin of fake, lying, finance-dominated "Americanism." Provost Moore heard the noises. His own one-hundred-per-cent-pure blue blood boiled. Enraged by the defiance of the Council, he determined to rid himself of its opposition with the most powerful weapon at his command. The patriots would like that. So would the Board of Regents. So would the backers of Merriam, to whom each new Red Scare was just so many votes in the bag of Big Business' friend.

That day there was a telephone conversation between Provost Moore and President Robert Sproul, at Berkeley, concerning the situation. I am assured of that by a student close to the scene—one who, incidentally, was not affiliated with any of the left-wing campus groups. The conversation is important because it indicates that President Sproul knew what was to happen the following day. It is barely possible that he tried to reason with Dr. Moore, but of this there is grave doubt. For although the president is a far more amiable, honest and well-intentioned man than the drill sergeant at Los Angeles, he is also sensitive to the voice from above, especially when it comes from the Regents and the State Legislature. He himself is a protégé of Guy Earle, prominent industrialist and ex-Regent, who engineered him into office several years before, to the consternation of the faculty. Aggressive, youthful in appearance, with a booming voice, he had been well trained in business offices before his university career and has mastered the Rotarian manner. But Sproul has his difficulties. As one writer noted,* each year he is forced to sell the idea of higher education to the Regents, who vote the biennial appropriation for the maintenance of the university. He is haunted by the fear of their displeasure; everything he does is calculated to mollify any dissatisfaction they may have or to work himself more deeply into their affection. When asked to comment on Governor Rolph's sanction of the outrageous San José lynching a few years ago, President Sproul said: "It is not my place to criticize my superiors on the Board of Regents." He has always exercised his function by that credo. He has to—if he wants to retain his job.

And on that afternoon late in October, President Sproul must have known what the entrenched citizens wanted when he received a telephone call from Dr. Moore of Los Angeles.

Twenty-four hours later five students were suspended from U.C.L.A. for "using your student offices to aid the National

* See Anna Wallace's summary of the situation in the January 9, 1935 issue of *The New Republic*.

276

Student League to destroy the university." The victims were four members of the Student Council, including its president, and the organizer of the National Student League chapter at the school.

The next day was the most tumultuous in the university's history. As word of the suspensions was transmitted, students had gathered throughout the night in excited, nervous groups to discuss the episode. In the morning hundreds assembled at a mass meeting called by the National Student League to protest the reprisals. It was a stormy assemblage. For in the interim, Provost Moore, aware that his act would not pass unnoticed, had begun to mobilize his followers both within the university and outside. They arrived on the scene full of vigor and inspiration, prepared to serve their Provost through any crisis and by the most vehement methods they could command. Their appearance was the signal for a bitter pitched battle. I quote from the description of a freshman, recently enrolled in the school and only vaguely familiar up till then with the issues involved:

"I stood on the steps of a college hall, a building of knowledge and free thought. . . . I listened as a boy spoke swiftly, eagerly to the noisy crowd. Suddenly we were no longer a curious gathering. Brawny athletes began shoving and pushing through to the speaker. . . . Cops bobbed up from nowhere. . . . Someone pushed a policeman into the bushes—he had struck a girl. Another cop seized a girl speaker, hurled her down into the shrubs. . . . Why the demonstration, the vicious attack, the violence of athletes and police? Five suspended students who believed in free speech—and the fighting, bitter attack on academic freedom. . . . I was not the only student shocked to realization of the truth on that day. . . . There is no such thing as freedom of thought, inquiry or expression on our campus." *

* From an article by Vera Cox in *The New Masses*, of June 4, 1935.

Dr. Moore had incited the counter-attack. He had denounced his own university as a hotbed of communism, pledging himself to carry on a relentless purge. And in this he needed help. He said so. He shouted it to reporters, fell over himself seconding his own opinion, beamed as his picture was splashed over the front pages of the press. In his zeal he did not forget the recruiting of allies. On the day of the suspensions the Dean of the Men's office is reported to have advised Robert Denton, president of the Interfraternity Council, that the administration would welcome its cooperation in the great cleansing of unpopular opinions. Simultaneously members of the football squad were reminded by Assistant Coach Fred Oster "to remember where your jobs and eligibility come from." Thus were born the U.C.L.A. Americans and the Vigilantes to counteract student indignation against the suspensions. They were free to do as they wanted in the execution of this task—and in the first protest meetings their future tactics were boldly defined. Provost Moore, having gone this far, was not to be repelled by the prospect of violence. He watched the police and his own lieutenants assault the throng of demonstrators and felt confident that the purge was on in earnest. According to the *Los Angeles Herald and Express:* "The Vigilantes came from the ranks of the husky, stern-faced athletes who met in a drizzling rain on the Westwood hillside last night and vowed to purge the campus of radicalism 'by force if necessary.'"

Meanwhile the Americans swore a solemn oath by torchlight, and in front of newspaper cameras, to join in the historic mission. It was to be no petty skirmish.

Although large numbers of his own students were bombarding him with demands for the reinstatement of the suspended five, and others were rallying to his side, there was scant doubt that those who mattered were full of approval for Dr. Moore's act. Harry Harper, president of the Chamber of Commerce, declared: "Every right-thinking American citizen will back up Dr. Moore in his determination to rid our state of all subversive influences." The Friday Morning Club, headed by the staunch Mrs. Louise Ward Watkins, expressed the hope that "all decent and law-abiding American citizens will support Dr. Moore."

From the Daughters of the American Revolution came a telegram:

"Our organization indorses the action of Dr. Moore in suspending five students for subversive activities on the campus at U.C.L.A. . . . The time has arrived for concerted action in behalf of American ideals and principles."

The American Legion:

"The action of the authorities at U.C.L.A. insures the people of California against their state educational institutions becoming hotbeds of communism."

Overnight Dr. Moore had become a hero among the people whose adulation he most cherished and needed.

Meanwhile terrorism of liberal and radical students continued apace. While Dr. Moore was delivering his virulent attacks before each meal, the situation at Berkeley was growing increasingly tense. Dean Louis O'Brien summoned ten leading students to his office, "recommending" to them that they intervene to smash the impending student strike against the suspensions. Alumni of Psi Upsilon fraternity offered a "sizeable sum" to the chapter if its members would "organize to suppress radicalism on the campus." Several days before the walkout one of the strike leaders was set upon at dusk by five Vigilantes who shouted, "Slug him!" and proceeded to administer a sound beating. And that took place on the campus proper without any administrative intervention.

279

Parallel with open violence was the elaborate network of espionage which developed. George A. Rader, a Legionnaire, glowed with pride as he described the spy system he commanded. He employed twenty-two students who were "mostly seniors, members of fraternities, level-headed and have been very carefully chosen." Under these twenty-two were subcommitteemen, designed to "aid in the gathering of information and the educational phase to fit in with the local organization." These were augmented by faculty men, acting under orders from Provost Deutsch of Berkeley, who served as informers; meanwhile university spies were photographing strike leaders and taking stenographic notes of all addresses.

Anti-semitism, which we shall find as an inevitable by-product of the growth of Vigilantism, was more pronounced at U.C.L.A. On November 2, students arriving on the campus were greeted by a band of stalwarts pinning small American flags on all within their reach, simultaneously offering an anti-Red pledge for signatures. When a Jewish student refused to accept a flag, he was loudly warned: "You dirty Jew, we'll run you off the campus along with the Reds!" That night a loud-speaker, heralding the arrival of alumni to the campus, blared forth his name for public scorn. There were few who refused the flags. As one student wrote: "How many accepted them because they were unaware of the factors behind the display of patriotism and how many others wore the flags reluctantly, under the influence of the prevailing fear psychosis, it is impossible to conjecture."

The day of the strike at Berkeley saw Vigilantism make its most determined bid. On the eve of the walkout, President Sproul announced that no meeting would be tolerated on the campus and that the police had been so informed. Reversing his earlier noncommittal stand, he issued his edict and hurriedly departed from the campus. That morning's issue of *The Daily Californian* carried his indictment of the strike; when its leaders sought to compromise and agreed at Provost Deutsch's suggestion to shift their session to Sather Gate, they believed that strife had been averted.

But in the meanwhile the administration had sent letters to professors demanding that they be present at their classes ten minutes earlier than usual, take the roll—an unusual procedure in most classes—and ascertain the names of all who left for the strike or sought to announce it in the time before the meeting began.

In that atmosphere, the inevitable occurred. The Vigilantes stormed the strike rally, transforming the scene into a sustained riot; speakers were attacked by missiles of every description; fights were frequent and usually bloody; organized booing choruses endeavored to drown out the speakers. The only declaration of opinion from the Vigilantes came when Stuart McClure rose to shout from the platform: "I don't see why this U.C.L.A. mess concerns us."

That afternoon Provost Deutsch publicly condoned the actions of the Vigilantes, declaring in a press statement:

". . . What happened today should at least make absolutely clear that upon the campus here at Berkeley the students have little sympathy with any effort of this kind to disrupt the work of the university."

As *The San Francisco News* commented: ". . . Dr. Deutsch seems to rejoice in the rowdyism of students who were not in sympathy with the protest movement."

Dr. Deutsch was not alone. From the outset of the dispute, every incitement had been given to the students. Out of either compulsion or ignorance, depending upon the individual case, they had responded. Yet their deeds served at least one notable function: they aroused honest and sensitive liberals to the perils of the situation and the grave portents implicit in it. From that realization was welded a concerted and unyielding protest in behalf of the suspended group. Unfortunately, four of the five suspended did not see the

281

need for organized opinion; they hoped to slip back into the university by testifying to their own purity. Thus, they went so far as to declare that Provost Moore had lost four valuable allies for his purge. One must acknowledge, however, that they had been subjected to a gruelling experience, of which they did not comprehend the total meaning. They were terrorized and brow-beaten; lacking an essential understanding of the events, they played directly into the hands of the red-baiters by isolating Miss Celeste Strack, the National Student League member who had been suspended —and who, incidentally, was the outstanding woman debater on the coast and a member of Phi Beta Kappa.

President Sproul, after maintaining his silence for two weeks after the strike, suddenly announced the reinstatement of the four Student Council members. His statement at the time was significant: "I find no evidence convincing me that the suspended students, either directly or indirectly, gave approval to the work of the National Student League." His implication was clear; if he had found such evidence, they would not have been so quickly restored to their posts.

But popular sentiment was gradually swinging; even Miss Strack could not be ignored. Whether the volume of protest, which was continually growing, was decisive in her reinstatement or whether the threat of legal action forced the university to capitulate cannot be estimated. It is probably safe to say that both, together with the fact that Merriam was by now snugly in office and the need for hysteria had diminished, conspired to insure her reinstatement. It is equally certain, however, that without the pressure of student and outside opinion, the administration would never have retreated.

Toward the end of March a group of students stood at Sather Gate, off the Berkeley campus, distributing leaflets which advertised the approaching peace strike. Prohibited from circulating literature on university grounds, virtually barred from any place in the college press, denied permits for meetings on and off the campus, they were resorting to their last method of presenting their views.

On March 20th the Berkeley police suddenly arrested nine of them for violating an ordinance passed in 1913 and never before invoked. The following day seven more were seized, rushed to the police station, photographed, fingerprinted and numbered with other "criminals."

The university administration endeavored to remain aloof from the incident. It described the arrests as a matter for the Berkeley authorities. It protested its innocence of the affair.

But on the Berkeley police blotter the following entries were registered: "U.C. by an unknown man says there will be distribution of leaflets tomorrow at—— (listing the time and place)."

On another page is written, under the caption "University of California": "The arrests made on the request of the above."

And twenty-four hours later, when fifteen students were handing out leaflets at the same place, only three were arrested—the three Jewish participants. The others protested that they were equally guilty. Two Christians, George Kelly and Jean Symes, went to the police station and offered themselves for custody. They were told to leave. When the story of the arrests was broadcast by one of the students, the word Jewish was censored by the radio officials.

Arraigned on March 25th, the defendants were informed by the judge that the contents of the leaflet had nothing to do with the arrests; he condemned their distribution because they were fire hazards and might "block up the storm drains." Yet the fact is that thousands of leaflets had been distributed before at the same place, in addition to volumes of commercial advertising. It is noteworthy that, although the last student arrested was a Jew by the name of Gertzel, his was the first case called. The reason was obvious. He had a pronounced semitic appearance and was afflicted with a

283

speech defect. He provided a good inaugural for the incitement of race hatred.

Provost Moore was somewhat becalmed. The furor over, his earlier act left him weary and indecisive as the strike against war approached. He wanted urgently to stop it. He would have liked to renew the purge at the expense of its leaders. But he could not view with equilibrium another storm such as he had just endured—at least not yet. Although he was plainly anxious to stem the movement at any cost, he did not see how that could be done without a repetition of the previous conflict. Hence he sought to have the student officers perform the task for him. When they refused, he turned to his old allies, The Americans. They were still replete with enthusiasm. At intervals they delivered threats against the peace leaders, warning that no demonstration would be tolerated. And the Provost did not intervene. In fact, John McElheney and Remington Omstead, Vigilante leaders, freely confessed that "Dr. Moore is always kept informed. . . . He knows all our plans." Again this great character in the educational world was readily assenting to the tactics of rowdyism. He seemed to enjoy the prospect.

At dawn on April 12th, the day of the strike, three fiery crosses were found on the campus of U.C.L.A. Simultaneously a deluge of handbills emerged, urging students to "unite and drive off the menace of communism."

Strife was narrowly averted. About 500 students gathered to hold a peace meeting without benefit of the Vigilantes, who had suddenly altered their plans. In the absence of the patriots, there was no "Red riot."

At Berkeley President Sproul was in a quandary. The day when appropriations would be voted was nearing, and there was a strong EPIC bloc in the house which had endorsed the anti-war strike. At the same time the Republicans were calling for drastic measures. Although the arrests had already taken place, Dr. Sproul was still reluctant to con-

demn the strike. He solved his dilemma by compromising
with himself. He merely had the regulations forbidding mass
meetings on the campus posted. But he was careful, in announcing that permission for the strike had not been granted,
to add that "neither has permission been given to break it
up." This was an advance over the earlier outbreak and it
served to insure that the day would pass without conflict.
Dr. Sproul had made the successful straddle. At Sather Gate,
scene of the October violence, several thousand undergraduates gathered to protest against war. The scope of the assemblage was a notable index of the advance of the insurgents.

One concluding item, which eloquently reveals the plight
of the faculties at these two institutions, should be mentioned. That spring a series of anti-Red bills was introduced
into the legislature. If enacted, these measures would have
made possession of liberal literature cause for a jail sentence.
Eighteen members of the University of California faculty
joined in a protest against the statutes, citing them as additional illustration of the tide of repression in the state.
Whereupon Assemblyman Martin, sponsor of the bills, wrote
an indignant letter to President Sproul, demanding that he
make a formal statement on the stand taken by his professors. He did. He disavowed any connection of the university
with the protest and hinted that such steps would not be
looked upon with favor in the future.

This was only an elaboration of his thesis of the summer
before when, in an address before several fraternal orders,
he devised what must be recorded as a classic interpretation
of the Bill of Rights. He said:

". . . The Bill of Rights in the Constitution guaran-
tees to all freedom of speech, . . . freedom of the
press, freedom of assembly. . . . There is no liberty
where those rights are denied. In order to protect this
freedom the university assumes the right to prevent exploitation of its prestige by unqualified persons, or by

285

those who would use it as a platform for propaganda. It therefore takes great care in the appointment of its teachers."

And that last sentence, as one writer remarked, "spells the doom of every teacher who dares to think independently and to express his thoughts." Like other institutions, California has its limited quota of progressive, forward-looking men—but they are exceptions. With startling regularity, dissenters find that they are "not reappointed" or that the path to advancement has been barred. A student at the institution depicts academic freedom there as "the freedom of students and teachers to think the thoughts and do the things of which the most conventional and respected members of the community approve." Granting the few exceptions cited, that has been inescapably true. The advance of repression has only accentuated that condition.

The 1935 Commencement at U.C.L.A. was a stirring performance. More than that, it was a characterization of the academic level for which Provost Moore and his cohorts are so earnestly striving. The Los Angeles press hailed the ceremonies; the perpetual alumnus felt just a little more proud to be a U.C.L.A. man. Sitting in his dignified administrative robes, Provost Moore smiled with the quiet jubilation of a man whose plans are maturing. The cause of this good humor was obvious; at his university, where students are being terrorized into submission, where faculty men live in fear of momentary exposure for nurturing an idea, the following press despatch related how extravagant was the Commencement program in June, 1935:

"Baby Le Roy and Virginia Weidler, Paramount child stars, were made honorary members of the graduating class of 1935 at the University of California. Baby Le Roy was voted Best Boy and Virginia was voted Movies Sweetheart."

286

VI. Students in Uniform

VIGILANTISM made its earliest headway in California. The circumstances of its arrival, however, were neither unique nor isolated. Although the coast was the first area to experience the full fury of the Red Scare, the hysteria rapidly travelled eastward. Out of that tension undergraduate Vigilantism arose, precipitating a cleavage more sweeping than the one—serious as it was—in California. And if the onrush of loyalty oaths, the terrorizing of professors and the outbreak of legislative inquisitions were identified with incipient fascism, the Vigilantes were the most palpable fulfillment of that trend. For their deeds had one distinguishing mark: the utilization of violence. Provost Moore had inspired precisely such strategy; the president of San José State had incited his loyal students to "take the radicals out and drop them off at the end of the campus." It was inevitable that the procedure should win its adherents in other territories where reaction was gaining a foothold. The Red Scare needed aid.

Although the Vigilantes were usually a spontaneous, local growth, their methods in each instance did not vary: the use of force was the essence of their theory, if such existed, and of their practice. That point is of crucial importance. The responsibility for violence should be fixed plainly and unequivocally, while there is a measure of sanity in the air, and the guilt rests with the Vigilantes and those educators and pressure-groups to whom they look for counsel and inspiration. Certainly the testimony of California supports that conclusion; even more striking are other cases which we shall investigate, in which the same performance is enacted. And the endeavors of the Vigilantes, although still decentralized, give no promise of subsiding. The possibilities of their growth are confirmed by reports from every part of the country where the need for a "purge" is being daily reiterated.

Who are the Campus Vigilantes? From what sections of

287

the undergraduate body are these terror-bands recruited? Why has it been so easy for the patrioteers, often abetted by university administrators, to organize the persecution of the insurgents? It is dangerous to over-simplify the answer. To see them as a regular pattern is to ignore the real import of their existence. They are as diverse in background, in credo and in purpose as the whole American undergraduate body. Once we acknowledge these complexities, however, we can still discover certain common denominators in the chart of their expansion. We will see, as already suggested in California, that three institutions form the main reservoir of the reactionary bloc: the Reserve Officers Training Corps, Fraternity Row and the Athletic Associations. Augmenting these, and often included within their ranks, is an even larger group, the "bribed aristocracy" of the undergraduate body—those who in one way or another are the recipients of rewards which administrators can furnish in jobs, scholarships and loans. Finally—and again let it be emphasized that these groupings are interspersed—there is the large contingent which acts from sheer ignorance and delusion; its members are vaguely dissatisfied with things as they are but have no clear comprehension of what they want. Hence they ease their own distemper by persecuting those whom conventional opinion repudiates.

I am not intimating that all fraternity men or R.O.T.C. followers are, per se, eager and willing to invoke violence against the student revolt. What will become evident, I suspect, is that these institutions are being utilized for that purpose, often to the dismay of their constituents. Each has a function as a camping-ground for reaction. If we understand their personnel, tradition and sponsorship, I believe that function will be clear.

Less than a month after the first student strike against war, several hundred representatives of R.O.T.C. units were summoned to an emergency session in Washington. It was not widely publicized. All that was openly announced was the launching of a nationwide assault on "subversive pacifists." How planned was the link between this conclave and the violence which became manifest within the following year is impossible to ascertain. It can safely be stated, however, that the formation of Vigilantes was immeasurably aided and often inspired by the R.O.T.C. functionaries.

From our earlier study of the expansion of the corps, this development proceeds with complete logic.* Ever since its inception, the campus military agency has displayed the symptoms of intolerance, of chauvinism and of mental rigidity. The concept of a "good soldier"—the man who obeys orders—is the keynote of R.O.T.C. doctrine in more than military matters. What happened in 1934 was a shift in strategy, rather than a change in viewpoint, the introduction of violence where administrative bans, moral compulsions and whispering campaigns had once sufficed.

As far back as 1929 a prelude to the present technique was furnished. Three high school students were seized by cadets for distributing literature on Soviet Russia. They were brought before Sergeant John Holly, U. S. Army instructor, who said he would let them free and count five before turning the R.O.T.C. men on them. The boys fled, but were overtaken and severely beaten. Commenting on the case, *The Baltimore Sun* remarked: ". . . Apparently the R.O.T.C. and its managers have evolved no gentler or cleverer way of dealing with persons whose opinions they dislike than resort to terrorism and strong-arm tactics."

Two years later a group styling itself Young America organized to "stamp out radical agitation" at Roosevelt high school, Los Angeles, Cal. When several students sought to circulate left-wing pamphlets, the R.O.T.C. men, aided by the American Legion, attacked and beat them, then smashed the cooperative restaurant where the radicals met.

Perhaps the most revealing statement of the case was made

* For the history of the R.O.T.C., see the chapter "A Pre-War Generation."

289

by Major Herbert Holton of C.C.N.Y., leader of the military department, who, in 1932, urged the formation of a vigilante committee to combat the radicals. Said Major Holton: "Force is the ultimate sanction in the world."

Nor has the corps hesitated to fulfill his suggestion. At City College and elsewhere the American philosophic counterpart of *Mein Kampf* has been swiftly translated into its practice. According to *The Army and Navy Register*, the R.O.T.C. has "developed a great educational mission as an antidote to the various forms of subversive activities which is (sic) spreading through our colleges." If its technique of education was once subtle intimidation, now more drastic methods have been inaugurated. It has not been a long step; the roots were there, waiting for the emergency which would call them forth. The rulers of the corps have been undeniably aroused by the spread of anti-war activity, and with eminent justification. For one of the major targets of this action has been the R.O.T.C. itself, the campus personification of war and repression. By its behavior in recent events, the corps has clearly vindicated this description.

For the past decade the fraternity system has been submitted to vehement criticism from a host of different quarters. So prolonged has been the attack that it has suffered from stereotype; of late, however, the terms of the critique have been vastly altered. The fraternity system has ceased to be the evil among evils, to be shattered above all else and at any cost. It is now merely one of a set of institutions firmly dedicated to the preservation of the status quo, and should be evaluated in those terms.

Why this tendency? The answer is largely two-fold, lying in the structure of the fraternity system and its present-day composition. It must be abundantly plain that the Greek-letter house is a refuge for alumni; it exists for them—and by them. Without their financial endowments scores of houses would have closed down long ago. Without their periodic drives for funds, Fraternity Row would be neither so elaborate nor well-equipped as it is today. In return the alumni preserve their link with their undergraduate days; the house is their medium for sentimentalizing, for recapturing that hallowed past when they too lived within the college walls. And to them anything which would change the scene beyond recognition is undesirable; it deprives them of a timeless symbol.

There is another, less sentimental reason for their bias against change. The alumnus who can afford to devote funds and energy to the perpetuation of a fraternity is likely to be a good business man; more often than not, he is a citizen of standing in the community, the man who has made his mark, the perfect incarnation of the success dream. He cannot fathom why there is discontent with an order which has given so freely to him; like Mr. Walgreen, he believes that America always was and continues to be a land of opportunity. This spirit pervades Fraternity Row. It is one of the last and most powerful hangovers of the golden era, replete with all the attitudes engendered by the time.

And the present inhabitants of Fraternity Row are gallantly pursuing the tradition. It is logical that they should be one of the last groups on the campus to respond to the fresh currents of a changing world. For they are indisputably, as a body, the most economically secure section of undergraduates. They have to be. Greek-letter dues, the demands of the social life so intimately connected with fraternities, the necessity for "keeping up appearances"—all take their toll in funds. Moreover, Greek-letter houses have always drawn the sons of the prosperous; the man who has to work his way through college is not likely to be engrossed by the prospect of a fraternity existence, with all its preoccupations and responsibilities.

This has had, as I have suggested, wide consequences in terms of ideas. It was in Fraternity Row that the most extravagant phases of the "jazz era" flourished; it was there that the notion of the college man as a curiously inert specimen took shape; it was there that the college, as a haven of retreat from any pressing political or social considerations, reached its highest stage. These conditions have persisted among Fraternities to a greater extent than anywhere else, for the very excellent reason that the average fraternity man has been the last to feel the effects of world disorder. Thus today the chapter house is probably the one place on the campus at which you will find relatively little difference in tone from the vanishing hey-day; there will be bridge-games, crap-shooting, backgammon and dances just the same as a decade ago; hardly a chair will appear to have been moved. Discussion will have veered only slightly from its ancient channels.

Just as these forms have prevailed, so has the classic prejudice against the intellectual. It was not fashionable to ponder external events ten years ago; the man who did so was likely to be branded an iconoclast or, more vividly, a "drip"; he would help neither the house nor its inmates and he was a good person to avoid. That hostility, in somewhat modified terms, has endured. It is encouraged by the back-slapping alumni who return to what they hope is the same old college; it is fostered by the moguls who, above all, want to save the "good name" of the house and want nothing which savors of non-conformity lest it interfere with next year's rushing. They want their dreamland undisturbed. Snobbery, of a peculiarly non-intellectual tone, is the dominant note; it is still based on clothes or family name or "smoothness," and the hundred associated virtues of a disappearing era.

Granting these initial conditions, one could easily have foreseen the fraternity's rôle in the resolution of undergraduate conflicts. For war, depression and fascism are unwarranted intrusions; to a man inured in the fraternity spirit, the response is likely to be a pained "why bring that up?" More than that, they are downright challenges to all that is sacred and worthwhile. Those who promote activity on such issues

292

are trouble-makers. They are fellows who couldn't get along anywhere. They don't belong in college. This may seem an extreme statement of the case and yet, as we shall see, that is what it simmers down to. The aura of the past rests heavily upon Fraternity Row and will not be easily dispelled.

The customary defense of the fraternity—that it provides a meeting-ground for individuals of common interest—only obscures its real nature. Friendships are neither formed nor preserved merely by the weird mumbo-jumbo of Greek-letter ritual. If real grounds for comradeship exist, they do not need a fraternity pin to enforce them.

Lest this analysis seem unfair, let me confirm it by the blunt declaration of a leader of the fraternity system at Columbia. He is, and has been for several years, an ardent advocate of the Greek-letter system. He has no desire to injure it by public avowals. And yet, perhaps tired of the endless rationalizations in which his brothers have indulged, he declared what he felt to be the truth. I quote from an article by Jerome B. Harrison, of Alpha Delta Phi which appeared in *The Columbia Jester* of October, 1934: "The fraternity is essentially a snobbish institution. . . . It is anathema to anyone with a Keen Sense of Social Responsibility." (Capitalization as in original.)

This was an unfortunate confession, swift to be repudiated by his colleagues. Its full force cannot be minimized. What he said so succinctly was more revelatory than a hundred lampoons by Greek-letter enemies. It was a disarmingly frank admission that the fraternity, by its very structure, will not usually harbor those who have broken from the time-worn paths.

This has been more than a passive war. For today, as we shall discover, Fraternity Row is lining up with the wholesome, conservative, healthy-minded boys to ward off the inroads of thought and dissent. It has been an utterly logical outgrowth of a system whose perspective is so clearly shaped by a dying past.

I have never been able to voice any genuine reformist rage at the "scandals" of commercialism in athletics. With each successive disclosure, I feel even more strongly that the athletes are an unhappy lot. They have to work for a living. They are not the pampered children of idleness. The only idleness most of them have ever known is the forced unemployment of their fathers. Drawn from mining towns, from lumber regions, from steel centers, they have been chosen for education because they are husky. Football scouts intermittently tour the industrial centers in the hope of finding some good, able-bodied material; when they discover such, the dragnet of scholarships, jobs and other inducements is quickly thrown out. That's how first-rate football teams are born.

And yet, as I have said, these do not seem shocking revelations. The boys do not get anything for nothing. It is true that they are often provided with soft jobs at which they appear only once a week to collect their pay. But this reward is really earned. They are subjected to five days a week of gruelling preparation for one big outing at which the college community, from Trustees down through boyish alumni and further, experiences an intensely vicarious form of exercise. They must endure the lash of a highly-paid coach whose major asset is his facility for cursing or his ingenuity in "getting the most out of the boys." They must suffer periodic injuries which lay them up on an infirmary bed for weeks at a time—causing damage often beyond repair. They have to "make the grade" on the gridiron or be gently informed that their college careers are over. This is a life of stress and strain, with pitfalls and despair in body and in mind. The athletes are more to be pitied than censured for asking a decent wage.

One might anticipate that the blows of the athletic speed-up would make the headline heroes a rebellious lot. But they aren't, and with good reason. For the patriots have been quick to capitalize on their forced subservience. In Hearst's

New York Journal there recently appeared an unexpected tribute to Columbia. It was not a bouquet for the 3,500 students who participated in the anti-war strike last April. It was a salute to her athletic warriors. The editorial decried the large group of noisy radicals at the institution but went on to draw solace because Columbia "still retains some of the old Columbia spirit which in the past made it eminent as a patriotic institution—and, incidentally, at various times, as the possessor of many first-rate fighting football teams." From this the writer proceeded to some more general observations on the relation of the athlete to the affairs of his time:

> "For some reason which the psychologist can perhaps explain, football and communism don't go well together. We never heard of a soap-box orator who made a team. We never heard of a good halfback who cared two straws for Marx or Lenin."

The explanation is not nearly so elusive as the editorial writer sought to make it. In the first place, the average gridman, compelled to devote most of his waking hours to preparing for the next game, is not likely to have much time or energy for politics. After a good day's scrimmage, he will more probably batter his head against a few French verbs and then fall lightly to sleep. The antics of foreign rulers or those closer to home will seem utterly alien in his condition. There are more pressing problems on his mind. After all, he isn't being financed through college to ponder Plato or politics; his task is to smash through left-tackle for at least seven yards every time he gets the ball.

If his own weariness is not enough to stifle rebellion, however, there will be those alert to see that he has some help. A gentle reminder, a hint or a forceful weekly address will convince him to stay away from Social Problems Club meetings. There is that matter of next year's scholarship to be borne in mind, or some other favor from Trustees and alumni who have no use for the Social Problems Club. There is the good name of the college to be remembered. Let an assistant coach spy his left end on a picket line and that end is through—unless he is either too spectacular to be sacrificed or quickly amenable to counsel.

It is but a short step from negative admonition to positive exhortation; the athletes turn to Vigilantism. In many instances they enlist at the friendly hint of the coach, who in turn has been advised from above to help "mop up" the radicals; in others the athletic hero will do so spontaneously, not because he has any awareness of what he is doing, but because he thinks it's a good way to ingratiate himself with the dispensers of funds. And as long as he is on the hurling end of the eggs, tossed indiscriminately at pacifists, liberals and communists alike, his interest in politics will not be curbed. It's healthy self-expression.

There is only one consoling aspect to this situation. Retrenchment in education is at last striking at the gridiron; even the wages of high-grade quarterbacks are going down. This descent in their living standards will have a fortunate effect if it rouses them to a sense of the purpose for which they are being utilized—against their own interests. For come war and reaction, not even the leading scorer in The Big Ten will be exempt from the collision of social forces. He may find just how transitory is the acclaim bestowed upon him by Trustee, alumnus and administrator alike. Let him assert his rights as a human being rather than as a football player and his enlightenment will be swift. But the awakening has hardly begun; for the present, the bearers of glory to alma mater are cheerfully performing an extra assignment —the forceful squelching of the insurgents. When a football stadium is picketed by striking gridmen, or when the intermission between the halves is devoted to a peace exhortation by the captain, then one of the last citadels of the old order will have fallen.

Such are the three bulwarks of Vigilantism. But they are not alone. For what applies to the athletic luminaries is often true of a far larger number of undergraduates who have never advanced to such headline fame. They are the receivers of scholarships, of jobs and loans, the men who could not go to college without financial aid—and are in constant danger of being reminded of the fact. They are the rank-and-file of the "bribed aristocracy," of which Saturday's heroes are the favorite sons. The extent to which this "obligation" is impressed upon the recipients varies from place to place; on some campuses it is quite overtly expressed, on others only subtly hinted. I am familiar with an example of the most glaring type which occurred in a university professedly devoted to the more liberal learning. From it we may deduce what takes place in institutions where the need for platitudes is not so acutely felt.

In February, 1935, two left-wing students at Columbia College were deprived of their scholarships because of a technicality whose merits we will not examine now. They proceeded to appeal for loans in order to continue their studies. And they were met with prompt refusal. Dean Hawkes did not hesitate to tell them the reason—and he has privately repeated it to me and several others. The explanation was simple: one of his informants had reported that these two students had been distributing leaflets condemning a recent increase in fees enacted by the Trustees. Since they had thus declared their criticism of university policy, he could not recommend them for loans. I asked him whether he would have preferred them to hide their convictions in so free an institution of learning. He hedged, stammered and concluded by reiterating his position. When I suggested that this was a form of bribery, he threw up his hands in despair. He could not fathom why I was so slow to understand his position on financial dispensations. The most revealing incident was yet to come. Upon further investigation, it was found that one of the two victims had not been distributing

297

the leaflets, although he was frank to say that, if he had been present, he would have done so. But, because he had committed "no overt act against the university," he was granted a loan. The other victim was punished. This delicate distinction probably does not exist in most universities.

That is what is expected in return for the favors of an administration: devoted and unquestioning loyalty to anything which the Trustees prescribe. It is not to be wondered that students, in need of financial aid, deliberately curry approval by joining the Vigilantes. These are times of stress, and a man must do unpleasant tasks to get along. When the choice lies between Vigilantism and abandoning college, only the brave or the far-sighted will accept the latter alternative. The long list of needy in our colleges provides reliable shock-troops for the assault on heresy.

But it should not be believed that the Vigilantes are prodded into action by administrators or alumni alone, and against their own will. Certainly there are such. Even more disconcerting, however, is the large number who join the ranks out of sheer misconception and ignorance. They do not fathom the significance or potentialities of their acts. They probably regard them as a new and more stimulating phase of college life. What they do is based upon the fierce prejudices of their homes, their communities and their colleges, and often nothing more. Recently a survey was conducted by Professors Brameld and Dudycha of Long Island University to determine how much the undergraduate knows or doesn't know of contemporary issues. Certainly the results were far more promising than they would have been ten years ago; on the other hand, there was a large group "quite ignorant of the meaning of socialism, communism, fascism, or, in any real sense, democracy." That survey was a comprehensive one, based upon the responses of 857 students in nine representative colleges to questions concerning the most immediate problems of the day. Of these issues, orthodox education had given them only a bare hint, surrounded by a series of prejudices and half-truths.

And the sponsors of Vigilantism have availed themselves of this confusion. They understand the dormant hatreds which incessant propaganda has instilled in the school, in the press, in the cinema. They realize the spectres which can be conjured up by a single word—"Red" or "Jew" or "Nigger," depending upon the locality. These are the inevitable instruments of reaction. The Vigilantes are often the innocent victims. For their stake in war and poverty is usually no different from that of their colleague. The dictates of self-interest, if allowed to operate unchecked, would align them on the side of the insurgents. Instead, they are again being mobilized to perform a task which, so they are told, is an imperative public service. The ensuing case histories are indicative of the process by which Vigilantes are made.

MICHIGAN STATE

About four years ago the national headquarters of the R.O.T.C. circulated a bulletin outlining the civic virtues of the corps. It was a document full of self-laudation; to confirm the officers' enthusiasm about themselves, however, a series of endorsements from prominent citizens was included. Among the contributors was President R. S. Shaw of Michigan State College who wrote:

"I have always been strongly in favor of required military drill for freshmen and sophomores. . . . By far too many American boys fail to appreciate the significance of discipline and obedience. If they do not learn to understand what these things mean at all in the elementary schools, it is time for the college to give them a proper impression."

There was more than passing importance to this utterance, signifying as it did the nature and end of education within the institution. Just four years after this declaration, an Ann Arbor minister, whose experiences at the school will later be detailed, wrote his own recommendation for the conduct of Michigan State: "Let the West Point of the West close its doors to the co-eds, honorary colonels included, and apply itself to the job of making good officers in its three units of infantry, cavalry and coast artillery."

President Shaw may denounce the suggestion as unwarranted and his resentment may be shared by sections of the student body. There is abundant justification for it, however, on the basis of comparatively recent developments.

Until the early spring of 1935, there had been no prolonged symptoms of thought on this "well-disciplined" campus. If one could conceive of a school smothering within the confines of its own narrowness, Michigan State might have been one of the earliest victims. The pattern of its life was simple, unhurried and free from controversy. Where there was dissent it was tactfully concealed, but I doubt that any considerable subterfuge was necessary. The vast majority of faculty members was too rigidly conservative to encounter any limitation on its activities and a small liberal group within its ranks soon became adapted to the routine. One student informs me that several faculty members have frankly confessed to him that they were "afraid to express any opinions." If sedition lurked within the college's walls, there was emphatically no classroom outlet for it; communism or any concept of basic social reform, far from being preached by the professorial staff, was virtually taboo as even a source of discussion. This zealous impartiality, however, does not extend to the power interests, which receive more than casually favorable mention in text-books, engineering classes and during "Farmers' Week" on the Campus. Recalling that the Federal Trade Commission disclosed a $6,500 payment by the Detroit Edison Co. and Consumers Power Co. for fellowships and scholarships, we find one concrete intimation of the friendship between the utility business and the school.

Holding primary sway, however, and far overshadowing any efforts of ordinary faculty members, is the military hierarchy represented by the R.O.T.C. Two years under its direction are compulsory for every student; what this means can perhaps most clearly be gleaned from a now celebrated remark of one of the professors in cavalry. Admonishing his pupils to bestow greater energies on their labors, he shouted: "Remember, when you ride down the field, you are not sticking a dummy with your sabre. That is a man and I want that sabre to be dripping with guts."

One can readily discern how President Shaw's plea for "discipline" and "obedience" has been taken to heart by the loyal functionaries of the military instruction department. The setting could hardly have been conducive to any independence of mind or scholarly zeal on the part of the student body. When in East Lansing, they understood, do as you are told to do. No explicit instructions were usually required. I asked the editor of the student newspaper there for any specific illustrations of repression of student thought in past years. That he is a fairly typical Michigan State student will soon become clear and hence his reply, more candid than I could have hoped, is striking: "There is no faculty repression of student thought here because there is no student thought. Students are free to get roaring drunk at any time and thus work off their discontentment, if they have any."

Another problem in Michigan was the infiltration of certain un-Aryan stock. While only about fifty to one hundred Jews are enrolled, Mr. Cleary, the editor of the student newspaper, informs me that "There is definite opposition to Jewish students here. It has developed because of the Jews' clannishness. . . ." He did not explain whether he believed the clannishness arose out of any peculiar race characteristics or the polarization which unconcealed prejudice quite naturally impells.

If these intruders were a perplexing group, however, they did not receive any undue attention until other events precipitated the feud into the open. In addition to the Jews, there are about twenty-five Negro students, of whom Mr. Cleary writes: "There is little prejudice against Negroes— they are allowed to take an active part in athletics and evince little interest in social life which would, of course, be discouraged. However, the East Lansing schools have refused to let Negroes do their practice teaching there."

In so tranquil and normal an atmosphere, the existence of any patriotic societies to reenforce the military department as a bulwark against treason may appear to be undue caution. Mr. Cleary contended that "a strong chapter of Scabbard and Blade, military honorary," seems to be sufficient. But it isn't. For his edification, for he indicates no knowledge of the fact, it should be revealed that there is also present at Michigan State a secret organization known as The Knights of the Sherwood Forest. Instrumental in fomenting the college's most acute case of mob spirit, it is an offshoot of the Ku Klux Klan; its members have pronounced anti-semitic leanings and they work, in many instances, hand in hand with the military department.

Finally, we should not neglect to observe that Michigan State is the producer of renowned football teams whose members are husky, patriotic and profoundly indebted to their administrators—a debt which they have paid with more than football victories.

Michigan State has prospered and expanded. Her students have been successfully weaned away from any preoccupation with worldly affairs; her faculty has surrendered whatever originality or critical capacity it may have possessed in return for a regular pay-check. The power interests have proved deeply grateful for the sympathy they have received. While her contributions to learning may have been undistinguished and sporadic, Michigan State can be secure in the knowledge that her military department graduates soldiers, men who can take orders.

That interval when a state university's appropriations bill is pending before the state legislature is the most precarious in the life of an administrator. No matter how cautious, sub-servient and humble he may be by profession, these traits will be augmented tenfold in that tortuous period. In the midst of the witch-hunt of 1935, President Shaw and his colleagues could find no rest.

Usually they would have had no specific source of concern. Even Mrs. Dilling's "Red Network" was unable to involve the conformist halls of East Lansing—and if she could discover no heresy there, one might suppose that there was none. The guiding figures of the school should have been remarkably serene, whatever the turmoil elsewhere. They weren't. And the reason was a group of young men who were organizing plans for a strike against war.

It is probable that President Shaw had heard very dimly, if at all, of the approaching nationwide demonstration. Such occurrences were normally of only remote interest to him. Perhaps his lack of awareness prompted him to grant permission for the conduct of a peace meeting in one of the campus halls. Either he was reprimanded for the error or saw the light himself; at any rate, he was swift to reverse his decision, warning that no such assemblage would be tolerated. That stand, of course, was more in tune with the environment and tradition of the school and the precepts of the military department. It was rigidly pursued after the initial mistake had been rectified.

For President Shaw and his underlings had never cared for the Social Problems Club. Its very name was sinister, foreign to the atmosphere. The topics with which it dealt, war, economic crisis, a profitless social order, seemed fit for only alien, unorthodox and probably morbid minds. A true Michigan State man, I have been given to understand, would firmly reject any link with it.

After his ill-fated grant of a campus building for the meeting, President Shaw soon set about to compensate for

303

his mistake. A cordial hatred for the proposed demonstration was swiftly inculcated among the administration and transmitted to the student body. Everyone was enlisted in an effort to convince the legislators that the peace meeting had neither the endorsement nor the sanction of a loyal and devout institution. In their haste to acquit themselves and reassert their purity, college officials publicly endorsed the Dunckel bill then before the legislature—a measure which would have made possession of a liberal periodical a criminal offense. Whether they liked it or not, the statute had the support of such compelling lobbies as the American Legion, the Chamber of Commerce and the Veterans of Foreign Wars. An aspiring administrator, especially in an hour when his appropriation is pending, must accord solemn tribute to such agencies; nor have we any reason to believe that the officialdom at State college had any secret opposition to the gag-bill.

So word was sped of the official position. Mr. Cleary somewhat obscurely explains: "The *State News* is relatively free from censorship. During the anti-war strike agitation I was told by the officials to do as I pleased. Only when appropriations are involved is there much guidance from the Administration."

Whether Mr. Cleary required "guidance" in this instance or whether he acted from instinct is still uncertain. The fact is, as he admitted: "As editor of the paper I received the first propaganda distributed about the strike but refrained from publicizing it because I saw no intelligent plan in it."

This discriminating news judgment was unquestionably a signal public service. Although later on an article on the event managed to break into the paper's columns, the journal was fairly consistent in its oblivion to the venture.

These preliminary discouragements, however, did not succeed. More naïve than their contemporaries and still believing that the right of assemblage was among the prerogatives extended a citizen, the members of the Social Problems

Club proceeded with their preparations. Such unfamiliarity with the ways of the world may have astonished more realistic sections of the college population, but they soon recovered their balance to organize their own views on the matter.

A young man named Louis Weisner was particularly indignant over the administration's ruling. So determined was he to obtain an explanation of the ban that he dared to go to the home of President Shaw for an interview. Now Michigan State is officially an agricultural college and President Shaw, I am informed, is an eminent authority on beef. His horizon did not extend very clearly, however, to the matter which was occupying Mr. Weisner's mind. After the student had submitted his inquiry, President Shaw lost any remaining restraint which he may have possessed. Turning upon Weisner, he bellowed: "Will you take an oath of loyalty to the constitution?"

The question might legitimately have been reversed. Weisner confessed that he saw no reason to be compelled to do so, and that, to his knowledge, the Bill of Rights was still a part of the document. President Shaw was utterly upset; he felt that he was being persecuted; he wanted to end the source of his troubles at once. Moreover, with the legislature still to enact his appropriation, continued discussion of peace seemed a distinctly lamentable matter.

Alternately enraged and panic-stricken, the Deans of Michigan State went to the legislature on the following day, asking the power to enforce the oath of allegiance in cases where they had "reason to be suspicious."

For several days before the anti-war meeting, there were intimations of impending violence. Telegrams were sent to parents of the boys participating, advising them that their sons were in danger because they had persisted in plans for the demonstration. The students themselves were apprised that they would encounter forcible resistance. On the eve of April 12th, however, the most inflammatory and bold gesture was staged by the patriots. I have mentioned the existence of anti-semitism at the school; after smouldering for years, it broke out that night in unconcealed terms. A contingent of 200 public-spirited students marched on the only Jewish fraternity at the school and, arrayed before it, shouted insults and threats to the occupants. It was an overwrought, serious throng. No one could confuse their deeds with college capers nor believe that the furor would quietly subside. From the crowd came vicious taunts and demands for the leaders of the peace meeting to surrender themselves for general maltreat-ment. There were caustic references to the ancestry of the fraternity members. There was unmistakable indication that the night's performance was only a preview of the day to come. It was probably disconcerting to this self-righteous band that the sponsors of the rally could not be intimidated.

If sufficient provocation had not already been extended by the military rulers of the college, the secretary of the school furnished the conclusive incitement. I have before me a clip-ping from the *Lansing State Journal* of April 12th in which that gentleman, J. A. Hannah, is quoted as declaiming: "This peace meeting is a blind for a radical gathering. The adminis-tration of the college will have no objection if other students toss these radicals in the river."

This was the temperate statement of a presumably sane officer of our higher education, in a school devoted to "disci-pline and obedience." The same newspaper, recounting the final phase of the pre-demonstration period, disclosed: "Around conference tables . . . deans and administrative officers were drawing up a plan of battle, football squad hus-kies were militantly assembling and governing bodies of campus societies were 'taking positions' on the peace issues."

Meanwhile, desperate efforts to find a suitable hall for the meeting proved futile; the interlocking directorate of town and college was functioning. *The Journal* reported: "The club has tried unsuccessfully for several days to obtain a place for a meeting. The college authorities denied use of any of the buildings and property owners of East Lansing followed suit."

President Shaw, trusting to the strong-arm tactics of his football players and soldiers, departed from the campus in the morning. Perhaps the ensuing spectacle might have been embarrassing to one so devoted to tranquillity. At any rate, there was no one in East Lansing unaware that President Shaw anticipated and condoned the brewing violence. Mr. Hannah had spoken for him in that morning's *Journal*.

It was exactly four o'clock in the afternoon when Weisner stood up before several hundred students and townspeople and opened the meeting. With no hall in either the college or East Lansing available to them, the demonstrators had met in the street.

Hardly had he begun, however, when it became clear, if any doubt still lingered, that the meeting would not proceed for long. The throng was dominantly hostile; most of those who were sympathetic were careful to conceal the fact. On the edge of the gathering was the student pastor of the People's Church, who had himself been expelled from the same campus years before for refusing to submit to military drill. Near him was a rabbi who had been warned by the conservative president of his synagogue to stay away from the assemblage or suffer the consequences. The college minister was there, tight-lipped, angry, yet unable to express his sympathy with the strike for fear of certain reprisal.

Weisner had started to speak but the tumultuous mob around him did not seem anxious to hear what he said. These stalwarts, far outnumbering the demonstrators and confident of their strength, contented themselves with cries of 'Comrade,' 'Back to Russia.' Suddenly a piece of fruit struck Weisner in the face; he casually removed his glasses, then continued. Whereupon another deluge of objects collected at the Kruger store in town was unleashed. The marksmen

307

had received most of their training in the R.O.T.C.; to their officers' consternation, their first attempts only rarely met with success.

The invaders had designated a leader who entrenched himself near the speaker, periodically raising his arm as a signal to his followers. At each gesture some new outbreak occurred. As Reverend Harold Marley, the principal speaker, whose address was never delivered, later wrote to me: "The military authorities who dominate the life of the Campus chose not to argue. . . . Rather, they decided to show the community and the legislature, in session a few miles away, who was boss of the Campus. There must be no discussion of peace to jeopardize appropriations."

As the uproar increased, the spirit of the hecklers rose until they received the signal to advance. Without further ceremony, they rushed toward the speaker's stand, grabbed hold of Weisner, four other students and Reverend Marley and started toward the Red Cedar river. The crowd trailed on behind, inspired by the scene.

"For the first time," said Reverend Marley, "I realized how Negroes must feel on the way to a solitary tree."

The network constructed by these patriotic bloods and their approving administrators was complete. Having set the stage for the capture, they were not to be deterred; the chief of police, long a foe of student pranks, would not move to defend the victims. A call was sent in for help from State police; but there was no response.

On the way to the river, the Knights of Sherwood Forest led the procession, their hats bearing an emblem of green sprigs. At their side was a bucket and a jug of tar—the American counterpart of castor-oil.

As the hysterical array tramped onward, the few who wanted to intervene realized how hopeless such action would have been. Nothing could have prevented the culmination of the long-planned foray.

The pastor and the rabbi provided dry clothes for the victims when they emerged from the river.

Mr. Cleary later assured me that "there was no violence at the demonstration, but only a considerable amount of garbage-throwing and the aforementioned ducking." It is true that those who were attacked have survived and will be able to profit by the fruit of that experience. That there were no fatalities, however, seems fairly irrelevant. As Reverend Marley commented: "If at East Lansing students can plan a military putsch in Washburn's smoke-shop and can fight with ammunition rejected by Kruger's drugstore, it is only a step to the armory across the street where more effective weapons are at hand."

Episodes like these are cumulative. When they are abetted by ignorance, by adherence to the dictates of a corrupt military caste, the possibilities become more menacingly outlined. The R.O.T.C. (Mr. Cleary says that it is "regarded with pride" on the Campus) was the primary instrument in the attack; it was not alone. The whole machinery of reaction in the town and in the college community was geared to stop this single peace meeting. Let us observe here, as we will in other colleges throughout the country and as we have already described in California, the source of "violence" in the controversy. And let us carefully note that this violence, so blithely and abstractly condemned by our educators goes unpunished when it comes from the right-wing.

Yet one cannot fix final responsibility upon the student Vigilantes. "Their teachers—the town and gown, were to blame," said Reverend Marley and in this there can be scant disagreement. Throughout the state patriots, represented by the Legion and its usual affiliates, had goaded the uprising; police officials turned their backs; and the educators who control the destinies of the school openly incited the outburst.

Shorty after the "ducking" was concluded, Mr. Fred Rush, a leader of the Junior Service League, an avowedly fascist

309

organization, appeared on the scene to launch a recruiting drive. His entry was symbolic. Whether the students knew it or not, a trained reactionary could perceive that they were ripe for his legion.

CONNECTICUT STATE

Among our more backward colleges, there are varying degrees of alertness to be discerned. Even our Jerkwater institutes have been compelled to recognize the serious disequilibrium of present-day life. Of course only the first glimmerings of enlightenment have penetrated; more often than not they are swiftly lost in the solemn campus affairs of the institute and the energetic efforts of its directors to avoid that which is even remotely fundamental.

Slumbering quietly on a hill overlooking Storrs, Connecticut, is Connecticut State College. Once it was known as an Agricultural school and received the abbreviated description of "Conn. Aggies." But more advanced spirits succeeded not long ago in effecting a decisive change; "Aggies" was neither a euphonious nor distinguished title; moreover, there were those in the Administration who were sufficiently heretical to believe that even a farmer should have a passing acquaintance with the liberal arts.

So Connecticut Aggies became Connecticut State College and, aside from certain reforms in its curriculum, resumed its placid, uneventful course. If, as I have said, a minimum of light has broken into almost every educational hall in recent years, Connecticut had been careful to prevent the infiltration of more than a chance beam. Its steadfast devotion to the ideal of simplicity, of seclusion, of divorce from the unpleasant strife of the world beyond the hill was vigorously maintained.

Yet agitation on campuses throughout the country was bound to produce reverberations even here and these cautious and upright Trustees responded more spontaneously to the omens than did the student body. In an effort to insure the respectability of the college with those dignitaries who matter, a bill was introduced into the Legislature early in 1935 to place the Adjutant-general on the board of overseers of the college.

Such a step was never envisaged, I am certain, as an incitement to rebellion among the students. Those accustomed to supervising their affairs had never been disturbed before and were hardly expectant that the lambs would rise up now. But a Social Problems Club had been recently formed there. To the dismay and bewilderment of the administration, this group had come into existence resolved to shatter some of the provincialism of the college in which its members resided. The nomination of the Adjutant-general first attracted attention to its activities.

Almost immediately after the nominations the club circulated a petition protesting the threatened appointment. Liberal groups throughout the state interested themselves in the campaign. Moreover, the Connecticut student body, inert and unenthusiastic as it was, managed to express a fairly unanimous sentiment. So overwhelming was the pressure for defeat of the bill that not even the determined lobbying of the American Legion could save it from oblivion. The episode, however encouraging to those who saw evidences of awakening among the Connecticut State students, enraged the petty moguls who are its Trustees. For they are not powerful business figures, much as they might like to be. Most of them are merely small-town Babbitts striving frantically to advance their prestige to the proportions of a big-college trustee; they have delusions of grandeur which are still far from realization. To this august body, with its deep-rooted local prejudices, its middle-class strivings, its eternal instinct to conform, the rebuff to the Adjutant-general was a source of no small displeasure.

Frustrated in this venture, the organizers of reaction throughout the state introduced a teachers' loyalty oath bill.

Again their efforts were blocked by the rising progressive onrush. Not that the American Legion was lacking in followers; but for once its foes met them on their own ground, speedily formed ranks, and stemmed the tide. With these two reverses a matter of general indignation, the Trustees at Storrs were obviously seeking to salvage something from the debacle. The nationwide student strike against war apparently gave them their cue.

There was no strike at Connecticut State. Whatever concern had been aroused over the two previous campaigns, the students were still too apathetic to continue their education. April 12 passed with only a meeting sponsored by the Social Problems Club in the evening. But this should not be minimized. It was only the second assemblage in the history of the college in which the problem was discussed; moreover, several hundred seemingly interested and wide-eyed students attended.

Even that was too much for the Trustees, already sensing an international plot in these unprecedented developments. Further, the advances which the peace movement had made in other colleges foreshadowed even more menacing spectacles at Connecticut. All these incidents accumulated in the Trustees' tortured minds. By the following Monday, the date of their regular meeting, they were prepared to crack down.

The resolution which was adopted at that now historic session of the Trustees has few parallels in the life of American Universities. Connecticut is the home of some of America's largest munitions interests. Outwardly this may have only symbolic bearing on the resolution, but if we understand the aspirations of the Trustees, the connection may appear more precise. The statute they handed down was explicit, reading:

"Military training is declared to be a part of the college instruction.. Any public agitation or formal public discussions on the campus promoted by individuals on the college staff or individual students, which reflect upon the college military instruction or training, will subject such individuals to cause for removal."

I can find no more frank and unequivocal admission in any of the decisions of Trustees of American colleges. Neither the origin nor the purpose of the measure was unique; what was unprecedented was the bold and unassuming way in which it was presented. Other schools have freely penalized anti-war leaders and invoked the harshest reprisals against them, but invariably they cloak their efforts in more altruistic garments. Whether inexperience or panic prompted this breach of disciplinary etiquette is uncertain. The fact is that the Trustees had announced that peace was too dangerous a subject for students to handle and that the War Department's emissaries on the campus were above criticism.

Nor did they conceal the intent of the move. In conversations with the press, the Trustees blandly stated that they were seeking to "prevent the disorders which have occurred in other colleges."

Charles C. McCracken, the president of the University, was not, by any definition, a radical. Yet he had enough perception to oppose the resolution and publicly to brand it "preventive and not remedial." His resignation, as we shall see, was announced less than a month afterward.

Having completed their task, the Trustees dispersed, hopeful that Connecticut State was once again safe for the sons of decent, self-respecting citizens. If there had been cause for uneasiness over the unrest of preceding months, however, the statute only brought forth a new phase in the extra-curricular education of the Connecticut undergraduates.

The faculty of this little New England college was long ago attuned to a career of shameless servility. Hemmed in on every side by the static rigidity of the community, they soon renounced any independence which might have once been theirs. The experience of one youthful member in his brief attempt to assert himself should suffice to demonstrate the attitude of his older colleagues. He is a relatively new member of the psychology faculty; after a trip to the Soviet Union, he returned impressed with the achievements of the Soviets in eliminating many of the neuroses and maladjustments so familiar to our society. In his enthusiasm he dared to state his views in the course of a public meeting; he suggested that all things Bolshevik were not inevitably undesirable, and that in the sphere with which he was most acquainted their accomplishments were manifold.

His respectable, ignorant and bigoted audience was horrified. With terrifying swiftness his remarks were circulated through the neighborhood, exaggerated, misconstrued, and finally communicated to the college authorities. Soon it was an open secret that his tenure at Connecticut was decidely precarious. Of course, if he had returned to relate the sad fate of the Russian people under communism, his welcome would have been very different.

More in harmony with the spirit of the institution is a loyal servant of the public utilities who is ironically described as a professor. So notorious was his pandering to the utility interests that when I later addressed a meeting of the school and referred sarcastically to "impartial" propagandists for the utilities, there was loud snickering in the hall. Even his students were on to him. Nevertheless—or consequently— he was the man whose tenure was safest in the institution. The remainder of the faculty was not far behind him in paying lip-service to the gods.

Confronted with the gag-rule which the Trustees had suddenly enacted, the students could hardly have been expected to display any considerable militance. Only the thoroughly unscrupulous, however, could accept it without a semblance of consideration. Moreover, the stand of President Mc-Cracken was known to them and may have served to bolster their spirits. Thus at its regular meeting the faculty proceeded to discuss the problem which had been raised. Meanwhile, the student newspaper, *The Campus*, had expressed, in humble and apologetic tones, its own opposition to the ruling; the Social Problems Club was simultaneously circulating a petition calling for its repeal and several hundred signatures had been obtained. But fear, the fear inculcated through years of subservience and boot-licking, overcame the faculty. It ultimately went on record with a weak-kneed plea to the Trustees for reconsideration. It did not even have the courage to appeal to the Association of University Professors, although the respectability and propriety of that organization is well known. The subtle reign of terror which had oppressed this backwoods faculty for years now appeared with all its fury. They were literally overwhelmed by the spectre of dismissal—and they behaved in the best manner of the kept servants of reaction. Upton Sinclair, discussing the actions of our professors in similar situations, once quoted the verse of a celebrated political prisoner. Vivid is its application to the scarecrows of Connecticut:

"... But rather mourn the apathetic throng,
     the cowed and meek
Who see the world's great anguish and its wrong
     and dare not speak."

While terror gripped the men of learning at Storrs, the gag-rule had become an issue of major proportions in liberal circles throughout the East. Students in other colleges, who had probably encountered similar measures and fought them at their own schools, were incensed at the edict. Leading educators, many of whom would have shied the issue if it had required defiance of their own administrators, were vigorous in their condemnation. To the astonishment and chagrin of the Connecticut Trustees, their deed had failed to settle anything except their own blundering. Faced with this arbitrary ultimatum, the student body was roused to more thoughtful inquiry than it had ever undertaken before.

315

In neighboring colleges, plans were set in motion for a delegation to Storrs to urge revocation of the Trustees' action. But these valiant squires did not propose to back down in disgrace. Apparatus to quell the protest was already being set up. Several weeks before the dispute arose, I had accepted an invitation to address the Social Problems Club on "Fascism on the Campus." Shortly after the ruling, a spokesman of the club was called in by an administrative official who suggested that it would be "tactful" to postpone my talk. This was agreed to in view of the impending arrival of the representatives of other schools.

Recognizing the critical nature of the situation, the Administration apparently deemed it advisable to work through its "level-headed" subordinates within the student body. For this task the Student Senate proved admirably fit. It was this body which devoted itself unreservedly to preserving the "dignity" and the "good name" of Connecticut State—without the help of outside agitators. The student newspaper ably cooperated.

The prospect of a delegation from other schools provided these groups with an opportunity to direct the wrath of the students away from the Trustees. It must be understood that the average Connecticut undergraduate had never been involved in a situation resembling this one; all his loyalties were on the side of his "great and revered college," his campus leaders and his administrators. Few perceived the full import of the resolution, its relation to broader trends or its basic design. Instinctively they resented it as an intrusion and a violation of abstract principles which they dimly harbored; but beyond that their feelings were vague and easily diverted.

There were those in the college community prepared to capitalize on these circumstances. Obviously the military officials had rallied to the side of the Trustees; the ruling itself was a flattery which merited their ardent support. Aligned with them were the more developed reactionaries—those who

316

were utterly unperturbed by the gag-rule and determined to halt any agitation against it. In this category were a few members of the Faculty, prominent athletes and certain student officers.

When news of the contemplated delegation reached them, these functionaries began their activities in earnest. Their rationalization can be traced to their essential conception of a college as an isolated entity separated from the interests and movements of fundamental social forces. This was the premise for their hostility to those championing the campaign in other institutions. The cry of "outside agitator" has been raised so often that it tends to become bromidic; but the frequency of its usage has not diminished either the strength or meaning of the slogan. Around it gathered a substantial bloc of the student body, prepared literally to fight off the intrusion. In their minds burned only the long-indoctrinated dread of interference, of unfavorable publicity, of injury to the reputation of the college. Let the Trustees enact the most brazen and contemptible of gag-rules; let the last remnants of student independence be banished, and still the proprieties must be observed, the illusion of one happy family held intact. Grimly they assured themselves that the Trustees had intended no repression, that only the twisted fancy of misinterpreters could discover a sinister motive behind the action.

When an advance guard of three spokesmen for the delegation visited Storrs three days before the others were to arrive, they discovered that plans were on foot for forcible ouster of the intruders. The road leading to the campus was to be barricaded; students would defend the blockade with missiles, ready to let fly at the first sign of the delegation. It is difficult to estimate how many at Connecticut were sympathetic to the maneuvers; certainly every effort was being made to incite the undergraduate body against those who were coming on a mission of aid.

But the three who had gone on ahead to survey the ground succeeded, miraculously enough, in averting the violence—

temporarily. Instead of evicting the delegation, the student leaders decided to attempt to emasculate its purpose. A cordial reception would be waiting. On the eve of the arrival, a leaflet was issued by the undergraduate functionaries which blandly declared, under the caption "Hold Steady!":

> ". . . It will be the responsibility of every loyal student to see to it that no trouble is started by an irresponsible group. These visitors are very certainly our guests. . . . We have a splendid opportunity . . . to establish friendly feelings, show off the college and make a good impression on our fellow New England institutions. . . .
>
> "Let's forget any thought of mass action and turn the whole idea into a good-will sightseeing tour. . . . Further action on our part is unnecessary at the present time."

Meanwhile, the Student Senate had despatched a communication to the Trustees recommending reconsideration of the ruling. Having performed its duty, it could now devote itself wholeheartedly to the task of quelling the protest movement. What these undergraduates, so conditioned against the idea of intrusion, had failed to see was that the very fact of "intrusion" alone, represented in hundreds of letters, telegrams, statements throughout the country, had compelled the Trustees to agree even to discuss the ruling again. What they avoided, consciously or not, was the realization that without the stir created in countless other municipalities, the Trustees would have dismissed any local sentiment on the matter.

But with child-like faith they remained confident that, "if we keep this among ourselves," the Trustees would rescind their statute and all would again be tranquil. Unalterably convinced of this, they decided to minimize the purpose of the delegation and to turn its presence into a tour of inspection.

They partially succeeded. Nearly 200 students from a dozen colleges visited Storrs, conducted a meeting in the Chapel and departed without any visible response from a large number of Connecticut students. Unquestionably there were many who were impressed with the gravity of the issue as represented in the widespread interest it had awakened. But the admonition of the Student Senate—"Hold Steady"— had accomplished its aim.

The following Wednesday the Trustees reconvened. Before them were the visible evidences of the storm their ruling had aroused—protests arriving from people and groups who before had only a distant knowledge that Connecticut State College existed. The aspiring, backwoods careerists could not remain silent on the issue.

They had, however, the solace afforded them by the fealty of their undergraduates. At the meeting representatives of the Student Senate were called in; I have no transcript of the discussion but I am assured that it was polite, weak-kneed and apologetic—on the side of the students. While they recommended repeal of the resolution, they were continuously saluting the mighty moguls. If the gentry had been moved by the expressions of indignation on their desk, they must have been rejuvenated by the spectacle the Senate afforded. Gradually the interview lost its formality; one Trustee leaned over to one of the boys and remarked ominously: "You don't realize the extent of the communist menace in this country."

And the pupil—whose information on communism was probably even more negligible than that of his Trustee, was appropriately awed. For the benefit of the outside world the Trustees then proceeded to redefine their edict. In the clause referring to agitation against the R.O.T.C., they inserted the phrase "by a small minority." Thus, when and if the "majority" of the student body simultaneously felt the urge

319

to criticize the military instruction, it would be technically legal to do so.

It should have been clear, of course, that this amplification of the ruling only reenforced the danger of it. All repressive movements begin with an attack on a minority; soon they branch out into more extended fields. Moreover, the definition of a "minority" is open to diverse interpretations; 4,000 students may go out on strike against the war at Columbia University and its administrators will attribute the disturbance to a "small but vocal minority"!

At this juncture, however, the Student Senate exhibited its most colossal piece of boot-licking. With a confident flourish it proceeded to announce to the student body that the Trustees' redefinition of the gag-rule was a victory for the student body.

It is often difficult to discern where innocence ends and corruption begins. I cannot believe that the administrative vassals in the Student Senate, who proclaimed their triumph really believed what they said, no matter how earnestly they may defend their point. In view of their desperate efforts to reduce or nullify protest against the edict, one can well understand their eagerness to terminate the battle—with as much glory as possible.

On the following Friday evening I arrived at Storrs to deliver my postponed address to the Social Problems Club. The influence of the Senate's pronouncement had already been felt; the Club's endeavors to reveal the actual meaning of the "amplified" resolution were counteracted by the strenuous soft-soaping of the figureheads. Small in numbers and viewed critically by their fellow-students, the Club members could hardly hope to combat this sentiment.

Meanwhile the military department was stepping in more decisively to assert itself as a force for law, order and inertia. Violence was openly predicted for several days. By the time I reached Storrs there was general knowledge of preparations for an outbreak. What form it would take was still concealed but that the evening would not proceed peaceably was guaranteed.

In the interim President McCracken had resigned. In making public his withdrawal he insisted that maintenance of the gag-rule was not the cause and, to some extent, this is true. There had been strong differences of opinion between him and the Trustees over educational matters and it is likely that bitterness over the edict only hurried his departure. With this announcement, a new device to rout the agitators had been discovered. Now, the students were told, all must bend their efforts toward securing a "strong man for the presidency" and any "agitation" would injure that objective. I have never been able to discover precisely what was meant by the term "strong man"; in the light of subsequent events I have a grave suspicion. All these factors contributed to the tension of the evening. In addition, the cry of "Hate-the-Jew" was beginning to be heard.

Since the meeting was being held in the community church, twenty feet off Campus property, it did not violate the letter of the regulation even if, as I intended, the R.O.T.C. was unfavorably discussed. The small room was crowded, partly because of the anticipation of trouble and also because there still lingered among a large number of students some dissatisfaction with the conclusion of the dispute. As I started to speak, automobiles began to drive up and down outside the window, their horns shrieking and their occupants yelling jubilantly, "We want war; . . . we want war!" This subsided after a while and there was no further interruption save for one incident. Having concluded their efforts outside, the boisterous spirits strode noisily into the back of the hall where they stood with arms folded.

When I proceeded to discuss the R.O.T.C., I observed one significant thing. I charged that in other institutions the corps had been used not merely as a military adjunct, but as an instrument for suppression of minority groups. To my dismay I discovered that these students either did not understand what I was saying or else regarded me as a liar. I could pick out the R.O.T.C. men in the hall by the expressions of disbelief on their faces; they refused even to consider the possibility that they might be serving the purpose of reaction.

Before the night was done they had demonstrated, I hope to their own satisfaction, the validity of the charge.

In the course of the question period one student urged that I go out on the Campus to make a test-case of the ruling. When I consented, a burly, threatening figure rose in the back of the hall, shouting: "There isn't going to be any test case tonight or there'll be a riot that you can tell your children about." His cohorts vigorously applauded. Similar sentiment was voiced in other parts of the hall. Recognizing that we were outnumbered, that, in fact, we could never have gotten out of the hall to fulfill our purpose, we were forced to abandon the test case. But the invaders, their spirits inflamed, would not be content.

When the meeting finally adjourned, I walked to the side of the stage. It was a fortunate step. There I was met by about a dozen students, not affiliated with the Social Problems Club but still eager to discuss the problem further. They were certainly not on the side of the rioters. Meanwhile, I saw the group which had stood in the back of the hall advancing menacingly toward the stage; I proceeded to engage the others in animated conversation. The discussion served its purpose momentarily. Seeing that they would have encountered opposition if they sought to reach me, the group went after the chairman of the meeting, started to pummel him and dragged him out of the building.

There the Reverend of the college interceded. He jumped up and urged the students to halt the attack—and they heeded him. He was the only man in the college that night who could have permanently averted the outbreak. But after a few brief remarks to the attentive throng, he suddenly either changed his mind or became fearful of his position, declaring: "Now fellows, I was a student once, and if you want to have a rough-house, go to it; all I ask is that you do it in a spirit of fun and not with hatred in your hearts."

That was sufficient inspiration. Several of us raced for our car and managed to drive off the campus before they could reach us; we headed for the house of one of the faculty members about eight miles away.

We returned in about half an hour to survey the scene. In the interim the student who had asked me to make the test case had been routed from his room and hurled into the lake by the guardians of the good name of Connecticut State. As we drove around the campus, we saw little knots of students assembled; intermittently there was the sound of students rushing through the dormitories to flee from their assailants. Anti-semitism was rife and increasing every moment. A faculty man sped up to the room of one of the Club members to get him off the campus; the mob followed and threatened to throw him in the lake along with the student.

Another professor appeared in his car and was surrounded by a hostile group which had suspected him of sympathies with the movement against the edict. Confident that the administration would ultimately uphold them, or at least refrain from any reprisals, they proceeded to denounce him as a "dirty Jew" and order him off the campus. It was nearly midnight when the state police finally arrived to patrol the school until dawn.

In the aftermath of the clash it was established that the marauders had acted in collusion with the military department of the college. I need not add that, aside from a mild censure from President McCracken, no discipline was invoked against those involved. Yet again they should not be too heavily blamed; they had acted in accordance with the prejudices and incitements of their education; taught to march in step by both their military officials and the other alleged educators on the faculty, drilled in dog-like faithfulness to middle-class misinformation and bigotry, it would have been surprising if they had adopted any other tactics. There were

323

many who repudiated the assault, who, whatever their views, were angered by the brutality and viciousness it represented. But they understood neither its roots nor its implications. The small, aware group was pitifully outnumbered, unable to shake the smug complacency of those whose education was a series of rigid, static formulæ.

The gag-rule, as I write, still stands. A new president is yet to be designated. If the Trustees have their way, and there is no reason to believe that they won't, I fear that they will choose a strong man in the same tradition as the strong man who guides the Italian fascist regime. The tragedy is that only a handful of students in the college will know what they are in for.

WISCONSIN

Over a long span of years, progressivism has made its most decisive inroads in the state of Wisconsin. No other area has had a tradition of similar dimensions. Viewed in terms of the formation of attitudes and responses over a considerable period of time, this atmosphere must be visualized as a singularly independent force.

Certainly the university which has matured in the state has been susceptible to the tradition. I am not suggesting that "untrammeled inquiry"—the inscription so proudly displayed by the school—has permanently prevailed. Even in this most illustrious home of progressive rule, there have been vivid illustrations of the omnipotence of the financial dynasty. When Upton Sinclair sought to deliver an address there a decade ago, the pressure-groups ceased to be invisible. Three years ago the student newspaper was declared "unofficial" because its policies were deemed too radical for the general welfare. There have been reported efforts to prevent the publication of a National Student League journal on the campus; several students claim that the Administration has endeavored to reach the printer and compel him to withdraw his services.

These incidents, however, seem to me merely indicative of the ultimate limitations of any institution within our social structure. Despite them, it would be foolhardy to categorize Wisconsin with Michigan State or Connecticut State. The whole spirit and temper of the University has reflected the territory in which it resides; if Wisconsin has been intermittently guilty of reprisals against non-conformists or subtly maneuvered to curb their efforts, it has at least cultivated a veneer of freedom unknown to most of its contemporaries. Students have been attuned to the idea and atmosphere of independence even if that notion has been contradicted by certain of the actualities of the University's life.

Thus, when Vigilantes first appeared in California and then penetrated more backward areas in other states, there were repeated assurances that Wisconsin and the handful of universities which resemble it would be prepared to counteract the trend. Within a brief space of time, a convincing refutation was at hand. From the student body nurtured in the state of progress, of enlightenment, of an advanced social outlook, came the same legion of reaction described at East Lansing and Storrs. The sequence of events and the aftermath was markedly different here. That does not alter the fact that the upheaval did occur. The source of Vigilantism is rooted far deeper than in the locality in which it arises and even our centers of progress are not immune to the condition.

When the managing editors of the Hearst press received word that "the old man wants us to get the professors," it was entirely logical that they should seize upon Wisconsin as a fruitful field of exploration. Embarking upon their crusade, they soon received the hearty sanction of one John Chapple, candidate for governor, senator and any other offices that were soon to be vacant.

Mr. Chapple's cooperation was so zealous, in fact, that his own history is worth recounting. Now he is described as a "Wisconsin witch-burner"; yet in 1927 Mr. Chapple, just returned from the Soviet Union, was, as he soon let everybody know, a confirmed radical. His subsequent conversion was a mysterious process which he has never publicly explained, and in the absence of any public avowal, rumor will have to suffice. The rumor, now generally accepted, is that Mr. Chapple's father, then the holder of a postmaster's job, informed his son that said job might disappear if the stigma of radicalism was attached to the family name. Furthermore, as Johnny should have known, the radicals offer little remuneration to their chieftains. So Johnny, after a trying struggle in his soul, turned to the road of Stalwart Republicanism.

Perhaps the shame was too great or the impulse of strategy shrewdly discerned. In either case young John Chapple remained out of sight for a while. When he had become only a distant and not too revered memory, the transformation began. One day, reading through the student newspaper at Wisconsin, he discovered a letter written by one Schofield, a freshman, in which the university was depicted as an adjunct of Moscow. Whereupon John Chapple, now wearing his new garb of Stalwart Republicanism, headed straight for the campus and, within several hours, organized a League for the Defense of American Principles. Summoning an assemblage of the student body—he received an encouraging turnout—he proceeded to expose the university. No one from Glenn Frank to the charladies was exempt from the fury of his attack. The audience enjoyed the meeting and demonstrated its pleasure by cat-calls and other shouts of derision. A beaten man in his home territory, John Chapple headed east, still undaunted, into the loving arms of the Daughters of the American Revolution. The old ladies and the patriots quickly made him a favorite son. Herbert Hoover, then residing in the White House, lunched with him and was reputedly enthusiastic over his plans. Following the luncheon, our hero announced that he was a candidate for the Senate if the Stalwart Republicans would have him.

Though John Chapple had been hooted off a platform at Wisconsin many months before, now he was a celebrated figure. In triumph he returned to his native state, organized his entourage and proceeded to tour the state. Young Schofield, who had flunked out of school by then, was one of his leading performers with a specialty entitled the "Reds at the University." A Mr. and Mrs. Waters, who charged that they had been cheated by the Soviets, related the horrors of life under Bolshevism. Chapple concluded the exhibition with the climactic revelation of the evening. His repertoire now included an unsigned letter to *The Daily Cardinal* in which a co-ed announced that she had entered into close sexual relationships with men while unmarried. The state was rapidly becoming Chapple-conscious.

Only one untoward incident marred the victory parade. Flushed with conquest, Chapple decided to turn loose his circus on the Wisconsin campus again. But the renegade Schofield, angered by Chapple's delayed payments, deserted and told all. He revealed that Chapple had written the speeches of the troupe; he announced the salaries, provided for delivering them. Without paying his landlady, Chapple abruptly left town.

Still defiant, he came back a few weeks later to address another meeting of students. His words were still less than persuasive. When he had ended his disclosures, the students took over the platform and ruthlessly debunked his accusations.

I have cited these episodes merely to illustrate the indomitable patience of Mr. Chapple. The students of Wisconsin may in 1932 have hooted him off the platform; yet the people of the state were paying heed. By 1935 his vicious nonsense was even beginning to attract support in the university.

Hence, when Mr. Hearst launched his most modern foray, John Chapple, still ambitious and energetic, was rushed into battle to take up the crusade. Prodded unceasingly by *The Wisconsin News,* a Hearst affiliate in Milwaukee, the State Senate early in 1935 voted an inquiry into "communism, atheism and other perversionisms" at the University of Wisconsin. Despite the refusal of the Progressive-controlled assembly to cooperate, the Senate committee undertook its labors with unconcealed ardor.

At this point Dean Snell, head of the Extension division, entered the arena. He had just been dropped from his post after a prolonged investigation by the Board of Regents; the Regents, representing Republicans, Democrats and Progressives, were unanimous in their decision and there appeared substantial reason to believe that his dismissal was merited. Testimony had been taken in private, however, to protect those witnesses still under Dean Snell's supervision from his natural wrath at their "insubordination."

The Senate investigating committee seized the opportunity. It did not matter that Dean Snell had been released for palpable failure in his job nor that there was hardly a soul in the university who would have moved to defend him. He was hurriedly summoned before the committee. The night that he appeared the Senate chamber was thronged; there was general apprehension that Snell, infuriated by his discharge, was about to obtain revenge. He did.

With reckless disregard for fact, he proceeded to libel almost everyone in sight. He accused a former Socialist regent of Nepotism and her daughter of immoral conduct with a member of the Extension faculty in Milwaukee. Similar innuendos were offered about his remaining list of enemies. The committee neglected to observe that not a single shred of proof was offered. Instead it observed with glee the chance to identify communism with free love and the university. The press went for the story in a big way. It was on the front page of every neighboring newspaper.

What had started out as comic opera now assumed the aspect of a grim and determined inquisition. In 1932 Wisconsin might not have been ripe for the invasion; then students might have laughed Chapple out of court. Now, however, the spectre of Moscow was literally haunting the country, abetted by the ghost stories in the Hearst press. Armed with the Snell "revelations," the committee appeared to be making headway.

It need hardly be reiterated that the university was disturbingly innocent of the charges. Not only is there a minimum of sedition there; even this comparatively progressive university does not have a single Communist on its faculty to state his case; in the two or three courses in which the subject is discussed, the presentation is with varying degrees of hostility; Professor Selig Perlman, labor theorist, is a pronounced anti-communist.

But the fact that a real measure of liberalism does, as I have said, prevail there in sharp contrast to most other schools accentuated the fever of the investigators. Most of them probably had only the vaguest notion of what communism really is; their acquaintance with it, in most instances, was probably through the Hearst picture-book. Unfortunately, however, in this more distinguished of our universities, a segment of the student body was no better off. Moreover, the whole tenor of the university's response to the probe was not to fight it as a symptom of a perilous trend in our national life, but to insure the acquittal of those being probed. It was Chicago all over again. The Senate committee and the big business forces behind it should have been on trial for ignorance, for corruption, for an attempt to stifle any vestige of independent thought; instead the university administration and the bulk of the student body sought only to defend the good name of the institution. Thus, nineteen undergraduate leaders signed a statement in which they declared:

"The committee of 19 represents that 99 per cent of the undergraduate body whose energies are normally completely absorbed in the serious business of education. . . . The moral standards of the university community are higher than those of the average community in Wisconsin or elsewhere . . . most of us here are intent on the serious purpose of training ourselves for life in a highly competitive and disordered world, to the exclusion of the more romantic and exciting diversions of which newspapers and senators suspect us; that despite the widely advertised charges of atheism, our campus churches are still among the best attended in the state, some 82 per cent of our students being affiliated with one or another of the 15 denominations represented; and that as heirs to the multiple throne of a democratic government, the institutions and traditions of this country are as dear to us as anyone."

Instead of meeting the challenge and striking back, Wisconsin chose to defend its lily-white, conformist purity. Rather than assert any distinctive independence of the university, these representative students preferred to reiterate their unequivocal devotion to what is, what has been and what vested interests hope always will be. "Bad publicity" was more terrifying a prospect than the inroads of repression. The fact is, of course, that much of this confession was true. In their eagerness to avert unfavorable public criticism, these student leaders inadvertently revealed that Wisconsin, like its brothers everywhere, was still turning out almost as regimented and Babbitt-like a product as little Jerkwater College in Podunk, Kansas. This fact, together with the frenzied attempt to broadcast it, set the stage for the outbreak of May 15th.

The sessions of the League for Industrial Democracy at Wisconsin are normally attended by only a small if interested group of partisans. The affairs with which these meetings deal have not yet received the absorbed attention of the student body even in this allegedly alert institution. On May 15th, however, in the heat of legislative inquiries, Red Scares and widespread panic, its activities were the object of almost unprecedented student interest. Monroe Sweetland was scheduled to address one of their meetings and, as he said in his opening remarks, he was gratified at the size of the turnout.

But if there were any who believed that the League for Industrial Democracy had suddenly seized the university by the force of its own reason, they were soon to be disillusioned. All through the evening preparations had been under way. "W" men, those who have achieved distinction on the field of sport, had scurried through Fraternity Row, mobilizing their supporters. I have no doubt that the American Peace Alliance, a patriotic organization formed with much fanfare in the Hearst press in March, contributed its strong-men to the impending assault.

Almost as Sweetland rose to speak, the hastily-recruited representatives of Americanism indicated that they would be loudly heard from. Hisses, heckling, a growing tumult greeted his sentences. Finally, in an effort to prevent more serious consequences, Sweetland offered to turn the floor over to a spokesman of the self-proclaimed Vigilantes, the defenders of the good name of Wisconsin.

After a momentary lull—the suggestion was probably discomforting—one Victor Pape strode to the platform. One of the most revealing things about all these episodes is the profundity of the addresses delivered by the patriots. Their catcalling is usually eloquent and well-timed; their fighting ability cannot be questioned; but their mastery of both the form and content of the English language is never a tribute to their educators. Pape was no exception. The first incisive utterance to come from his lips was the pertinent question: "Are we Americans or are we Reds?"

331

In bellowing tones his followers cried that they were "Americans." Pape, after calling for a vote of disfavor against the L.I.D., then returned to his questioning: "Shall we listen to the next speaker?"

Again the loyal, upright and indignant standard-bearers of all that is American, shouted back a firm "no."

The chairman, a young man by the name of Crews, endeavored to define Americanism in more historic terms. The Americans were too wrought up to hear him.

Sweetland made one more effort to continue his speech. The uproar was too loud and threatening. When he declared that "this is the first time I've ever talked to a bunch of rowdies," there was a sullen, menacing response; then the attack which had been so carefully nurtured in the minds of Wisconsin's ardent flag-wavers began.

The trek to the water, the same lynch-march which we have witnessed at Michigan State and Connecticut, ensued. It did not end until four persons, including Sweetland and a young medical research student who sought to intervene, had been immersed in the chill waters of the adjacent lake. The remonstrances of two faculty members were in vain. Shouting and cursing, the Vigilantes carried their plan to its hysterical conclusion.

The lake at Wisconsin has frequently witnessed student pranks. But, as one observer later wrote, "this episode was entirely different." Never before had women students been manhandled and threatened; one girl was, in fact, hurled over a railing and others narrowly escaped similar treatment.

More ominous, perhaps, than all these attacks was the blatant declaration of several leaders of the mob that they were members of the "Silver Shirts," an avowedly fascist, anti-semitic, anti-Negro organization. Their procedure gave credence to the announcement.

For already the first forebodings of rampant race hatred were visible. Witnesses have unanimously agreed that an anti-semitic fever pervaded the whole scene. One prominent student leader later told me that, while race prejudice had always existed on the Campus, he never realized its ugly potentialities until that night. How much of the feeling had been calculatingly incited by the sponsors of the mob and how much was a spontaneous expression of deep-rooted bigotry cannot now be estimated. Even more clearly was the tendency to be exhibited the following day.

Lola Lebow was described in *The Cardinal* as a "quiet, highly intelligent student earning her way through school through her art work." For several weeks she had been confined to the university infirmary and it was the day after the outbreak when she was finally able to leave.

Starting back for the campus, she was passing slowly around Beacon Hill when suddenly a student wearing the numerals "1935" (awarded for athletic accomplishment) suddenly confronted her. Without any warning, he slapped her in the face and struck her several times in the ribs. The attack was accompanied by a stream of derogatory references to the fact that she was a Jewess, echoing the sentiments of the rioters of the night before. Having inflicted sufficient injury upon her, the athlete then quietly turned and strode away. Momentarily stunned, Miss Lebow sought to follow him, but he raced towards one of the Campus buildings and soon eluded her.

If anyone had suggested several years ago that an American student would be capable of so unwarranted and brutal an act, he would have been summarily disregarded as an alarmist. In the progressive shades of Wisconsin was demonstrated how imminent is the unbelievable.

When Glenn Frank assumed the presidency of the University of Wisconsin, it was well-known that he regarded the post as a stepping-stone to the White House. With the passage of years his hopes have ebbed, but the aspiration still lingers; occasionally his name is mentioned in political gossip and this has served to bolster his dwindling confidence. The ambition is to be lamented in a university president; a man with his eye on the White House, whatever his original forthrightness, must understand the dictates of respectability and humility even more keenly than the ordinary college official. It is particularly to be deplored in one of the few universities where a liberal environment prevails.

Again let us carefully distinguish between President Frank and the average hick-college functionary; he is far more alert, intelligent and conversant with both educational and political forces. At the same time he is not nearly so bold and decisive in his actions as a progressive stronghold might imply—a fact which was eminently borne out in the days after May 15th.

To the outside world his stand was firmly taken. A university convocation was summoned for the Friday after the upheaval and the President agreed to deliver the principal address. But the inside story of the calling of the convocation is far less impressive than this might signify.

Immediately after the riot the League for Industrial Democracy and the National Student Legue voted to conduct a protest meeting the following night, Thursday. It was a step which President Frank did not greet with any favor. With the attack on the Lebow girl and increasing tension on the campus, he feared another episode which would have made his position even more difficult and augmented his mounting obligation to speak out. Moreover, he did not fancy the assumption of leadership by the radical groups with a substantial section of undergraduate opinion prepared to follow them. There was, in addition, considerable pressure from the Teachers Union, urging him to take drastic measures against the Vigilantes. When the District Attorney refused to intervene, blithely declaring that the matter was "a student prank," President Frank was compelled to act. And yet the impression was unmistakable that he did not enjoy the rôle.

It was at that point that he decided upon the university convocation. He had originally consented to permit speakers from the National Student League and the League for Industrial Democracy to appear at the session; later he sought to withdraw this agreement, but he was held to his promise. Still treading warily, he suggested that all addresses be submitted to him before they were delivered. And finally, as a last and lamentable gesture, he endeavored to transform the meeting from a discussion of the Vigilante attacks to a more judiciously abstract level. Thus, *The Daily Cardinal* announced: "The meeting is not a protest meeting over the Wednesday evening incident, its leaders announced, but a meeting at which leaders of the university, city and perhaps state will give their views on academic freedom." President Frank admonished the speakers to follow this understanding.

On the night of the convocation more than 1,200 students assembled in the hall. Sentiment had swung sharply against the Vigilantes, especially in the light of the vicious beating administered to the Lebow girl. But President Frank's speech was a shocking evasion of the issue. He almost disregarded the Vigilante outburst, contenting himself with a general discussion of political theory. Even more extraordinary was the fact that he did not mention fascism in the course of his address, although the Vigilante uprising was significant precisely because it was so inextricably linked with fascist tendencies in this country. These things were subordinated. President Frank's address was primarily a tirade against communism!

But Dean Sellery did not heed the cue. The Dean is a conservative and he has never hesitated to say so; on the other hand, he was too independent and forthright to participate in the sham battle which his president was carrying on in a situation which called for a bold offensive. Without any exhaustive preliminaries, Dean Sellery vigorously declared: "We have been a great university. . . . But the deeds of two nights ago will wreck the university unless we wreck the individuals who supported such a principle."

Three separate witnesses of that scene have testified to me

335

that, in the course of Sellery's address, President Frank literally turned pale. But the tumultuous ovation which the students gave their Dean partially compensated for their president's timidity. To that extent the night was a sharp repudiation of the Vigilantes, far more encouraging than the performances of undergraduates elsewhere.

The Vigilantes, temporarily routed, did not make themselves heard at the convocation nor in the following weeks. That does not alter the significance of their arrival and the forces which seemed to be abetting them—the District Attorney's refusal to act and President Frank's endeavor to minimize the conflict. It is reported, although this has never been confirmed, that a prominent business man in Madison was instrumental in fomenting the disorder. Whether such backing was present or not, the Vigilantes were a meaningful storm signal in the "most progressive state in the country." Their next outburst will be better prepared—and the remainder of the student body will have to be prepared for it. I am certain that President Frank does not believe in Vigilante methods; but whether he will speak out more decisively is far from assured. The beginnings of his retreat seem to be discernible. Next time the Vigilantes may have more influential sponsorship—and the Republican Party may still be in search of a candidate. That is the dilemma of "progressivism."

M.I.T.

When the late Dr. Stratton presided over the destinies of the Massachusetts Institute of Technology, there was only one enemy to the routine complacence of the institution. It was a small, limited but tireless Liberal Club whose efforts were devoted almost exclusively to a campaign against the R.O.T.C. Dr. Stratton was irritated; the club was an unwanted, burdensome agency for which he could display no sympathy. In 1928 these students invited a representative of a pacifist organization to deliver an indictment of the

R.O.T.C. at a campus meeting. Apprised of the plan, Dr. Stratton immediately conveyed his disapproval to the leader of the group, informing him that: "There are three subjects that should not be discussed. They are religion, politics and military preparedness. There is no argument about preparedness. Every intelligent person knows that it is the only way to peace, and discussion about it would only cause confusion and hard feeling."

Although its specific application may have changed, that principle survived Dr. Stratton's death. One of M.I.T.'s most revered contributors—to the extent of twenty million dollars —was George Eastman, Kodak magnate, whose philanthropy was prompted by his "great confidence in the material you turn out at the institution." Karl Taylor Compton, Dr. Stratton's successor, has assiduously striven to justify the trust with a full quota of sound "material." M.I.T. is a celebrated engineering school, and it typifies the conservatism which is more pronounced in such institutions than in others. Its directors propose to train engineers, not enlightened citizens, and this is adequately reflected in the curriculum, of which a student writes:

"There is intense concentration on engineering and professional subjects. Since all students (except those in architectural courses) are required to take the same freshman subjects, this schedule may be taken as typical: only eight out of forty hours per week of combined classroom work and preparation are allotted to subjects of a genuinely cultural character, i.e. English. The rest, with the exception of one hour for physical training and three for R.O.T.C. are strictly scientific subjects, physics, chemistry, calculus and engineering drawing. Moreover, the proportion of cultural subjects diminishes through the succeeding years. . . . Such a description of the curriculum will not be found in the official announcements of the administration. . . . But when it is observed that

337

under the heading of the 'Humanities' come such items as military science, the exaggeration of these claims becomes apparent. . . ."

The "Corporation" (Board of Trustees) which controls the Institute is one of the most corporation-laden in the country. That is the secret of M.I.T.'s achievements, "a liaison between the engineering school and those corporations which absorb the finished product." It is impossible here to detail the affiliations of the overseers; they include the officers and directors of thirteen railroads and transit lines, two locomotive works, United States Steel corporation, General Electric, five major telephone and telegraph companies, General Motors and Mack Truck, six power companies, six textile mills, United Fruit Co., two large refineries, E. I. Du Pont de Nemours and affiliates, seven mining companies, four shipbuilding firms, five steamship lines and a host of others. Moreover, most of the Institute's academic staff have had extensive industrial experience and continue to maintain close contact with their former associates: "There is no cloistered scholasticism about Tech. It is an integral part of the industrial system itself, an extension of various plant and factory research departments."

The faculty, logically enough, is overwhelmingly conservative; before the 1932 national election a poll showed that ninety per cent of its members favored the Republican candidate. The most noted reactionary is F. K. Morris, a first-rate geologist who has refused to confine himself to that field and has strayed into realms of which he is grossly uninformed. He is supremely certain of the inevitability of war, prides himself on being "tough-minded" about it and has repeatedly demonstrated his hostility to any anti-war activity among the student body. But he is not alone. Although there is a small group of liberal professors, it is patently outnumbered and its views subordinated to the prevailing tone of the institution.

338

M.I.T. boasts that seventy per cent of its graduates attain executive posts within fourteen years after their graduation. This is entirely understandable. The Institute draws a comparatively wealthy enrollment. A professor recently cited the fact that a large number of students graduate into their fathers' offices—and those offices are in the highest strata of American industry. The captains of industry are agile at perpetuating the family tradition. They can afford to be.

Among the "commuters," those who live in Greater Boston, the economic status is not so high as among others; there is a moderate group of lower middle-class representatives recruited from this sector. At the other extreme is the fraternity ensemble, the "cream" of the school, rulers of campus social life and extra-curricular activities.

It should not be assumed, however, that all M.I.T. men automatically receive ranking industrial posts. Even they have not been able to escape the effects of the "contraction." According to an estimate made by the school in October, 1934, for example, twenty-six per cent of those who received bachelors' degrees the previous June were still unemployed, and although there is said to have been an upturn the following year, the fact remains that for a varying percentage of the student body the outlook is shrouded in far more uncertainty than the glowing self-laudation of the Institute would indicate. On the other hand, compared to the colleges we have just examined, the men of M.I.T. are, as a whole, better situated than a large majority of their contemporaries. It was in that setting that a leftward student bloc made its appearance in 1933.

Shortly after the formation of a National Student League chapter that year, the local Hearst press and the R.O.T.C. officialdom organized a "united front" to end its existence. *The Boston Advertiser* was the medium. When its reporter was barred from a meeting of the club because of her consistently garbled reports of events at other schools, a secretary of the R.O.T.C. department was despatched in her stead. Her identity unknown to most of the students, she managed to attend the meeting; the following item in *The Advertiser* was the lurid and fantastic product of her mind: "Class war, revolution, bloodshed and an overturning of the government were preached to M.I.T. students at an organization meeting to form a Tech. unit of the National Student League."

This was only one of a series of inventions circulated in the press with the talented cooperation of an R.O.T.C. representative. Even more startling was a weird legend that some "unnamed citizens" were financing "scholarships" for members of the League. Despite these ingenious devices, an anti-war conference was held at M.I.T. in 1934, arousing more authentic and controversial opinion than any episode in her recent history and causing the R.O.T.C. officials to intervene. A "skeleton in uniform" had been placed on the campus to dramatize the approach of the conference and this provided Major Gatchell, acting for Colonel Vestal, with an excuse for oratory. He summoned leaders of the peace committee, demanding that they remove the skeleton or face a penitentiary sentence for desecrating an army uniform. When the students refused to obey his dictates, they were called before Colonel Vestal himself who informed them that they were "playing upon the chords of cowardice," and that—literally—they were being subsidized by Moscow gold. The uniform was finally removed.

In the Spring of 1934 a Nazi cruiser, the Karlsruhe, visited Boston and was tended a reception by city functionaires, at a time when reports of Nazi terrorism were widely prevalent throughout the press. Nearly 5,000 Boston anti-fascists gathered near the place where the ship was moored, planning to conduct a protest demonstration, and among the throng was a large contingent of students from M.I.T. and Harvard. That meeting witnessed a notorious display of police bru-

tality.* The crowd was dispersed before any addresses were
delivered; the "tactics of the police in scattering the crowd
were unenlightened, uncalled for and brutal"; "arrests were
made without due cause and with completely unjustified violence"; "three of the arrested men were slugged after they
had reached the station house." † But the officialdom of
M.I.T. was simultaneously entertaining cadets from the ship
with Dean Lobdell as their personal supervisor. The Dean
was distraught. He scurried through the building tearing
down posters announcing the anti-Nazi demonstration. When
one student accosted him during this performance, the Dean
explained that the sponsors of the protest were not a recognized group—although they had been even granted official
permission by the Institute committee to use the bulletin
boards.

After the arrests, Dean Lobdell was in perpetual distress.
Learning that the victims of the police round-up included
several M.I.T. students, Dean Lobdell rushed to the Boston
newspapers with pleas for them to avoid any mention of the
connection. I need hardly add that neither he nor his fellow
administrators were indignant over the unrestrained violence
practiced by the police or the unfairness of the trial procedure.
Although a group of faculty men responded valiantly to the
defense campaign, the official stand of the Institute was characterized by the ingratiating reception to the cadets of the
Karlsruhe.

It was not until a year later, however, that the most ruth-
less attempt to quell undergraduate activity was carried out.
And it was engineered by M.I.T.'s own version of Vigilantes.

One week before the 1935 strike against war, a group of
students at M.I.T. came into possession of a set of pass-keys
to the dormitory rooms. That was on April 5. Late that night

* A detailed report of this event was issued by a group of Harvard professors and amply confirms this accusation. The report was published in
pamphlet form and copies are in the possession of the Civil Liberties Union.
† Quoted from the report of the investigating committee.

the band slipped through the corridors and into the room of Robert Landay, a member of the National Student League. Landay was immediately blind-folded, bound and gagged and, after a series of blows had been administered, his head was shaved. While he lay there, the invaders proceeded to disarrange his belongings and, when the room was sufficiently in turmoil, they proceeded on another expedition. This time they were partially frustrated; they entered the room of Robert Newman, secretary of the anti-war strike committee and a member of the League for Industrial Democracy, only to discover that he was staying elsewhere for the night. To assuage their disappointment, the vandals smashed furniture, tore up notes, books and pictures and in an assortment of ways imitated a conventional Nazi assault on culture. Even this did not soothe their fury; the following Monday night they returned and found Newman at home. It was late and, with no one to interrupt their plans, Newman received more drastic punishment than Landay, perhaps in retribution for his earlier absence. The crowd, about twenty in number, set upon him, knocked him unconscious, and proceeded to shave his head. As a final stroke, a swastika was cut in the stubble remaining at the top of his skull. Leaving their victim to take care of himself, they abruptly departed with a few final warnings on the anti-war situation.

Dr. Compton betrayed no anguish at the news. When a student urged him to seek out and discipline the assailants, he murmured that it was out of his province; he protested that he didn't know who the culprits were and huffily refused to issue any statement discouraging future acts of that nature. Finally, since the anti-war strike was "counter to Institute regulations," he could not afford any protection to its participants. He was even more threatening on the general subject of the strike; if any violence occurred during it, he asserted, the strike committee would be held responsible, possibly to the point of expulsion. And that responsibility remained whether the R.O.T.C. or any other group provoked a disturbance by attacking the strike meeting!

Two days before the strike, however, a fortunate circumstance compelled Dr. Compton to alter his position. Newman had mentioned the attacks to a member of the Simmons College strike committee who immediately prevailed upon her friends to communicate with Mrs. Compton. The pressure was effective; shortly after it had been exerted, Dr. Compton agreed to issue public condemnation of any further violence. Dissuaded momentarily from their intention, the Vigilantes contented themselves with more rational methods on the day of the walkout. They appeared on the roof of one of the neighboring buildings bearing the slogans: "GROW BEARDS IN PROTEST AGAINST WAR"; "DOWN WITH HAIRLESS PACIFISTS"; "FOR BIGGER AND BETTER WARS."

The members of the Vigilante-gang were never identified, nor was there any intensive administrative attempt to find them. It is known that an avowedly fascist group exists at M.I.T., led by Harry Sommer, a spirited Nazi propagandist. Its members meet regularly with outsiders who have similar views and together they maintained a room at the Riverbank Court Hotel during the first semester of the 1934-35 school year. But there is no conclusive evidence that this array was responsible for the assaults. It may have been as spontaneous and confused an hysteria as the other risings we have witnessed. One thing, however, distinguished the M.I.T. exhibition from all others: the incredible, furious brutality of the participants. There was no humor in their demeanor. With a minimum of added incitment, they might have inflicted permanent damage on their victims.

M.I.T. breeds engineers. It does not purport to do much else. When the students were confronted with an issue of which they had only dim comprehension, they reacted by instinct and prejudice—and violence. Others stood around trying to fathom what was taking place. M.I.T.'s "material" is turned out on the assumption that the social system is static, fixed and prepared to absorb these talented graduates.

The graduates, in turn, are expected to believe the same things. If there is to be any resistance to the next assault of the Vigilantes, it will come only because a percentage of students have been prodded by their colleagues into a semblance of consciousness. Until then reaction will find a receptive audience at the Institute—and the executioner's axe will continue to be poised for recalcitrants.

OREGON

When Richard L. Neuberger became editor of *The Oregon Emerald* three years ago, one of his major campaigns was for abolition of a compulsory athletic fee. He contended that, in the light of growing economic depression, the statute was an unwarranted burden on needy students. For his zeal he was almost deposed from his editorship; the athletic officialdom cried for his dismissal and the educational office appeared to heed the appeal. But Neuberger went to court and, despite the opposition of reactionary blocs throughout the state, proved that the fee rule was illegal. The victory was noticeably effective; it enabled a large number of "border-line" students to remain in college and others, who would not have been able to afford the cost, could enter.

But in 1935 the State Legislature, prompted by the Chamber of Commerce and its associates, enacted another notorious piece of "class legislation" for the university. It passed a bill which made both compulsory athletic and dance fees legal. The measure would have forced certain students to leave college and compelled others to pay for events in which they were not remotely interested. It was a move vigorously endorsed by the athletic moguls and the campus "socialites."

Neuberger, by then a student at the law school, hurriedly formed a Student Relief committee to combat the edict, ultimately aiming to secure a state-wide referendum. To do this a petition signed by thousands of voters was required, and the liberal group at the university immediately proceeded to circulate such a petition. Governor Martin denounced the plan as "a crazy idea," adding that its sponsors "should be ashamed of themselves" and ridiculing the possibility of success. The conservative press was equally vehement in its denunciations.

Several weeks later the students arrived at the State Capitol with one and a half times as many signatures as were needed. *The Oregon Voter* commented: ". . . It was a smashing rebuke to the little clique of society people and jingoists who have attempted to turn the state schools into glorified country clubs and athletic camps."

The backers of the legislation were angered by the defeat. University administrators were plainly lukewarm over the initiative of their students. It remained for the directors of the athletic system, however, to manifest their resentment most vividly.

Shortly after the petitions had been submitted, a mob of Oregon athletes invaded the residence of Howard V. Ohmart, chairman of the fee referendum campaign. He was dragged from his room and vigorously beaten by the emissaries of the athletic office. When he protested, the attack was intensified until his resistance ceased.

The Vigilantes were never apprehended nor were any steps taken to prevent a repetition of their acts. *Everybody's Business*, a liberal weekly, remarked: "C. V. Boyer, president of the university; Charles H. Martin, governor of Oregon; W. J. Kerr, chancellor of education, may have issued protests—but nobody heard them do so."

VIRGINIA

A unique form of agitation occurred at the University of Virginia late in 1934 when a group of undergraduates circulated a petition urging the introduction of an R.O.T.C. unit at the school. Whether this was done on their own initiative or at the behest of outside patrioteers has never been ascer-

345

tained; whatever its origin, the campaign was an arduous one which awakened only a minimum of sympathy among the remainder of the undergraduate body. It did not succeed and there is still no R.O.T.C. at Virginia. But the sponsors of the move, balked in that effort, proceeded to even more vigorous measures. They made virtually no headway at the anti-war strike which had the enthusiastic support of a large section of the college, but when Clarence Hathaway, communist leader, was invited to address a student group several weeks afterward, the defenders of the commonwealth decided to make their presence more acutely felt.

Hathaway's address was scheduled for Cabell Hall. Shortly after he began to speak, however, the opposition announced its sentiments. I quote from the account in the student newspaper: "From the very outset Mr. Hathaway was heckled and interrupted by an organized band of noise-makers situated at strategic points in the audience as well as by various noises from the surrounding fire-escapes."

Although a large group of undergraduates sought to silence the intruders, at one time forcing them to leave the hall, the lecture could not be completed. The Vigilantes reappeared and launched an even more vociferous series of outbursts. At this juncture, when a pitched battle seemed imminent, the directors of the meeting urged the assemblage to move to Jefferson Hall. The Vigilantes did not return. And the following day the Administration and undergraduate leaders bitterly berated them for their performance.

The incident was important for two reasons: it signified the temper and behavior of those who believe in the R.O.T.C. as a social safeguard; it was also one of the few occasions on which a university administration was prepared to deal forthrightly with rioters when the rioters are acting in the name of "patriotism."

These are representative institutions in which Vigilantism has begun to advance; numerous other cases could be cited

346

to illustrate the same tendency. There seems indisputable evidence that a reactionary youth movement on our shores will be founded upon precisely such blocs, and operating in the guise of "Americanism." It is true that a large number of centralized, semi-fascist agencies have already arisen in this country, but they have not yet captured the Vigilantes. One of the inevitable characteristics of these groups is their proclamations against "fascism and communism alike." Many of their constituents, only vaguely aware of what either term implies, rally to the standard; suddenly they discover that they are being utilized against communists alone, and serving the ends of fascism. They also find that communism means what the American Legion defines it as—any liberal social reform, any critical inquiry or non-conformist opinion.

The Vigilantes do not depict themselves as fascists; it would be absurd to believe that most of their members believe in fascism or anything resembling it. They don't know what they believe in. But they will be, and are, quick to follow leaders who give them a semblance of promise and a maximum of incitement. Which of the countless arrays now emerging will fulfill that mission cannot be prophesied. The Vigilantes will not stand still. They have adopted the essential tactic of fascist reaction: violence against critics of the status quo, and from that premise they can go far. If and when the tide of Vigilantism becomes nationwide, with a coordinating agency to give it organization and purpose, it will be a formidable foe. For such a movement would have powerful financial backing, not of Moscow gold, but the gold of rugged American industrialists who have decided that reaction pays dividends.

VII. Goose-Step at Harvard

WHILE Professor Harold Laski was lecturing at Harvard in the period immediately after the World War, a strike of

347

the Boston police agitated the Massachusetts plutocracy. Conservative journals delivered unremitting indictments of the walkout, declaring that it was inspired by the newly-triumphant Russian revolutionaries. In that hour, when it was so emphatically unsafe to betray sympathy for the strikers, Professor Laski did. And his utterances brought down the condemnation of the whole Back Bay financial network. Warning the foreigner to "go back where he came from," *The Boston Transcript* led the procession of outraged virtue. At dinner-tables and in drawing-rooms Professor Laski's status became the center of respectable, meaningful frowns.

A. Lawrence Lowell, then president of the university, refused to oust the heretic. But the noted English scholar was hounded from his post by unceasing pressure, of which no single gesture was more decisive than the performance of *The Harvard Lampoon,* undergraduate humor magazine. It published a special anti-Soviet number which announced that Lenin owned 148 personal motor cars, Trotsky 52—and that Dr. Laski was one of the Bolsheviks' chosen emissaries. The journal also explained that the visiting lecturer was an ardent exponent of free love.

The ensuing uproar, half-comic, half-serious, proved overwhelming. A distinguished scholar departed from Cambridge, Boston's solid citizens relaxed, and the Harvard undergraduates could feel secure in the knowledge that their "joke" had done the job.

On the morning of April 13, 1934, the day of the first student anti-war strike, there appeared in *The Harvard Crimson* an announcement of the impending arrival of the Michael Mullins Marching and Chowder Club.

By 10:30 groups of students were gathering in front of the Widener Steps, scheduled scene of the peace meeting. Their mission was not a solemn one. If there were 200 students in the university genuinely anxious to conduct a protest

348

against war, there were hundreds more who were drawn by no such serious intention. For days there had been reports of the approaching intrusion and Harvard, in its best carnival spirit, prepared for the outing.

At exactly eleven o'clock the meeting began. Within three minutes could be heard the oncoming tread of the men of Michael Mullins who strode on to the grounds with large, flamboyant placards. As they marched in goose-step fashion, they raised their arms in Hitler salutes while the men in front lifted a placard:

DOWN WITH PEACE.

One of the leaders was draped in towels; another wore a full-fledged Nazi uniform; still a third, dressed in Boy Scout attire, tooted a bugle. When a speaker sought to address the crowd, the men of Mullins rushed forward to present him an engraved medal. When another arose, he was immediately pelted by missiles and shouted down. A professor's wife attempted to quell the invaders, and for her efforts she was roughly handled and silenced. Tiring of this exhibit, the marchers adjourned to another section of the quad to conduct their own mock-meeting; speakers, somewhat self-conscious but gradually won over by the force of their own personalities, heiled Hitler, war and the extermination of heretics. And hundreds of residents of Harvard University joined enthusiastically in the show, halting only momentarily to shout final defiance at the outnumbered, hapless sponsors of the anti-war meeting. There were students who rebelled at the invasion; admittedly indifferent at the outset, they found themselves drawn to the side of the peace demonstrators. Despite these desertions, the troops of Michael Mullins carried the day, successfully averting any possibility of Harvard's alignment with the strike movement. That was the first act of the burlesque.

Several weeks later the press announced that Ernst (Putzy) Hanfstaengl had been designated a marshal for the approaching Commencement exercises. "Putzy," subsequent to his graduation from Harvard, had made his way in the world; by 1934 he was something of a celebrity. He had risen so rapidly in the estimation of his chief that he was now a member of the cabinet. His chief, of course, was Adolph Hitler. With his background of Harvard culture, he had supervised book-burnings and other festivals of Naziland and now he was returning to the university of his youth. From the moment of his appointment, a chorus of protest emerged from anti-Nazi groups and individuals throughout the country who regarded the designation as an incongruous educational award for merit. But to the editors of *The Harvard Crimson*, "Putzy" was a hero, a man of some talent, a distinguished son; the protest was an affront, a sign of "bad manners," an unbecoming attitude. In an effort to assuage Hanfstaengl's feelings, *The Crimson* proposed the awarding of an honorary degree to Hitler's protégé. The boy had made good.

The Crimson's proposal was not accepted; it was deemed adequate for the celebrity to be a marshal and nothing more. But the spirit expressed by the Michael Mullins array and *The Crimson* survived and, in the fall of 1934, another outlet for its appearance was provided. President Conant, in a stand which few of his contemporaries have equalled, rejected a scholarship fund heavily laden with Nazi strings. Under the terms of the offer, Harvard would have despatched a student each year to study in the universities of Hitlerism—and President Conant stated quite boldly that he did not believe Nazi education to be worth the journey. Again *The Crimson* and its followers were indignant, berating their president for his outspokenness and his lack of "good taste." That was not, they argued, the "gentleman's way." When President Conant adhered to his position, the men of Harvard returned to disgruntled hibernation until the following April.

But their performance on that occasion was neither as humorous nor as effective as their earlier outing. After the first strike, one eyewitness had written: "Their first weapon is ridicule. But that can't be kept up. Another strike may witness violence and injury. The fun will turn into bitterness and there were lots in the audience who would have joined in a fighting rush."

His prophecy, if not fulfilled in detail, was borne out by the atmosphere in April of 1935. The men of Michael Mullins were, in the first place, limited by the intervention of the "Yard police"; they found, moreover, that a fairly large segment of undergraduates was no longer receptive to their exhibition. And the demeanor of the invaders was slowly changing. A group of them rode around the campus with a machine-gun, stolen from a neighboring armory, mounted in their car. The occupants of the car, the press related, were "New York socialites." I am glad to report that the gun was never fired nor do I believe that it was intended for such use. But its presence was a notable addition which symbolized the transformation in mood.

The intruders sought to repeat their burlesque; they were eminently less successful. Even *The Crimson* reported:

HECKLERS FAIL AS STRIKE FOR PEACE GOES OFF QUIETLY

There were the customary interruptions, described by one newspaper as the barks and yelps of the Mullins men. There were missiles hurled, accompanied by chants of "We Want Hitler." To an increasing number, however, the Nazis were no longer quite the thing—and the Nazis, divested of humor, were becoming more conscious of purpose.

It will be protested that the loud-spoken opponents of the peace strike, the admirers of Hanfstaengl, the men who gave

351

the Hitler salute, were primarily out for a good time. That is partially true. Only a few are members of the Harvard chapter of the Friends of New Germany, Hitler's American agency; whether they gave the initiative to the outbursts cannot be ascertained—but the overwhelming number of the disrupters did not have either such direct affiliation or developed convictions. They are, significantly enough, drawn most noticeably from the wealthier sections of the student body; that fact cannot be minimized. They are men who have had no personal experience with the inroads of depression and are consequently oblivious to its implications. To them, Harvard is what it was to their predecessors—a happy interim between two altogether satisfying worlds. Their mock-meetings are still shrouded in satire; their approach is vague, ill-defined, the response of prejudice rather than of philosophic completeness. If you assure them that they are behaving as the students of Germany did during Hitler's rise, they will ridicule the charge. And yet the joke is ceasing to go over. There is a serious, inescapable aspect to it which those in the university have felt. The tactics and temper of the Harvard invaders is not identical to the average Vigilante throng; it retains a veneer of sophistication, an air of superiority to the rabble, a political portrayal of those traits which they regard distinctive to the Harvard man. Elsewhere Vigilantes are patriots, firmly convinced that they are fighting off a menace and animated by a definite conviction on the issues involved. They have suffered, in varying degrees, from economic deprivation, and they hope, by some valiant crusade, to ease their dissatisfactions. These factors are not the motivations of the Michael Mullins contingent, students whose essential concern is to avoid the facing of extraneous issues, to silence the nuisances who are trying to bring these problems before them, students whose status is still relatively fixed without fear of immediate disarrangement.

And the Harvard intellectual reflects that feeling in different terms. One student writes:

"To Harvard, still groping under the slender shadow of Eliot's 1933 lectures, the religious issue is of far greater importance than even the political and economic problems of the immediate present. It is more important to the Harvard student to check the decline of the faith than to arrest the decline of capitalism. The topic of bull-sessions is more likely to be T. S. Eliot or the Orozco murals than sex or politics. . . . The greatest topic for polemics is religion." *

The result is a dominant conservatism, whether manifested by the "collegians" in Michael Mullins parades or by the intellectuals in disdain for all political activity. The answer cannot be oversimplified by saying that all Harvard men are the sons of privilege; although there is a large section which can be so classified, there are also great numbers without such certainty, particularly the "commuters" who reside in the neighboring communities. The left-wing group is small, partly because of its deficient handling of specific situations, but even more so because of the atmosphere in which it is operating. There has been some notable headway; the larger group of interested participants in the 1935 strike testifies to that circumstance; the demonstration against the reception to the Karlsruhe received some marked undergraduate sympathy, especially in the light of the flagrant behavior of the police and the courts. But the pervading tone of the institution is still more broadly summarized by other currents, of which the left wing is only a restricted murmur.

One of the most curious paradoxes is that liberal sentiment and concern for social issues is probably more pronounced among faculty members than among students. The professors have to maintain reserve to the extent that a New England whispering campaign can be more damaging than administrative intervention. But far more influential is the spirit

* From "Varied Glimpses of the Collegiate Mind," by Evelyn Seeley in *The Literary Digest*, of May, 1935.

and custom of Harvard undergraduate life itself, rooted in the social tradition of the undergraduates. They are being divided just as perceptibly as the residents of less enlightened institutions. The left wing, whatever its progress, is still restricted. The Harvard intellectual is seeking the revival of the Faith—for worldliness is akin to Philistinism. Meanwhile the men of Michael Mullins continue to reassert that "air" which sixteen years ago drove Harold Laski from Cambridge. Today the conflict is more profound and critical, although only the first simmerings are yet visible. Burlesque quickly loses its outer dressing in that setting. When the Marching Club sets out in greater clarity to end the "nuisance," its veneer may remain—but the purport of Vigilantism will be unmistakable.

VIII. The "Theory" of Vigilantism

ONE of the most uniform and alarming accompaniments of Vigilantism has been the rise of the pogrom-spirit. It flared on the West Coast and again at Connecticut, Michigan State and Wisconsin; there are a host of other places where similar attacks are brewing, although their symptoms have not yet been so dramatically bared. This impression has been confirmed by students and teachers throughout the country. On almost every campus the same judgment is expressed: the cry of "Hate-the-Jew" is growing more intense and ominous.

Anti-semitism is not a latter-day development in American colleges. It has been nourished persistently, with varying degrees of intensity, by the educational structure. The distinction to be noted today is in the methods by which it is expressed and the purposes for which it is utilized. These are more menacing than ever before. From a passive, static prejudice it has grown into an overt, violence-inspiring, fascistic weapon.

There is a large body of conservative opinion—both Jewish and Christian—which has always protested any discussion of the problem. To do so, it is argued, only heightens the antagonism, bringing to the surface feelings which presumably will remain dormant. And yet I am more than ever convinced that only frank and bold treatment will curb the outbreaks. For the sponsors of anti-semitism, those who today are invoking it as an antidote to discontent and the advance of progressive social opinion, are only abetted by the continued ignorance of their subjects; they will operate effectively only so long as this ignorance of genuine issues prevails; to remain silent in the face of their efforts, far from discouraging them, serves their deeds beyond measure. The "conspiracy of silence" has not halted anti-semitism nor will it ever succeed in doing so. It provides *carte blanche* for the disseminators of prejudice. It enables them to flourish without fear of contradiction. It paves the way for an ever-increasing storm which is more imminent than we commonly realize.

Several years ago Heywood Broun and George Britt published *Christians Only,* a notable exposé of the extent of anti-semitism in this country; one of the phases of the theme most copiously treated was the anti-Jewish tenor of American universities. This, they found, was partly inherent in administrative policy; it was also reflected in activities over which undergraduates had undisputed control:

"Discrimination in colleges goes deeper than the official attitude of the faculty. I have always felt that part of student prejudice might be traced to professorial or presidential policy. But I grant that even in the most liberally administered institution students could kick up rows under their own steam. . . ."

One of the aspects of undergraduate life most conducive to the breach is the fraternity system:

355

"The fraternity system bears harshly upon the Jewish undergraduate. . . . Jewish fraternities set up a dangerous duality of existence. If there are to be Gentile fraternities and Jewish fraternities, it might also be logical to have within the same institution a Gentile baseball team and a Jewish baseball team and to carry this division through."

In 1927 an intercollegiate group conducted a survey of the methods by which anti-semitic feeling in the student body is evinced. The findings were based on reports from schools throughout the country and indicated the following array of techniques:

". . . slurring remarks, social aloofness, exclusion from honorary fraternities, glee clubs, managerships of social organizations, difficulty of election to honorary fraternities, discrimination in campus politics . . . offensive jokes in student publications, general unfriendliness, admonitions given to non-Jewish girl students not to associate with Jewish young men."

Six hundred and sixty-five institutions were covered in the analysis; they were attended by 236,395 students, of whom 10.72 per cent were Jewish. Broun's inquiry disclosed essentially the same circumstances. From the University of California a student wrote: "I might enjoy many of the university privileges without being discriminated against, yet there is always a feeling that Jewish students can never attain the highest student body offices."

He was told by an undergraduate at Bowdoin that "Jewish students are treated as intellectual equals and social inferiors"—and they soon learned not to attend campus dances. It was a lament repeated on every side over a condition which seemed incapable of solution.

If undergraduates were susceptible to the prejudice and

356

betrayed their feeling in a host of ways, university policy only widened the breach. The most glaring example of this tendency was—and is—reflected in the Admission office. "After all the Gentiles are seated, in effect, Jews may have the vacancies." In tax-supported institutions there is presumably no discrimination in admissions—"in many cases, however, it does not go much farther." When confronted with this accusation, Broun reported, "the usual practice of the colleges is silence, evasion and denial." At Rutgers University Julius Kass, an alumnus, interviewed Dean Metzger and placed before him this situation: a Jew in the upper quarter of his prep school class and a non-Jew in the lower three-quarters both applied for admission to Rutgers after the Jewish quota was full. Who, Kass inquired, would be admitted? The Dean did not hesitate to reply that the non-Jew would be chosen.

The quota system is common to both large and small universities; it is usually invoked when a large number of Jewish students seem to be converging on a single institution. The result, of course, is that educational standards and integrity are thrown overboard; no matter how able and earnest the Jewish student, he finds himself shunted around, desperately searching for a school which will harbor him. If he seeks to enter professional schools—particularly medical colleges—he will usually find the limitations even more pronounced. Concluding his findings, Broun observed:

"Prejudice in colleges generally may be said to correspond to the area of density of Jewish population. It is strong in the big Eastern colleges—Columbia, Yale, Harvard, Pennsylvania, the New England schools as a whole. Princeton nips the problem in the bud by holding down Jewish admissions far below the percentages in any of the others mentioned. And although there are scores of institutions away from the Jewish centers where there is no overt ban or discrimination, the number seems to be exceedingly small and decreasing where Jews can be accepted on their merits. . . ."

That is the background of the present attacks. It is not a praiseworthy aspect of an allegedly democratic system—and yet there is rarely an educator who will challenge even the most flagrant principles of discrimination. He cannot afford to do so. The prejudice, he understands, is embedded in the economic system which dominates our higher learning.

But the present outbreaks of "Jew-baiting" violence are far more sinister than the denial of ordinary, every-day rights to Jewish students. These assaults, symbolized by the pogrom-cry of the Vigilantes, are primarily an attempt to damage and destroy the whole leftward student movement. When all other remonstrances have failed, this whispering campaign begins. The theme of the incitement is familiar: all Jews, according to the legend, are radicals; all radicals are Jews; good "Aryans" should hence avoid any relationship with activities in which the despised species is involved. This is the crux of the myth, stated as simply as it is set forth by its most rabid exponents. And it is founded on two deliberate, provocative untruths; they should be faced, not by humble apologies, but by a plain enunciation of fact. All Jews are not radicals; all radicals are not Jews. The first should be understood by anyone with a bare familiarity with the essence and aims of radicalism; the second can be demonstrated by a study of the rosters of any left-wing organization. On the other hand, there are among the insurgents a definite number of Jews, just as the camp of reaction will find followers of the same creed. This division is rudimentary and ancient—and it flows from a very elementary set of circumstances.

Among the Jewish people there are bankers, paupers, industrialists and workers, the privileged and the poverty-stricken. The cleavage is discernible among any section of the populace; it is, above all, an economic dividing-line as clear-cut as that which pervades any social order in which property rights belong to a limited segment.

But—and this is indisputable—a large number of those who inaugurated the left-wing student movement, for example, were Jews. That, remember, was late in 1931. How is this disproportion to be explained? Is "discontent" a "tribal characteristic" as anti-semites so vigorously proclaim? It is not. Jewish students reacted to the economic crisis in greater numbers than did others because the burden of that decline, in its inception, fell most heavily upon them. Even in times of comparative prosperity, they did not enjoy many of the benefits which accrued to their Christian colleagues; they were barred from jobs because of their religion, professional schools systematically rejected their applications, advertisements concluded with the age-old warning: "Christians only need apply." That was true in 1928; it was far more poignantly felt two years later when "industrial contraction" was under way. But it must be emphasized that this was essentially the problem of lower-middle class and working-class Jews; it did not confront those whose fathers were owners of industry, large-scale merchants and bankers, men whose economic status was the equivalent of any member of America's financial oligarchy. Even the latter might sense a social prejudice—but they were not the victims of wholesale economic reprisals. The fact is that there are Jewish firms in every sphere which practice the same discrimination as their Gentile partners—they keep down their quota of Jewish employees!

If there is an "instinctive" radicalism among certain sections of the Jewish community, it is the product of centuries of economic torment, lessened in degree, but not in kind, in this country. Of that there can be no doubt. But there is nothing "instinctively radical" about the behavior of Jewish vested interests; they are motivated by the same aspirations as the entire propertied-class. In this present and most crucial crisis, their loyalties are to that class because they operate on the simplest principles of self-interest. They, like their Gentile comrades-in-finance, are prepared to invoke the most furious reactionary force to safeguard their own stature. And they will do that, not as Jews or as Mohammedans, but as owners aligned against those whose only request is the right to work. The performance of Trustee Falk at the University of Pittsburgh was highly revealing of that common credo.

The vast majority of American students are bound together by common insecurity, by the steady retrogression of their own status in the economic scale. Ten years ago the Jewish student was likely to experience that oppression almost alone in the undergraduate community; today it is a visitation being steadily imposed upon the overwhelming number. The whole student upsurge is an offspring of their plight. Those who raise the shout of "Down With the Jew," are endeavoring to divide an entity which should, for the sake of its members, be indivisible. So long as anti-semitism persists unchecked, the student revolt—and the broader social movement of which it is a part—will be shorn of its natural solidity. The effect will avail no one save the beneficiaries of the status quo. It will provide a major keynote for the development of a fascist upheaval in this country.

I am frankly pessimistic over the immediate outlook on this issue at least. All the testimony I have gathered reveals how deep-seated and intense is the spirit of anti-semitism in the American college. What one student writes from a fairly large mid-western university is characteristic:

"There will probably be trouble this year. I have noticed a pronounced increase in 'Jew-baiting' even among fellows who should know what they are doing. They are subtly encouraged by important administrators and their activities will, I am afraid, be condoned by others. The prevailing attitude seems to be: 'a harmless anti-semitic riot will take the boys' minds off other things'.

These threats are almost intangible—and yet I can feel them in the air. So do others; and, if it comes, it will be primarily because the boys are ignorant and are being used by vicious, unscrupulous fascists—American brand or otherwise."

That apprehension exists everywhere, foreboding violence and terrorism of the most brazen sort. From De Pauw University a student writes that a leading official has referred to the National Student League as "a bunch of neurotic Hebrews." These are the innuendos and epithets employed in an effort to stifle undergraduate action—and they fit harmoniously into the network of repression by force. The fever will subside only to the extent that ignorance, and the intolerance which flows from it, can be alleviated and an insight into the cause of prejudice can be spread. That is an acute and solemn task, inseparable from the economic derivation of the problem. That this derivation be realized is imperative to the future of the Jewish student—but it is equally pressing to the outlook of all students in quest of a fruitful, satisfying order.

For the pogrom-hysteria which the Jewish undergraduate faces will not be alleviated by his "keeping quiet" or "proving his conservatism." That formula is advocated by those who would accept discrimination—and urge that nothing be said about it. Again I suspect that they are deluding themselves. The "hate-the-Jew" credo will be circulated whether the Jew is radical or not. It is a weapon which will not be combatted by conceding to it. Anti-semitism has a fairly precise, inescapable economic base; it will be utilized just as viciously and in the same terms even if the Jewish student does nothing to justify the accusation of "red." To the practitioners of fascism, the Jew is a logical scapegoat and will continue to be so as long as the roots of fascism persist. His salvation will not be achieved by meticulous adherence to the existing order—for that order does not want him, no matter how ardent his devotion. He can be more useful to it as a target for discontent.

More than 150 years ago a band of revolutionaries proclaimed that all men are equal, embodying this conviction in a notorious manifesto of the time. It was called a "Declaration of Independence"; the author was Thomas Jefferson, the man who was later to establish the University of Virginia. His statue is still proudly displayed on her campus. There is an annual series of ceremonies conducted at the institution to commemorate his sponsorship. And that university, the self-styled exponent of the Jefferson tradition, rigidly excludes Negroes from its halls.

The paradox is pointed and tragic; but Virginia's guilt is shared by the whole educational system, even in those schools which pay lip-service to the credo by maintaining no official ban. For decades the plight of the Negro student was evaded by liberals and radicals alike who refused to come to grips with an issue so fraught with "dynamite." Today it is projected into immediate significance, not for the Negro alone, but for the whole student insurgence. The cry of "Hate-the-Jew" has already been noted as an incitement to reaction; lynch-law against the Negro bears an even more deep-seated and perilous relationship to the panorama of social change.

There are three glaring manifestations of the problem. The first is the most pronounced and, in a sense, explains the others: only a fragment of the Negro population is economically able to secure higher education even within the limited zones prescribed. That is so obvious an infringement that it hardly bears reiteration—and yet the trumpeters of democracy continue to profess adherence to the idea of universal education. It is plainly true that the restriction essentially applies on a far wider front—to the whole working population. But the Negroes are victims of a special, more emphatic curb within the general pattern of discrimination, reflecting the more intense, distinct persecution of an entire people.

362

The Negroes were never "emancipated"; their bondage was transferred from the auction-block to the wage-market—but with the conditions of servitude imposed upon them as a national minority still retained. They did not become equivalent to white wage-workers nor were they endowed with any of the privileges accorded whites; they were still a separate category with distinguishing circumstances of employment. That formal change, however dynamic in terms of social processes, was not the end of the Negro problem; oppression was shifted to new levels, more vividly exposed because it was now directed against a "citizen."

Granting the initial curtailment of educational opportunity, most perniciously evident in the relative handful of Negroes who are part of the collegiate structure, those Negroes who are enabled to obtain a college degree are not automatically rescued from the discriminatory scheme. Their "uniqueness" is evidenced in two ways: within those colleges which do admit Negroes, and in the essence of the principle of the "separate" school—the Jim-Crow principle enacted into law in nineteen states of the Union.

It is unmistakably clear that discrimination in "mixed" colleges is carried on as vigorously by white students themselves as by their educators. Student behavior, however, is an inevitable outgrowth of the preachments handed down from above: education has developed a formula of prejudice which is implicit—and explicit—in every classroom doctrine. Enlightened anthropologists may demolish the concept of white superiority—but it persists as one of the most widespread and deeply-rooted tenets of American learning. From grammar school onward, it is impressed upon the white until, in the stimulating halls of university life, he readily and willingly embraces it. Prejudice is predominantly made, not born; one of the primary functions of advanced American learning has been to perpetuate it. A multitude of instances could be cited to illustrate the American counterpart of the "Aryan" myth; the example of the University of Cincinnati

363

should provide a fairly complete introduction, indicating how the anti-Negro spirit pervades every phase of the institution's operation.

In 1934 the sponsors of the Junior Promenade scheduled that fête for the Netherland-Plaza hotel—which systematically excludes Negroes. Several Negro students, desiring to participate in this function, one of the major events of university activity, bought tickets at the university book-store. When their purchases were made known to the president of the student council, he and several others immediately sought to "persuade" them not to attend, warning that it would "hurt their own cause." The Negroes went to interview the president of the school who assured them that they had a "perfect right" to attend—and then strenuously endeavored to prevail upon them to remain away. He even offered to repay double the price of their tickets. They rejected the offer. But the following year adequate "precautions" were taken to prevent Negroes from appearing at the Prom. The event was shifted to the auspices of several honorary fraternities, making it a "private function" for which the sponsors could choose their own guests. No Negroes were present.

The secretary of the University Y. M. C. A. upholds the same principle, stubbornly refusing to allow Negroes to eat in the Y. M. C. A. cafeteria on the grounds that the people who donated the building specified this provision. He has never substantiated that claim; but Negroes do not eat there.

The most prominent Negro student at the university is Donald Spencer who wrote a musical comedy produced by a Negro society there, an effort which received considerable local renown. Shortly afterward a group of white students put on a performance of their own; Spencer went to the opening production only to be told at the ticket-office that he would not be admitted. He protested to the faculty advisor who instructed that Spencer be sold a ticket; the custodians obliged by giving him a seventy-five cent seat for one dollar—a seat in the last row of the auditorium, two rows removed from every other occupant of the theatre.

In the university pool neither Negro men nor women are allowed to swim when whites are there. The R.O.T.C. is one of the most vigorous proponents of Jim-Crowism in every part of the country; at Cincinnati, for example, all Negroes are barred from its ranks—even the War Department is careful about "mixing" its cannon-fodder. A Negro who was eligible, on the basis of earlier training, to serve as an officer in the corps was just as rigidly banned; it would have been too degrading for the whites to serve under a Negro leader. These are the daily experiences of Negro students at Cincinnati, of the men who have been endowed with the privilege of a college education.

And this sentiment is duplicated at every university which condescends to admit members of the Negro race or is compelled by legal statute to do so. The University of Michigan has concentrated its energies on athletic discrimination. When Eddie Tolan, well-known trackman, served on the Michigan team, he was consistently sent to separate sleeping quarters during all the squad's journeys. In 1934 Willis Ward became one of the most celebrated athletes in this country; after two years of brilliance in football and track, he clearly merited the captaincy of one of the teams. Whereupon the football coach told his players not to elect Ward gridiron head because the trackmen intended to name him as their leader. When the elections for the track team were held, Ward was not chosen; the voting is done by secret ballot and, although the majority of the men later said they had voted for him, the outcome, as announced by the coach, was not in his favor. And in the same year, when Michigan played Georgia in football, Ward was withdrawn from the line-up "out of deference to Georgia."

Ohio State is one of the major centers of anti-Negro practices. Doris Weaver, a Negro student, sought to major in domestic science which would have required her residence in the social science hall—from which other Negroes had previously been barred. Miss Weaver took her case to the State court which decided in her favor. To solve this dilemma, the university authorities placed her in a separate wing of the building; the court upheld this move. At the same university Jesse Owens, one of the school's most famous athletes, was summarily barred from election to Bucket and Dipper, honorary athletic fraternity.

At Barnard College—the girls' division of Columbia University—there is an established rule that out-of-town students must reside in the dormitories. When Evelyn Yetman, a Negress, applied for admission to the dormitories in 1934, she—an out-of-town student—was assigned to living quarters in Harlem, the Negro center of New York.

Several years ago George Fleming, a prominent Negro debater at the University of Wisconsin, was elected to Delta Sigma Rho, honorary debate fraternity. A clause was then discovered in the constitution forbidding the admission of Negroes; it took three years for a concerted protest to secure the removal of the clause and Fleming's initiation.

Welford Wilson was a star on the City College track team in 1934; the squad travelled to Philadelphia for a meet and took up headquarters at a hotel which bars Negroes, sending Wilson to special quarters. Wilson at once resigned from the team.

In the same year Roy Thurston was initiated into Theta Sigma Rho, a University of Minnesota fraternity. Indignant alumni immediately demanded his withdrawal, claiming that a clause in the fraternity constitution forbade the entrance of Negroes. Thurston was forced to relinquish his place in the fraternity. But that statute could never be found in the fraternity's published constitution and, when this oversight was noted, the provision was hurriedly inserted.

Fraternities, with scarcely an exception, do not admit Negroes; separate Negro fraternities are rarely, if ever, given charters in national Greek-letter organizations. And the athletic system strenuously encourages the same condition: throughout the "Big Ten," Negroes are barred from participation in basketball. This spirit is not confined to any specific types of schools nor is it fought in more liberal institutions. Even at Oberlin—where the Abolitionist movement was so strong seventy years ago and where perhaps the most liberal environment in the country prevails—the Negro is not freely and cordially accepted. A student writes that there is pronounced discrimination in the dormitories and that the quota of Negroes entering diminishes each year. A bloc of faculty members has repeatedly expressed the view that "Negroes should be excluded."

To these cases could be added hundreds more; they are outright, unrestrained results of a disease which is deeply rooted in the social structure but which education, far from combatting, has encouraged and intensified. When Jean Blackwell was barred from the Michigan dormitories four years ago, she was experiencing a rebuff which scores of others have felt. When the University of Kansas prevents Negroes from participating in the R.O.T.C., from swimming in the university pool, from engaging in extra-mural or intra-mural athletics, when it raises funds among them to build a "Student Union" and then segregates them in the dining-hall of the edifice, it merely carries the tradition to its logical conclusion. The Negro is not wanted; educators demonstrate their hostility to him by a network of university restrictions—and white students are nurtured in the ideas by which these restrictions are rationalized.

But in nineteen states discrimination is solved by abject surrender. Negroes are not the victims of prejudice and subtle retardation in colleges whose administrators "tolerate" them; they are herded into the "separate" school—from primary education to college. It should not be imagined that these facilities, in the first place, are equivalent to those accorded whites; in 1900 it was estimated that the disparity in per capita expenditure upon Negro and white pupils was sixty per cent in favor of the whites; by 1930 this disparity had increased to 253 per cent. And the emphasis is all toward "mechanical and agricultural" training as opposed to study in the fine arts. There are seventeen states—including the sixteen southern states—in which such institutes are set up to prepare the Negro student for his career as a wage-worker and to destroy any illusions he may have held about a more secure place in society. Among those liberal arts colleges which do exist, there are many without adequate equipment, with insufficient funds and able to provide merely for bare fragments of educational work.

The "separate" college is vicious in principle: it establishes and reenforces the doctrine of segregation; it caters to the myth of "white superiority"; it is a final and decisive concession to Negro persecution. But it is even more pernicious in the influence it wields over the thought of the Negroes who are enrolled. They are taught that most cherished slogan of the Bourbons—"be a good nigger." They are continually warned to avoid "controversial issues," to "accept their place" or to refrain from any thought or gesture which would indicate dissatisfaction with their status. Perhaps the most dramatic illustration of the tendency is given when Negro student drama groups present performances open to outsiders. The Negro administrators often segregate the audiences. When, a few years ago, Negro students at Fiske University protested several flagrantly discriminatory acts in the neighboring territory, the leader of the protest was expelled because his behavior was "detrimental to the best interests of the university." On the one hand, the Negro is warned in state-supported separate colleges that the legislature will punish him for "insubordination"; meanwhile, those colleges dependent upon private funds—of which the Rosenwald and Rockefeller families are a major and dominating source— are admonished to conform to the credo of those who pay the bills. And the sponsors of these institutions are invariably citizens who believe in the economic advantages—to them-

368

selves—of segregation; administrators adhere to the principle because it is the condition of their existence.

There were several notable uprisings in the Negro colleges in the post-war decade, centering primarily around the social rules of the institutions and the willingness of their over-seers—sometimes Negroes and occasionally whites—to uphold segregation as a first and irrevocable standard of the school's relationship to whites. These upheavals, however important because of the oppression they signified, were usually short-lived; without the cooperation of whites, there could be no genuine or concerted resistance—and even left-wing groups were not then eager to touch "dynamite."

With the advent of crisis, Negroes were naturally con-fronted with its most intolerable burdens. And yet the Negro college, for the first few years, remained comparatively quiet, stirred by only sporadic dissent. In 1932 the National Stu-dent League was formed, setting forth as one of its major tasks the alignment of Negro students with whites on the common issues of their lives.

"Because of their comparatively greater freedom, it is the duty of white students to take the initiative in the struggle to break down these barriers of race prejudice and discrimination which tend to divide the student body and weaken its fight."

This was fairly unique language in a nation which was accustomed to accept Jim-Crow as a permanent, immutable tradition, and in an educational system which had valiantly perpetuated the breach. Nor was its effect instantaneously visible. The white student believed in the ancient, sacred shibboleths; he held on to "white superiority" as one of the last and most pronounced vestiges of his vanishing middle-class stature; he could not readily break with a prejudice which his home, his school and his environment had so vig-orously imposed. And the Negro was equally wary, suspi-

369

cious, uncertain of the few who came to him with a pledge of cooperation.

There were beginnings. At the University of Virginia, white students joined with Negroes at Virginia Union, a Negro school, and together they went to the legislature with a demand for increased appropriations for Negro students. At Virginia State College, another Negro school, undergraduates conducted an organized, militant strike against the Victorian atmosphere and convent-like restrictions which Dr. Gandy, the college head, had so mercilessly enacted. In 1933 the National Student League, at the invitation of several faculty members, held its convention at Howard University, one of the leading Negro schools in the country; but the president was reported to have disapproved of the step, the conservative Negro press denounced the congress and a large number of Negro students were successfully weaned away from it. Nevertheless, a group of Howard undergraduates did attend and it is they who have subsequently aroused more critical, independent opinion in Howard than probably at any previous time. For, whatever the difficulties, there was progress being made. One of the most impressive examples was an anti-war conference conducted jointly by undergraduates at Maryland, George Washington and Howard; at that conclave these Negroes and whites stood side by side, declaring that "We solemnly pledge ourselves not to support the government of the United States in any war it may conduct." At Virginia Union a similar conference was held.

On April 12, 1935, there were anti-war strikes at Howard, Virginia Union, Virginia State, Morgan and several others. In some places white students from neighboring colleges joined together with the Negro demonstrators; in others messages of cooperation were transmitted. These were among the most hopeful signs the American campus has ever witnessed—and they came, not at the inspiration of educators, often with their disapproval and only rarely with their aid. The problem is an enormous one; only the first inroads have been registered. There will be an increasingly bitter attempt to stifle the movement in the Negro colleges, to set it apart from the endeavors of white students, to invoke more furiously the warning: "be a good nigger." As I write, a Congressional investigation is being conducted into "radicalism" at Howard. These efforts will succeed primarily to the extent that they are condoned by white students; they will not be defeated by Negroes alone nor will the ferment in the Negro college grow unless it is assured of the honest and genuine support of whites.

The Negro's future is more dismal than that of any other segment of students; he has always been subject to discrimination by professional schools, particularly the Medical centers. At the University of Pennsylvania, for example, Negroes are rigidly barred from medical work; at Kansas they are allowed to take the preliminary years of study—but are refused permission to serve as internes in the University-owned hospital. That discrimination, however, is only the prelude to his experiences if he does obtain a medical degree; there are relatively few opportunities for doctors of any race or creed—but the Negro can virtually abandon all hope. He is not wanted after graduation any more than he was during his studies. Recently the National Association for the Advancement of Colored People compelled, by court procedure, the admission of a Negro to the University of Maryland Law School—a suit which the University fought by every device at its command. That is a notable victory on a single front; but isolated court procedure is significant primarily in terms of the popular opinion organized around it and the accompanying assault on those conditions which make the procedure necessary. The courts will not decide the basic issue; it will be resolved only by that crystallization of thinking and effort which the Bourbons fear. The Negro stands at the cross-roads, confronted on one side with economic impoverishment and on the other by lynch-rule. But neither will be ended by acquiescence; humility provokes new humili-

371

ations. He cannot, of course, make a fight for his life single-handed; he will be able—and willing—to do so only with the cooperation of the white.

That joint endeavor is begun, not because white students are "philanthropic" or "humanitarian," but because they recognize the Negro as an ally in a common cause; those who were once secure—while Negroes were enduring their present form of bondage—now find themselves menaced by essentially the same perils. I do not want to exaggerate the scope of this union; it is still in its infancy. For every case in which white students devote their energies to combatting discrimination against Negroes, there will be twenty in which the whites themselves condone and practice it. If at City College undergraduates vigorously repudiated the segregation of Welford Wilson during the track team's journey, many more have been the occasions on which such gestures went unnoticed. The student insurgence is probably weakest in the South—where anti-Negro feeling is most deeply embedded. But it cannot neglect the problem nor hope that "time will solve it." The approach of fascism foreshadows lynch-hatred on a scale never before witnessed; its results threaten Negro and white alike. And the burden of the counter-attack will rest in large measure upon the white. He will often have to take the initiative in the campaign against Jim-Crow schools, against reduced appropriations for Negro education and on those every-day, repeated evidences of discrimination in "mixed" universities.

Vigilantism uses the Negro; in many places it will employ him as a scapegoat far more fiercely and unremittingly than the Jew. And many American students, unless awareness is sped more swiftly than ever before, will be more likely to join the lynch-mob than to stand on the other side. Education has laid the setting for the reactionary outbreak of the "pure whites" and economic rulers are frantically endeavoring to preserve the split. In the South undergraduates have been known to participate in lynchings before. Although these conditions have altered somewhat in recent years and there are students who have broken through the sham of the great white myth, vast roads remain to be travelled if American learning is not to raise her own banner of "Aryanism," flying it above the whole parade of reaction. Students whose sympathies—and interests—often rest on the side of progress may often be converted into Vigilantes by the lynch-cry. For that cry can and will be widely utilized. Minorities are the first— and only the first—victims of fascism.

IX. "Free" Education

REBELLION—and repression—are the ancient heritage of the sons of the College of the City of New York. Long before the residents of our established universities awoke to social disorder, these undergraduates were at war—with the administration, with the city officialdom, with the intolerable condition of their own existence. Depression has not been a sudden interlude; in the age of collegiate country clubs, of extravagance in dress and custom, of get-rich-quick formulae, the City College man was scraping together funds for his carfare and lunches. Crisis has only accentuated his discomfort, exaggerating even more bitterly his original economic grievances. Today it is literally true that scores of students there are under-fed, emaciated, often forced to remain away from school because they cannot afford the luxury of travel —ten cents a day. Outside of academic hours, they search for jobs and, if successful, run elevators at night, serve as errand boys and perform countless other tasks to obtain their "living expenses" for the pursuit of higher learning.

To the die-hards of the community, City College is gripped by constant turmoil, without cause or meaning. There has been a recurrent effort among real estate interests and politicians to "close down the school" as punishment for the "agi-

tators." On the Board of Higher Education * which controls
the policies of the institution are men like Charles Tuttle,
noted lawyer for large corporations and a long-time spokesman for their directors. These are the men against whom the
students are aligned—and there have been singularly few
voices to confess that the conflict may represent more than
youthful intransigence.

There is reason in the unrest. Whatever else the Hearstlings have said about the City College student, they cannot
dismiss him as an incompetent or a "scatter-brained non-conformist." Repeated surveys have substantiated the belief that,
on the whole, this undergraduate body is the most talented
and earnest in the academic system. Professors who might
otherwise have transferred to more appealing posts admit
that they remain at C. C. N. Y. only because of the quality
of the material they teach. Perhaps nowhere in the country
can there be found a community of more alert, devoted scholars than among these students. And this is entirely logical.
The City College students go to college to learn, enduring a
host of privations and inconveniences to do so; if they were
in quest of "college life," or could afford to be, they would
have matriculated elsewhere. City College has never produced an All-American football player; although President
Robinson has recently been dubbed the "All-American Ass,"
the deeds which merited him this award were not associated
with the gridiron.

To understand the turbulence in which the college is involved, more than its glaring symptoms should be scrutinized. I think that a suggestion of the explanation has been
given; for a more comprehensive insight into these affairs,
so deliberately distorted in the popular press and in the testimony of college functionaries themselves, the whole growth
of the college is pertinent, tracing back to the turn of the
last century.

* The Board of Higher Education of the city serves as the equivalent of a
Board of Trustees for the college.

Up through the early part of the 1890's, City College was comparable to most centers of higher learning of the period— a school for the sons of at least moderately secure middle-class families. It was predominantly a civilian military academy, without distinction in scholarship, devoted to the disbursement of a minimum of knowledge and a maximum of respectability. Its ideas were antiquated, its procedure utterly routine, its minority of true scholars hemmed in by the rigidities of military-academic life. To the undergraduates, this barrenness was inconsequential. They were receiving the same training as their brothers at other institutions—and without paying for it.

Toward the end of the century, however, an unmistakable social cleavage began to take place in the undergraduate body, on the impetus of widespread immigration from terror-ruled foreign lands. There was a concerted influx of Russian Jewish boys into the college, students whose families had arrived in the preceding decades in ever-increasing numbers. They were not wealthy. Coming from lower middle class and proletarian homes in which the saga of "opportunity" had made only slight imprints, the students had failed to cultivate the social amenities to which the better families were accustomed. It was no minor jolt to the respectable citizens to discover their sons attending college with the off-spring of fish-peddlers. They believed in equality, of course, but that was barbarism.

So perceptible was the influx that the "gentlemen" decided to look elsewhere for education. Augmenting their feeling of loss of caste, there was another factor to speed their departure. That was the matter of grades. City College had always inspired fierce competition among its students, often not more than ten per cent of those who matriculated remaining to receive their degrees. And the poorer boys, who came with a zeal for study, began to outdistance the "gentlemen"; in one class, only 138 of 1800 entrants were graduated—and the majority were the ill-dressed, socially untutored boys from New York's lower East Side.

375

The better people retreated. Their sons were shunted to other institutions where they might find more harmonious surroundings. And, in 1902, General Webb resigned the presidency of what, to his discomfort, was being described as a "Jewish institution."

Among the older alumni this trend had been the cause of acute dissatisfaction and, with Webb's departure, they set out to rectify the situation. The first task was the selection of a new president, a "distinguished educator" who would restore a tone of "class" to the school. At the recommendation of Grover Cleveland, John Finley became the new head of City College.

Finley, with great outlines for his own future, intended the post as a stepping-stone to greater distinction. Afflicted with visions of later eminence, he never hesitated to advertise his own modesty. Despite these traits, or perhaps because of them, he did seek to introduce several important and noteworthy reforms in the habits of the institution. The "civilian military" aspects of the curriculum were the first to go; a host of other "modern" methods were inaugurated to replace the archaic structure, to transform the college into a genuine center of learning.

But Finley could not combat the "Jewish problem." Registration was increasing; a modicum of increased prosperity in all sections of the population sped the intrusion of "foreign" elements. Further, an increasing number of law schools now required college degrees for admission, thus augmenting the influx. These developments did not coincide with Finley's aspirations. Like his predecessor he sensed the contempt of established citizens for his school and Finley was even more sensitive to the attitude than Webb had been. Perhaps the decisive blow was furnished in the course of a visit he made to the Yale campus. Invited to deliver an address at a banquet there, he delivered a rhapsodic tribute to the "slumbering, restful" shades of the New Haven community.

The chairman, commenting on these remarks, looked solemnly at Finley and then observed to the audience: " 'He sleepeth not, the watcher of Israel.' "

Disturbed by this and similar references, Finley became restless at the limitations of his position. He felt that it was an impediment, rather than an aid to his ambitions. He desired far more prestige than his office at the college seemed capable of providing. When that restriction of his horizon became too intolerable, he withdrew, leaving the presidency to Dr. Sydney Mezes, fresh from the University of Texas.

Mezes was a man of moderate scholarship, often willing to heed the advice of his faculty and relatively unobtrusive in his relationships with students. Appointed largely through the political maneuvering of Colonel House, his regime is notable, not for his own place in it, but for the beginning of a not too modest drama—the rise of one Frederick B. Robinson. Under Finley's stewardship, Robinson had been an ordinary member of the staff, without distinction or any noticeable aspirations. Finley commonly called him a "whipper-snapper," possessing no more outstanding traits than that of grim persistence. With Mezes' arrival, however, the status and the ambitions of the "whipper-snapper" were markedly altered. He was suddenly elevated to the post of assistant professor. Spurred by this achievement, Robinson conceived a far more elaborate aim: the assumption of the post which Mezes held. That may seem to have been a fantastic hope for a man so lately lifted from the ranks but Robinson, it will be observed, was a genuinely unique personality.

That goal animated every one of his subsequent moves. He ingratiated his presence everywhere; he did petty favors for anyone who seemed capable of repaying him later. When Mezes adopted the habit of assigning minor phases of administrative work to faculty members, the staff resented the burden; whereupon Robinson stepped into the breach and performed all unwanted duties, never neglecting to announce that he was doing so.

377

REACTION

This determination, this patience, this unexcelled boot-licking was destined to attain its end. When Mezes betrayed signs of age and illness in 1925, Robinson embarked upon the final, most treacherous phase of the advance. Mezes having taken a six weeks' leave early in that year, Robinson maneuvered himself into the acting presidency. The academic community did not take his ascendancy too seriously, confident that it was only a temporary replacement. Robinson assiduously labored to preserve the impression; he ridiculed reports that a new president was in the making; he vigorously discouraged the suggestion of candidates for Mezes' post, declaring that Mezes was coming back and that to speak of a successor was "bad taste."

The details of the ensuing weeks have never been brought to light and many legends have sprung up around them. But one fact was forthcoming. Shortly before Mezes' anticipated return to office, the Board of Higher Education announced that Frederick B. Robinson had been named to the presidency of City College, with all the powers and duties incumbent upon that office.

Robinson was a man of diverse talents. So the newspapers, the Sunday supplements, the Success Magazines, reported in redundant succession in the period after his election. A great ballyhoo campaign had begun. Entertaining an increasingly affectionate estimate of his own prowess and possibilities, Robinson was proceeding to impress his presence upon the community. Thus one interview blared forth:

SCHOLAR AND EXECUTIVE TOO, DR. FREDERICK B. ROBINSON APPLIES UP-TO-DATE BUSINESS METHODS TO EDUCATION

Another story recited his accomplishments as a cellist: within sixty days and without previous musical training to help him, Dr. Robinson learned to play the cello. A third un-

378

folded his capacities as an etcher. "In his spare time one Summer he became a capable etcher." For public edification, there were pictures of him arrayed in a smock and intent on his easel, or in a black suit with a cello bow in his hand. Perhaps the most spectacular tid-bit was his declaration that he had discovered a flaw in Einstein's theory months before scientists in Southern California did!

This was, the press emphasized, no ordinary figure on whom the Trustees had imposed the direction of City College.

Even before his rise, Robinson had never been looked upon with admiration by his students. While in an executive post at the School of Business, he had pushed through a system of compulsory fees which the students could ill afford to pay. On numerous other occasions he had displayed equal disregard for their economic plight and their scholarly aspirations. In return, they neither respected him as an administrator nor manifested any affection toward him as a person. He had, moreover, aroused their bitter enmity in the course of an intense dispute in the year of his official elevation to the presidency, at the time when, with Mezes either absent or ill, he was in virtual command of the institution.

In the summer of 1925 Felix Cohen had attended a conference of college editors in which the discussion centered around military training. Cohen was, at the time, editor of the City College student newspaper, *The Campus*. Deeply impressed by the tenor of discussion at the congress, he determined to raise the issue squarely on his own campus where drill was an established force.

Returning to school in the Fall of 1926, he planned to wait until Armistice Day as the most effective occasion for inaugurating his campaign. On that day *The Campus* appeared with what proved to be an edition of nationwide importance. Its editorial columns were left blank save for several excerpts from the *Manual of Military Training*,*

* These are quoted in greater detail in the chapter: "A Pre-war Generation."

379

headed by this selection: "The inherent desire to fight and kill must be carefully watched for and encouraged by the instructor."

With the appearance of the issue, a sustained outcry descended upon the heads of the editors. Resentment against drill at City College had grown throughout the preceding years; the students were alert, not merely to its unwarranted immediate drudgery, but also to its political and social implications. While the local patriots began to demand the decapitation of the editors, the Student Council conducted a referendum which disclosed that 2,092 were opposed to compulsory R.O.T.C. and only 345 were in favor of it. Two days after the outcome of the survey, President Mezes ordered *The Campus* to refrain from any further mention of the course in its columns. Whereupon the paper appeared with three blank columns, draped in black as a protest against his edict.

Meanwhile, Robinson was scurrying about, desperately attempting to stifle the uprising, bring acclaim to himself and clinch his grip on Mezes' post. He succeeded. Each time the Administration seemed to have bungled the affair, he was careful to let it be known that Mezes was responsible; when a victory was scored, he was quick to assume the credit.

A faculty committee headed by Professor Morris Cohen was appointed to study the situation. It voted down the demand of the students for optional drill. But Major Holton, of the Military Science Department, knew that the end of the conflict was not in sight. After the vote was taken, he remarked: "This is only the first skirmish."

It was. Today military science is optional at City College.

That was the first clash, foreshadowing hostilities over a far wider range of issues. For Robinson was frankly panic-stricken. As a result of the episode, the college had become "news," reporters clustering about to await the next outbreak. And Robinson, his own reputation with the right people uppermost in his mind, set about to avoid any publicity which might offend those interests and endanger his own status.

An incident in the Spring of 1926 was typical of those to come, in ever-swifter succession. At that time a strike was in progress in Passaic and one student, who had been present there, was invited by the Social Problems Club to deliver a report. Robinson, in accord with his deliberate and frequently reiterated policy, announced that the meeting could not be held. Embittered by his stand, the students determined to conduct it anyway and gathered in the "alcove" for the session. At this juncture a member of The Newman Club arrived and promptly tossed a stench-bomb into the room in an effort to disperse the crowd.

The Campus, apprised of the details, went to press with the report, including Robinson's original provocation. But the Acting President had erected an elaborate spy system throughout the school to keep himself informed of such developments. When he learned that *The Campus* planned to publish the account, he immediately contacted one of the "Alumni editors"—under the paper's constitution several alumni were instrumental in controlling its affairs—and ordered him to have the issue suppressed.

Some weeks later *The Campus* editorially appealed for a student representative at faculty meetings. A professor was quoted as saying, with reference to the request, that the "faculty is entitled to privacy at its meetings. Its announcements should have oracular mysticism." The editor gently ridiculed this notion. For that—and the preceding incident— he was removed from office.

Thus was renewed the guerilla warfare. *The Campus'* staff, aroused by the reprisal, went out on strike and published an independent newspaper, obtaining newsboy licenses to hawk it on the streets. The alumni—who had performed the execution for Robinson—refused to yield. The deft Robinson rule was achieving results.

Such incidents occurred repeatedly through the remainder

381

of the decade, invariably following the same pattern. In each Robinson demonstrated that he was neither competent as an educator, remotely liberal in principle nor in the least desirous of cultivating independent thought within the college. He came to be cordially despised by his students; the faculty split into two camps, those willing to accept his dictates in the hope of promotion and others who, finding the atmosphere unbearable, either left or resolved to wage war against him.

The onset of depression immeasurably heightened the tension. Many students were forced to drop out to devote all their time to the search for employment. Those who remained were confronted by the remorseless deprivations of the present and the uncertain, chaotic outlines of the future.

Out of that disorder, their groping, desperate curiosity about the nature of society was vastly intensified. They did not at once and in a body despair of this social structure; even today a majority of City College students have not proceeded that far. But they were impelled into activity on such immediate, concrete issues of their lives as the threat of the imposition of fees and the menace of a war which would solve the "surplus population." These things were particularly real and meaningful to them. But as they translated their inquiries into action—whether in the newly-formed National Student League or the League for Industrial Democracy—their enlightenment advanced. Robinson stepped to the fore more boldly. He sought to curtail every attempt at social investigation. He tried to disrupt and terrorize every left-wing student group. He erected an even more oppressive network of espionage and intimidation. When these devices were first introduced on a large scale, one writer remarked that "either President Robinson or the student body will have to go." As events progressed, the suspicion spread that Robinson would ultimately stand alone in a deserted empire. For behind him in every gesture, endorsing his most arbitrary

382

endeavors, refusing to heed a growing demand for his ouster was the Board of Higher Education of the city.

Among the more flagrant instances of repression in the early depression period can be cited the following:

In 1931 the editor of *The Campus* was suspended for criticizing the Dean of the Business School.

The following year the Social Problems Club and Liberal Club were unable to function for several months because no faculty member dared to lend them his services as advisor; later the groups were entirely suppressed.

The Dramatic Society was forbidden to produce "Merry-Go-Round," a satire of Tammany political rule. Dr. Robinson, of course, is a Tammany appointee.

In October 1932 the Student Forum was denied the right to hold a political symposium with speakers from the four parties—Republican, Democrat, Socialist and Communist.

The Student Forum was denied permission to issue a publication in March, 1933.

The Ticker, publication at the school of business, was suppressed by Dean Moore because it refused to accept the condition that its faculty advisor be allowed to "reject editorial comment that is directed against any administrative officer."

When Oakley Johnson, faculty advisor to the Social Problems Club, was dismissed from the faculty in 1932, students met on the college grounds to protest his dismissal. They were dispersed by police. They thereupon engaged a hall—off the campus—and conducted a "mock trial" of President Robinson. Previously ten students had been suspended for the campus meetings which resulted in arrests. Upon the holding of the "mock trial" nineteen more were suspended by the Board of Higher Education.

When the Student Forum planned a meeting to pro-

test the suspensions, it was warned that "to criticize the
Board of Higher Education constitutes in itself a breach
of discipline."

But despite all these and similar steps Robinson still maintained a minimum of discretion. Thus, in the spring of 1931
several members of the Social Problems Club were suspended
for publishing a magazine against the orders of the administration. Later he reinstated all but one, known to be a communist. One of those reinstated wrote a letter to *The Campus*
accusing Robinson of political discrimination—whereupon he
was again suspended. Outraged by this high-handedness, a
group of leaders in extra-curricular affairs signed a letter
asserting that they were equally guilty since they too accused
Robinson of discrimination. When a reporter asked him
whether he would take any action against the signers, Robinson waved him away: "Pish, pish, just a boyish prank."

But there was a valid reason for this unusual display of
tact. At the head of the list was America's one mile champion
runner, George Bullwinkle! Robinson did not forget. He
simply rejected the bludgeon for his more treacherous, de-
ceitful strategy. While openly promising that there would be
no discipline, he informed faculty members that those twenty-
five were not to receive favorable recommendations for jobs
and loans. And on their record cards was written: "signed
insubordination letter to *The Campus.*"

There was another significant indication of Robinson's
capacity for deception which occurred at about that time.
An intensive campaign was being waged by students in the
city colleges against one of the frequent moves to impose fees.
Morton Gottschall, then the registrar, announced that the college was instituting a fee of five dollars for every point
in excess of 128 accumulated by students before graduation.
Since extra points at the college are awarded for high grades
(the administration was trying to avoid the appearance of
direct tuition fees) this constituted a tax on scholarship and

384

was criticized as such. During the early stages of the dispute, Robinson had been out of town and on his return, when students carried their protests to him, he betrayed great indignation over the ruling. He assured them it must have been the work of some "irresponsible subordinate." When these students returned to Dean Gottschall, he showed them documents proving conclusively that the measure had been originated with Robinson's knowledge and cooperation.

These episodes rapidly mounted, engendering an atmosphere of bitter distrust, suspicion and enmity. By 1933 the college was riddled with rulings which virtually barred any semblance of undergraduate expression on the issues of their immediate environment or of larger spheres. The students were constantly reminded that they were the recipients of a "free education" and hence expected to renounce any of the ostensible rights of citizens. It was not until the spring of 1933, however, that Robinson introduced the umbrella as a technique of the higher learning.

City College, like most other institutions where the R.O.T.C. is firmly entrenched, has its annual military exercises. On that day the life of the college is customarily transferred—officially—to the hands of the War Department, the patriotic societies and anyone else who believes that all men are enemies. The demonstration had always been a source of profound annoyance to the vast majority of City College students who are opposed to drill and all that it represents. They have regarded it as an emblem of their own persecution and the bias of the administration. To them the ceremony is "Jingo Day."

By May, 1933, they felt that they could not tolerate the procedure any longer without some overt counter-demonstration to voice their sentiments. And so, on the appointed day, more than 500 students gathered on a street opposite the campus grounds to conduct an anti-war meeting. Meanwhile, the traditional parade of the R.O.T.C. having been launched, the police ordered the mass meeting to disperse. The students then formed a picket line around the stadium, carrying anti-war placards, only to be again instructed to leave. All students having been invited to attend the exercises, held inside the stadium, they dropped their placards and sought to gain admission. Again they were rebuffed; whereupon they moved across the street opposite the stadium to conduct an orderly protest assemblage.

At this point two things must be understood about Robinson. He is a hot-tempered, easily aroused man whose rage frequently seems beyond ordinary control. And he is a blunderer. He often does things which, in the calm aftermath, he is likely to regret—not because they were unethical or unreasonable but because they seem to have damaged his reputation.

That afternoon, while the meeting was in progress, President Robinson approached the stadium, accompanied by Colonel Lewis, head of the Military Science Department, General John Byrne, two Daughters of the American Revolution and several police officers. As the party neared, the students uttered in unison the shouts which have become the battlecries of the City College campus: "Down with the R.O.T.C. Drive Military Training Out of City College."

President Robinson glanced at his companions, saw their disapproving frowns. He envisaged his great plans for himself suffering another reverse. And he was, moreover, afflicted with an uncontrollable burst of temper. Abruptly leaving his guests, he rushed out into the street and began to strike at the group of undergraduates with the weapon which has become the symbol of his regime—an umbrella.

After numerous heads had been soundly thumped by the savant, students came over, pinioned the hands of their president and wrenched the umbrella away. In the melee it fell to the ground, to be rescued by a quiet-voiced freshman who returned it to Robinson, with a brief comment: "Here is your club, Dr. Robinson."

386

The educator strode back to his guests and marched them proudly into the stadium. That gesture had summarized the status of learning in city college and the relationship of students to their administration.

Under an ancient code of educational procedure, an educator who invokes force against his own students has ceased to be of any value to the community. When that violence has been personally engineered, even a Board of Trustees should be compelled to recognize that his usefulness is past. But at City College the standards of conduct once presumed to govern administration were long ago abridged—months before other institutions made the same concession to immediacy. Following the "Jingo Day" outbreak a faculty meeting was hurriedly summoned at which Robinson was greeted by his loyal subordinates as a hero. Only a handful were distressed at his performance and they, to the everlasting dismay of their students, did not speak out. A tribunal of three was immediately appointed to investigate the "incident," a probe which was quickly transformed into a star-chamber proceeding against the whole insurgent movement in the college. Students were questioned, not merely about their presence on the scene when Dr. Robinson made history, but about all their past activities and their political beliefs. The aim was to end radicalism at the college—not to discover the causes of the "Jingo Day" conflict.

Meanwhile, Vigilantes were being organized under the direction of Major Holton, R.O.T.C. functionary, who incited his underlings to use "controlled force" against the rebels. But the Vigilantes were hopelessly outnumbered. The undergraduate body, repelled by their deeds, was united in condemnation of the president's behavior. One witness wrote:

"Policemen sit in the shade of the trees on the campus. . . . Faculty members walk rapidly and cringe at their own shadows. It is only the policemen who are self-confident and sure of themselves. It is they who have inherited the college."

Following the faculty "investigation," twenty-one students were expelled and nine suspended for "conduct unbecoming a college student and not in the best interests of the college." The three clubs devoted to discussion of social problems were deprived of their charters. A similar ban was placed upon *The Campus.*

If the faculty had stated its position more explicitly, the basis of the reprisals might have been described thus: "Inciting President Robinson—a sensitive soul—to riot."

The following year served to advance the conflict to a crisis which cannot long endure. For the student body began to rally behind one almost unanimous declaration: "Oust Robinson." And Robinson, who had been discovering how difficult it was to "expel" unrest from City College, enacted his most glaring invasion of the students' now almost invisible rights.

That Fall—1934—Robinson had attained his pinnacle of extra-curricular achievement when Bernarr McFadden, litterateur extraordinary, invited him to write a special article for *True Story* magazine. With that versatility so typical of his career, the president of City College responded, thus adding pulp-writing to his amazing repertoire. Once started on this literary expedition, however, it seemed highly doubtful that he would ever stop. Before long one could find his "by-line" prominently featured on the editorial pages of the Hearst press, with all the trimmings which Mr. Hearst can bestow upon talent he has "discovered." A new double-play combination, Robinson to McFadden to Hearst, was being formed to snuff out the infidels.

In the midst of these accomplishments, Robinson again found himself distracted by affairs at home; perhaps his subsequent pique was attributable to his eagerness to prepare another tid-bit for *True Story*, a desire which this intrusion halted. For early in October Robinson was informed that several hundred student emissaries from fascist Italy were arriving in New York and that a reception for them at City College would be in order.

To understand the fervor of anti-fascist sentiment among City College students, two things must be emphasized. In the first place, in their own educational halls, they have received an intimation of what education under fascism implies. For nearly ten years Robinson had pursued its credo: silencing dissent, shutting off criticism, upholding all the myths and sanctities of the status quo. Secondly, these students could not disassociate fascism from the American scene; they saw its coming as the final phase of their economic enslavement, the more drastic perpetuation of the conditions which they had so long experienced.

And now the man responsible for reactionary terrorism at the college was calling an assembly to do homage to the bearers of the propaganda of fascist Italy. That such was their mission, although there were frantic denials by their American representatives, has been adequately revealed. If there be any doubt, let us turn to the pages of *La Stampa* of Turin on the occasion of the students' return to Italy. There, on October 24, 1934, we find:

> "Today we salute in you the dear comrades in study and in faith who by the Duce's will have marked a brilliant new phase in the triumphal march of Fascism throughout the world."

Or to the account of Il Duce's greeting to them in the same journal:

> ". . . At twelve o'clock the Duce appeared in the reception hall, where, in triple file, were lined up the students. They greeted His appearance with a tremen-

dous 'To Us' in which vibrated the youths' consciousness of having fulfilled their honorable mission of representing fascist Italy on the other side of the Atlantic. . . ."

It was to serve as a spring-board for this "triumphal march of fascism" that the assembly had been called. From the moment that the reception was announced, the student body declared its position quite firmly. The Student Council sent a letter to the President urging him to cancel so brazen an attempt to propagandize for fascism. There were similar protests filed by undergraduate groups throughout the college. As Dean Gottschall later wrote: *

"To them (the City College students) the menace of fascism in America looms very close. . . . They cannot afford to wait, they feel, until the Fascist movement has grown stronger, but must combat its every manifestation. . . ."

But President Robinson refused to cancel the visit; as in so many of his performances, the convictions of his students appeared only to accentuate his own support for whatever they disliked. He proceeded with preparations for the reception—and damn the student body!

In this stand he was ardently endorsed by Mark Eisner, chairman of the Board of Higher Education, who had returned the year before from Italy with the belief that the New Deal should copy many of the outlines of Italian fascism.

President Robinson and his Trustees ought to have anticipated what was to take place. Perhaps they did. As the fascist students strode to the platform, a chorus of hissing broke out in the audience, to be followed by even more vigorous exclamations when Robinson rose to speak.

Less than two years before the President of City College

* From his report on the ensuing incident.

390

had been seized with uncontrollable fury. On that occasion he used an umbrella; this time, fortunately, he was unarmed. All that he could muster was a frantic expostulation, sonorously delivered: "Guttersnipes. . . . Your conduct is worse than guttersnipes."

The crowd was amazed by his outburst. But even astonishment could not restrain laughter at the spectacle he was making of himself. Then the uproar subsided, he concluded his address and fiercely strode back to his seat on the platform. The next speaker was a representative of the Student Council. It should be emphasized that, in all their statements, the protestants had declared no hostility to the Italian students as such; they were directing their protest against the mission of the visit. Had he been allowed to finish, the student council speaker would have said so. But he got only as far as: "I do not intend to be discourteous to our guests. I wish merely to bring anti-fascist greetings from the student body of City College to the tricked, enslaved student body of Italy. . . ."

He was allowed to go no further. Someone struck him in the eye; several others proceeded to drag him from the platform. Enraged by the performance, the student body streamed out of the hall to the stadium where it resumed its protest against a bitter symbol: the partnership between the City College administration and the agents of Italian fascism. That was not a fantasy; it had been created by years of repression, of unceasing provocations.

Robinson had refused to heed the overwhelming request of his undergraduates for cancellation of the visit; he—and his overseers—had insisted upon a performance which they knew could not pass unnoticed; when the results of this dictatorship emerged, the president could only vilify his own students and condone the forceful ejection of a spokesman for the student council.

In accord with the precepts of City College tradition, the

students paid for the outburst of their president. There were twenty-one expulsions; the council was disbanded; an investigation was begun into the conduct of student publications.

It is noteworthy that the faculty overrode the recommendations contained in the report of Dean Gottschall. That document was an important one because, although it did not clear the students, it at least endeavored to trace the causes and meaning of the undergraduate revolt. The faculty, as one member explained, was not interested in these "extraneous items." The Dean had been instrumental in many of the earlier disciplinary steps; now his demeanor was changing, perhaps because he saw the inevitable end of his efforts—complete alignment with Robinson. And hence it is significant that, beginning in the Fall of 1935, a new man—Turner of West Virginia—is to come to City College to direct "social affairs." No one has ever heard of him before; but the reason for his arrival probably lies in Dean Gottschall's report. The Dean is no longer the man for the job of repression.

The following spring, when the military department launched its customary preparations for "Jingo Day," the City College student body again sought to intervene; but to no avail. The Student Council proposed a compromise whereby R.O.T.C. men would be replaced as ushers by honor students to remove some of the more flagrant military aspects of the fete. When its suggestion was bruskly pushed aside, the Council called for an undergraduate boycott of the ceremonies.

Only a handful failed to obey the boycott. Virtually the only people in the stadium were a few hundred emissaries of various patriotic societies. When President Robinson called upon Lester Rosner, president of the Student Council, to award the extra-curricular insignia, there was no reply. Robinson fluttered for a moment, stamped impatiently, then the great truth descended upon him.

Rosner, too, had boycotted the exercises.

Commencement is a peculiarly festive occasion at City College. It is the day upon which students can once more prepare to enter a world in which a measure of freedom prevails. Whether they are on bread-lines or in soup-kitchens, they will henceforth at least be removed from the danger zone, the campus where each successive thought is suspect, where they live in momentary dread of execution. They do not love their alma mater. What they remember most vividly about her are the repressive orgies of a dictatorial president, the strangling atmosphere of apprehension, the wholesale legislation aimed at silencing their dissent. If there are faculty men whom they admire and with whom they have enjoyed fruitful hours, these memories are swept aside by more turbulent recollections. They have come from homes in which poverty is rampant to a school which does everything in its power to conceal the cause and prevent the relief of that poverty. Their discontent has encountered, not the elementary aspects of sympathy, but vicious antagonism. To them the college has been a prison, its rulers wardens, its procedure one of ever increasing regimentation.

It is not to be wondered that on Commencement Night they have the demeanor of men released from long incarceration. Their sentiments were vividly expressed at the exercises of June, 1935. That class had matriculated in 1931 when the most crushing stage of Robinson's regime was launched; it had lived through four years of unrelenting confinement, surrounded by constant dread and panic. It had neither affection nor esteem for the dispenser of degrees.

Dr. Robinson knew it. He tried to make the ceremonies as brief and inoffensive as possible. But he has never been capable of a graceful, unmarred performance. And so he forgot that Colonel Lewis of the R.O.T.C. was one of the major enemies of the student body; he forgot that the Colonel's appearance was bound to create a ferment. In accordance with custom, he introduced the Colonel to present the awards to the members of the corps. A storm of booing broke out.

393

Colonel Lewis rose slowly, his manuscript in his hand; but the speech was never delivered. Confronted with this protest, Dr. Robinson, in despair, waved him back to his seat.

But there was to be still another blunder. Colonel Maurice Simmons, representing the Spanish American War Veterans, had appeared to present a cup to the college (a prize, incidentally, which went to Dr. Robinson's son). Mr. Simmons did not know that his remarks were to be brief; moreover, he felt in the mood for discourse. He began by attacking "students who practice violence"—a reference which was emphatically hissed; he delivered a long eulogy of "preparedness"—and again was greeted with disfavor; when he mentioned Soviet Russia, the students decided to end their college careers with one final salvo. They vigorously applauded socialism.

At the conclusion of the exercises, Robinson was a flustered, shaken, angry man. He could not make peace with his students—because his terms demanded abject surrender.

Early in his academic career, Frederick B. Robinson issued the following pronouncement:

"The most illiberal thing a man can do is to impose upon a student body his views and theories. . . . Here at the college we do not wish to be tyrannical. Our regulations are not meant to be oppressive but are necessary to preserve law and order."

It is highly illuminating that the most "orderly" display of student expression at City College occurred on April 12, 1935. That was the day on which virtually the entire student body joined in an anti-war assemblage in the Great Hall— and on that day, Frederick B. Robinson was recuperating from an illness out in California.

But the blame does not rest on his shoulders alone. There is a pronounced tendency in some quarters to regard Rob-

394

inson as the lone source of reaction at City College. He is not. He is speaking for a banker-controlled Board of Higher Education which has always reenforced his stand. Even more revealing of that is the fact that, in 1932, when students were punished for conducting a "mock trial" of school officials, a trial held miles away from the campus, the reprisals were handed down by that Board. There is no essential conflict between its policies and those of Robinson; if on occasion he has acted too crudely, without adequate finesse, the Board members have realized how praiseworthy were his motives. They placed him in office despite his meagre qualifications; they have kept him there in the face of palpable student resentment and his own clear incapacity.

Ten years of terror—and "subversive activities" have not been "stamped out." The explanation is more basic than any peculiar truculence of the City College student. He is the victim of a disordered social pattern; he will continue to be restive and rebellious so long as the circumstances of his bondage persist. His passion for social issues, his concern for the tides of world forces, his refusal to be silenced by the threat of expulsion arise from that cause—and that alone. The left-wing student groups at the school have survived every attempt to demolish them because they give concrete, realistic expression to the needs of the undergraduate body.

Certainly Robinson has only aggravated the unrest; it is he who is responsible for recurrent disorders and strife. His administration, fraught with intolerance and cruelty, carried on under the educational principles of the R.O.T.C., defended by squads of club-waving police, has precipitated repeated violence in the institution. But he continues to rule with the approval of Tuttle and Co.; together they are still endeavoring to solve discontent by destroying the discontented.

Meanwhile, the entrenched citizenry clamors for closing of the college, warning that this will occur unless the "agitation" ceases. Destruction of the school would be a calamity of real dimensions; but it will be more damaging to the reputation of this social order than to the minds of the students. They will learn somehow—and men like Robinson will never teach them.

HUNTER

Shortly before Frederick B. Robinson delivered his famous coup de grâce by umbrella, the Board of Higher Education convened to designate a new president for Hunter College. Their choice was to be placed in command of the largest women's college in the world, where 5000 pupils attend the day session alone and 15,000 more are enrolled in sub-divisions. The post, it might have been assumed, merited the services of a distinguished educator.

But the Board of Higher Education—the same one which rules City College—operates under the standards of any other directorate of learning throughout the country. Its members are not educators: they are men who have risen to prominence in the sphere of business and whose concept of the school is based upon the dictates of their own self-interest and prejudice. They are, moreover, closely interwoven with the politics of the city. Constantly harried by demands for patronage, compelled to pay political debts whenever a vacancy arises, their range of selection is even more drastically curtailed—although it is doubtful that, if left to their own initiative, they would do any better. It was such a debt which was exacted late in the Spring of 1933 when Dr. Eugene Colligan became president of Hunter College.

Colligan was described by one journal, at the time of his appointment, as an "amiable mediocrity." Another remarked that "nothing in his career or in his hitherto revealed qualifications entitled him to what might well be the most important post in the education of women in the United States." But Colligan possessed all the "non-educational" requirements. His brother was a Tammany district leader. In his own right he was known to be "amenable" to "advice." He had never been guilty of an utterance which could be construed as an affront to conventional modes of thinking, acting and living. His life had been attuned to that subservience imperative to the acquisition of such rewards as a college presidency. When a new director was needed at Hunter, Eugene V. Colligan had proved himself sufficiently mediocre, undistinguished and orthodox. He got the job.

Looking uptown to the campus of City College, Colligan may have discerned the path by which an aspiring college president makes his way among the upper two per cent of the world. Whether he proceeded from envy, from ambition or from sheer common sense will never be known. The fact is that before two years had elapsed, Frederick B. Robinson was confronted with a formidable rival in reaction. It was the amiable, hot-headed, exciteable director of Hunter College. And the Board of Higher Education was saluting a new hero.

Colligan moved slowly in his first year, adapting himself to strange surroundings. But he could not refrain from a few meaningful preludes. In December, 1933, one of his students was arrested in the course of an anti-Nazi demonstration at Columbia; she was promptly suspended. The expansive president strongly intimated that her conduct was repugnant to his concept of social action and that future offenders would bring out the worst in him. Shortly afterward a large number of girls planned to hold an anti-war conference; they were immediately informed that no dangerously specific or militant resolutions would be tolerated. Later they were deprived of a meeting-place, forced to assemble in the locker-rooms and impeded by faculty "guidance." Meanwhile, Colligan was sniping at the International Relations Club, plainly aiming at its abolition. But he was still advancing with discretion, with temperance, with the slow, calculating outlook of a Tammany politician who wants to know where he is leaping.

After a year of office, Dr. Colligan gradually abandoned restraint. His amicable, under-handed methods had not availed except to acquaint him with the enormity of the problem. He was charting a more decisive, spectacular course. And thus there began, in March, 1935, a wholesale assault on every vestige of self-assertion at Hunter College. The campaign endured for the remainder of the term with no hint that it would subside in the future.

That month, it will be remembered, the patriots were re-gathering their forces after the invasion of Syracuse, Columbia and Chicago; having exhausted the possibilities of "exposing" professors, they were turning to the more general device of "investigations"; and throughout the country college administrators were preparing to "cope with" the impending strike against war.

Certainly the setting encouraged Hunter's president; but, even without these accompaniments, it is fairly safe to say that he would have been ready for the siege. Early in March Dr. Colligan, at a meeting with a few picked students and faculty members, warned that the "control" of an "organized minority" over student affairs would have to be broken—or else the Student Council would be dissolved. One week later the pledge was fulfilled. The faculty submitted to the council a document entitled—strangely enough—"grant of powers" in which student self-government was officially doomed. Faculty advisors, chosen by President Colligan, were to be superimposed on all clubs and publications; control was centralized in a council whose acts were to be "reviewed" by the faculty. Finally and perhaps most significant, the Peace Council, spear-head of anti-war agitation, was summarily abolished. It is noteworthy that, although other sections of the report were not put into immediate effect, the Peace Council's appeal for a room was denied until "it has reorganized in accordance with the faculty report."

There was instantaneous revolt among the students. The Student Council condemned the report as "a complete nullification of student self-government." More than twenty other campus groups avowed similar sentiments. Whereupon Beatrice Shapiro, freshman scholarship student and prominent in anti-war activities, was abruptly suspended. The official statement explained that she was "unteachable."

With this there was inaugurated an unbridled reign of espionage and terror from which no one suspected of liberal sympathies was exempt. Peace Council reconvened, refusing to acknowledge the validity of its dissolution and reasserting its right to exist. For several weeks it conducted meetings and no overt administrative intervention took place. It was not until April 11, the day before the nationwide strike, that Dr. Colligan moved decisively. On that day a representative of the Women's League for Peace and Freedom was scheduled to address a session of the council; hardly had she begun when a "representative" of Dr. Colligan appeared, demanding that the speaker appear before him at once—without concluding her talk. Since the speaker, Mrs. Samuel Sollender, was not familiar with the situation, she requested that the group accompany her. Upon arriving at Dr. Colligan's office, the girls were immediately ordered to leave; the President announced he would see Mrs. Sollender alone. The latter at once protested, citing the fact that she was unaware of preceding developments and felt that the girls were entitled to be present. At her request Dr. Colligan only grew more impressed with his own authority, more irate at the students, more overbearing in his demeanor. He shouted at Mrs. Sollender in an effort to make her "understand." She remained obdurate. At this juncture one of the girls quietly urged him to display a measure of courtesy to a woman whom they had invited to the college and who was therefore a guest of the institution. Her request was important because "good manners," the need for the amenities has been so long the weapon of the Board of Higher Education in disciplining holders of unpopular opinions. For suggesting that Dr. Colligan practice what the school system preaches, the girl was thereupon suspended from school. Another member of the group was ordered to the Dean's office where she was told that she too had been suspended—for calling an "illegal" meeting of the Peace Council and for blowing a whistle in the student exchange. (Thousands of whistles have been blown in the student exchange in Hunter's history to attract attention to an announcement—but this one was different!) There were now three suspensions engraved on Dr. Colligan's promising record.

Despite the suspensions, despite repeated harangues by Dr. Colligan and other administrators, accompanied by a series of threats and intimidation, 2200 students joined in the nationwide anti-war strike the following day. Denied a meeting-place on the campus, they convened in a midtown hall. From their mass meeting, a delegation of 200 proceeded to Dr. Colligan's office to present a resolution condemning the suspensions. The students waited patiently outside until he had finished with routine business; then, when he seemed unoccupied, they walked in. The President of the Junior class, standing at the head of the delegation, began: "We have come to present to you. . . ."

Dr. Colligan was suddenly inflamed; with each passing day he had grown more short-tempered, restless, dissatisfied with the failures of his efforts to silence protest. Striding toward the leader, he demanded: "Were you invited into this office?"

The student responded that she had merely come as the bearer of a resolution; she was quickly interrupted and ordered to leave the office. The girl asked whether he would interview the delegation later in the day. Drawing himself up, fuming audibly, the full dignity of his stature and his role overcoming him, the president shouted: "I will not be dictated to by any group of students."

Two other students thereupon endeavored to state the case; they repeated that their mission was simply one of protest against the earlier suspensions.

Within twenty-four hours those three girls received letters informing them that they had been suspended from the institution.

Meanwhile, detectives were assigned to the scene. The campus became conscious of a group of plainclothesmen who patrolled the area waiting for a call from administrative offices. When the Peace Council met on April 30, the summons came. According to the account in the student newspaper:

". . . Dean Egan entered accompanied by two police. Mr. Cadden (the speaker) was told to leave with the Dean, while the police agents stood at the door and did not permit students to leave or enter the room. . . .

"The Dean then returned and wrote down the names of some of the students present and then dismissed the group. . . ."

The Herald-Tribune reported that the men who stood guard at the door were representatives of the Alien Radical Squad.

Open repression was only one phase of the performance. With the ease developed by years of diligent preparation, Dr. Colligan then embarked upon a campaign of unrestrained slander. When a group of parents interviewed him to ascertain the cause of the reprisals, he assumed his best, confidential, bed-side manner and assured them that he possessed certain "nauseating facts" about the "private lives" of the suspended students. He was careful to see that the libel was not recorded; the stenographer was told to omit that sentence from her notes. But on repeated occasions he did not hesitate to invoke the most contemptible and fraudulent weapon at his command: aspersions on the "private lives" of the victimized girls. It was a performance which Frederick B. Robinson had never excelled.

401

And on May 16th another session of the Peace Council was invaded by police and its speaker forcibly removed from the building. The incident was striking because, outside of their meeting-room the peace leaders had posted a large sign: "This is NOT Nazi Germany. . . . Peace Council WILL Meet Today."

What of the faculty members? Dr. Colligan had not forgotten them. At intermittent periods they were reminded that, if they wanted to preserve their jobs, they would have to enlist in his holy war "to stamp out radicalism." His edict presented a difficult alternative which few have been willing thus far to face. Many are outraged by the events; they have seen the school transformed into a camping-ground for police, plainclothesmen and members of the Radical squad. They are, moreover, aware that the repression will not cease but will gather momentum as Dr. Colligan becomes surer of his ground. On the other side, they see scores of girls risking their academic careers, enduring every form of intimidation and brutality, to speak out on issues which they hold to be vital.

Like their brothers at City College, the Hunter girls are not the offspring of aristocracy. Each phase of depression has caught their families in its grip, leaving them bewildered, dispossessed, restless. Dr. Colligan is discovering—or should be—the lesson of every institution: that all the force and viciousness he can muster fails to "expel" the issues of suffering, of poverty and war from the minds of his pupils. But the banker-dominated Board of Higher Education—the same one which has so enthusiastically endorsed the persecution-drive of Frederick B. Robinson—has stood fast by Robinson's disciple at Hunter. He is their man.

Not long ago Mussolini awarded the Order of Merit to Dr. Eugene Colligan.

402

x. The Liberal Learning

It is difficult to appraise with detachment that great monument to the search for truth—Columbia University. I am so familiar with the deceit and corruption in which it is steeped and there are so many relevant details which must, for reasons of space, be omitted that I hesitate to attempt a portrayal. The university's status, however, is of vastly more than personal or sentimental concern; for Columbia has come to represent certain educational standards, certain precepts of conduct and conviction that are looked upon with envy by the occupants of an unhappy academic world. Its contributions to light—or darkness—in the present crisis are significant precisely because of the esteem in which it is popularly held.

And at the outset I shall record a series of virtues which the institution undoubtedly possesses and which render its extra-curricular behavior even more revealing. Columbia is among the leading centers of education in this country, far outdistancing hundreds of small, primitive communities where the torch of scholarship has never even flickered: of that superiority there can be no question. Her classrooms are endowed with almost unrestricted freedom: within them discussion and controversy are allowed to flourish to a degree seldom attained elsewhere. The curriculum—and now I speak of the college and graduate faculties, not the mail-order disbursement of knowledge in the Extension—is diverse, comparatively well-organized and receptive to a measure of fresh approach. These are no incidental distinctions; the more that I study scores of letters and recall conversations with students throughout the country, their importance is emphasized.

Having recorded these attributes, however, I fear that the basis of unequivocal praise is almost exhausted. For beyond them the university is—in essence—guided by fundamentally the same dictates and conventions as little Podunk Aggies. The point cannot be reiterated too often; for in this divergence between the methods of classroom liberalism and extra-curricular intolerances rests the fundamental and tragic dichotomy of the institution. That division confronts teacher and student alike; both may speak their minds in the class-room on oppression in Patagonia; let them declare themselves outside that secluded province on the same issue or on a more immediate phase of university policy and they encounter the same enmity which has haunted universities everywhere. The opposition will be expressed in far more restrained terms than the umbrella-waving of a Frederick B. Robinson; Columbia must ride two horses at once, satisfying the elementary needs of a "liberal tradition" and simultaneously catering to ortho-dox opinion. Both are sources of endowments; now, when the latter is more lucrative than the appeal to "liberal philan-thropists," I suspect that a change in strategy is occurring. It has yet to be fully synthesized.

I cannot hope to recount here the history of repression at Columbia; moreover, many of its most flagrant manifesta-tions—such as the war ousters of Dana, Beard and Cattell—are fairly well known; earlier, in another connection, the expulsion of Reed Harris was outlined. There occurred on Morningside Heights, however, three incidents of pre-emi-nent importance in the year 1934-35; these are related, not for any peculiar individual qualities, but because, together, they demonstrate the nature and direction of Columbia policy at this interval in world affairs. With these episodes under-stood, I believe the ensuing discussion of university principle and personnel will be entirely vindicated. Each development occurred, it should be noted, at a time when the student insurgence had reached some dimensions, when increasing numbers of students had begun to think—and act—on those issues once confined to the horizon of Nicholas Murray Butler.

Dean Hawkes expelled Reed Harris on what administra-tors now recall as a "Bad Friday" in 1932; but the policies of *The Spectator* which Harris edited continued to move progressively leftward. That tendency was an unceasing aggravation to the university overlords and they were seldom reluctant to say so. On the other hand, they did nothing about it which could have been construed as "censorship," a timidity in no way related to any revival of integrity or reaffirmation of principle. Several months after I became editor, Dean Hawkes stated his views to me with amiable frankness. These were his words as accurately as I recall them; the meaning is scrupulously retained:

"You know, a faculty man was in here today. He asked me why we didn't close you fellows up and stop all these meetings on the campus. I told him that, if we did, we would have meetings twice as large and a picket line outside my door."

I assured him that his judgment was sound. And it was that apprehension which had kept *The Spectator* alive despite the increasing vigor of its editorial pronouncements. This was, it will be noted, the spirit of university policy: retention of an independent newspaper is a lesser evil to the dangers of undergraduate protest. Since 1932 two undergraduate strikes had occurred at Columbia—against the dismissal of Reed Harris and, the following year, of Donald Henderson, an instructor. A third strike, it was feared, and the "liberal tradition" would be out! No one wanted that to happen— least of all the man who had precipitated the storm of 1932.

But if tact prevented drastic intervention, I hasten to add that the existence of *The Spectator* was not regarded as a permanent insoluble. Hoping to solve the administrative dilemma, a group of public-spirited undergraduates attempted to kidnap me late in the Spring of 1934. The attempt failed; whereupon Associate Dean McKnight recommended that I move from the dormitories to prevent any "disorder." He

405

could not comprehend the assertion that I was being punished for the rowdyism of the university's favorite sons.

It should not be imagined that the administration endorsed the kidnapping; as one official remarked, it would have been "damn bad publicity for the school." That was not the solution, everyone agreed. And so, late in that year, there began the most concerted and energetic effort to silence *The Spectator* by more constitutional methods—to prepare the way for "censorship" without providing grounds for suspicion that such an aim was being sought. Earlier I have discussed the "bribed aristocracy" of undergraduates, the men who can be relied upon to do what an administration finds uncomfortable to do in person. At Columbia this rôle was to be entrusted to the Student Board—and, with only two dissenting voices, the responsibility was accepted.

The first venture was a dismal failure. In an effort to obtain the authority of their constituents for repressive measures, the Board conducted a poll on the policies of *The Spectator*. On the eve of the vote there appeared a vitriolic leaflet signed by a group of "undergraduate leaders" in which the student body was warned that, unless *The Spectator* was curbed, the paper would be transferred to direct administrative supervision at the School of Journalism. That was not merely rumor; it was a project which the administration had long hoped to accomplish if it could be done peacefully and with finesse. Now the board was endeavoring to stampede an anti-*Spectator* vote by submitting this as an alternative. And the printing of that leaflet, I am reliably informed, was paid for by a University Trustee—Rogers Bacon. But the maneuver did not succeed, the board failing to receive the quota which had been previously agreed upon as a prerequisite for any action. The "great indignation" of the student body against our policies was nowhere to be found.

The next step was the formation of a committee "to revise the constitutions of campus publications." Now one point about the composition of the Student Board must be understood; every one of its seven members was receiving, in one form or another, financial aid from the university. I do not believe that this club was actually invoked; its effect, whether conscious or not, however, was unmistakable. Only one member of the group—an avowed radical—consistently opposed these moves; another vacillated from one side to the other; the remainder never retreated from the administrative fold. On the "constitution committee" were Associate Dean McKnight, Benjamin A. Hubbard, director of non-athletic activities and three members of the board. Mr. Hubbard and Mr. McKnight knew what they wanted; the students proved so amenable that the body gradually became known as an "administration-stooge" committee. Its members met in secret; no representative of *The Spectator* staff was invited to participate in the deliberations. And then, out of those conclaves there emerged one day a set of "proposals" for changes in *The Spectator's* conduct.

These proposals were, in themselves, relatively inconsequential; they would not have drastically affected the operation of *The Spectator* at once. They signified—and this was perfectly clear—the beginning of outside control over the journal, the precedent by which more direct censorship would gradually be imposed. It remained for "Ike" Lovejoy, backslapping, humble, football-mad, reactionary Alumni secretary to fortify our fears. *The Alumni News* appeared with a jubilant article hailing the labors of the "constitutional committee" as the event for which all loyal Alumni had so long been waiting.

Our subsequent endeavors were dedicated to one primary aim: the calling of a student referendum on the "proposals." We did not particularly care who won the referendum; we wanted the precedent of a vote by the undergraduate body fixed to combat the future steps of any similar committee, acting on the inspiration of this procedure. And that was precisely what neither the administration nor their spokesmen desired. Such a referendum would have negated their purpose: the charting of a technique by which *The Spectator* could be transformed into an administration newspaper. For days the dispute went on; finally the Board announced that, whether we liked it or not, the provisions were to be enacted as law. (Under these proposals, the power of the editor would have been divided, to rest in the hands of the five members of the managing board. As I have emphasized, this was no startling move nor one which would have influenced the policies of my régime; I think the Board members understood that; they were primarily interested, as we were, in the aspect of precedent.)

Confronted with this ultimatum, the staff immediately reconvened to outline a counter-attack. The essential problem was to arouse broad student opinion; without such aid, the provisions would have been railroaded into existence and the beginning of *The Spectator's* demise recorded. These were the considerations which prompted the unanimous strike-vote of the staff—the strike tentatively scheduled to last for only one day as a protest gesture.

The following morning *The Spectator* appeared with its columns virtually blank, broken only by an editorial explanation and short comments by columnists. One hour after the issue was circulated, two of the student committee members were closeted with Mr. McKnight, discussing suitable strategy; that afternoon an emergency session of the Board was summoned at which, in reprisal for our strike, publication of the paper was officially suspended. There was no one present who did not suspect that the decision had been formulated in Mr. McKnight's office that morning.

With this move, we were stripped of all funds for publication since our money came from a subsidy paid each year by students and administered by Mr. Hubbard. Dean Hawkes issued a statement hailing the "thoughtful" action of the Board; it had done a far more skillful job than he could have performed alone. The University Publicity Office, with eloquent journalistic fairness, prepared a release containing the

Dean's statement, the "explanation" of the Board—and no word of the strikers' position. I suspect that, at that point, the administration believed the long siege was over. A new, more amenable staff would be recruited; *The Spectator* would be restored to that state of tranquillity and subservience which Mr. McKnight had so ably demonstrated in his editorship fifteen years before—and which had prevailed until 1931.

But, if *The Spectator* was the eternal grievance of the administration, there were hundreds of students and faculty members prepared to lend their support. The extent of its influence was never more vividly revealed than in the ensuing twenty-four hours. Funds—in nickels, dimes and dollar bills —poured into our offices to enable us to publish on our own initiative. By the following morning an independent newspaper was being sold on the campus, the staff members hawking it themselves. And at noon a mass meeting was held in front of Hamilton Hall where the Dean's office is located.

That meeting was the decisive point. The Administration and the Board had remained supremely confident, up till then, that their elaborate venture would not be protested by the undergraduate body, that, if "censorship" was an inflammatory word, "constitutional changes" were not. Now more than 600 students assembled in almost unanimous disapproval of the edict. While that meeting was taking place, Dean Hawkes was heatedly conferring with William Lozier at the faculty club; Lozier was one of the Board's most vociferous assistants—he had gone to report on the progress of the protest session. And, from beneath the shades of distant dormitory windows, two Board members were seeing their moves condemned.

The undergraduate response forced a retreat. By that afternoon the Board proposed a "compromise"—an arbitration committee to include even the most radical instructor in the university. The offer was another dramatic indication of their frantic effort to avoid the referendum. It was unanimously rejected by the staff. Meanwhile, telegrams, letters and petitions of protest were descending upon the university. One administrator murmured that the job had been "bungled again." There were repeated conferences between the student officers and the university officialdom in search of "a way out." Within a day it was clear that they were about to surrender. The Board convened on Saturday evening, voting to reinstate *The Spectator* and to grant a referendum on one face-saving condition—that the revisions be accepted until the referendum was held. We willingly assented. I shall never forget the demeanor of the chairman of the board before that step was taken. He did not hesitate to confess that he was "sick of the mess." The job of pleasing the administration and preserving his own conscience—which was, I fear, surging to the fore—had been too much for him. He had become bitterly aware of his rôle; I doubt that he had fully comprehended it until then. On Monday *The Spectator* resumed publication. It did not matter that, in the referendum, the changes were ratified by a six-to-five majority. They had been deprived of all meaning; once the vote was granted, the question was merely one of abstract controversy over journalistic methods. The paper still belonged to the undergraduate body, to determine its future course and to prevent any sweeping controls.

The Spectator remains—unless there has been a new effort to silence it since this manuscript was completed—the most independent, outspoken college paper in the country. Its present editor is carrying on its most valued and notable tradition—critical, forthright inquiry into the students' environment. And, if the paper survives, it will be because of the awareness of a student body which long ago learned that, even in the "most liberal university world," academic freedom endures only so long as it is militantly defended.

The Columbia College of Physicians and Surgeons is situated nearly three miles from the Morningside campus, a distance which has exerted marked influence on the conduct of its affairs. Up till the late months of 1934, the Medical School was seldom penetrated by the issues which were agitating students in other parts of the university; it was one of the last strongholds to heed the challenge of external events. And with their students amiably aloof from such considerations, the Medical School administrators could allow free passage to undergraduate thought; Dean Willard Rappleye could write in *The Columbia Quarterly:*

"The responsibility of the universities is to help shape economic and political conditions, to influence public opinion and to train our professional workers to render the largest possible measure of public service. The challenge is for unselfish, thoughtful and courageous leadership which is the function of the university to contribute to present-day society."

These utterances were adequately abstract; they were in the hallowed spirit of university declamations—and they were rarely tested. If students on Morningside Heights were beginning to formulate dissenting, unconventional opinions, Dean Rappleye was disturbed by no such evidence. For student apathy, like faculty conservatism, required no administrative intervention. Consequently the Medical administrators were untrained in the skills which Dean Hawkes and his colleagues were so laboriously developing—the ability to restrain without appearing to do so, the art of camouflaged "supervision" over undergraduate affairs. That naïveté partially explains Dean Rappleye's subsequent crudities; but there is another phase to it. When anti-war activity was inaugurated at the Medical Center, the peace movement had already gained pronounced headway in other Columbia departments. Those who desired to intervene in other sections were faced with organized, concerted sentiment; no reprisals could have been undertaken without evoking a loud chorus of disapproval. At the Medical Center students felt themselves rela-

REACTION

tively isolated—and, unfortunately, they preserved that isolation when they ought to have appealed for help. It was inevitable that the first drastic suppression against the anti-war bloc should have occurred at its weakest link: Dean Rappleye's school where men are trained to provide "unselfish, thoughtful and courageous leadership."

Early in April of 1934 there gathered at Bard Hall of the Medical Center four hundred students and faculty members, convened to organize the first anti-war committee in the school's history. Two of the principal speakers were Dr. Hans T. Clarke, head of the Department of Biochemistry and Dr. Alvin Pappenheimer of the Department of Pathology. At this session were mapped extensive plans for work throughout the school, including the holding of forums, lectures and the publication of a bulletin. Activities were immediately launched and carried on for the remainder of the spring and through the summer months.

Returning to its efforts in the fall, the committee again charted another program of forums to be held in the University amphitheatre. In the midst of these arrangements, however, came the first warning, when Dean Rappleye's secretary informed the group that its accustomed facilities had been withdrawn: the amphitheatre was henceforth barred to its meetings. Unable to fathom the reason behind this development, the committee endeavored repeatedly to obtain an interview with the Dean but was, for weeks, unsuccessful. Finally he assented; in that conference he advised that a list of proposed speakers and topics be submitted to him for approval, which was readily done. Shortly afterward, however, the list was returned accompanied by the disclosure that the Committee on Administration had passed a resolution reserving the facilities of the school for activities with "a major medical interest." The anti-war committee did not, in its judgment, fulfill the requirements; the Medical School was apparently too absorbed with the struggle against disease to notice a danger which would bring more death, injury and

412

suffering in one skirmish than humanity might otherwise endure in a year.

Banned from the amphitheatres, the peace committee continued to publish its bulletin and to hold weekly meetings in the Student Room, shifting its forums to halls off the campus. On March 28 one of these forums was held and was addressed by Dr. Frankwood Williams, noted psychiatrist. Almost immediately afterward, a leading member of the committee, summoned to Dean Rappleye's office, was informed that the Hospital authorities objected to the distribution of the peace bulletin there and to the use of the name "Medical Center" in connection with the group's activities. Since this was the second occasion on which the Dean had warned a committee member, the entire body then asked for an interview in which the dispute could be settled. The session took place on April 11, 1935—the day before the student strike against war, the day on which Charles Walgreen rescued his niece from the University of Chicago and the month in which the witch-hunt was being launched in half a dozen states.

It was in that interview that Dean Rappleye issued the most frank and illuminating confession in the history of the University.* He began by setting forth three edicts: there could be no further appeal for the use of the amphitheatres; the committee would have to apply to the Hospital Authorities to obtain permission to call itself the "Medical Center Anti-War Committee"—and this permission, he was certain would not be granted; the committee's right to distribute its bulletins to students and to hold its own meetings in the Students' Room would be decided upon by the Committee on Administration.

Confronted with these orders, the delegation proceeded to inquire into their origins, to ascertain the reasons behind this

---

* All statements attributed to him in this interview are attested by sworn affidavits of all those present. The affidavits are in the possession of Professor Karl N. Llewelyn of the Columbia Law School.

incessant attempt to negate their efforts. Dean Rappleye's answer was an avowal which no Columbia administrator had ever before dared to make; citing the school's need for endowments, he remarked that "big money interests"—those were his exact words—had expressed disapproval of the group's deeds and, consequently, he was compelled to intercede. That statement has caused him many uncomfortable moments—but he has never retracted or even sought to deny that he had said it. For Dean Rappleye was new to the University disciplinary method, unskilled in its fine points, accustomed to saying what he thought without qualifying phrases, quotations from Aristotle or the sanction of pure learning. He accompanied this disclosure with the usual allegation that the committee was "window-dressing for communist propaganda." But that was a feeble anti-climax.

After this interview, the committee realized that it could advance no further by tête-à-têtes with the Dean or his aides, however revealing they might be. And so, that afternoon, it submitted a history of its difficulties to *The Spectator* for publication in the special anti-war issue of the following day.

The article, which has never been questioned in any detail of its factual content, immediately brought out the latent energies of the administrative machinery. Three hours after its appearance, the Dean summoned a leader of the committee and announced that responsibility for the document was to be placed upon him—a threat whose meaning required no elaboration.

When the committee reconvened, it voted at once to assume joint responsibility for the article. At that session one member remarked, as a sheet of paper was passed around for the signatures of all those willing to share the burden of the incident, that they were signing their academic death-warrants. Their gloom was well-merited. Six years before at the University of Pittsburgh a similar letter had been signed and its signers remorselessly weeded out, one by one, in the following years. P. & S. required only a month for the purge.

On May 9, Dean Rappleye received the letter with the list of signatures. The day before, the committee, having received no word of the Committee on Administration's action, had met in the Student Room to formulate plans for another symposium at which Stuart Chase was to speak, the forum to be held in a hall off the campus. In announcing the lecture, the group had retained its original name—again because there had been no word of an Administration decision on that matter. Whereupon Dean Rappleye called in one spokesman and declared that these steps were a "defiance" of the University, implying that no further mercy could be expected. He was reminded that the Committee on Administration was still to render these acts illegal.

Four days later that body met to act on the status of the peace group. It rejected a plea to permit the defendants a voice in the proceedings or an opportunity to hear the charges. When the session ended, the Dean informed the anti-war society that a unanimous verdict had been reached but could not yet be divulged.

Within five days from that meeting, two technicians in the Department of Biochemistry were dismissed from their jobs. Their removal was communicated to them by Dr. Hans T. Clarke—the same man who had addressed the opening session of the anti-war group one year before. While informing them of their status, he added that the decision came from the Committee on Administration and was attributable to the technicians' association with the peace committee. He also disclosed that a recommendation had been sent to the faculty to drop students with similar connections from the rolls.

On May 21, Gustave Bethke, instructor in Medical Art, was asked by Dr. H. H. Dunnington to resign. When pressed for an explanation of the request, Dr. Dunnington said that he was merely conveying Dean Rappleye's orders; Dr. Bethke was being banished for his participation in the "anti-

415

war melee," he was told. Later in the same day Hadley Kirkman, instructor in Anatomy, was also requested to withdraw from the institution. His name, with Bethke's, had been affixed to the letter in which responsibility for *The Spectator's* article was assumed.

Miss Eva Saper, another technician, received word of her discharge on May 24 from Dr. Charles F. Bodecker, head of her department, who remarked: "You did a foolish thing in signing that letter."

And during the first week of June, the remnants of the anti-war committee were wiped out. Six students received official letters informing them that they would not be readmitted in the Fall because they were "unsuited to the conditions of study at the institution." One of the victims had worked his way through school for seven years to gain entrance to the medical profession.

That was early in June. The residents of the university had already dispersed for the Summer. It was then too late to mobilize the protest which Columbia, caught in the network of its own sham, so desperately fears.

On Morningside Heights there stands a structure known as the Casa Italiana, officially dedicated as a gathering place for Italians and a center of Italian educational endeavor. The institution is a subsidiary of the University; it is partially financed by Columbia funds and hailed as another testimony to the "cosmopolitanism" which the University glowingly advertises. It fulfills none of these functions in any genuine sense.

The Casa, in actuality, is one of the prime sources of fascist propaganda in this country. That fact is no longer disputable. Early in 1935 a representative of *The Nation* conducted an exhaustive survey of the unit's operation, tracing its affiliations, its history and its present conduct. Among the charges which he later set forth were these:

1. That the Casa is dominated by representatives of the Italian fascist government and serves as a virtual adjunct to the consul-general's office in New York.

2. That anti-fascists are systematically barred from its platforms and seldom, if ever, invited to speak from its platforms or participate in its activities.

3. That anti-fascist students, once their sympathies become known, are the victims of steady discrimination.

4. There are no anti-fascists in the Columbia Italian department; Professor Arthur Livingston, the foremost American scholar in the field of Italian literature and culture, has been edged out of the Italian department into French—because he is anti-fascist.

5. The official publication of the Casa Italiana is overtly fascist in tone; in nine preceding months it had not carried an article in any way critical of the fascist régime.

6. The "educational bureau" of the Casa is primarily utilized for the dissemination of fascist propaganda among New York Italians.

7. Giuseppe Prezzollini, present director of the Casa, was forced to do years of penance for his earlier anti-fascist views before he could obtain the post.

8. In "return for services," the Italian Consul-general gave $3,000 to the Casa in 1933.

These were the highlights of the document, fortified by specific instances and abundant references. The existence of these conditions had been rumored for many years; it was not until 1934 that they were brought to light in their full setting—at a time when men and women throughout the world were realizing how swift was the advance of fascism.

Twenty years ago, Dr. Prezzollini was a rebellious spirit, imbued with the democratic ideal. He wrote a "Eulogy of Violence" in which he set forth his bitter contempt for any man who, under the fire of criticism, refused to reply to his

417

adversary. But time has mellowed him, security has cemented his bond with Mussolini, dispelling his youthful vigor. In the face of *The Nation's* charges, Dr. Prezzollini maintained a steadfast silence.

But Nicholas Murray Butler spoke for him. Eighteen years after the ousters of Beard, Dana and Cattell, three years after the dismissal of Reed Harris, two years after the removal of Donald Henderson and six months before the purge at the Medical Center, Dr. Butler issued an ardent defense of the Casa, pointing out that the university "has never questioned the opinions of any professor or student." It did not matter that every hint of anti-fascist thought was being stifled in the Casa; it was irrelevant that Columbia was serving as an instrument for the spread of fascist ideas and method; it was inconsequential that no item of disproof could be found to weaken the accusations. Dr. Butler, personally and with bravado, rescued the Casa. And an unceasing stream of student protest could not shake him.

Nicholas Murray Butler dominates Columbia University. Although he has frequently sought to shift responsibility for its troubled affairs to his subordinates, every university functionary will testify that the President is constantly supervising any important decisions. It will be remembered that two days after Reed Harris' expulsion, Dr. Butler assured a reporter that he had never heard of Harris—only to have Dean Hawkes disclose that Dr. Butler had been consulted before the dismissal. At the time of the Medical Center ousters, Dr. Butler, by some lamentable paradox, was sailing for a conference of the Carnegie Endowment for International Peace. *The Herald-Tribune* described his departure thus:

"Dr. Butler was not in the best of moods when the reporters located him. . . . He turned a shade pinker when they brought up the question of how his own peace activities could be reconciled with the Medical School incident.

" 'I have nothing to say about that,' he said, 'I know nothing about it.'

" 'The newspapers are sure to comment on the situation,' he was told.

" 'I don't read the newspapers,' he replied curtly."

And yet no one in the university believes that Dr. Butler was unaware of what Dean Rappleye was doing. It is barely possible that the Dean had first acted without consulting him; certainly, before the students were ousted several weeks later, the university President must have apprised himself of the situation. Columbia's behavior in crucial controversies expresses the convictions of Dr. Butler. His Trustees do not have to guide him; I am certain that he is far more instrumental in the formulation of policy than are his overseers. His presence—although he is virtually never seen by an undergraduate—pervades the whole university. If we understand his prejudices, his weaknesses and his preferences, we may comprehend the tragic plight of liberal education at Morningside.

Dr. Butler is not, by any realistic estimate, a liberal; that is a vague, undefined term but it signifies certain things— tolerance, an interest in social reform, at least a moderate willingness to defy entrenched interest, a recognition of the rights of the oppressed. If he once was a liberal, then he has damaged the credo beyond repair. Today there is no more loyal, devout and useful servant of vested wealth than Columbia's president. He has bitterly opposed the Child Labor amendment, invoking the bogey of "state's rights" to justify the exploitation of children. He has repeatedly denounced every prospect of taxation on large incomes because such measures "tax the thrifty." About a year ago he invented a new formula for solving distress to the satisfaction of his banker cohorts; with almost incredible seriousness, Dr. Butler announced that "maldistribution of wealth is an invention of radicals." And he laboriously sought to prove the thesis that

419

no one was actually suffering from the crisis. When criticism of capitalism as the source of economic disorder began to fill the air, Dr. Butler again prepared the decisive reply: "there is no such thing as capitalism; it is a debating term invented by Karl Marx."

These outbursts will be less bewildering if it is understood that one ambition has animated his life: to secure the favor of "the better people." He has always wanted to invade the circles of the economic elite; that could be done only by incessant pandering to their prejudices, a task in which he has achieved a considerable degree of success. He has allowed nothing to impede his progress. Before the World War he was a close friend of the Kaiser's; when the United States entered the conflict, the people whose esteem he courted had aligned themselves against the Kaiser—and so Dr. Butler became one of the most vicious, unrestrained partners in the heresy-hunt, warning that "there is no place in this university for anyone who is not committed with whole heart and mind to the struggle for democracy." That was not his first surrender nor was it to be his last.

And yet he has desperately tried to root himself in the popular imagination as a standard-bearer of liberalism. If there was any substance on which this reputation could be built, it was his opposition to the Prohibition Amendment. His stand on that issue was singularly forthright; but it should be remembered that he was residing in a state where the "Wet" interests were unquestionably strong. His other major claim rests in his support of the League of Nations; but advocacy of the League of Nations could hardly be viewed as a basic affront to the established order. Even granting the merits of these crusades, however, they indicate nothing profoundly insurgent in his nature. If there were years when a trace of rebellion might have been discernible, that has long ago vanished. Dr. Butler seldom speaks of the League of Nations any more, except as an alternative to active, mass resistance to war. His efforts in behalf of peace are limited to that eminently respectable, inoffensive Carnegie Endowment.

The League of Nations was an idiosyncrasy to be condoned by the better people. They have been rewarded for their faith. Dr. Butler has become a Tory in the front lines of reaction, his declarations enthusiastically quoted in the Hearst press, his subservience shrouded in a diminishing cloak of scholarly mysticism. A prominent administrator once told me that Mussolini regarded Dr. Butler as an invaluable advisor, a man whom he could trust in the tangle of diplomacy. Dr. Butler enjoys that trust; it is the epitome of his life-work—compensation for the pain caused by his failure to achieve the G.O.P. presidential nomination. That hope is gone; he must be content with more modest rewards.

I do not know whether Dr. Butler entirely approved the Medical Center dismissals, flagrant and indefensible as they were; I do know that, when a group of Columbia students protested a reception to Hans Luther, Nazi ambassador, Dr. Butler at first wanted to expel the sponsors of the demonstration, his fury subsiding only when other administrators soothed him. For Dr. Butler has a short, bitter temper; an affront to the people he cherishes quickly rouses him to an uncontrollable pitch and only the presence of understanding subordinates has prevented him from more glaring acts.

The faculty leads a difficult life, although it is rapidly becoming resigned to it. Its members are granted the right to say what they think in the classroom, as I have emphasized. But they are warned that the adventure ceases once the class is over. One incident was characteristic of their status. When the student delegation went to the Kentucky coal-fields in 1932, some of the most ardent sponsors of the trip were Columbia professors. A group of them had gathered at a camp for a brief vacation while the students headed for Kentucky when suddenly a wire was received informing the faculty members that the students were in danger and urging that a protest telegram be sent to President Hoover. The staff men were quick to draft the protest; as they were preparing to send it out, however, John J. Coss intervened. Dr. Coss is the Director of the Summer Session, an administrative figurehead and a possible successor to Dr. Butler. And Dr. Coss abruptly informed the group that no such message could be sent because "it would link Columbia's name with the Kentucky delegation." He did not have to say any more. Only two members of the Columbia faculty signed that telegram—from "the most liberal university in the world."

That is the philosophy which dominates the school. Donald Henderson was an instructor in economics; he was not a great teacher nor did he purport to be; he was equal to scores of other men whose positions have never been questioned. But Henderson was one of the founders of the National Student League; he organized unemployed workers in Harlem; he refused to accept the breach between thought and action to which his colleagues were inured. Dr. Butler's comrades began to inquire into the situation, demanding to know why the heretic was being retained and clamoring for prompt intervention. The University dismissed Henderson and, in an effort to prevent any protest he might make, offered him a fellowship to Soviet Russia. Henderson rejected the "bribe." I repeat that this man was not an extraordinary instructor; neither were eighty per cent of his colleagues. I am emphatically convinced that, if he had not been a communist, he would still be teaching economics at Columbia. And the strike of nearly 2,000 students in his behalf was a singular tribute to undergraduate realization of that fact.

Now Dr. Butler finds himself defending the fascist Casa Italiana and upholding the dismissal of anti-war leaders at the Medical Center. That was the inevitable destiny of a career devoted to the quest for "respectability." It is the synthesis of his prejudices and aspirations. While he dismisses depression as a "radical invention," while he solves the dilemma of capitalism by announcing that capitalism does not exist, Dr. Butler flays the "bad manners" of the "younger generation." Manners, the amenities, the stuffed-shirt and the top hat—these have become the symbols of his régime. Perhaps the most encouraging aspect of the scene is the swiftness with which his own student body is repudiating him. In April, 1935, Dr. Butler delivered a bitter indictment of the anti-war strike; he resorted to the ludicrously petty device of banning it from the Library Steps, where preceding rallies were always held, and invoked a dead-letter statute to support the ban. Whereupon 3,500 Columbia students thronged the university gymnasium to join the strike meeting.

Meanwhile, Columbia's liberal reputation is becoming a burden to her administrators. They will not adhere to it forever. The standards which apply to extra-curricular conduct may soon be applied to the classroom, ending an incongruous breach of long duration. But her students have already learned that the quality of freedom is precariously strained. It is not true that an overwhelming number of students have renounced the old faiths and illusions; Columbia College men are still uncertain, wary, tentative in their convictions. They are more receptive to fresh ideas, however, than many of their contemporaries. In the graduate schools, where the effects of economic deprivation are more visible, the ferment is even more pronounced. That awareness is the most promising safeguard against the day when Nicholas Murray Butler finally relinquishes his flirtation with liberalism and firmly embraces that solid, steady, well-to-do citizen: reaction.

XI. "Haven of Fascism?"

Princeton has always been envisaged as the ultimate in country club education. Long before the boom in culture and its lavish accompaniments, this institution had majestically awed the rank-and-file of the citizenry. There, so the populace imagined, brightly-groomed young men literally wallowed in luxury; their incessant whirl of diversions was interrupted only by infrequent migrations to classrooms—and these grew steadily more irregular. It was a college to which the common man did not aspire; only the best could walk on its long stretches of well-preserved grass or sip cocktails at its fountain of learning. With the arrival of rah-rahism, Princeton became even more celebrated; thousands of little Jerkwater institutions cast yearning, envious glances in its direction. The average depiction of the "collegiate," the raccoon-coated, flash-bearing, dare-devil fellow, had its most literal incarnation at this New Jersey cultural resort. For Princeton was the supreme, the elite, the unparalleled in American education: 1925 model.

Nor was the vision utterly unfounded in fact. Like all such popular idolatries, exaggeration did play a part in its expansion and legends multiplied with astonishing rapidity. Yet, granting these fictions, Princeton was—"Princeton." Nowhere in the nation could one find a student body on the whole as wealthy as the undergraduates of Tigertown. Certainly Harvard had its millionaires; but it also had a large number who were no better than moderately off. At Princeton the latter were almost exceptions; there was a handful of men who came from less aristocratic backgrounds and who earned part of their way through college; but, meeting the average Princeton student in the Fall of 1925, it would be difficult to detect the grime of labor on his hands or the oppression of poverty in his eyes. It was more likely that one could find his name in the Social Register. For the fathers of Princeton men were only rarely even the nouveau riche of the period; they were long-established moguls of industry and finance, men who had made their mark many decades before, offspring of the First Families of Virginia and points North, East and West.

The lust for learning never seriously afflicted any more than a minute segment of the community. In this respect, of course, Princeton was only a little more sterile than most American institutions of the era. The yawning gap of emptiness was most perceptible there, however, because of the

424

extravagant attention bestowed upon non-educational aspects of undergraduate life. It could hardly have been otherwise. The young men of Princeton had no grave personal dissatisfactions for which they might seek a cure; theirs was an emphatically comfortable place with adequate diversion to make life both assured and stimulating. If there were faculty men who might be disturbed by the lavish smugness of the atmosphere, by the utter disregard for either the things of the spirit or the destiny of man, they were a hopeless minority. Thinking was neither an art nor an object of much adulation. The "thinker" was likely to find himself outside the realm of affairs, looked upon with suspicion or contempt by his colleagues. I must emphasize that this was not unique to Princeton; but it was manifested there in its most extreme form. Only an occasional flurry over a national election, a momentary "fad" for some popular figure of the day or a stir occasioned by some new revelation in manners and morals ever penetrated the environment. If the university's educational techniques were more notable in some respects than in many other schools, no one seemed highly engrossed in them.

Princeton was the epitome of the cloistered tradition; with monotonous regularity, its sons stepped from the campus into relatively sound and remunerative posts—in banking houses, in industry, in commerce or any other branch of life in which their fathers were located. They left the university with only a feeble glimmer of light and the odds were high that even that ray would be dispelled by the routine of their post-collegiate activity. It was, they said, great to be a Princeton man. Everyone thought so.

There occurred in the fall of 1929 a severe dislocation in the affairs of society, a crisis which grew progressively worse with the passage of months. Men began to question, to view with a measure of criticism the structure which had once been so infallible. There was doubt and fear and the beginnings of panic in the minds of even the most stolid. But in Tigertown nothing had substantially changed. Certainly there was some dim recognition of a tension in the distant atmosphere; but such attention as was bestowed upon it was fragmentary and aloof. The men of Princeton were neither stunned nor alarmed. They had no immediate reason to be apprehensive. Nor had they any basis for believing that the crisis was of more than transitory nature. Such things occurred, as they always had, and ultimately calm was restored. Meanwhile, Princeton offered a snug and eminently well-equipped retreat from incidents which, at best, were unnecessarily troublesome.

Three years after the first symptoms of the economic debacle, Franklin D. Roosevelt was elected president of the United States. With the deepest chagrin it could muster, Princeton condemned the choice. In the undergraduate straw poll the Great Engineer from Palto Alto had swept the campus. Even after his defeat, Princeton eagerly awaited his appearance in newsreels to demonstrate how abiding was its faith. When his wistful smile was flashed upon the screen, there was concerted applause throughout the theatre, testifying to his magnetic power in the hour of defeat. For Hoover was a Republican, the standard-bearer of prosperity, of sound business principle, of the ancient practices of economic regulation. Roosevelt, it was murmured in Tigertown, had Stalinist leanings. And it need hardly be observed that the sons of Princeton were still to be persuaded by anti-capitalist doctrine. There was only one rebel for whom they displayed tolerance; his name was Norman Thomas and he was endured, not because he was a Socialist leader, but because, in the year 1905, he had received his diploma at the university. Princeton men are sentimental even about erring cohorts. Thomas, despite his subsequent deviations, would always be a "Princeton man."

Even the disclosure that Franklin D. Roosevelt, far from being a Stalinist, was not much more of a social engineer than

426

his predecessor, failed to evoke any immediate response at Princeton. There was neither rejoicing in his failures nor gleeful anticipation of his downfall. There was just sheer boredom. For the fact of the matter was that Princeton wished the strife and tumult of crisis were past. It got on a man's nerves to hear so much talk about the subject; it was not much spiritual consolation to know that the situation would not work too great a hardship on oneself. The whole picture was awry and a trifle perplexing. Someone, it was hoped, would do something about affairs in the very near future.

But nobody did. As depression wore on without any sign of relief, the problem became extraordinarily vexing. It was reported that a Princeton man of the previous graduating class was still in search of a job.

Despite these occurrences, there was no pronounced ferment arising. If you were in search of seclusion, of privacy, of mellow tranquillity broken only by the innocent screams of a prom guest; if you were looking for a place to ease your nerves without constant reminders of the cause of disorder; if you envisaged a shelter where men still dreamed the dreams of their ancestors, their fathers and their older brothers, you journeyed to the railroad station and hopped a train for Princeton, New Jersey.

In April, 1934 there was an upheaval. It is true that, prior to its coming, certain shifts could be felt in the atmosphere, auguring a change of still unpredictable dimensions. But that month a minor earthquake occurred. *The Student Review*, organ of the National Student League, carried an article entitled "Tiger, Tiger!" and written by a graduate student at the university. Many of the assertions contained in it had been made before; there were the customary references to the entrenched status of the students' families, their own resultant serenity in a chaotic world and the general temper of intense inertia which gripped their minds. But the con-

427

cluding sentence represented what was then a comparatively new formulation: "Fascism will find a readier home in Princeton than in any other university in the country."

Princeton did not enjoy that allegation—nor was it content to drop the matter. There was a student editor at the university who took up the dispute quite readily. He drafted a long editorial reply; when that reply was concluded, he found that he had assented to the charges of the "impudent communist."

In the light of subsequent events, that editorial was of real importance and I will quote some of its salient sections:

"Our first desire after reading the article was to leap to the defense of our Alma Mater and to administer to this impudent Communist a well-deserved pen-lashing. But the harder we fumed and the longer we muttered, the more we became convinced of the fact that, despite a few factual errors and considerable exaggeration, the main points in Mr. French's diatribe were tragically and undeniably true. . . .

"The author's accusations as to the superficial brand of culture that most graduates carry away from Princeton are all too devastating. . . . The idiotic manner in which so many alumni and students have, under the guise of attempting to keep Princeton a 'college', opposed any attempt to heighten her educational and intellectual standards, are all evidences of the strong Philistine spirit which remains to be overcome here. . . .

"We proceed to what is—to our minds—the most damning attack of all: the total lack of comprehension by any considerable group of men here of the social realities of the time. The continuance of the R.O.T.C. and the apparent absence of any organized opposition to militarism on this campus, shows that there is nowhere in Princeton a strong sentiment against the greatest of our modern vestiges of savagery. The International Relations Club, to which the author sneeringly refers, has done little worthy of mention along these lines, either toward fighting war or attacking its fundamental economic causes. . . .

"And as for resentment against the horrendous nature of the present economic system, there is only the feeblest kind at Princeton. . . .

"Worse than the spirit of conservatism in Princeton, however, is the smug intolerance which laughs off any attempt to fight economic maladjustments and social evils. This is well-demonstrated by the terroristic tactics used by students, 'townies' and Borough officials in attempts to break up Communist meetings in Princeton.

"All in all there can be little doubt that the 'sympathies of the people here are case-hardened capitalist' and that 'Fascism will find a readier home in Princeton than in any other University in the East.' "

It was an honest, penetrating and altogether refreshing document. Moreover, its author, far from being a lone iconoclast, was one of the most popular men on the Princeton campus. What he said could not be blandly dismissed as the work of a heretic. For he was of and by Princeton, distinct only in his willingness to depart from a pattern which Princeton men, since its inception, did not question.

Further, the charge of "fascism" was more disconcerting than the usual line of attack. For decades Princeton men had been assailed as the pampered offspring of plutocracy; they were accustomed to the description—and they reasoned that their place was an eternal one in an everlasting scheme of things. They could not feel any great indignation at their own wealth; those who were conscience-stricken were reassured by White House pronouncements of "permanent prosperity" and "wealth for everyone." Now this fixed ritual was being severely tried. And here was the accusation that, to defend their established rôle in the social order, they would accept—even abet—the rise of fascism. Certainly the majority of Princeton men were not too familiar with the precise nature of fascism; they had before them, that year, however, the inescapable indications of what fascism, in practice, implied. For that was the year of Hitler's further consolidation of power with all the desperate, remorseless persecution which accompanied it.

Now it must be remembered that a substantial number of Princeton men hail from the land of Jeffersonian democracy—the South. Although the spirit of Jefferson's credo has hardly been strictly observed by the modern Southern barons, its flavor is somewhere entwined in their consciousness. There was, in addition, the tone of Woodrow Wilson's stewardship still lingering in the air; and Wilson, to the Princeton man of 1934, was still a valiant example of idealism, however frustrated. His *New Freedom* meant something to them in a vague but irrepressible fashion. It would be absurd to imply that "Tiger, Tiger!" and the assenting editorial immediately called forth visions of Jefferson, Wilson, and the democratic spirit. I do suggest that these things were present in the ensuing response, whether by direct acknowledgment or long adaptation.

The impression of this exchange of notes between Mr. French and *The Princetonian* was felt throughout the college community. Princeton stirred, rubbed its eyes. On May 2nd the news columns of *The Princetonian* disclosed that:

"An anti-war society, as a direct answer to Arthur French's criticism in the April issue of *The Student Review* . . . will be officially organized at a meeting tonight."

Editorially the plan was greeted thus:

"Such a move deserves the support of every undergraduate who wants to wage a fight on the forces which,

430

unless checked and checked soon, are bound to result in the downfall of that perhaps pitiful object we term modern civilization."

The following day it was reported that the meeting was "highly successful," attended by both Faculty and students and had laid the groundwork for concerted activity. There were already sixty enrolled members in the society.

It was during this interval that Ruby Bates, a principal figure in the famous Scottsboro case, delivered an address at Princeton to an audience of several hundred which jammed the meeting-room to the doors. Of course, many had come out of curiosity, expecting a "sensation" of one sort or another. The important point is that they listened attentively and sympathetically to this girl, a spokesman of the South's "po' white trash." When she had concluded, they tendered her an ovation. And one more phase in Princeton's awakening had been enacted.

I am unable to report that, since those episodes, the barricades have risen at Princeton; neither are students sniping at their Trustees with private machine-guns from dormitory windows. If the transformation is less spectacular in form, however, it has been more deep-rooted and widespread than anyone could have conceived five years before. *The Princetonian* in 1935 became an ardent critic of New Deal policies— not because Roosevelt was Moscow-directed but because he was seeking to prop up capitalism at the expense of the mass of workers and farmers throughout the country. With equal fervor it denounced the war preparations of the Roosevelt government and the parallel drift to reaction. These currents of thought filtered through the ranks of the students, rousing larger numbers of them to a social awareness than had ever given heed to anything beyond their own horizon before. A substantial quota of the unimpressed and disinterested remained; that was to be anticipated. But even they experienced some repercussions of the trend.

On April 12, 1935, the following paragraphs appeared on the front page of *The Princetonian:*

"Today over 100,000 students representing colleges and universities will hold strikes and meetings in solemn protest against the black pall of war that today enshrouds the world.

"Although the storm spots shift, the threat of war remains ever present. Imperialists still cry for new lands and markets and are willing to sacrifice the youth of the world to get them. At present fresh contingents of troops are embarking for Abyssinia; conflicting oil interests prolong the war in the Gran Chaco between Bolivia and Paraguay. . . . Our government professes peace, but brings in the largest peace-time military budget. . . .

"At this time, with the atmosphere so ominously like that of 1914, the progressive and liberal forces on the campuses of the nation are called upon to assemble in protest against war. As a student of Princeton University you are urged to attend the meeting to be held at 4 P.M. on the steps of Whig Hall. . . ."

That declaration was signed by The St. Paul's Society, *The Daily Princetonian,* The Westminster Society, the Nassau Literary Magazine, the Undergraduate Council, Whig-Clio halls, the Student-Faculty Association, the International Relations Club, the Anti-War society and others.

And at the appointed hour hundreds of Princeton students trooped to the meeting-place to join their voices with students all over the nation. One could not hope that Princeton would shelve all the proprieties in so swift a time. A "strike" was vetoed in favor of the afternoon assembly. And the principal speaker was a distinguished graduate of 1905—Norman Thomas! Granting these hangovers of tradition, so overt a display of opinion on social matters was without precedent in Tigertown. More than that, it presaged greater things for the future. Perhaps with that in mind, President Dodds, when asked for a statement on the demonstration, judiciously hedged. He made no direct reference to the assemblage, contenting himself with the age-old assurance that "the causes of war lie deeply in human nature" and warning against "hysteria and personal abuse." It was reported that he did not too greatly enjoy the proceedings. Princeton needs abundant endowments to keep its structure well-preserved and its reputation intact. Dean Gauss expressed equal assurance that "the great majority realize how old is this problem and how deeply its roots strike down into the nature of men and society."

One concluding event must be recorded. A young man was travelling toward New York on the evening of Princeton's 1935 Commencement exercises. Boarding the train at Princeton was an elderly, well-dressed, austere and utterly respectable old lady. She was patently disconsolate. Seating herself opposite him, she twirled her pince-nez nervously and stared out the window. The young man watched her for a moment, then resumed his reading. But the old lady did not relax. Finally, because she could contain herself no longer, she sought to engage him in conversation. Gradually, the source of her concern emerged. As later recounted:

". . . And then, when the boys from the R.O.T.C.— you know what that is?—went up to get their awards, these young good-for-nothings started to hiss. I have been to twenty-six Princeton Commencements and I never seen the like of that performance. They kept on hissing—and booing—until the awards had been given. That's what their education has done for them."

And then she leaned over confidentially, warmed up to her subject, murmuring: "You know—that's the kind of thing we expect from Jews and Communists. I didn't expect to find them at Princeton."

433

Thus did this grand old dame, a Daughter of the American Revolution, a Social Registerite, a clubwoman, a patriot and a defender of the family, unburden herself.

Her grief was shared by others. For the facts were essentially as she stated them. A number of Princeton men had awakened to a contempt for and opposition to the R.O.T.C., and on the staid, traditional-laden afternoon of Commencement, that sentiment had been voiced. Several hundred gray-bearded men and soft-voiced women in their best ceremonial attire, squirmed nervously, searching for bombs beneath their seats.

To climax this outrageous affront, the senior orator had denounced the "Eating Clubs"—Princeton's most exclusive counterpart of the fraternity—as "havens of snobbery." The 1935 Commencement at Tigertown was unlike anything which had gone before. In Newport and adjacent points the upheaval was said to be a topic of subdued, anxious contemplation.

I must reiterate that these phenomena are hardly symptomatic of Princeton as a whole. There were students equally outraged by the proceedings at Commencement as their elders. There are hundreds still wary or skeptical of the first awakening of their cohorts and there are others who are hardly aware that it has taken place. But among other hundreds there is a ferment such as was exhibited at the final exercises. And it is of more than passing significance. For the men of Princeton have been less affected by crisis, as a group, than any student body in the country. Certainly there are more today than ever before whose status is shrouded in uncertainty; a larger number than usual are compelled to aid in the financing of their own education; but even these are no vast group. The dominant body of Princeton students is still drawn from families which have survived—with dividends—the general decline. Aristocracy has not fallen; Wall Street barons eke out a living. These considerations only enhance the importance of the stir at Princeton. For it provides the most clean-cut example of an intellectual unrest, fomented, not by personal privation or duress, but a conviction that the world today is a retrogressive, distorted and barren structure, in the grip of a clique which will sacrifice every vestige of human decency before its own material comfort. The menace of fascism implies more than economic tyranny; it foreshadows the destruction of everything which human beings hold important and worth-while in the realm of the mind. These are some of the motivations behind the dissension at Princeton, born, I have said, not out of personal suffering but of a growing anxiety over the threatened retreat to barbarism.

Princeton is not solidly aligned behind the quest for a new social order; its gropings are still in their infancy, directed against the most flagrant symptoms of decline. But there has been sufficient evidence to warrant the rumor—conveyed to me by a student there who insists that it be regarded as no more than that—that the Administration is preparing to invoke measures to quiet the scene. If that occurs, another eloquent admission of entrenched fright will have been recorded. For, when Princeton, the famed stronghold of plutocracy, cracks down, the old system must be nearer debacle than even the most lurid mind has believed. It will be acknowledging that even those to whom it can offer material advantage want none of its responsibilities of financial rule—the preservation of a system at such a cost to human learning and social progress.

XII. Survivals of "Freedom"

WHENEVER the academic world is assailed for the narrowness and outright repression it fosters, there will always be a chorus of self-righteousness emanating from widely separated quarters. Some pedagogue or business agent who has

435

climbed the ladder of success until he is now the Trustees' favorite son will exclaim:

"Look at our university. Come to Podunk and see for yourself. We have never expelled a student or dismissed a teacher. We have always given our boys and girls the chance to say whatever they thought. You will not find a case on record of any discipline of a man for his opinions."

And there are still hosts of institutions—ever diminishing in number—where this is relatively true. The fact is, as we have already suggested, that reactionaries have never encountered the displeasure of university authority. But there is more than that. In scores of American colleges, even in the year 1935, no reprisals have been invoked—because there are no opinions of any shade flourishing among the student body. These citadels of knowledge are the nearest approach to a vacuum that man could conceive; nothing stirs, nary a flutter, never a raised eyebrow, an inquiring voice or a rumble of dissension. This cannot forever prevail; ultimately the chaotic tides of the outside world will make their impact felt. For the present, however, this has not occurred. To believe that it has would be to present an utterly false and dangerous picture of the educational structure. This is not merely a negative fact; ignorance has already, in other places, begun to assume an ugly form. Where and how this has happened has been, I think, adequately discussed in the survey of Vigilantes, indicating clearly to what purposes it can be utilized. Elsewhere this consequence has not been perceived; the tenor of life proceeds almost as smoothly and undisturbed as it did in the year when a college education was heralded as the sure qualification for success. Here we will discuss only a few representative examples, but it should be borne in mind that their prototypes are many and far-flung. I have received dozens of letters from campuses throughout the country;

almost invariably, when a student claimed that his university was free from any symptoms of repression, he would add: "... because there is nothing to repress." Disaster has shaken the roots of the world, the issues of poverty amidst plenty, of property rights and human rights have surged to the center of men's minds; still do these empires of learning remain barren and unmoved and unaware of what is taking place.

From the University of Missouri came the most dramatic expression of this condition. It is from a student who is almost alone in sensing the inadequacy and narrowness of her educational environment.

The campus is a typical one. About three thousand students inhabit it and they have erected a vast superstructure of fraternities to which more than half the undergraduate body is affiliated. In their classrooms they encounter little which is challenging or dynamic; among the readings in general economics is the "Communist Manifesto" but the political theory and economic philosophy implicit in it is "treated as too ridiculous to be discussed at length." Of major concern to the Administration is the welfare of the R.O.T.C.; several years ago, in a hearing before the House Committe on Appropriations in Washington, the President of the university made this touching denunciation of the move to provide "inferior uniforms" for the corps:

> "The drastic change in the commutation of uniform in the R.O.T.C. units is a matter of vital concern to the authorities of this institution and unless changed by suitable legislation will prove a source of embarrassment to the University."

There have been a few minor flurries, none of which have evoked any sustained interest among the students but do reflect the tone of the atmosphere. In May, 1929, Professors Max Meyer and Harmon De Graffe and O. H.

437

Mowrer, a student assistant, were punished for circulating a questionnaire on sex. One question asked whether a man would marry a woman who was "no better than she should be." Meyer and Mowrer were dismissed outright, De Graffe was suspended for a year. This action had been no doubt spurred by the protest of 200 citizens of Columbia, Mo., where the college is situated. Complying with this outraged civic virtue, the Board of Curators of the University announced that the school must always cherish its "sane and wholesome atmosphere." From that time on they have had little cause for anguish. In 1934 another momentary dispute was occasioned by the barring of a conference against war and fascism from the university grounds. This, too, quickly receded from the students' horizon. And finally, the following year, a peace meeting was planned for eleven o'clock on the day of the student strike; the Administration denied permission to hold it then and instead there was a gathering in the afternoon. What the average undergraduate's response to this intrusion was can be gleaned from an editorial in the student newspaper:

"H. I. Phillips' simile—as futile as a college parade against war—characterizes the campus peace meeting last month. Two hundred lack-lustre listeners, with tepid enthusiasm, received the demonstration of Henry Clay's 'Peacemaking Modern Counterpart,' Fred Graham, with indifference, and spirited appeals against war and fascism fell on unspirited ears."

Such was the bored sophistication with which the student body of the University of Missouri disposed of the two most pressing evils of the era. At about that time a survey was conducted disclosing that the average Missouri undergraduate attends the movies three times a week.

How can one explain this invulnerable inertia? Certainly one factor is the presence of the R.O.T.C. with the goose-step

438

doctrine it so avidly preaches. The student paper, when it is not bored, is likely to blare forth an editorial against "agitators," accompanying this with a plea for revival of "100-per-cent-Americanism." But the reign of the military is far from decisive. There are even more acute reasons for the fact that the most concerted intellectual effort on the campus has been a drive against a local movie operator for consistently unattractive productions. They explain why the undergraduate body is apathetic, not merely to the challenge of war, but to the whole series of economic disturbances which today hold the nation in their grip. The student whom I mentioned earlier can depict these far more vividly than I can and this is what she writes:

". . . My own outlook is that the problem must be resolved into a whole complex. First, these students come from middle-class homes where they have been taught to react and not to think. The majority come neither from extremely wealthy homes nor laborers' homes. They come from environments in which the family life has been based upon standards of materialism or striving for social prestige. The student's daily routine of life is merely a continuation and an imitation of that way of living which they have seen in their homes; they strive outside of class hours for local prominence; on their own isolated little campus, they strive for social 'popularity'. . . . They have come to college because their parents wanted them to have those 'opportunities' or because it is 'the thing to do.' . . . Having come with no particular intellectual curiosity, they turn to that which is the most interesting to them and requires the least amount of effort. Their interests, crudely, are sexual, a hey-day atmosphere of rah-rah collegian and the glory of the football and basketball team."

The point to be understood is that, even now, they are better off than many of their colleagues elsewhere. For a

439

variety of reasons they, as individuals, have not yet encountered the real effects of economic disaster in terms of their
personal lives. Thus:

"Perhaps the only way in which the economic crisis has
affected these students is that generous fathers and
mothers are not contributing grand pianos and funds for
luxurious sorority and fraternity houses as in the '20's.
As far as the students themselves are concerned, they
feel fairly comfortable. . . . They accept the depression
as all good Americans should accept what they are
pleased to look at as the inevitable cycle of prosperity
and decline."

Nor is this complacence solely attributable to their own
comparative security. Their professors have done nothing to
arouse them, to encourage a sense of doubt or skepticism:

"The professors are dependent for their livelihood on
the administration, which in turn is controlled by the
state legislature, which in turn is made up of and controlled by those same unawakened middle-class west-
erners of similar philosophy and thought as the parents
of the students of the university. . . . The classroom is
an opiate, with very few exceptions. . . . One cannot
blame the students themselves. They have never had a
chance. And they see no industrial strife, no unrest, no
particularly pressing problems in Europe or nationally,
because those problems are too far away, too remote in
comparison with their individual business of playing
and achieving 'grades' and social prominence on the
campus. They've never been hungry; they've never
seen hunger; such things are fantasy. . . . And their re-
actions are long built-up reflexes all the way from home
influence primarily in babyhood through grammar and
high-school in adolescence to college, with probably no

upset in mode of living or thought except—occasionally
—the theory of evolution. . . . They refuse to be intellectually or emotionally aroused by any problem on the
doorsteps of their houses. It has to be in the house
before they will notice it."

The same interests and preoccupations, the identical aspirations, prejudices and delusions which were almost uniform on
the American campus in 1928 still pervade Missouri. All is
quiet, all is wholesome.

I talked to a student from the University of Arizona, returned to New York for the summer vacation. He is amazed
to learn of what is taking place in other universities; he
reads of a student revolt, of upheavals on the campus—and
he thinks mournfully of the university in Tucson where 2,200
young men and women are still clinging aimlessly to a vanishing past: "There is no repression of a political nature—
because there is no political movement and never has been
one at the school."

Nor has there been any perceptible change in outlook in-
duced by recent developments. They do not even figure in
discussion among undergraduates. At Arizona the impending
football game, a social function, fraternity politics are the
immediacies and ultimates of life. In the editorials of the college newspaper this isolation is most plainly evident; were
the editor to urge the loosening of freshmen rules, his stand
would be greeted as progressive, ultra-liberal. What is going
on outside does not filter into its pages or cause the faintest
reaction among its editors. On one theme alone are they
rhapsodic—the preservation of university tradition, of the
habits, customs and allegiances of the Arizona man—who
never changes.

What of the faculty? A handful of its members might be
called "not conservative" and nothing more. In an economics
course the student will learn classical doctrine, the tenets of

441

Adam Smith and his followers who regarded capitalism, property rights and economic relationships as fixed offspring of "natural law." And that will, with minor qualification, be the accepted credo of the undergraduate body.

Over all the R.O.T.C. stands unchecked; freshmen and sophomores are compelled to enroll; of great campus eminence is Scabbard and Blade, the honorary society of the military department. No one has ever questioned the origin or the meaning of the corps; it is accepted as naturally and unreservedly as the rising sun. Even while the peace movement was sweeping through other colleges, not more than a handful bestowed the slightest attention upon it or were aware of its existence. To them the R.O.T.C., and the doctrines synonymous with it, are far more indigenous to a university than any semblance of counter-attack.

What further need be said? Arizona is another landmark; it testifies to the success with which educators have fought off the approach of a world with which they want no relationship. Studying the composition of the student body, one can understand why the isolation has been preserved. The college population is drawn almost exclusively from the upper strata of the middle class; if the students' parents, most of them stockholders in copper mines or the like, have experienced anything of depression, it has been in negligible terms. Certainly the value of their stocks may have fallen but they themselves are still to undergo any pronounced decline in habits of living as a result.

Talk to an average Arizona student, seek to draw him out on the glaring disequilibrium of our times, ask him his observations about the immediate future. The replies will be almost equivalent to those which you would have received from his predecessors ten—or twenty—years ago. I asked one of them who came from the East and was among the more enlightened what would happen if a radical suddenly appeared to address the student body. How would they respond if he talked to them of a drastic revision in our social system, of

442

combatting the imperialist roots of war, of the challenging advances in the Soviet Union? The answer was quite certain: "Half the students would be ready to lynch him; the other half would not even be interested enough to do that. They would laugh out loud and continue to wonder who the girl was in the third row on the left."

Envisage an institution without sight, without hearing, without the ability to say anything—and without anything worth-while to say. You will find it in Tucson, where Harding's assurance that we have returned to normalcy is still ardently believed. So certain are the inhabitants, in fact, that nothing of grave import ever occurs, that they long ago ceased to regard such speculations as worthy of note. The world is a solid, static and enduring fact.

Another report of the same general condition—although no two sets of circumstances are alike in detail—comes from the South, from little Hampden-Sydney college in Virginia. Again it begins with the declaration: "There is relatively complete freedom of thought at Hampden-Sydney, though I strongly suspect that most of that freedom is due to the fact that there are very few who do enough independent thinking to be obnoxious."

Whatever the currents which animate discussion and activity elsewhere, they have not yet penetrated here: ". . . The interest in politics at Hampden-Sydney is confined to a very small minority who debate among themselves but are not numerous enough to form any societies. . . . The great majority of students are completely indifferent to such matters."

For part of the explanation, at least, we must turn to the classroom. The only mention of Marxism occurs in a course in general economics and that is limited, academic, without any emphatic interest to the average student. Like most of his studies, it is another course which serves as an interruption to the social and athletic life of the institution. It is not a coincidence that the coach of the varsity football team is

443

listed as a member of the faculty. He is probably more in-spiring a personality than most of his colleagues, most of whom are conservative democrats. They have not encoun-tered any interference with their expression of the sentiments of conservative democracy.

One of the subjects on which the undergraduates feel most deeply is that of Jews. Not that the problem is a local one: "There is no anti-semitism here for the simple reason that there are never any Jewish students here."

But: "Many students at Hampden-Sydney are disgusted with the way many southern colleges, especially in this state, are stocking up with Jews, and that antagonism is increasing —but there is no concerted feeling because there is no direct contact with the problem."

Occasionally the campus newspaper, in recent years, has expressed doubts about the stolidity of the student body and voiced opinions faintly reminiscent of liberalism—for which its editors have been severely criticized. On the occasion of the strike against war—which did not take place at the school but whose echoes were dimly heard there—the student editor asked:

"The most interesting thing about the situation seems to us to be the fact that students of Hampden-Sydney seemed hardly aware that their fellow-students all over the country were uniting in this great move to express student sentiment against the great evil, war, and cer-tainly cared not enough to make any move or even any suggestion of cooperation. Is Hampden-Sydney so se-cluded, so sheltered, so cut off from the world that in the event of a sudden world crisis with entry by our country we would not be called on to serve as cannon-fodder along with the rest of the nation's young men? No, we would. . . . Can we afford to remain disinterested spectators?"

444

His was a solitary cry. Among his colleagues, the omens of catastrophe are still unnoticed. They are ensconsed in a dreamland which not even the rude shocks of the past six years have seriously perturbed. Steadfast in their pursuit of irrelevance, the young men of Hampden-Sydney have not encountered any considerable administrative intervention.

In the spring of 1933 a writer visited three mid-western colleges and returned to record his impressions. These are striking now because they are so similar to the documents I have received from a number of little, and big, institutions throughout the country. Back from his journey, he observed at the time:

". . . For the most, they (the students) know that no jobs await them. For the most part, perhaps, they study a little harder and perform a little more conscientiously their routine tasks because parents back home expect at least academic results. But there is, so I was told, no new spirit abroad, no changed attitude assumed toward a much-changed world . . . student bodies as such are much as student bodies have always been. They are not rebellious or cynical or even melancholy. They do what they are told, believe what they are told and hope for the best. . . . In the colleges which I visited the spirit was still the spirit of a youth which has been favored too long to believe that the favors could so suddenly be forever withdrawn." *

It is entirely possible that, were he to return there today, his observations would need only minor revision, although it is conceivable that drastic changes have taken place in, say, one of the three institutions. The others, like Missouri and Hampden-Sydney, will still be carrying on in the best of the ancient tradition.

* From *The Nation,* June 21, 1933.

445

Look, for instance, at the replies to a questionnaire I sent to a student at Colorado State Teachers College. The answers are laconic; he gives no detailed explanation of the situation; all that can be gleaned from his letter is:

1. There are no liberal or radical student groups on the campus.
2. No student agitation on any issues has occurred on the campus.
3. The faculty is free from any hint of radicalism—and no courses dealing with Marxism or any basic theory of social change are offered.
4. Fraternities exert a powerful influence over student affairs—such as they are.
5. The student newspaper is directed by a student-faculty committee with students in the majority.
6. No peace strike or demonstration of any kind took place in 1934 or 1935.
7. Students and faculty members have not been curtailed in the expression of their opinions!

Perhaps the largest group of institutions which have remained inert to contemporary issues is the Catholic colleges. This was proudly testified to in a recent address by Rev. Eugene Callahan, spiritual director of the Archdiocesan Union Holy Name Society of New York:

"As we assemble here this afternoon to pledge loyalty to God and to country, I cannot help but think that within a stone's throw of this historic ground we have a certain young element that rises in disobedience, an element for whose education we help pay, avowed atheists and pacifists. (He was referring to the students of C.C.N.Y.)

"You will find no picketing, no communistic rebellions on the campuses of Fordham or Notre Dame Universities. President Robinson (of City College) is to be applauded for maintaining, in the face of difficulty, our best traditions for law and order."

Nor have any events belied his words. Fordham, Notre Dame and the host of other Catholic colleges situated throughout the country have remained fortresses of retreat. The point is all the more disconcerting because one might anticipate that religious institutions would take issue with the flagrant injustices and distortions of the day. As I write the Catholic Church in Germany is paying the price of non-resistance with Hitlerism pledging its swift and decisive extinction. Yet, despite the gathering omens of American reaction, the consequences of which will be equally disastrous for Catholicism, these schools are fervently devoted to the ideal of surrender.

In 1935 the student newspaper at Georgetown University waged the most bitter crusade in its history. Against poverty? Against war? Against repression? No, against the sinister "Un-American activities" pervading the higher learning elsewhere. I have not met the editor but, judging from his use of capital letters and hysterical rhetoric, I suspect that he is under the persuasive influence of that great religionist, William Randolph Hearst. Most of his diatribes were directed against the undergraduate anti-war movement—in which, Georgetown, unhappily, has played no part. Listen to certain of his more flowing declarations:

"Very few realize the extensive scope of this Communistic propaganda campaign and follow unknowingly as disciplines (sic) fostering the dreaded Red menace. But why should we Americans continue in ignorance of this approaching crisis, when any logical thought by Americans on this subject would lead us immediately to expel this menace from our country. Now is the time to fight against this impending danger, and not wait until cherished American traditions, homes and rights

447

have been swept away from us by our own ignorance. . . .

"You may ask 'What can we do?' Probably the most
efficient way for Americans to rid themselves of this
Red menace is to educate themselves to the program
and activities of the communists. Then they would realize the real meaning of the Red menace. But one thing
is essential. Act Now!"

It might be added, for those who are entranced by these
expostulations, that *The Hoya's* editorials on this and related subjects, have been published in pamphlet form. I am
assured that they can be obtained and reprinted without
payment.

The experience of a young man at Xavier, a Catholic
University in Cincinnati, was indicative of the status of
thought in these institutions. He was the editor of the undergraduate newspaper and, before each edition, he found that
a priest would come in to read all material before it went
to press. After repeated intervention, the student resigned
and transferred to another university. The paper is still censored; its editorial column has been completely eliminated
and, in its stead, appear a series of advertisements.

How long will this persist? Will professors at these schools
tell their pupils this year that Hitlerism has placed the "Red
Menace" and the Catholic Church in the same concentration
camp? Or will they continue to invent new atrocities committed by the Bolsheviks against mythical sanctities? Up to
the present there has been neither restlessness nor curiosity
manifested among these undergraduate bodies. But they must
ultimately become conscious that all is not so placid as they
have been told. They may take the preachments of religion
at face value. To correlate them with the facts of the existing
world may incite rebellion even in the shades of Fordham—
where the student editor last year ably imitated the antics of
his colleague at Georgetown.

448

Out at the University of Nebraska, scene of the pajama parade described elsewhere * an equivalent inertia prevails. Discussing the student peace strike, *The Daily Nebraskan* recently wrote: "If it was lethargy (which explains the absence of a peace demonstration at Nebraska) then *The Daily Nebraskan* for once duly thanks that usually abhorred spirit."

And further down the column it voiced its disapproval of a "bunch of college boys abruptly cutting classes for an hour and holding soap-box meetings." Would *The Nebraskan* have been equally pained if the meetings had been devoted to the sale of Liberty Bonds or enrollment pleas for the R.O.T.C.—or recruiting for the American army?

These are remnants of a tradition which we are too prone to regard as dead. They are the hangovers of that all-inclusive rah-rah decade in which the college man had no particular reason to concern himself with anything remotely fundamental. Rushing to the defense of their alma maters, there will be scores of students and teachers who will deny that the repression depicted elsewhere exists on their own campuses. Before they become too heated in their enthusiasm, let them ponder these questions:

1. Is there any opinion on the campus sufficiently original and independent to merit repression?

2. Are there student or faculty members who have come forward with proposals for activity on the crucial issues of the hour?

3. Has there been any event or campaign to challenge conformity and its local symptoms?

If not, it is entirely likely that there has been unqualified freedom of opinion granted by the Administration. Nor will these campuses have been seriously affected by the onrush of reaction throughout the country either in its steady, long-time form or its current expression. What will happen

* See Chapter I.

449

when these students are confronted with serious choices and decisions is an ominous problem to ponder and one which will have crucial bearing on the whole future of national insurgence.

XIII. The Outlook

SO precarious is the future for the inhabitants of the academic world that there should be no need to sound an alarm. And yet precisely that alarm is most urgently needed. Nowhere is self-deception, false hope and illusion more rampant than in our faculties; these traits have inevitably persisted among large numbers of students. Certainly the insurgence has been of real scope and impact, far exceeding any movement which the American campus has heretofore witnessed. But the uncertainties of the contemporary scene have multiplied even more rapidly.

Academic freedom has thus assumed an altogether new relevance and content. We have come to realize that it is neither a divine, inexorable right nor one which is possessed by all groups and the holders of all opinions. In the face of this most unremitting advance of repression, the nature of freedom has become more clearly defined. For the Hearstlings are declaring what Austria's Francis II said long ago: "New ideas are being promulgated of which I cannot and will not approve. Abide by the old; for they are good and our fathers have prospered under them—why should not we?"

The derivation of this credo is plain. It is the last resort of that diminishing segment whose interests can still be served by the preservation of the existing framework. Those who control the destinies of society cannot, with safety, allow freedom to flourish any longer; the heroic cries of 1776 are the enemies of the Tories of 1935. Once again it is evident that this liberty belongs to those who rule, to be disbursed by them in limited quantities. They readily confer it upon their mouthpieces; they deny it those who threaten their supremacy. Today the political expression of this attempt is fascism, a technique which bolsters profits and plunder at any sacrifice in the general welfare and in progressive thinking. Those who sponsor it speak in state legislatures, in the public press and in administrative chambers; they are motivated by a fear which springs from authentic roots. Confronted by the paradoxes and inanities of a declining social scheme, they are desperately striving to maintain it, and they realize that they can do so only by removing the possibility of a more ordered arrangement. To them education suggests inquiry and criticism; having established an educational structure, they are now terrified by what its researches may bring forth. Hence the inquisition, hence the loyalty oath, hence the Red Scare. These are the preludes of fascism.

All the tumult cannot conceal the fact that, underlying the agony of the patriots, is a fundamental crisis within the economic system. There are now more than ten million American citizens deprived of any avenue of employment; yet government spokesmen continue to announce that recovery is approaching. It is entirely possible that recovery, in the terms in which it is now conceived, will be temporarily attained and it will only serve to emphasize how pitiful is the effort. We are already warned to accept, as a necessary truth, the permanently forced unemployment of from five to seven million people; if that number is miraculously reached, the orthodox economists will pronounce the dawn of revival. The situation to which they would have us reconcile ourselves is that the past will never be recaptured and that whatever gains may be made will be on successively lower levels from that which was once viewed as the base of eternal prosperity. But there is a further inevitable to which we must become accustomed: international warfare at recurrent intervals. There must be markets for surplus goods; there must be outlets for capital; now, when all fields of imperialism

451

have been explored, the struggle for redivision must be regularly renewed.

Let us accept one premise: the past cannot be embraced and a period of steady decline has set in, a movement which may, on occasion, rise upward but always with decreased tempo and to lower heights. Granting that prospect—and that is substantially the best we are offered—the idea of change assumes new prominence. If we are faced by war and reaction, and these as the outgrowth of economic decay, then, whether our fathers have prospered under this system or not is irrelevant. We can hope for no more than a temporary breathing-spell, assuming that we survive the chaos of conflict. To the student this should be adequate inspiration to a search for a more fruitful order; to the teacher, both as a scholar and as a human being in need of the material requisites of life, the path should be fairly obvious. Neither can hope to regain the past which, for the student at least, was one of privilege and for the teacher one of comparative peace. It is true that a limited number of undergraduates can still move into the executive offices of their father's plant; there are faculty men who will be well paid to rationalize the status quo. They will be a fragment and they will be forced to surrender a fund of integrity for a minimum of luxury. The remainder cannot even anticipate that consolation.

But this plight is not the problem of the student and teacher alone. They are merely sharing that burden which, in more intense fashion, was earlier visited upon millions of people throughout the land. In that common disaster lies their hope. Large numbers of students have begun to perceive the possibilities inherent in an alliance; the same realization has pervaded a less widespread company of faculty men. If the student movement has partially accomplished one primary aim, it has been to demonstrate the need of that union and its inherent power. Vested interest has its united front; those aligned on the other side have begun to follow the example. As I write, the amalgamation of the League for Industrial

Democracy and the National Student League appears imminent. Two years ago the N.S.L. proposed this move; events since then have adequately revealed how timely was the proposal. Together these groups have been primarily responsible for an awakening in the colleges and in recent months they have acted almost as a unit on specific fronts. It is both logical and necessary that their efforts be further consolidated into an organization which will enroll far more than their present constituencies. Their task is manifold; they must do for education what educators have assiduously refused to do—face the issues of our time boldly and uncompromisingly. And yet they must combat both factionalism and snobbery which have often characterized left-wing ventures and repelled those not committed to the complete tenets of their position. Today the most imminent and menacing danger is the approach of fascism; to resist it will require more than the isolated protests of the left. There are thousands of students who have begun to sense the peril, who are prepared to act against it. They will do so only to the extent that they are convinced of the sincerity of those who offer them cooperation.

The new "American Student Union," as the amalgamated body will be called, faces these almost terrifying tasks, responsibilities, pitfalls. There is, however, so exigent a need for its formation that the step cannot be delayed or the responsibility shifted; no one else—least of all the educational hierarchy— will fulfill that rôle. The Union can, if we proceed steadfastly and clear-sightedly, if we develop an even broader sense of purposeful activity, if we refuse to be set apart from the main streams of campus life, become the voice of a groping undergraduate world. And it will be wanted and welcome by those thousands for whom the present seems only a faint prelude to a more devastating future.

Those whose perspective is directed toward a wholesale realignment of the social system must prove that action on one front, where agreement can be reached, is no sinister or deep-dyed plot. For the Tories will call it that at every turn; they will blame the "Reds" for economic disequilibrium; they will try to prove that their own incapabilities can be traced to Moscow rather than to the nature and direction of capitalism. The insurgents can dispel these fictions, but to do so will require patience and zeal. We believe that the liberal will acknowledge, if he moves to deter the sweep of fascism, that he is ultimately compelled to seek out its roots —the economic system. We contend that, if he hopes to stem war, he will be led to a similar discovery. And we are prepared to lead him through that process of enlightenment. On the other hand, if we are wrong, then let him prove us to be so by engaging in joint activity. If capitalism can be restored to health, reaction stifled and war averted within this order, then let us find that out together by combatting the symptoms. Certainly there is an abundance of testimony to support our pessimism. Only let it be clear that there is no divergence between our interests and those of the vast body of students; our problems are alike and our quest for a solution inspired by the same conditions.

There is a genuine ferment on the campus and its most dramatic expressions have herein been detailed. But the final form which it will take is far from assured. If there is an increasing number of students alert to social evils, if there are many hundreds, even thousands eager to explore new ideas and to labor for a revised social pattern, there are still vast, unbroken terrains in which no such purpose has stirred or in which the logical conclusions of first principles are disregarded. Thus, even where the student has experienced the effects of crisis, he is susceptible to ancient myths. He may acknowledge the scope and enormity of the problem but he will miss its most elementary corollaries. For example, even where he admits that entrenched interest is inaugurating its last-ditch offensive, he will not see its relationship to his own Board of Trustees. He will protest that the overlords finance education and are consequently entitled to impose whatever manner of education they desire. That is indisputably the logic of the Trustee's position, but it does not alter the student's insecurity. If the perpetuation of the status quo is the motivation behind endowments to education—and I believe I have strongly suggested that it is—then the student has an equivalent right to demonstrate his own relationship to that objective; if today the Tories are literally buying education to prevent its utilization on the side of progress, then we should not remain the innocent victims of the transaction. If and when they decide to close down the universities because they discover their occupants to be promoting social readjustment, then they will be confessing the bankruptcy of their own position. The point is that education, per se, is not deserving of blind worship at a time when our economic rulers have determined to assert the rights of ownership more forcibly.

I have emphasized these reservations and doubts common to a large number of students because it is important that no fantastic estimate of the scene be accepted. Certainly almost every student has, in one way or another, been affected by some phase of external upheavals. The crucial number, however, have still not adopted any decisive stand; they are adrift in the middle, cajoled by their administrators to remain inert, incited by the Vigilantes to joint the foray against the "Reds," still unwilling to dedicate themselves to the task of social revision. Enormous inroads have been made by the insurgents; anyone familiar with the American campus of a decade ago is astounded by the change in mood and interests. But these are only beginnings; there are far more critical conflicts ahead.

On one thing there is general accord: the student alone will not "save the world." It was the fatal delusion of *The New Student* fifteen years ago to believe that he could. He is part of a far-flung army located in every sphere of our national life, advancing with first faltering steps toward a new frontier. The path to an ordered, cooperative, profitless so-

REACTION

ciety is a long and perilous one; once attained, that goal will
not be a wonderland of sweetness and light. It will be, let
us say, the closest we can now conceive of the best of all
possible worlds—without perfection or unbroken bliss or
undiminished joy. It will provide the base upon which a
civilization can be built; it is a prerequisite to that civilization
but not the end-all of it. With the achievement of such a
system our possibilities and progress will only be potential;
but we cannot begin to emerge from our present dilemma
without the erection of such a foundation.

Whether a dominant number of students will be aligned in
that quest or whether they will be recruited to uphold a de-
caying order cannot now be prophesied. If the decision rests
with the overlords of education, then the undergraduate is
doomed to serve in another holy war. But there is another
hope and it is one which I have endeavored to depict in these
pages. It is that of students breaking from a confining fold
to learn about the outside world—and to do something about
it. They have done so, not as a martyred band, but as people
whose future is a post-graduate course in war, unemployment
and reaction. Having set out to educate themselves, they have
begun to ponder the unmentionables of our academic world.
It has not been a happy season for the educational hierarchy.
The fury of administrators, the outcries of the Hearst press
and its allies, the distemper of Trustees have only accentuated
the significance of the movement; its survival has testified
to a more basic strength than they ever visualized. And that
is the promise of the coming years.

INDEX

457

AMERICANA LIBRARY

The City: The Hope of Democracy
By Frederic C. Howe
With a new introduction by Otis A. Pease

Bourbon Democracy of the Middle West, 1865–1896
By Horace Samuel Merrill
With a new introduction by the author

*The Deflation of American Ideals: An Ethical Guide
for New Dealers*
By Edgar Kemler
With a new introduction by Otis L. Graham, Jr.

Borah of Idaho
By Claudius O. Johnson
With a new introduction by the author

The Fight for Conservation
By Gifford Pinchot
With a new introduction by Gerald D. Nash

Upbuilders
By Lincoln Steffens
With a new introduction by Earl Pomeroy

The Progressive Movement
By Benjamin Parke De Witt
With a new introduction by Arthur Mann

*Coxey's Army: A Study of the
Industrial Army Movement of 1894*
By Donald L. McMurry
With a new introduction by John D. Hicks

*Jack London and His Times: An Unconventional
Biography*
By Joan London
With a new introduction by the author

San Francisco's Literary Frontier
By Franklin Walker
With a new introduction by the author

Growth and Decadence of Constitutional Government
By J. Allen Smith
With a new introduction by Dennis L Thompson

Breaking New Ground
By Gifford Pinchot
With a new introduction by James Penick, Jr.

Spending to Save: The Complete Story of Relief
By Harry L. Hopkins
With a new introduction by Roger Daniels

A Victorian in the Modern World
By Hutchins Hapgood
With a new introduction by Robert Allen Skotheim

The Casual Laborer and Other Essays
By Carleton H. Parker
With a new introduction by Harold M. Hyman

Revolt on the Campus
By James Wechsler
With a new introduction by the author

American World Policies
By Walter E. Weyl
With a new introduction by Wilton B. Fowler

The Revolt of Modern Youth
By Ben B. Lindsey and Wainwright Evans
With a new introduction by Charles E. Larsen